MW00572368

A Mac
For the Teacher:
ClarisWorks®
Version
Second Edition

A Mac for the Teacher: ClarisWorks® Version Second Edition

Gregg Brownell
Director of Clinical and Computer Labs
College of Education and Allied Professions
Bowling Green State University

Jan Metzger
Director of Technology
Maumee City Schools

Carol Youngs
Coordinator, Computer Services
Washington Local Schools

Nancy Brownell
Department of Educational Curriculum and Instruction
Bowling Green State University

WEST PUBLISHING COMPANY
Minneapolis/St. Paul   *New York*   *Los Angeles*   *San Francisco*

Production Credits:
Cover image: © David Young-Wolff/PhotoEdit
Interior text design: Roslyn M. Stendahl, Dapper Design
Copyeditor: Kathy Pruno
Index: Schroeder Indexing Services
Composition: Carlisle Communications, Ltd.

Claris is a registered trademark of Claris Corporation.
ClarisWorks is a trademark of Claris Corporation.
HyperCard and HyperTalk are registered trademarks of Apple Computer, Inc.
HyperStudio is a registered trademark for Roger Wagner Publishing, Inc.

WEST'S COMMITMENT TO THE ENVIRONMENT

In 1906, West Publishing Company began recycling materials left over from the production of books. This began a tradition of efficient and responsible use of resources. Today, 100% of our legal bound volumes are printed on acid-free, recycled paper consisting of 50% new fibers. West recycles nearly 27,700,000 pounds of scrap paper annually—the equivalent of 229,300 trees. Since the 1960s, West has devised ways to capture and recycle waste inks, solvents, oils, and vapors created in the printing process. We also recycle plastics of all kinds, wood, glass, corrugated cardboard, and batteries, and have eliminated the use of polystyrene book packaging. We at West are proud of the longevity and the scope of our commitment to the environment.

West pocket parts and advance sheets are printed on recyclable paper and can be collected and recycled with newspapers. Staples do not have to be removed. Bound volumes can be recycled after removing the cover.

Production, Prepress, Printing and Binding by West Publishing Company.

British Library Cataloguing-in-Publication Data. A catalogue record for this book is available from the British Library.

 TEXT IS PRINTED ON 10% POST CONSUMER RECYCLED PAPER

COPYRIGHT © 1994   By WEST PUBLISHING COMPANY
COPYRIGHT © 1997   By WEST PUBLISHING COMPANY
                    610 Opperman Drive
                    P. O. Box 64526
                    St. Paul, MN 55164-0526

All rights reserved

Printed in the United States of America

04 03 02 01 00 99 98   8 7 6 5 4 3

Library of Congress Cataloging-in-Publication Data
A Mac for the teacher : ClarisWorks version/Gregg Brownell . . . [et al.].—2nd ed.
        p.   cm.
    Includes index.
    ISBN 0-314-20057-6 (soft : alk. paper)
    1. Integrated software. 2. ClarisWorks. 3. Macintosh (Computer)
I. Brownell, Gregg.
QA76.76.I57M33   1997
005.365–dc20   96-19129
                                                CIP

Dedication

For Nancy, whose support, energy, intelligence, and constancy continually amaze me, and for Sandy and Justin, who make us a family and who always bring me back to what is really important. Also, special thanks to Les Sternberg and Leigh Chiarelott, both for their support and for their work as true leaders in education.

Gregg Brownell

This book is dedicated to our families: the Metzgers—Den, Brianne, and Dustin; and the Youngs—Bill, Beau, and Betsy. Thank you for your support through all the long hours we have spent sitting in front of a computer rather than spending time with you. We appreciate your assistance with this project in all the large and small ways that you have contributed to the finished product.

Jan Metzger
Carol Youngs

For my family, whose love and support are always present and always appreciated.

Nancy Brownell

CONTENTS

3   ClarisWorks Graphics—Draw & Paint   71

4   ClarisWorks—Database   115

5   ClarisWorks—Spreadsheet   175

6   ClarisWorks—Additional Features   211

7   Introduction to HyperStudio   235

8   HyperCard—Introduction to Stacks, Fields, and Buttons   265

9   HyperCard—Backgrounds, New Stacks, and Added Features   303

10   In the Classroom   343

Preface

This text is designed as an introduction to the Macintosh computer for both preservice and inservice teachers. As such, it covers key concepts and skills related to computers and the tasks teachers commonly perform. Software covered includes ClarisWorks, Version 4.0, a popular integrated software package on the Mac that offers word processing, spreadsheet, database, graphics, and telecommunications applications; HyperCard, a popular, powerful Mac program for creating interactive software on the Mac, as well as Mac-based presentations; and HyperStudio, another interactive program for producing presentations and interactive software that provides for easily integrating images from videotape or videodisc. Examples and practice exercises have been carefully chosen to reflect the types of activities teachers need to perform. Throughout these chapters references are made to make a connection between the tutorial activities and possible classroom activities in sections called Classroom Connection. In addition to the skills-oriented tutorial chapters on these three programs, information about educational computer use in general and the use of different types of computer programs with students is also covered. The text assumes that the user is working on a Macintosh with a hard drive and is operating under System 7.5. Tutorial chapters are written for ClarisWorks, Version 4.0; HyperCard, Version 2.3; and HyperStudio, Version 3.0.6. A brief chapter summary follows.

Chapter 1 Getting to Know the Mac

> Introduction to a teacher's perspective on software and to the Macintosh desktop interface.

Chapter 2 ClarisWorks—Word Processing

> Editing text, handling documents, using rulers, using font options, finding/changing text, checking spelling and making outlines.

Chapter 3 ClarisWorks Graphics—Draw and Paint

> Using draw and paint tools, moving object layers, and using Arrange and Transform menu options.

Chapter 4 ClarisWorks—Database

> Browsing and editing data, creating new databases and fields, sorting records, finding and matching records, and creating and editing layouts.

Chapter 5 ClarisWorks—Spreadsheet

> Entering and editing data, using formulas and functions, pasting and inserting columns and rows, using absolute and relative references, and making charts and grids.

Chapter 6 ClarisWorks—Additional Features

> Using ClarisWorks Stationery and Assistants to help create documents. Introduction to telecommunications, networks, and basic steps for making connections with ClarisWorks.

Chapter 7 Introduction to HyperStudio

> Creating cards, adding text and graphic objects, creating buttons, and creating stacks.

Chapter 8 HyperCard - Introduction to Stacks, Fields, and Buttons

> Browsing, setting user levels, editing fields, adding cards, using paint tools, adding buttons, and printing stacks.

One basic premise of this text is that the best initial place for a computer in the classroom is on the teacher's desk. For teachers to comfortably and effectively integrate technology into the classroom, they must themselves be comfortable with the technology and able to use it effectively. This can often be accomplished by first providing teachers with the technology and training on how to use it, then providing teachers with time to think about how to use the technology and time to implement the use of technology in accordance with their own teaching styles.

The authors are sensitive to the realities of the classroom as they affect both teachers and students and have all spent considerable time in K through 12 education. We hope that an awareness of the reality is reflected in this work. One major strength of the project, from our perspective, has been its collaborative nature. Carol Youngs is currently Coordinator of Computer Services for Washington Local Schools in Toledo, Ohio, and has spent 20 years previously as a classroom teacher. Jan Metzger is Director of Technology at Maumee City Schools in Ohio and also has over 23 years of classroom experience. Nancy Brownell teaches computer education courses in the Department of Educational Curriculum and Instruction at Bowling Green State University and has previously worked as a math teacher and in industry as a programmer and systems analyst. Gregg Brownell is Director of the Clinical and Computer Labs in the College of Education and Allied Professions at Bowling Green State University and has taught in elementary and secondary education, as well as at the community college and university levels. From these various perspectives we sought to offer a text that would be useful and practical to both the beginning and practicing teacher interested in making use of technology in the schools.

As with any project like this, the comments and suggestions of the reviewers have helped to guide us and, we hope, make a better product. We wish to thank the following people who reviewed our first edition and whose suggestions were insightful, knowledgeable, and much appreciated.

Dale A. Banks, St. Mary's College
Donna J. Fremont, University of Calgary
Tim Smith, Brigham Young University
Norman Sterchele, Saginaw Valley State University
Suzanne Sullivan, California State University at Hayward
Jean G. Ulman, Ball State University
Angie Wilson, Samford University
Roger D. Wolff, Black Hills State University

We would also like to thank our friends and colleagues who read our early drafts of the new text and offered suggestions. Rita Barcus, Daneen Cole, Wendy Cushnie, Mary Schalitz, Sylvia Washburn, Karen Zach, and the Maumee City Schools teachers who attended the staff development programs at the Shuer Center provided very helpful feedback as we were working through the initial stages of the text.

We would also like to thank the people at West Publishing Company who have been so helpful in making this book a reality: Clark Baxter, whose insights are always appreciated; and Linda Poirier, whose competence and support have always been a great help. A special thanks to Matt Thurber, whose timely responses, great support, and willingness to explain the fine points of the production process has made this an exciting experience.

In closing, we hope your experiences with technology are both positive and productive, and that this text helps that to be so. We welcome comments or suggestions related to this work and may be contacted at the following postal and e-mail addresses:

Gregg Brownell
Clinical Lab
215 Education
Bowling Green State University
Bowling Green, Ohio 43403
e-mail: gbrowne@edap.bgsu.edu

Jan Metzger
e-mail: ma_jmm@mavca.ohio.gov

Carol Youngs
e-mail: wl_cay@mavca.ohio.gov

Nancy Brownell
e-mail: nbrowne@bgnet.bgsu.edu
Bowling Green, Ohio
March, 1996

1

Getting to Know the Mac

Introduction

Exciting developments have occurred in the educational computing and technology field over the last decade. The quality of materials available for use by teachers and students has increased steadily. The machines and programs available now are easier to use and more powerful; more educationally meaningful things can be done with them and yet they are friendlier, more humanlike in the way they work. Perhaps even more important, instructors and administrators now understand that for teachers to use computers with students, the teachers must first be comfortable using technology themselves. The best first place for a computer in the classroom is on the teacher's desk.

This book is designed to bring these trends to teachers by introducing three software packages on the Macintosh computer—ClarisWorks, HyperStudio, and HyperCard—in ways that are meaningful and useful to teachers. This first chapter is an orientation to the Macintosh, its place in education, and how people interact, or interface, with it. This chapter also briefly introduces some concepts about computer **software**—the programs, or instructions, that make computer **hardware** (machines) perform as intended. Chapters 2 through 9 provide instruction in ClarisWorks, HyperStudio, and HyperCard. Examples, exercises, and activities are geared to teachers and demonstrate ways to perform practical, relevant functions on the computer, functions that teachers often need to perform. The final chapter provides a selected overview of other Macintosh programs teachers will find valuable for their own use and for use with students.

In Chapters 2 through 9 the presentation is a tutorial format in which you can learn by doing. The contents of this and the last chapter are presented as an overview.

A Computer System

A computer system refers to a computer plus attached **peripheral devices** such as a keyboard, printer, and monitor. A computer system also may include CD-ROM and a modem. Figure 1-1 shows a typical computer system. In this figure the system consists of the computer, a keyboard, a mouse, a monitor, a printer, and disk drives. There is a **hard disk** drive inside the machine to save

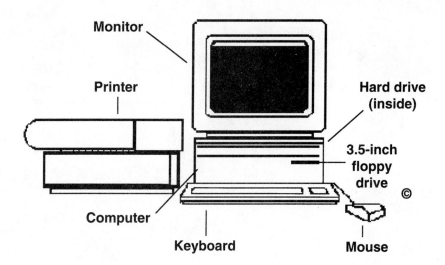

FIGURE 1–1

An example of a computer system.

and retrieve information. There is also a slot on the front of the computer where a 3.5-inch **floppy disk** may be inserted into a floppy disk drive. These disk drives are referred to as **storage devices** because they allow information to be saved, or stored, and retrieved for later use by the computer. The software, or instructions, that the computer needs to perform a task, is read by the computer from either the floppy disk or the hard disk in the machine.

A hard disk can store millions of characters, or bytes, of information. Think of a character or **byte** as one letter or numeral. A double-sided, double-density, 3.5-inch floppy disk can store a total of 819,200 bytes of information; a high-density, 3.5-inch floppy disk can store a total of 1,474,560 bytes of information. A typical Macintosh computer system may have a hard disk that stores 520 million (or more) bytes of information, plus a floppy disk drive. One million bytes are often referred to as a **megabyte**, so a hard disk with a capacity of 520 million characters is called an 520-megabyte hard disk.

The Friendly Computer

One of the most important things about the Macintosh is the way the computer user communicates, or interfaces, with the computer. The Macintosh makes use of a **Graphical User Interface** (GUI, pronounced gooey). This means that icons, or pictures, are presented on the screen. The **icons** represent available functions that the computer may perform. To accomplish a task you choose or move the appropriate icon. For example, if you wish to remove a document from the computer's memory, you would move the document icon to an icon that represents a trash can.

The GUI of the Macintosh is implemented using a **desktop metaphor**. If you were working with pencil and paper on an ordinary desktop, imagine what the desktop would look like. There would be papers, with some papers probably in folders, and papers and folders might be partially on top of one another. Various tools might be on the desk, such as pens, pencils, and maybe scissors. Certainly a trash can would be near the desk. The desktop metaphor is aimed at making the computer screen analogous to a physical desktop. Keep this in mind as you progress through a few initial concepts about using the Macintosh.

The intention of a GUI that is analogous to a desktop is part of a philosophy of making the computer as easy to use, as friendly, as possible. Ideally, the interface, the way a user communicates with the computer, will be intuitive; the user will simply understand how to perform the desired function or task by looking at the screen. In fact, this approach is vastly different from the way earlier computers worked. In the past, users had to know and carefully type very specific commands, or remember particular sets of keystrokes, to perform any task. Less friendly machines often required the user to spend hours studying manuals and memorizing commands to make the computer perform as desired. Most modern personal computers attempt to use some form of a GUI.

Of the many programs available for Macintosh machines, most follow a fairly consistent implementation of a GUI. This has great dividends for Macintosh users and especially for educators. Once a student or teacher becomes familiar with the Mac environment, with the way the Macintosh works, using new programs on the Mac will be much easier. With other computers, the interface may be greatly different from program to program, requiring more time to learn how each new program works. In the Mac environment the interface is, for the most part, standardized; that extra learning time is often not necessary when going from one program to the next. One high school computer teacher estimated that with his students using the Mac, the time to introduce new software was about 20 percent of that needed when using some other machines.

Initial Concepts

The basic concepts of using the Macintosh interface are presented here. This presentation assumes the use of a Macintosh with a hard disk plus a floppy disk drive. It also assumes that the **system software** (the software that actually runs the machine) is System 7.5. The number 7.5 is the version of the system software. If you are using a version of system software other than System 7.5, your instructor will point out to you any important differences.

In some computer labs Macintosh machines are left on at all times. If you need to turn on the Macintosh, press the switch or switches at the back. A Macintosh, such as a Performa 575, has a single switch. On a modular Mac, such as a Performa 6220, where the computer and monitor are separate pieces of equipment, press the switch on the monitor and then the switch on the computer. Some models can be turned on from the keyboard. Ask the instructor if you are not sure about yours.

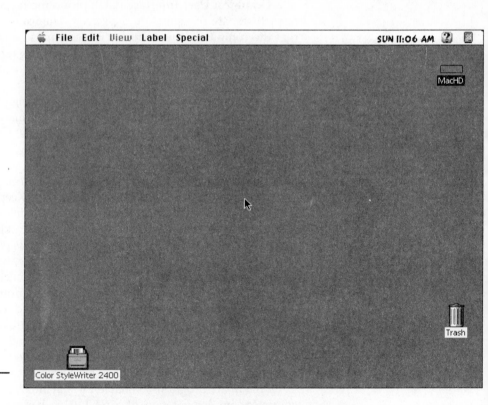

FIGURE 1-2

The Macintosh Desktop.

THE POINTER: POINTING, CLICKING, AND DRAGGING

Once the computer has booted (started up), the first screen shown is called the **Desktop**. Figure 1-2 shows the Macintosh Desktop. Notice the arrow, called the **pointer,** that is near the center of the screen in Figure 1-2. Connected to the computer is a device called a **mouse**. On the bottom of the mouse is a ball; on the top of the mouse is a rectangular button. Moving the mouse on a desk or table causes the ball to roll and the pointer on the screen to move. In this way, the pointer can be moved anywhere on the screen. This is referred to as **pointing**.

On the gray portion of the Desktop in Figure 1-2 are three icons. The one at the upper right represents the hard disk inside the Mac and on this particular machine is labeled MacHD. The one at the lower right represents a trash can and is always labeled Trash. The one in the bottom left corner is the printer icon. If the pointer is moved to an icon and the button on the mouse is clicked, the icon darkens. This is called **clicking,** and the darkened icon indicates that you have chosen to work with this icon—you have selected it. In Figure 1-3, the Trash icon has been selected. In the Mac environment, you **select** an icon, or some text, or a graphic (a picture), in order to do something with it. The act of selecting does not change anything except the color of the icon. It simply indicates that the selection is what you will be working with—using, editing, or changing. In most cases you must select something before you can work with it.

FIGURE 1-3

An icon is highlighted (darkened) when it has been selected.

If the pointer is moved to an icon and the mouse button is pressed and held, the icon can be moved to another location on the Desktop. Simply point to an icon, hold down the mouse button and, while the button is held down, move the mouse. The icon will, correspondingly, move on the screen. When the icon is in the desired position, release the button on the mouse. This is called **dragging**. In Figure 1-4, the Trash icon is being dragged to a location nearer to the hard disk icon. These three skills—pointing, clicking, and dragging—are used repeatedly in the Mac environment.

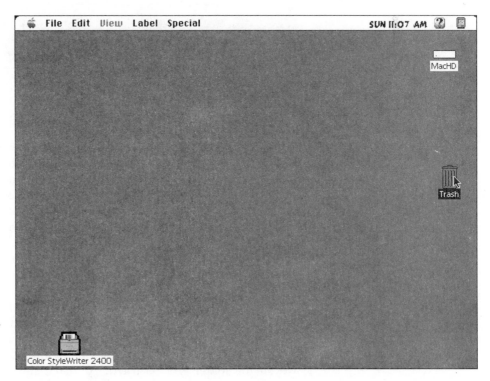

FIGURE 1-4

The Trash icon has been dragged to a new location on the screen.

MORE ON THE DESKTOP

To gain access to the data and information on the Mac, you must **open** the disk on which the items are stored. One way to open a disk is to point to the icon, such as the hard disk icon, and **double-click**, which means to click twice in quick succession. When this is done, a window is superimposed on the Desktop as shown in Figure 1-5. This particular window provides a catalog of what is stored on the hard disk. **Windows** are an important concept in the Mac environment. Think of a window as a way to look into something. In this instance the window allows you to look into the hard disk to see a listing of what is stored there. The top line of the window is called the **title bar** and the area where the title for the window is displayed (in this instance the title is MacHD) is called the title box.

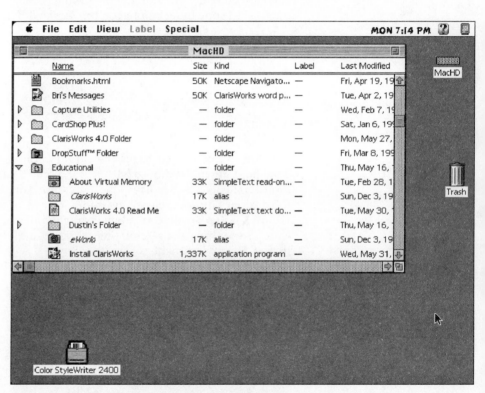

FIGURE 1-5

The hard drive named MacHD has been opened and a window displays its contents.

Notice that within the MacHD window the Name, Size, Kind, Label, and Last Modified columns give particular information for each item available on the hard disk. The types of items available are documents, applications, and folders. A **document** is an item, or file, created with a program such as a word processor. An **application** is a program, such as a word processor, that allows you to do something with the computer, to use it in a particular way. A **folder** is a place to store documents, applications, or other folders. For example, just as in a file cabinet you might have a folder containing all the work related to a project, say a field trip, you can create a folder on the Mac, name it Field Trip, and then keep all related work in it.

Notice the triangles that appear to the left of some of the names listed in Figure 1-5. A triangle that points to the right indicates that the item is a folder containing other items. (Notice that the icon for a folder looks like a small file folder.) By clicking once on a triangle pointing to the right, the items contained within the folder will be listed. At that point the triangle will point down, indicating that the contents of the folder are being displayed. See the folder named Educational in Figure 1-5 for an example.

Notice at the top of Figure 1-6 the apple at the upper left, followed by the words File, Edit, View, Label, and Special; the time display; and two additional icons at the upper right of the screen. This is called the **menu bar**. The menu bar lists the task choices available to you. The choices will vary, depending on what you have been doing and what program you are using.

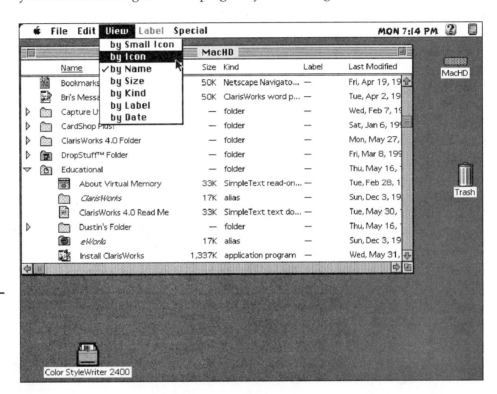

FIGURE 1-6

The View menu is pulled down and by Icon is being selected. The checkmark on the menu shows that the contents of the window currently are being displayed by name.

If the pointer is positioned over any of these eight items and the mouse button is pressed and held, a menu will "pull down" like a window shade. In Figure 1-6 the **pull-down menu** is the View menu. If you continue to depress the mouse button and drag the pointer down the options on the menu, each option will in turn be highlighted (selected) while the pointer is on that particular option. By releasing the mouse button when the desired option is selected, the computer will perform that selection. For instance, this View menu allows the information in the MacHD window to be displayed in different ways. In Figures 1-5 and 1-6, the information is displayed by name. If the you point to the View menu and drag the pointer until by Icon is highlighted (selected) as shown in Figure 1-6, then release the mouse button, the information in the MacHD window will be displayed by icon, as shown in Figure 1-7.

Figure 1-8 shows the options in the **File menu**. Note that some of the options are gray. When a menu option is gray, it is not available for use at present. For instance, the Open option is not available here because no icon has been selected to indicate what could be opened. Also notice that some pull-down menu options have a symbol and letter to the right of the option name. You can execute such options by pressing the indicated keys on the keyboard rather than using the pull-down menu. For example, to open a document, folder, or application from the Desktop, you first select the icon for it. Then you either drag the File menu down

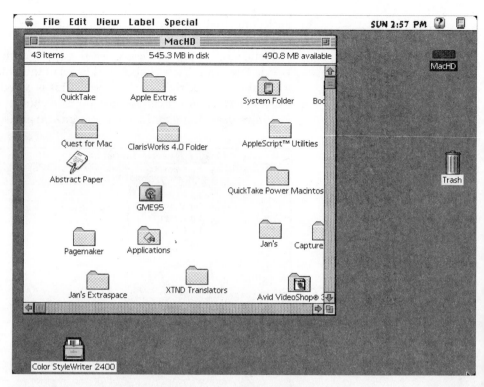

FIGURE 1-7

The contents of the window are being displayed by icon.

to the Open option or you press and hold the **Command key** (the one resembling a four-leaf clover) and simultaneously press the O key. Another way to open a document, folder, or application from the Desktop is to double-click its icon. Other items on the menu bar will be covered later in the text.

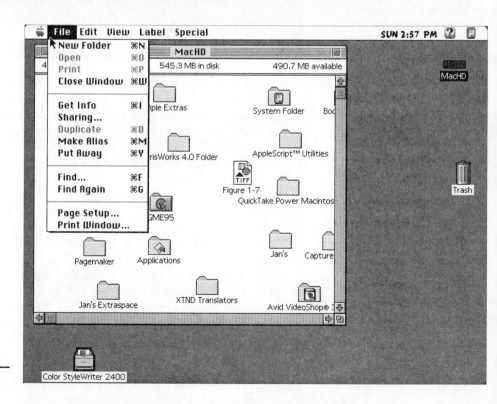

FIGURE 1-8

The File menu is pulled down.

INSERTING AND EJECTING FLOPPY DISKS

Floppy disks usually have a small arrow imprinted on the top, left side. To insert a floppy disk into the floppy drive simply point the arrow at the drive and slide it in. There are several ways to remove a floppy disk. The easiest is to drag its icon to the **Trash** icon, releasing it when the Trash is highlighted. A second way is by selecting Put Away from the File menu. Both of these methods remove any memory of the floppy disk and are the best methods for removing a disk. Another way to remove a floppy disk is to choose Eject Disk from the Special menu. This method will leave a gray disk icon on the Desktop. This last method is not recommended because later on the Mac may ask you to reinsert the floppy disk, then eject it, and then ask for the disk again. This process may be repeated several times and can be frustrating when you are trying to work.

MORE ON WINDOWS

You will be using windows in all your Macintosh work. To make your work easier, you can scroll to view information that does not fit in a window. You can also move and resize windows to suit your needs.

Scrolling Windows

Often more information is available in a window than can be displayed on the screen at one time. In Figure 1-8 a vertical **scroll bar** can be seen along the right edge of the window. The bar is gray, which indicates that there is more information above or below what is displayed in the window. By placing the pointer on the top or bottom arrow of the bar and holding down the mouse button, you can scroll through all the information in the window. Also, to scroll more rapidly, the gray areas of the scroll bar can be clicked, and the square within the scroll bar can be dragged anywhere between the up and down arrows. Scroll bars may also be horizontal to allow you to view segments of information that are too wide for the computer screen.(In Figure 1-10 in the area at the bottom of the window there is a horizontal scroll bar. In this case it is white, which indicates that no horizontal scrolling is necessary because the width of the information in the window can fit on the screen.)

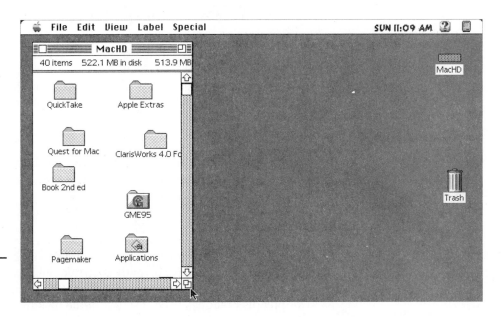

FIGURE 1-9

The pointer is on the size box, which has been dragged to change the size of the window.

Resizing Windows

Windows can be resized by using either the size box or the zoom box. The **size box** is located at the lower right corner of the window. By dragging the size box, the window can be made smaller or larger. Figure 1-9 shows the MacHD window resized by using the size box.

The **zoom box** is located at the top right of the window, at the end of the title bar. By clicking on the zoom box icon, the window will automatically adjust to show as much of its contents as possible. By clicking the zoom box again, the window will resume its previous size. Figure 1-10 shows a window enlarged by use of the zoom box.

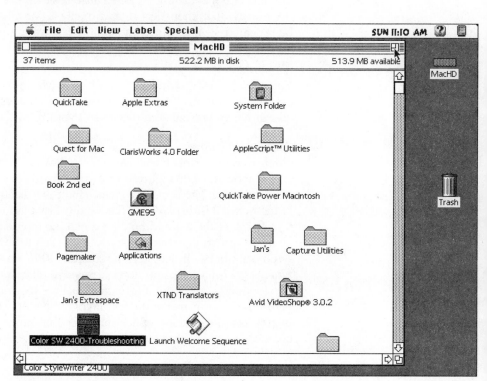

FIGURE 1-10

The pointer is on the zoom box, which has been clicked to enlarge the window.

Moving Windows

You can also move windows around, or reposition them on the screen. By placing the pointer anywhere on the title bar except the zoom box or the small, white box at the left side of the title box, you can drag the window to the desired location on the screen. In Figure 1-11, the window from Figure 1-9 has been moved to a new location.

Closing Windows

To close or exit a window, click once in the **close box**, located at the left side of the title bar (see Figure 1-11). Another way to close a window is to open the File menu and drag down to select Close.

Multiple Windows

So far you have seen only one window open at a time. You can have multiple windows open. However, only one window can be the **active window**, the window in which you may currently do work. In Figure 1-12 notice that a floppy disk icon, titled MyWork, is displayed with the hard drive icon. This icon represents a floppy disk that has been inserted in the disk drive. Figure 1-13 shows both the

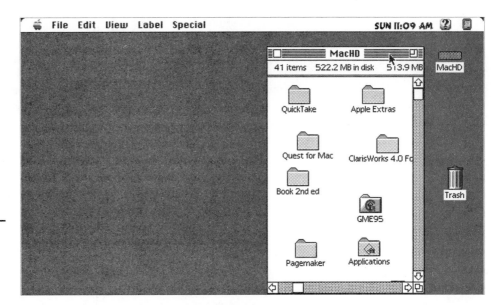

FIGURE 1-11

By dragging the title bar, the MacHD window has been moved. The white box on the left of the title bar is the close box.

MacHD and the MyWork disk opened at the same time. Notice that both these icons are shaded, but not darkly highlighted, to indicate that they are open. The MacHD icon was opened first, then the MyWork icon was opened. Parallel lines in the title bar indicate the active window. Notice that the active window in this case is the one for the MyWork disk. To make the MacHD window active, simply click anywhere within its window. When more than one window is shown on the screen, the ability to resize and move windows around becomes important.

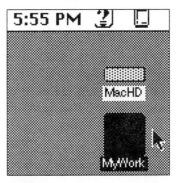

FIGURE 1-12

The floppy disk icon, labeled MyWork here, looks like a 3.5 inch disk.

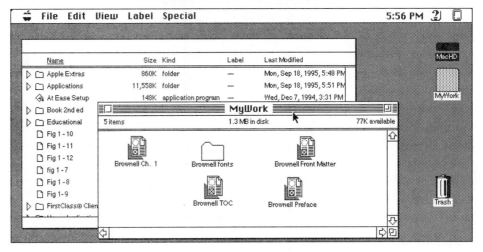

FIGURE 1-13

Both the MacHD and the MyWork disks have been opened. MyWork is the active window, as indicated by the parallel lines on the title bar.

ALERT AND DIALOG BOXES

Two other types of boxes are important. Two **alert boxes**, shown in Figure 1-14, simply alert the user to important information. In this case, as a document is being printed, the lower alert box informs you of the keystrokes needed to cancel the printing of the document. A **dialog box**, shown in Figure 1-15, provides the user with information and the opportunity to do something, and it requires a response. Some of the options available on this dialog box from the ClarisWorks program are to assign a new name to a document before the document is saved (stored) on disk, to Save the document, or to Cancel the procedure.

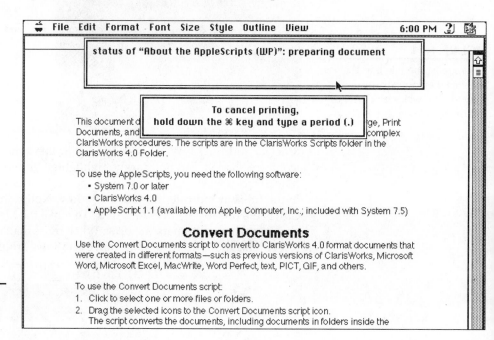

FIGURE 1-14

Alert boxes such as the ones shown here alert you to important information.

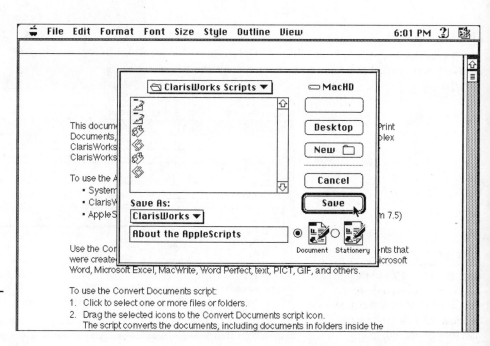

FIGURE 1-15

A dialog box such as this provides information and requires a response.

COPYING AND REMOVING FILES ON THE DESKTOP

You often may need to copy an item from one disk to another. One way to copy from a hard disk to a floppy disk is first to open the hard disk. Next, drag the desired item from the hard disk to either the closed floppy disk icon or to the window of the open floppy disk. This leaves the original on the hard disk and a copy on the floppy disk. To copy from the floppy disk to the hard disk, just reverse the process. A document, application, or folder can be copied into a folder on the receiving disk, the disk you are copying to, by dragging the item to the closed receiving folder icon and releasing the mouse button when the folder is highlighted.

You can also copy multiple items at the same time. Select the icon for one of the items to be copied. Then place the pointer on the icon of another item to be copied. Press the Shift key on the keyboard and continue to hold it as you click the mouse button (this is referred to as **shift-clicking**). That item will also be selected for copying. Continue to do this for each item to be copied. When all items are selected in this way, drag one item to the receiving disk. By dragging one item, all items will follow and will be copied onto the receiving disk.

To remove files from a disk, simply drag the desired file to the Trash icon. Release the mouse button when the Trash icon is highlighted. Multiple files may be removed at once by shift-clicking as many as desired and then dragging one to the Trash. The Trash will bulge when one or more files are deposited there. Files will stay in the Trash (the Trash will not be emptied) until Empty Trash is selected from the **Special menu**. If the Trash has not been emptied, you can retrieve the file(s) last sent there. Double-click on the Trash to open it, select the file you wish to retreive by clicking on it. From the File menu, select Put Away and the file returns to where it was before you put it in the trash.

EDITING ON THE DESKTOP

To change the name of a document, folder, or program, click on the name that is to be changed to select it. The name becomes highlighted with a box around it and the arrow pointer changes to an I-shaped pointer, called an **I-beam**, when it is moved over the name. To replace the whole name, start typing and what is typed will replace the existing name. When you know how to use the I-beam for text editing (as you will learn in Chapter 2), you will also be able to edit part of the name by using the I-beam as you do for any other text editing.

FILE HANDLING—OPEN, FIND, AND GET INFO

As mentioned previously, a document that already exists (is stored on a disk in the computer) must be opened for you to work with it. From the Desktop you may either double-click on its icon, or you may click on the icon to select it and then pull down the File menu and choose Open.

An application program must also be opened to use it. You open the program in the same way that you open documents from the Desktop. In a program, this is also called launching the program or, in older computer terminology, booting the program. If you use an application such as a word processor, the program usually can also be launched automatically by opening a document that was created by it.

You may sometimes need to find where a file, a document, or a program is located on a disk. Perhaps the file was created some time ago and is located on a hard disk drive with a lot of information stored on it. Rather than laboriously scrolling through all the files on the disk, you can use the Find... option located under the File menu from the Desktop to quickly locate the file. Simply choose Find... from the File menu and then type in the file name (see Figure 1-16) or part of the file name. The Mac will create a list of all files containing that word. You may then select the file you want. The Find option also allows you to search for a file using a variety of attributes.

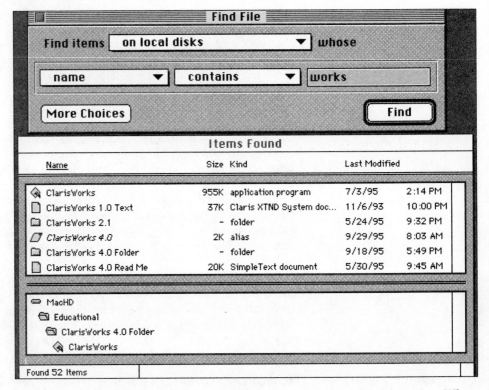

FIGURE 1-16

Selecting Find... on the File menu displays this dialog box. Clicking the Find button locates all files with the typed name.

Another useful file-handling tool is Get Info, located on the File menu. When you select a file icon such as a document, folder, or program, and then choose Get Info from the File menu, the Mac will return information about the file as shown in Figure 1-17.

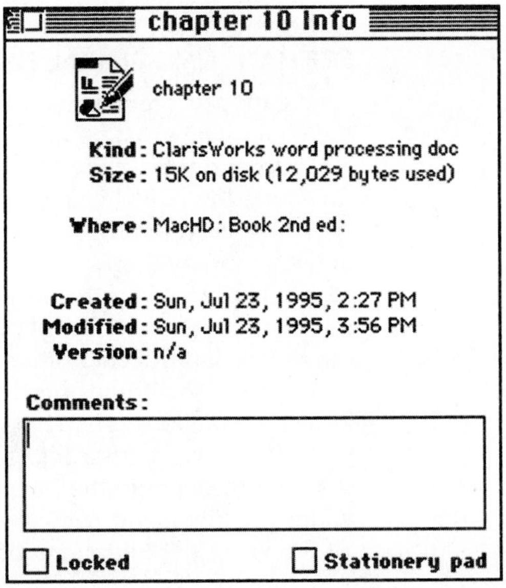

FIGURE 1-17

Choosing Get Info from the File menu displays this window describing the file.

APPLE GUIDE

System 7.5 includes a comprehensive help system called **Apple Guide**. The Guide menu, located under the question mark on the right side of the menu bar, gives help on using the computer. By choosing Show Balloons (Figure 1-18) from the Apple Guide menu, you turn on **Balloon Help**. Application programs that support this feature of Apple's System 7.5 software will provide you with help balloons for menus and other items within the particular program. Simply position the pointer over the item in question (but do not click the mouse) to see the help balloon. For pull-down menus, press and hold the mouse button, without releasing it. To turn off this feature, choose Hide Balloons from the Apple Guide menu.

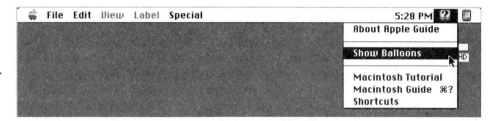

FIGURE 1-18

Choosing Show Balloons from the Apple Guide menu turns on the Balloon Help function.

The **Macintosh Tutorial** is also located under the Apple Guide menu. It will teach you the basic skills needed to use a Macintosh computer effectively. You should go through the tutorial even if you have used other Macintoshes, as this is a good way to find out about new features in System 7.5.

The **Macintosh Guide** gives indepth information on all the features of the Macintosh. To use this guide, select Macintosh Guide from the Apple Guide menu located on the right side of the menu bar. The Guide screen, shown in Figure 1-19, gives you three options: Topics, Index, and Look For. Topics shows general categories; by clicking on one of the topics a list of specific questions appears. Select Index to see an alphabetical listing of keywords. By scrolling through this list you can find the specific word you wish to learn. The

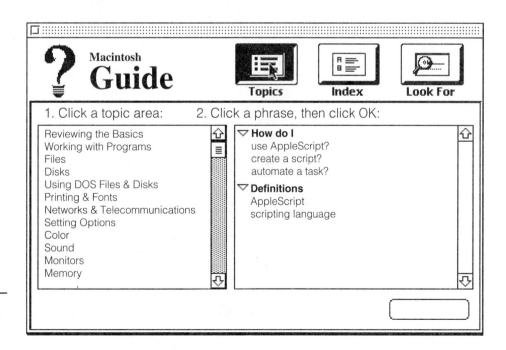

FIGURE 1-19

Choosing Topics from the Macintosh Guide dialog box displays topics and questions.

Look For option allows you to type in the keyword and search for it directly. When a question has been selected, instructions appear. These instructions include tips, extra help, and even step-by-step instructions on the screen as you are performing the procedure.

Many programs also have other help features available through one of the pull-down menus. Often this feature is under the Apple Guide, as it is in ClarisWorks. An explanation of ClarisWorks's Help is presented in Chapter 2.

SHUTTING DOWN

A hard disk contains a mechanism that includes a **read/write head** that floats over a rotating platter (disk). If the read/write head comes into contact with the disk when not in use, the disk may be damaged and information stored on it may be lost. For this reason, the head must be parked when the machine is turned off. To safely shut off the machine, first quit every application and close every window that is open. Next, go to the Special menu and choose **Shut Down.** The computer will then automatically park the read/write head. A message will appear on the screen to inform you that it is safe to shut off the machine. You may then turn the machine off. On many Macintoshes a Shut Down option is also located under the Apple menu.

In some computer labs and on some types of networks, the machines should not be turned off. Also, some models will turn off by themselves when you choose Shut Down. Ask your instructor about yours.

Preparing to Work with the Data Disk

In Chapters 2 through 9 of this book, you will be using files from the Data Disk that accompanies the book. This disk has been permanently locked to avoid all possible viruses (programs specifically designed to copy themselves to your computer and potentially cause problems for you). A locked disk allows you to open documents, but you cannot save anything on the disk. Because you will need to save most of the work you do, you should copy all the Data Disk files to your own disk. If you have your own computer, you may wish to copy the disk contents to the hard disk and work on the files from there. If you are working in a standard lab setting, you will not be able to leave your personal documents on the computer's hard disk, so you will need to copy them from the floppy Data Disk to another floppy.

This copying can be done in several ways. Unfortunately, when you have one floppy drive the most direct method to copy from floppy disk to floppy disk— dragging an icon from one floppy disk to another—is also the most time consuming because it requires switching the disks in the drive many, many times. Another method—copying the disk contents temporarily to the hard disk, then to your floppy disk—is more efficient in the long run, but requires more steps and can be confusing to the novice Macintosh user. An alternative to copying the disk (but, again, not the best for the novice) is to open documents from the Data Disk that comes with the book and to switch to your floppy disk whenever you are required to save. (Saving in this way is described in Chapter 2, "Saving Documents.")

You should check with your instructor to find which of these or other methods is best for you. If you choose, you may use the following steps to copy the Data Disk contents to your floppy disk. However, you should go through these steps with your instructor if you have not worked with a Macintosh previously. With these steps you will copy the contents of the Data Disk to your hard disk, then copy the same contents from your hard disk to your floppy disk, and finally delete the copy on your hard disk. If you will be working from your hard disk, you may just do the steps under "Copying the Data Disk to the Hard Disk." Keep in mind that these steps are written for a system with one hard drive and one floppy drive.

COPYING THE DATA DISK TO THE HARD DISK

1. With your closed hard disk icon visible on the Desktop, insert the Data Disk that came with this book into the floppy drive.
2. Position the pointer on the closed Data Disk icon, press the mouse button down and drag the disk icon to the hard disk icon, releasing the mouse button when the hard disk icon is highlighted.
3. The files on the Data Disk will be copied to the hard drive.
4. Position the pointer on the Data Disk and drag (with the mouse button down) until the Trash is selected (highlighted). This ejects the disk.

COPYING FROM THE HARD DISK TO THE FLOPPY DISK

1. Insert your floppy disk into the floppy drive.
2. If your disk is a new, unused disk, you will automatically be asked if you wish to initialize it. Initialization places indexing and other information on the disk to prepare it for use with the Macintosh.
   a. Click Two-Sided, then Click Erase in response to the prompts. When you are warned that the disk will be erased, this is all right—a new disk has nothing on it to erase.
   b. Type **Data Disk** when prompted for a disk name.
   c. Click OK to complete the initialization of the disk.
3. Double-click (click twice in succession) on the hard disk icon to open it. You should see a folder labeled Data Disk somewhere in the hard drive window.
4. Double-click (click twice in succession) on the Data Disk folder to open it.
5. Position the pointer on the Edit menu and drag (with the mouse button down) until the Select All command is selected. All the documents in the window should be highlighted when you release the mouse button.
6. Position the pointer on any one of the document icons and drag the icon (with the mouse button down) until your floppy disk icon is selected. This copies all the selected documents when you release the mouse button.
7. Position the pointer on the File menu and drag (with the mouse button down) until the Close Window command is selected to close the Data Disk folder.
8. Position the pointer on the Data Disk folder on the hard disk and drag the folder icon (with the mouse button down) until the Trash icon is selected. This removes the folder from your hard disk.
9. Your disk should be ready to use.

Conclusion

The intention of this first chapter is to provide an orientation to the Macintosh. If you have used the Mac before, much of this information will be familiar. If you have never used any computer before, all the information may be new. This chapter is presented as an overview. In the following chapters (except for the last chapter) the presentation is different. Information is presented in a tutorial format. In those chapters you will learn by doing, and many of the ideas presented here will become more familiar as you work with the computer. Don't be concerned with memorizing everything in this chapter if it is new to you. As you use the Mac, your understanding of the machine, these ideas, and the value of educational computing will develop through practice and hands-on experience.

KEY TERMS

active window	floppy disk	pointing
alert box	folder	pull-down menu
Apple Guide	Graphical User	read/write head
application	Interface (GUI)	scroll bar
Balloon Help	hard disk	select
byte	hardware	shift-clicking
clicking	I-beam	Shut Down
close box	icon	size box
Command key	Macintosh Guide	software
Desktop	Macintosh Tutorial	Special menu
desktop metaphor	megabyte	storage device
dialog box	menu bar	system software
document	mouse	title bar
double-click	open	Trash
dragging	peripheral device	window
File menu	pointer	zoom box

2 ClarisWorks— Word Processing

OUTLINE

Introduction

Teachers today have many demands on their time. Handouts and tests must be created, teaching materials must be organized, and grades must be calculated. Reports are required, not only for the classroom, but also for various organizations and activities. Learning to use a computer can give a teacher more control over the management of these tasks. Harnessing the power of the computer can allow more time for what is most important—teaching and interacting with students.

ClarisWorks is an integrated software package that provides teachers with an opportunity to use the power of the computer. **Integrated software** combines a variety of tool programs—word processing, spreadsheet, database, and sometimes others—into one program. The advantages of this are that commands for the different tools are similar and that data can be passed between the different types of documents. As a result, one integrated program is easier to learn and more efficient than using all the separate programs.

ClarisWorks includes word processing, database, spreadsheets, graphics, and communications in one program. The **word processing** function allows for the creation of letters, handouts, tests, flyers, and even individualized reports and newsletters. The graphics mode allows for the creation of drawings and illustrations. The **database** application can be used to keep information about students, to maintain an inventory of equipment, to keep track of teaching materials, or to prepare presentations about particular topics. The **spreadsheet** tool can be invaluable in calculating grades, doing classroom or club budgets, working with money-making projects, and teaching about problem solving using mathematical calculations. The communications package, when combined with additional hardware, allows the teacher to connect with local and distant banks, libraries, bulletin boards, and other resources to obtain information through a home or classroom computer.

Because ClarisWorks is an integrated package, the procedures used in the various applications work in the same manner. Also, information from one area can be used in another. More specifically, student names and information in a database can be placed in personalized letters or progress reports, and budget information managed within a spreadsheet can be copied to memos or used to create graphs that can be placed within a newsletter or printed report.

Learning ClarisWorks is easy. The software comes with a ClarisWorks User's Guide and provides an on-line tutorial, *Introduction to ClarisWorks*. This on-line tutorial will lead the new user through some of the features of ClarisWorks and will provide a good overview of the capabilities of the program. Another helpful feature is the ClarisWorks Assistants that provide automated assistance in creating certain types of documents such as a calendar, a certificate, an envelope, home financial calculations, a presentation, or a newsletter. ClarisWorks also has a variety of stationery documents that serve as a template or guide for you to create documents such as an annual report, certificates, newsletters, an expense report sheet, a home budget, a lease versus purchase analyzer, a fax cover sheet and several others. ClarisWorks has an on-line **Help** feature that allows you to look up information without having to go to a manual. This feature can be accessed at almost any time. If you can't remember how to do something while you are working on a document, you can look up references using the Help feature without closing your document.

In this chapter, you will begin by working with word processing. Of all the features available from ClarisWorks, word processing is probably the most useful, in general, to the teacher. Think of all the time teachers devote to creating letters, handouts, quizzes, and tests. Whether they are typed or handwritten, a great deal of time is taken up creating this type of material. Using the word processor can simplify these tasks by allowing changes to be made quickly and easily. Also, using the Spell Checker and Thesaurus can ease the actual writing process.

The ClarisWorks chapters in this book have been written with ClarisWorks Version 4.0. The assumption is made that ClarisWorks has been installed on your hard disk. You are going to find the word processor a valuable tool. It is time to begin discovering how the word processor will work for you.

Beginning ClarisWorks — Opening a Disk or Document

One way to launch the ClarisWorks program is by opening a document created by the program. Begin by opening, with the following steps, the document labeled A Welcome on the Data Disk (or the copy of the Data Disk that you made in Chapter 1) that accompanies this book.

1. Start with the Macintosh turned on. The hard drive and trash should be displayed on your Desktop.

2. Insert your Data Disk in the floppy drive of your computer.

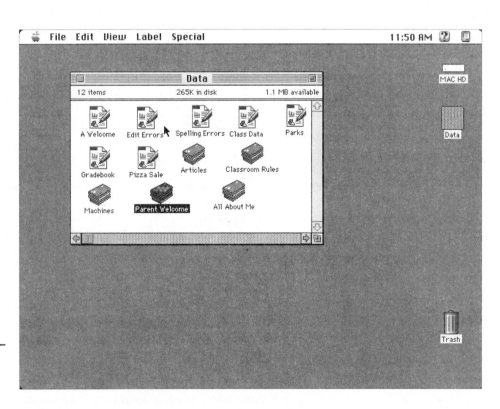

FIGURE 2-1

The Data Disk has been opened. Its contents are displayed in the window.

3. The Data Disk may automatically open so that a window displays its contents, as shown in Figure 2-1. If it does not open automatically, double-click (click twice in succession) on the Data Disk icon to open it. You should see the Data Disk window displayed.

4. Open the A Welcome document by double-clicking on the document icon labeled A Welcome. The window that appears on the screen should be similar to Figure 2-2. Because A Welcome was created with the ClarisWorks program, when you open the document, the ClarisWorks program is launched or started at the same time.

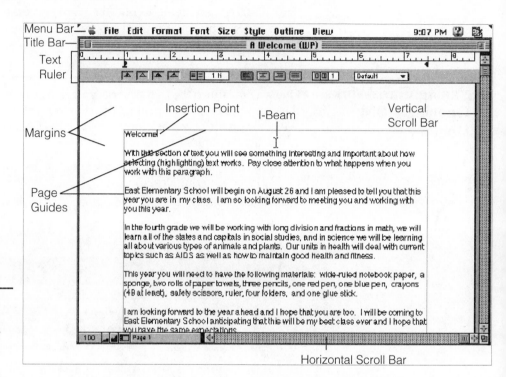

FIGURE 2-2

The ClarisWorks word processing screen with the A Welcome document displayed. Note the various parts that are labeled.

Using the Mouse

What you see on the screen is a word processing document, or file, along with a variety of features that will help you create and format your document. To use these features, you must know how to use the mouse to obtain an **insertion point** and to drag the mouse to select (**highlight**) text or features.

INSERTING TEXT

Often when you read through a document you have written, you find you may want to add words to make your meaning more clear. In this section you will learn how to coordinate use of the mouse and the keyboard to insert words into your document.

1. Move the mouse around on your desk or mouse pad.

   Notice how the symbol that appears on the screen changes when the mouse is in different areas of the screen. When the mouse is on the outer edges of the screen, you see an arrow. When the mouse is over the text at the center, you see a different symbol. The new symbol is called an I-beam pointer and indicates that the mouse is in a text area where typing can be done. An I-beam pointer is shown in Figure 2-2.

2. Position the I-beam immediately before the word **interesting** in the first paragraph of the A Welcome document.

3. Click the mouse, then move the I-beam to any other position. A flashing bar remains at the point where you clicked. This is called the text insertion point. This is the location where text will be inserted when you type.

4. Type **very,** then press the space bar. **Very** is inserted at the insertion point. Notice that everything following **very** automatically moves over to allow room for the new word. Notice also that the I-beam can be anywhere on the screen when you type. The text insertion point controls where the typing will be done, not the I-beam.

5. To move the insertion point to a new location, simply move the I-beam and click the mouse in the new location.

SELECTING TEXT

You will be using the mouse to insert text and to select words, lines, or even large sections of text. As described in Chapter 1, you can move the I-beam to the beginning of a certain section of text and then drag the mouse over any text you wish to select, releasing the mouse at the end of the text. This works even if the text extends above or below the window—the window will scroll. These methods work in any Macintosh program. Try this method of selection with the following steps.

1. Position the I-beam before **Pay** in the first paragraph.

2. Press and hold the mouse button down as you drag the mouse.

3. Notice that you can move the mouse in any direction. If you move the mouse up or down, each line of text that you pass is selected.

4. Release the mouse button—everything between the location where you started dragging and the location where you stopped is selected.

5. Repeat these steps with any text on the screen. Try to select each of the following: a letter, a word, a line, a portion of a line, a paragraph, and more than a paragraph. When you start a new selection, the prior selection is no longer selected—it is deselected.

6. Click anywhere within the window to again have the insertion point with no text selected.

In ClarisWorks there are also some shortcuts that may be used to select certain sections of text. These shortcuts can save you time and are often especially helpful when you find the mouse awkward to use.

1. Place the I-beam anywhere on the word **attention** in the first paragraph.

2. Double-click the mouse button. The word **attention** should now be selected. Double-clicking on a word will select that word, as shown in Figure 2–3.

3. With the I-beam again on the word **attention**, click the mouse button three times. The entire line containing the word is now selected. Clicking three times selects the entire line where the I-beam is located.

4. With the I-beam again on the word **attention**, click the mouse button four times. The entire paragraph containing the word is now selected. Clicking four times selects the entire paragraph where the I-beam is located.

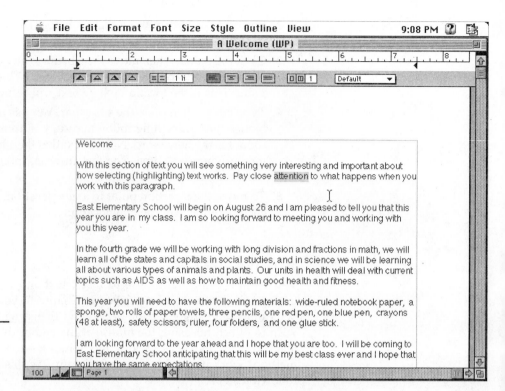

FIGURE 2-3

A word can be selected (highlighted) by dragging the I-beam over it or by double-clicking on it.

5. Practice the skills you have learned in selecting various portions of the text. First select a letter. Then select a word, a paragraph, and finally two paragraphs. Practice dragging the mouse and also using the shortcuts. You must be able to select specific sections of text within your document, because that is the only way to make changes to existing text. Continue practicing until you are confident that you can select any text you want.

6. Click anywhere to deselect the highlighted text when you are finished practicing.

Using these shortcuts can often save you time when you are working with your word processing document. Remember, double-clicking selects the word where the I-beam is located, clicking three times selects the entire line, and clicking four times selects the paragraph.

Word Processing Screen Features

As mentioned earlier, what you see on the screen is a word processing document along with a variety of symbols, such as menus, scroll bars, and a ruler, that represent features available in ClarisWorks. A brief overview of these features will give you a clearer picture of the word processor and some of your options (refer back to the labels in Figure 2-2 during this discussion).

MENUS

The menu bar at the very top of the screen displays menus that deal with actions related to the word processing application. These menus pull down to provide further options. Notice that some of the menus differ from those found on the Desktop when you are not in the ClarisWorks program.

Choosing Pull-Down Menu Options

You will frequently use pull-down menus during the process of editing. The following steps demonstrate how to select a menu option, in this case the Select All option on the **Edit menu** (the word Edit on the menu bar). The **Select All** option selects (highlights) all text in the document.

1. Position the mouse pointer over the Edit menu.
2. Press the mouse button down and continue to hold it. You can see your menu options (Undo Typing, Cut, Copy, etc.) displayed.
3. Drag the mouse pointer down over the Edit menu options. Notice that as you pass the pointer over black options, the option becomes highlighted. Gray options do not become highlighted, because they are not available to use at this time.
4. When Select All is highlighted, as shown in Figure 2-4, release the mouse button. All text in the document should now be highlighted.

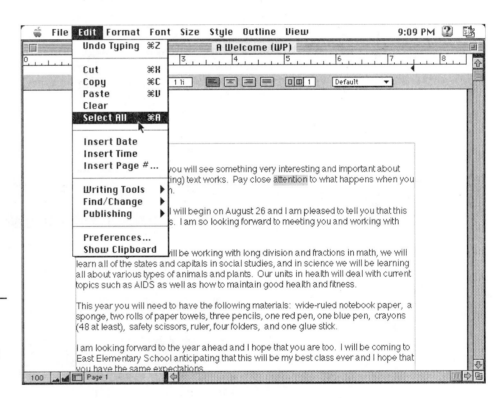

FIGURE 2-4

The menu bar for the word processor displays nine menu titles (including the Apple). The Edit menu has been pulled down and the pointer dragged to Select All.

5. Click anywhere on the text to remove the selection.
6. Sometimes you will pull a menu down, then decide not to use it. If this happens, simply continue to drag the pointer anywhere off the menu, then release the mouse button. No option will be chosen. Try it by pulling down the Format menu and dragging the pointer off the menu to the left, then releasing the mouse.
7. Pull down other menus, observe their options, then release them as you just did in Step 6.

TITLE BAR

Under the menu bar you see a bar with the name A Welcome in the middle. This is the title bar, which is always at the top of any open window. It shows the name of the current document or file being used, followed in parentheses by the type of document. In this case, (WP) indicates that this is a word processing file.

TEXT RULER

Under the title bar you see the text **ruler**. In addition to an actual ruler showing the width of your page, the text ruler includes some symbols on the blank line under the ruler and more symbols on the shaded area below the blank line. The ruler is used to control characteristics of paragraphs, such as spacing, tabs, indentations, and text alignment. These will be considered in detail later.

MARGINS AND PAGE GUIDES

The actual text is found in the area below the text ruler. Notice that there is a white area on the outside of the text. That area is the **margin**. The gray lines surrounding the text are the **page guides** that indicate the edges of the margins. This allows you to see on the screen what your text will look like when it is printed on paper. This is sometimes called What You See Is What You Get or WYSIWYG (pronounced WIS-EE-WIG).

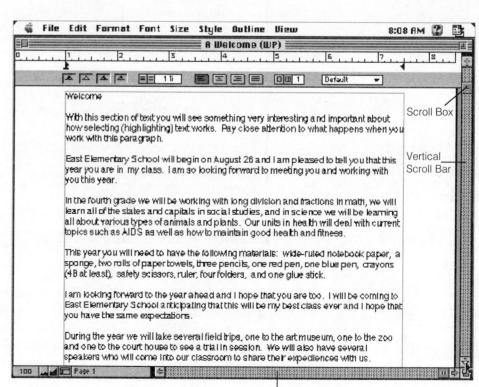

FIGURE 2-5

The A Welcome document has been scrolled up a few lines through the use of the arrow at the bottom of the vertical scroll bar. Notice that the scroll box is no longer at the top of the scroll bar.

SCROLL BARS

Only a small portion of the text is currently displayed on the computer screen. To see additional portions, you can use the horizontal and vertical scroll bars, the gray areas at the bottom and right of the screen with arrows on each end. These help you move through your text. The following steps demonstrate how to use the scroll bars.

1. Click the bottom arrow of the **vertical scroll bar** (at the right of the screen) as shown in Figure 2-5. This moves the text toward the top of the screen one line at a time.

2. Continue clicking, or hold the mouse button down to continue moving through the text.

3. Click the arrow at the top of the vertical scroll bar to move text back down. Notice that the scroll box—the small, white square on the scroll bar—moves as the text scrolls.

4. Drag the scroll box to the bottom of the scroll bar. This allows you to move quickly to the end of the document. Drag it back up about half way to move to approximately the middle of the document. Dragging the scroll box is particularly useful if you are working with a long document with many pages.

5. Click on the gray area of the vertical scroll bar. This moves the document approximately one screen at a time. If you click above the scroll box, the document moves one screen higher in the text. If you click below the scroll box, the document moves one screen lower in the text. Try it!

6. If the document does not fit horizontally on the screen, the **horizontal scroll bar** (at the bottom of the screen) moves the document horizontally in a similar manner. Practice the horizontal and vertical screen movements until you are comfortable with them.

7. Position the document in the window so that you can see both right and left page guides.

Note that at the bottom of the screen just to the left of the horizontal scroll bar you see the **page indicator**, as shown in Figure 2-6. When working with a multipage document, this indicator will show you what page is being displayed. If you double-click on the page indicator, a dialog box appears that allows you to move to a specific page in a multipage document.

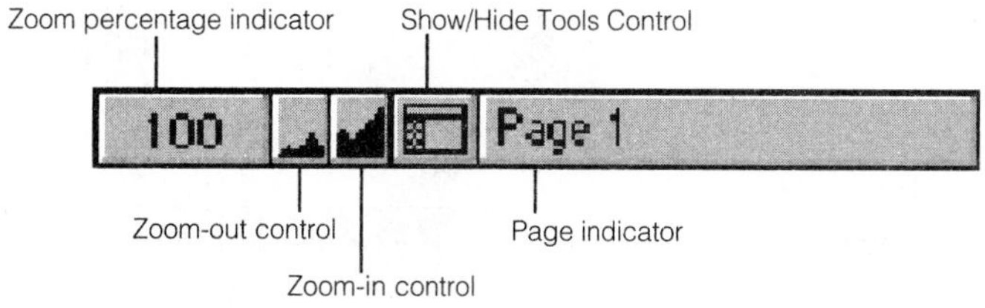

FIGURE 2-6

The bottom left portion of the screen contains the zoom controls, the page indicator, and the show/hide tools control.

ZOOM CONTROLS

Currently the text is displayed in fairly large, readable type, but unfortunately you can't see how this text will look when it is printed on paper because you can't see enough of it at a time. To remedy this situation you have the capability of "zooming in" or "zooming out" of the text. This is like zooming in or out with a movie camera or VCR camcorder—you get a closer view or a more distant view. When you look closer you can see more clearly, but you can't see as broad a range.

On the bottom left-hand side of the screen you should see the number 100. This area is called the **zoom percentage indicator**. Next to it are two icons. The left, smaller icon is the **zoom-out control**, and the right, larger icon is the **zoom-in control**. These are shown in Figure 2-6. Experiment a moment by following the steps below.

1. Click on the zoom-out control (the smaller one). The text should become smaller and more of the page should be visible. The zoom percentage box should now indicate 66.7, meaning the screen image is reduced to 66.7 percent of actual size.

2. Click on the zoom-out control again. The text becomes even smaller and the zoom percentage box indicates 50 percent.

3. Click yet again on the zoom-out control. The text again becomes smaller. Now the indicator displays 33.3. The document should appear on the screen as in Figure 2-7.

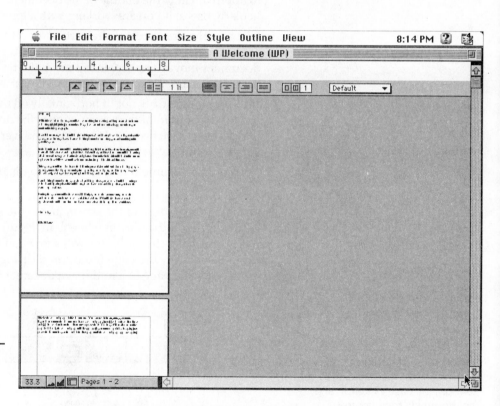

FIGURE 2-7

The A Welcome document has been zoomed out to 33.3 percent of its actual size.

Zooming out allows you to see what the general layout of a page is without concentrating on the text in the page itself. It gives you thumbnail sketches, which can be helpful in determining whether there is enough white space and whether the general arrangement of text or graphics is pleasing to the eye.

4. When you are ready to go back to 100 percent viewing, point to the zoom percentage indicator and hold down the mouse button. You will see a zoom percentage pop-up menu, as shown in Figure 2-8.

```
 ┌──────────┐
 │  25%     │
 │  33%     │
 │  50%     │
 │  67%     │
 │  75%     │
 │ ✓100%    │
 │  200%    │
 │  400%    │
 │  800%    │
 │  Other...│
 └──────────┘
```

FIGURE 2-8

The zoom percentage pop-up menu allows the easy selection of a particular viewing scale.

5. Choose 100%. Note that you can quickly zoom to a particular zoom percentage using the pop-up menu, or you can choose Other... to enter your own viewing scale.

6. Click on the zoom-in control. The text becomes much larger and the zoom percentage indicator displays 200. Zooming in gives you the opportunity to see more clearly what is on the display as you are editing text or graphics. You can zoom in as closely as you need to.

7. Continue practicing with the zoom features until you are easily able to change to different views.

8. When you are finished practicing, click on the zoom percentage indicator to place the view back to 100 percent. Use the scroll bar, if necessary, to center the document horizontally on the screen.

SHOWING/HIDING TOOLS

Another control available at the bottom of the screen is the **Show/Hide Tools control** (see Figure 2-6). The tools are currently hidden from display on the screen.

1. Click on the Show/Hide Tools control (to the left of the page indicator).

FIGURE 2-9

Tools for graphics are displayed on the screen through use of the Show/Hide Tools control.

2. You should see a display of tools on the left side of the screen as shown in Figure 2-9. These tools are useful for creating graphic illustrations and enhancements within the various types of ClarisWorks documents. You will use these tools in the Graphics chapter.

3. Click on the Show/Hide Tools control again to remove the tools from the display.

Editing Text

Now that you are familiar with the layout of the screen and the use of the mouse, it's time to begin making some changes to the text. Inserting, deleting, changing, and moving text are some of the activities most commonly needed for editing.

INSERTING TEXT

You have already learned how to insert text. Try this procedure with the following steps. There are some changes that need to be made in the welcome letter for this current school year; the activities have changed for this year. Begin by following the steps below to add the phrase **and drug and alcohol abuse** after the word **AIDS** in the third paragraph.

1. If the third paragraph is not visible on the screen, use the vertical scroll bar to bring it into view.

2. Move the text insertion point to the right of the word **AIDS** in the third paragraph. (Remember, to move the insertion point, position the I-beam just past the **S**, then click the mouse button.)

3. If a space is needed after the word **AIDS** press the space bar. Then type the phrase **and drug and alcohol abuse** to indicate that these additional topics will be covered this year. Notice that the new phrase has been inserted and the rest of the sentence has moved right. Notice also that at the right margin the text wrapped automatically to the next line.

4. Now add information about a book the students will be reading. Move the text insertion point to the right of the period at the end of the same sentence after **... good health and fitness.**

5. Press the space bar once; then type the following sentence: **We will also be reading the book, The Silver Star, and writing a personal biography in English.** Don't worry about typing errors—you will be able to correct them later.

DELETING TEXT

In the last paragraph, which begins **During the year ...,** the word **experiences** has been typed incorrectly as **expediences.** You can delete the **d** and replace it with an **r** to correct the error.

1. Use the vertical scroll bar to bring the last paragraph into view.

2. Position the text insertion point immediately after the **d** in **expediences.**

3. Press the Delete key on the keyboard. The Delete key deletes characters to the left of the text insertion point.

4. Type **r** to insert the correction.

Another way to delete is to use the Cut option on the Edit menu. This is especially useful if you have a large segment of text to delete. To use Cut, you must first select (or highlight) the text to be cut. If you don't make a selection, the program won't know what you want to cut, and the Cut option will remain gray on the menu.

1. Use the vertical scroll bar to bring the first paragraph into view.

2. Select the first paragraph either by dragging the mouse down through the lines or by moving the I-beam anywhere within the paragraph and clicking the mouse four times.

3. From the Edit menu choose Cut.

4. You will notice that the text that was selected has disappeared from the screen. It has been moved out of the document to an area called the Clipboard.

5. To see what's on the Clipboard, choose Show Clipboard from the Edit menu. The cut text is saved here temporarily, in case you want to use it later. Figure 2-10 shows the open Clipboard window.

6. To remove the Clipboard from view, click on the close box, the small square box at the left end of the Clipboard title bar.

7. If you wish to take out the extra line between **Welcome** and the first paragraph, press the Delete key while the insertion point is at the beginning of the line above **East Elementary School.**

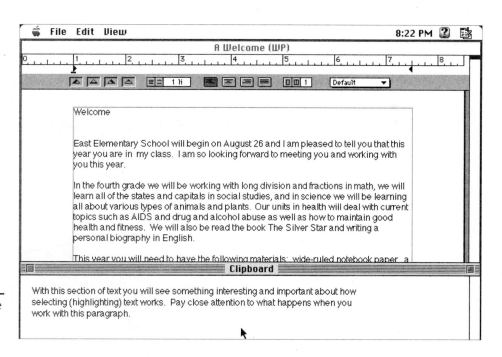

FIGURE 2-10

The Clipboard is displayed on the screen by using Show Clipboard from the Edit menu.

REPLACING TEXT

Sometimes it is easier to replace text rather than to go through steps of deleting or cutting before retyping. This is done by selecting text to be replaced and typing the new text. This year school begins on September 1. You need to correct the date at the beginning of the letter.

1. Select **August 26.**
2. Type **September 1.**

Whenever text has been selected, pressing any key replaces the selecte text with what was just typed. In this case typing **S** deleted the selected te and replaced it with **S**. Also an insertion point appears so that addition typing is automatically inserted, as was the remainder of the dat **eptember 1**.

Note that if you select text and then press the Delete key, all of the selecte text is then removed from your document. If you wish to erase a section of tex this is an easy way to do it.

UNDOING ERRORS

Beware! If you have a section of text selected and accidentally type anoth character on the keyboard, the entire selected text will be replaced by th character! Selecting your entire text and carelessly typing could cause you to los everything in your document.

About the only choice you have in a situation such as this is to use the Und option on the Edit menu. **Undo** lets you *undo* what you just did. It works n only with typed characters but also with some other functions, such as Cut an Paste. If you pasted in the wrong place, you can select Undo Paste and get bac to what you had before. You must, however, use Undo immediately after yo make the mistake. Try it:

1. From the Edit menu choose Select All. This highlights all text in your docu ment.
2. Press the space bar. OOPS! Only a space is left on the screen!
3. From the Edit menu choose Undo Typing, as shown in Figure 2-11. All th text is back in the document. Notice that the cursor is now at the end of th document. You may move the vertical scroll box to the top of the scroll ba to go to the beginning of the document.
4. Click anywhere to deselect the highlighted text.

FIGURE 2-11

The Undo option allows you to undo most errors.

Saving Documents

You may want to save the changes you have made to the A Welcome document. All the edits you have just made are stored in the memory of your computer. If someone accidentally kicks out the power cord, if the electricity goes out, or if you just turn off the computer, all your work will be lost. To avoid this problem, you must store your work someplace else. You do this by saving your document on a disk. When you save a document or file, you are essentially copying it to a disk. The first time you save a new document, you give it a name and tell the computer what disk to use for the save. Once your document has been saved, you can edit it again, then save it again with the same name. This saves the document with the new edits, replacing (deleting) the older version that is no longer needed.

Saving your work often is generally a good idea in case of unexpected computer or power problems. Saving a document before editing large sections of it also helps if text is accidentally deleted. When you have a copy of the text saved on disk, you can simply reopen it and start over with your editing.

There are two save options on the File menu, as shown in Figure 2-12. One option, **Save**, is used when a document has been previously saved. It will cause the old document to be replaced by the current, edited version. In most cases, when you make revisions to an existing document, you will use Save to replace the original version with the corrected one—the version without the edits will no longer be useful to you. If the Save option is used for a document that has never been saved before, a Save dialog box is displayed. This dialog box is the same as that displayed with the second Save option (Save As...) and allows you to name the document and to choose the disk where the document will be saved.

The second option, **Save As...**, displays the Save dialog box every time it is used. This allows you to save a new document that has never been saved. It also allows you to save an already named (previously saved) document, such as the one you have been working with, on a different disk or with a different name. Saving in this manner leaves the original, unedited document intact on the original disk and saves the edited version under a different name or on a different disk.

File	Edit	Format	Font
New...			⌘N
Open...			⌘O
Insert...			
Close			⌘W
Save			⌘S
Save As...			⇧⌘S
Revert			
Document Summary Info			
Shortcuts			▶
Library			▶
Mail			▶
Mail Merge...			⇧⌘M
Page Setup...			
Print...			⌘P
Quit			⌘Q

FIGURE 2-12

The File menu has two save options, Save and Save As....

In general, you will use Save As… with most of the sample files on your Data Disk to save the files with a new name. This will allow you to keep a copy of your edits and will also keep the sample files in their original, unedited form, available for you to reuse if you wish to go through these lessons again. When you start typing your own documents and making revisions, you will use Save to replace the original version with the corrected one.

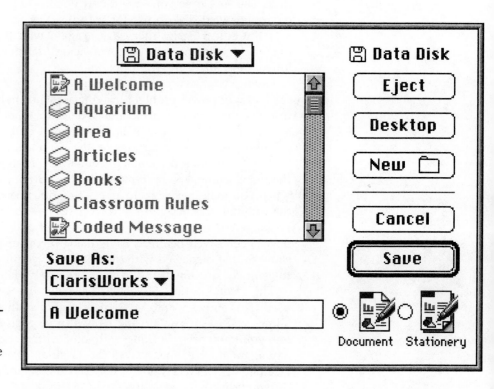

FIGURE 2-13

By using the Save As… dialog box, the name of the document and/or the disk drive used for the save can be changed.

Follow the steps below to save the corrections you have made in a document with a new name, leaving the original document unchanged on the Data Disk.

1. From the File menu, choose Save As…. A dialog box similar to Figure 2-13 should be displayed.

2. Note that the name Data Disk is displayed on the right side of the dialog box next to the diskette symbol above the Eject button. This is the disk that you took the file from originally. The name Data Disk also appears at the top of the dialog box, above the list of files. The name in this location currently shows the disk, but it will show a folder name if files within a folder are listed. Folders are used much as file folders are used to organize documents. You can create folders for subject areas, students, and personal records. You will notice that within the Save As dialog box there is an option to create a new folder. This allows you to create a folder and then save your document in that folder. Right now you won't create a new folder, but once you begin creating your own documents you may wish to place them in folders. There is also an option to save the document as a document or as stationery. Generally you will be saving items you create as documents. You also have the option to save the document as stationery, a template document. When you open a stationery document, it opens as Untitled and the original docu-

ment does not change. This is helpful for form letters and other items for which you have a general template.

You must know which drive you are saving your document on. For instance, if you thought you were saving a document on a floppy disk, but saved it on a hard disk, it wouldn't be on that floppy disk when you tried to finish your edits. And if you were working on a school computer, you would be extremely lucky if no one deleted the document. However, if you work on your own computer, you will probably want to save documents on the hard drive. Or, you may want to save your document on the floppy drive but on a disk different from the one currently in the machine.

CHANGING DISKS AND FOLDERS

You will be saving this document on the Data Disk, but to be sure you understand how to change drives if you need to, follow these steps:

1. Within the Save dialog box click on Desktop. Your hard drive name will now be on the right above the Eject button and the label Desktop will be above the listing. Notice that now the list contains only Desktop objects that can be opened: the hard drive, the floppy drive (Data Disk), the Trash, and perhaps other drives, if you have others attached.

2. Double-click on the hard drive name to open the hard drive (or click the hard drive name once to select it and then click on Open). You should see the hard drive name above the Eject button and above the list of folders and documents contained on your hard drive. If you were to click the Save button now, your document would be saved on your hard drive (do not do this now).

3. Double-click on one of the folders listed. You should see the hard drive name still above the Eject button. The name here always indicates the Desktop or the name of the disk you are using. The name of the folder you opened should be above the list of folders and documents that are in that folder. If you were to click Save now, your document would be saved in that folder, on your hard drive (again—do not do this now). Notice the small triangle to the right of the folder name at the top of the dialog box. This indicates that you can see more information.

4. Point to the small triangle beside the folder name and hold the mouse button down. The hard disk name and the Desktop should be listed. If the folder were inside other folders, all folders would be displayed, with each inside the one named below it. By highlighting any of these and releasing the mouse button, you could display the contents of the highlighted folder.

5. Click Desktop again.

6. Double-click Data Disk. Notice that Data Disk appears once more in both locations at the top of the dialog box. If you wanted to save this file on another disk, you could click on Eject and place a different disk in the drive. If you used the original write-protected disk that came with this book, you will need to eject that disk and replace it with another disk that is not write-protected before proceeding. If you wanted to save within a folder, you could open a folder, as you did the folder on the hard drive. You will be saving your document now on the Data Disk, and not in a folder.

SAVING WITH A NEW NAME

Because you do not want to replace the original document, you need a new name for the document. You will save it with the name New Welcome.

1. Be sure the name Data Disk appears in both locations at the top of the dialog box. If it doesn't, repeat Steps 5 and 6 above until you see it.
2. Select the word **A** in the name **A Welcome.** The name here can be edited in the same way that text in the document can be edited.
3. Type **New** to replace the **A**.
4. Click Save. The Save dialog box disappears with no messages, but now the name New Welcome is on the title bar and also New Welcome is on the Data Disk. It contains your edited changes. A Welcome has been automatically closed. It is still on the disk also, and if you were to open it now, it would be exactly as it was when you first opened it. If you wanted to save the file in a folder but had not yet created the folder, you could create one by clicking on the New folder button. After creating the folder, the document could be saved in it. From now on you can edit the New Welcome document.

> **CLASSROOM ←——→ CONNECTION**
>
> How can you use what you have learned so far in the classroom? A good way to begin is with a story starter. Give students basic instructions on how to insert and delete text, then let them create a story. Save the story starter as stationary, then as students write their endings they can each save the story with their own names, leaving the template intact.

CLOSING A DOCUMENT

Once you know how to get in and out of ClarisWorks and to open, save, and close documents you will be able to stop and restart your work at almost any time. To close the New Welcome document do the following:

1. From the File menu choose **Close**—you can also click on the close box, the small square on the left in the title bar. The document window closes and the Desktop items that were under the window can be seen.

Closing documents does not stop the program. By using the File menu you could return to the New Welcome document or any other document. To stop the program you must specifically tell it to quit.

Quitting ClarisWorks

When you finish, or just need a break, you must know how to quit using the program. Exit ClarisWorks by following the steps listed below.

1. Choose **Quit** from the File menu.
2. You have just saved all your changes, so there should be no messages. If you had made edits and not saved them, you would see a dialog box asking if you wished to save changes. You could click Yes, No, or Cancel, depending on what you needed to do. Clicking Yes would save the changes with the current document name on the current disk. If you wanted to change the

document name or disk before saving, you would cancel and use Save As... on the File menu.

Now you are surely ready to stretch! This may be a good place to take a break. You have accomplished a great deal so far, especially if you are a novice with the Macintosh. What you've just done is the basis for all your work with ClarisWorks. As you continue with these exercises, you will have plenty of opportunity to practice these skills. You will discover that they gradually become familiar and easy. As you continue these exercises, refer back to earlier steps whenever you need to.

CLASSROOM ← → CONNECTION

Have students open a document that is a letter. Their assignment is to insert, delete, and change certain features of the letter and then save it using their name or initials as a part of the name.

Returning to ClarisWorks

You will now be working with additional editing features in the New Welcome document that you saved. To return to ClarisWorks and the document, simply open the New Welcome document in the same manner that you opened the A Welcome document earlier in this chapter. (If the Data Disk is closed, you can double-click to open it. Then double-click the New Welcome document to open it and launch ClarisWorks.) Refer to "Beginning ClarisWorks—Opening a Disk or Document" on page 23, if you need to.

Additional Editing Options

With what you have learned so far you can successfully edit any text. However, some editing could be done more easily with additional commands available in ClarisWorks. A few of these are introduced in the following exercises.

MOVING TEXT

The next to the last paragraph of the New Welcome letter would work better as the last paragraph. You don't need to erase it and retype it; you can simply move it. To do this, "cut" it out of its current location and "paste" it into its new location.

1. Select/highlight the paragraph that begins **I am looking forward to the year ahead and ....**

2. From the Edit menu choose **Cut**. (If you forget to select the text, Cut or Copy will not be darkened. By selecting you are identifying what it is you want to cut or copy.)

3. The paragraph has been cut from the document and placed on the Clipboard. (What was previously on the Clipboard is no longer there. The Clipboard only holds one set of text at a time. Check it with Show Clipboard if you like and then close the Clipboard.)

4. To put the text into the new position below the last paragraph, move the text insertion point to a location below the last paragraph of the letter.

5. From the Edit menu choose **Paste**. You should see the text appear at its new location.

6. If the spacing below the paragraph needs to be adjusted, do so by placing the text insertion point at the beginning of a paragraph. Press the Return key to add a blank line or the Delete key to remove a blank line.

Note that in copying the paragraph you may have left a blank line above and below the paragraph. This causes extra spacing in your document. When you paste, you may not have the extra space you need between paragraphs. This can all be adjusted as noted in Step 6 above.

COPYING TEXT

Sometimes two or more sections of text are similar, with only a few differences. In cases such as this it is useful to copy text from one location to another. In the coming year, students will be keeping some materials that should have names placed on them. Other materials will be shared by the whole class on an as-needed basis. One way to tell the parents this without retyping the list of materials is to simply copy it. To do this you "copy" the text and "paste" it into its new location.

1. Select part of the list of materials in the third paragraph, highlighting **three pencils** through **one glue stick.**

2. From the Edit menu choose **Copy**.

3. The text is still in the document, but it has also been copied to the Clipboard. Anything previously on the Clipboard is now gone. (Use Show Clipboard to see this and then close the Clipboard.)

4. Place the text insertion point at the end of the paragraph after **one glue stick.**

FIGURE 2-14

The selected text **three pencils** through **one glue stick**. was copied and pasted immediately after glue stick. The copied portion can now be edited.

This year you will need to have the following materials: wide-ruled notebook paper, a sponge, two rolls of paper towels, three pencils, one red pen, one blue pen, crayons (48 at least), safety scissors, ruler, four folders, and one glue stick. Although it may be a little difficult, many problems can be avoided if you put your name on each piece of the following: three pencils, one red pen, one blue pen, crayons (48 at least), safety scissors, ruler, four folders, and one glue stick.

5. Press the space bar and type the following: **Although it may be a little difficult, many problems can be avoided if you put your name on each piece of the following:** and then press the space bar again.

6. From the Edit menu choose Paste. Your paragraph should contain the text shown in Figure 2-14.

7. Practice the rest of your editing skills. Insert text, punctuation, and so on, so that the rest of the paragraph reads as follows:

   On the package of notebook paper a name may be simply written on the package. The other materials will be stocked

and used as needed by the class. Names do not need to be placed on the sponge and the two rolls of paper towels.

When you paste text, always be sure that the insertion point is positioned in the location where you want to place the text. If there is no insertion point, but text is selected when you paste, the selected text will be replaced by the pasted text. Remember that you can undo the paste if the results are not what you expect.

Saving a Document Periodically

At this point you should save the document again, because you have made more changes. It is a good idea to save your work often to avoid the possibility of losing your changes—every 10 or 15 minutes is a good interval. You never know when something might interrupt your program!

1. From the File menu, choose Save.

2. There is no dialog box. The document with the changes made is stored under the same name, New Welcome. The version of New Welcome saved earlier is replaced by this version with the new edits. The document name and the storage disk are not changed by this type of save.

CLASSROOM ←———→ CONNECTION

Scramble a familiar nursery rhyme or any other familiar song or poem. Have the students use copy, cut, and paste to correct it. Possible examples are *Mary Had A Little Lamb*; *Row, Row, Row Your Boat*; or *Twinkle, Twinkle Little Star*.

Using Return Markers

You may have noticed that as you type, words at the end of a line **wrap** around to the beginning of the next line and sentences immediately follow other sentences. However, some sentences start on new lines as new paragraphs. To start a new paragraph, you press the Return key. ClarisWorks inserts an invisible return marker when Return is pressed. This forces everything typed after the Return to go to a new line. Typing an extra Return inserts a blank line. Return markers can be deleted in the same manner as any other character. Other keys, such as the Tab key and the space bar, also cause the insertion of invisible characters. ClarisWorks gives you the option of displaying these invisible markers.

1. Choose **Preferences...** from the Edit menu. A dialog box displays options for the document (see Figure 2-15).

2. Click **Show Invisibles** to select it. An X should be displayed in the box once it is selected.

3. Click on OK.

4. The letter should now look like Figure 2-16. Note the symbols used to indicate use of the Return key and space bar. Tabs also would show here, if they were used.

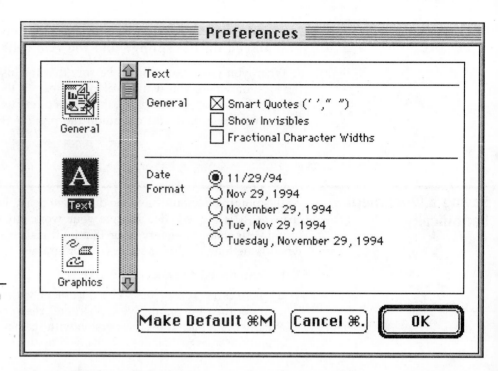

FIGURE 2-15

The Preferences dialog box with an X in the boxes of selected text Options and a darkened circle showing the date format selected.

5. In this letter it would be nice to have one blank line between paragraphs for better readability. If you have extra blank lines in the letter, put the text insertion point at the beginning of a blank line and press the Delete or back-space key to erase the Return marker.

6. If you have two paragraphs that do not have a blank line between them, place the text insertion point at the beginning of the second paragraph and press the Return key to create a blank line.

7. To remove the invisible characters from view, choose Preferences… from the Edit menu.

8. Click again on Show Invisibles. This will deselect it. (Note that the X is no longer displayed in the box.)

9. Click on OK. The text should be displayed without the invisible characters.

Seeing the invisible characters can be helpful when editing, but may be distracting when you are creating or reading a document. The symbols used for the invisible characters will not print when you print the document even though they may be displayed on the screen.

Using Font, Size, and Style Menus

Font refers to the design of the letters and the characters in the text. A font may include very fancy or very plain letters and symbols. The fonts you have available depend on which ones have been installed in your system folder. These fonts are listed in the **Font menu**. Size refers to how large or small the characters are and can be adjusted using the **Size menu**. Style refers to attributes such as italic, bold, underline, or the color of the text. The **Style menu** lists these options. When you first start a new document, font, size, and style are already set for prechosen

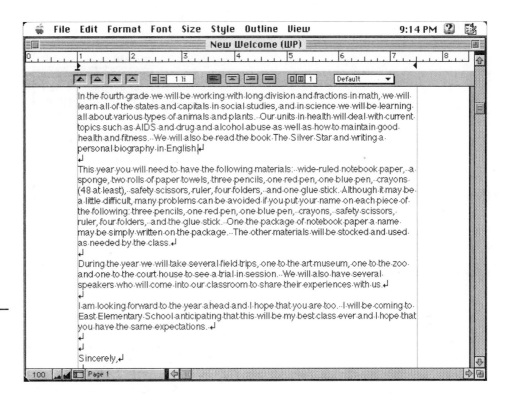

FIGURE 2-16

The New Welcome document with the previously invisible characters displayed. Notice that spaces are represented by dots and returns by arrows.

default values. If you start typing, all text will match the default settings. If you do not want these settings, you must change them.

EDITING FONT, SIZE, AND STYLE

To change these features in previously typed text, select the text to be changed, then make choices from the menus. The choices you make will affect only the text you have selected. For instance, in the New Welcome document the title of the book **The Silver Star,** should be italicized. In addition, the heading **Welcome** at the beginning of the letter can be changed to a different font and enlarged to make it more attractive, eye-catching, and interesting.

1. Select the title **The Silver Star** in the paragraph beginning **In the fourth grade ....**
2. From the Style menu choose Italic, as shown in Figure 2-17. You should then be able to see **The Silver Star** in italics.
3. Look at the Style menu again. Notice that Italic is checked. This indicates the current style for the selected text.
4. Select the word **Welcome** at the beginning of the letter.
5. From the Size menu choose 18 Point to change the size of the current font.
6. From the Font menu choose any font that is not currently checked. (See Figure 2-18.) **Welcome** should appear in the new font.
7. From the Style menu choose Text Color. From the colors shown choose a color you like.
8. Experiment with other changes in font, size, and style to make the letter more interesting.

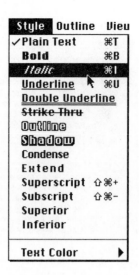

FIGURE 2-17

The Style menu provides options that control the way text characters are displayed and printed.

FIGURE 2-18

The checkmark on this Font menu indicates the selected text is in the Helvetica font. The text will be changed to the Chicago font when the mouse button is released.

INSERTING NEW FONT, SIZE, OR STYLE

Normally, what you type will have the same font, size, and style as whatever text immediately precedes the insertion point. However, you may want to insert text using a font, size, or style different from that currently being used. To do this, place the insertion point in the desired position, choose the desired font, style, and size, then type. (Note: This works not just within previously typed text but also when you are inserting text at the end of a document or at the beginning of a new document.)

1. Place the text insertion point in the second paragraph after **In the fourth grade we will be.**
2. From the Style menu choose Bold.

3. Press the space bar and type **very.** It should appear on the screen in bold text.

4. From the Style menu choose Outline. (Notice that Bold continues to be chosen as well.)

5. Press the space bar and type **busy**.

C L A S S R O O M ◀━━━━▶ C O N N E C T I O N

Have your students experiment with different fonts, sizes, styles, and colors by writing an advertisement for their favorite television show, a subject in school, or some other topic that would appeal to them.

Practice

To be able to use ClarisWorks successfully, you will need to be comfortable with the skills you have just learned. Practice will provide that comfort. Take some time now to do more editing. Continue this tutorial when you feel confident about your ability to select, insert, delete, cut, copy, paste, and use the Font, Size, and Style menus.

1. Open the document labeled Edit Errors that is found on the Data Disk. (Leave New Welcome on your screen. Choose Open from the File menu. From the dialog box that appears, select the file Edit Errors by clicking it and then clicking on Open.) Follow the instructions in the document.

2. Scroll to the second page of the New Welcome document. Play with what you know so far about ClarisWorks. You can do anything you want on this page or at the end of it. Type a holiday note to your students, a poster advertising a school activity, a list of classroom rules, or whatever you want. Edit it and use lots of fonts and styles.

Using the Ruler

The text ruler is at the top of the screen just below the title bar, as shown in Figure 2-19. The markings on it show the width of your page. However, the text ruler also has several other functions. Below the rule marks, the shaded area of the ruler contains four sets of symbols, or icons. The triangular icons on the left side of the shaded area are the various tab settings available. (You will use the tabs later in this chapter.) The second set of three icons in the shaded area allow you to control the spacing of the lines of text. The four icons to the right of the spacing icons determine how the text is aligned (how it lines up with margins) on the page. The two icons at the right allow you to change the number of columns in your document. The status box at the right displays the number of columns currently set. The pop-up menu at the far right allows for easily making changes in the style of your paragraphs.

Except for the column control, the ruler settings apply to paragraphs. As you remember, the end of each paragraph is marked with an invisible paragraph (Return) marker. So, a ruler displays settings for one paragraph—all the text between two paragraph markers. If a ruler is changed, it changes all the text between paragraph markers. The way ClarisWorks knows which paragraph to

---

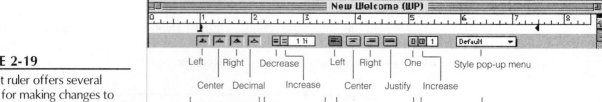

FIGURE 2-19

The text ruler offers several options for making changes to paragraphs in the document.

apply the ruler to is through the insertion point and selection of text. If no text is selected, the ruler applies to the paragraph containing the text insertion point. If text is selected, the ruler applies to a paragraph that is partially or completely selected. If text in more than one paragraph is selected, the ruler displays settings for the first paragraph containing selected text, and any changes made on the ruler apply to all paragraphs containing selected text.

CHANGING LINE SPACING

Take a look at the second group of symbols under the text ruler, the line **spacing** controls. These allow single spacing, double spacing, or other custom spacing to be used. You may change the spacing of an already typed document or parts of a document by selecting paragraphs to be changed and clicking on one of these symbols. The symbol with three lines decreases the spacing and the symbol with two bars increases the spacing by half a line for each click. The status box to the right of these symbols indicates the current line spacing in lines or in points. A point is a unit of measure that is often used by printers and artists. You may have noticed that font size is also based on points. In Figure 2-19 the spacing is one line (1 li), which is single spaced.

Change paragraphs from single spaced to double spaced with the following steps.

1. Place your insertion point anywhere within the paragraph beginning **East Elementary School will begin....**
2. Click on the increase spacing tool (the one with 2 lines). The status box should indicate 1.5 li and more space should have appeared between the lines of text for this paragraph only, as shown in Figure 2-20. Notice that other paragraphs are not changed.
3. Select all the text from **This year you will need...** through **During the year** (Stop the selection at **year**—don't select that entire paragraph).
4. Click on the increase spacing tool once, and then again. Now the status box should indicate 2 li, which means that the text is double spaced. Notice that the entire paragraph beginning **This year...** has been double spaced. Also the other paragraph containing selected text has also been double spaced, even though only a portion of the paragraph was selected.
5. From the Edit menu choose Select All to select the entire document.
6. Click on the increase spacing tool until it indicates the text is double spaced. All text should now be double spaced.
7. Click anywhere to deselect the text.

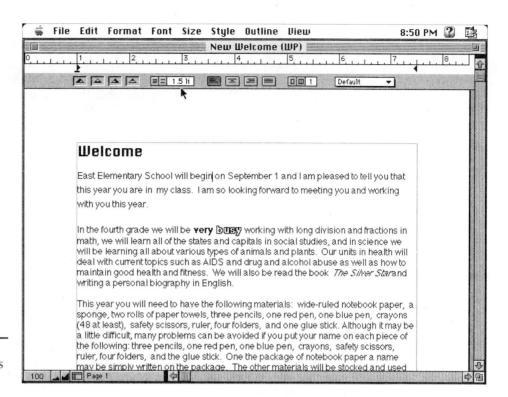

FIGURE 2-20

The spacing of the paragraph containing the insertion point has been increased to 1.5 lines.

CHANGING THE ALIGNMENT OF TEXT

Alignment, or justification, refers to the way a line of text lines up with other lines of text. For instance, when text is aligned at the left margin, or left justified, it forms a straight line down the left side of the page. Many times you will want one section of text, such as a title or subtitle, to be centered horizontally on the page while the remaining text is left justified. Examples of the various types of alignment are shown in Figure 2-21.

Left Alignment
Notice that this text is flush (even) on the left and ragged on the right. The alignment of text can enhance the look of your document. It can highlight certain important features of the text and can make reading the text easier.

Center Alignment
Notice that this text is centered on an imaginary vertical line running down the center of the text. The alignment of text can enhance the look of your document. It can highlight certain important features of the text.

Right Alignment
Notice that this text is flush (even) on the right and ragged on the left. The alignment of text can enhance the look of your document. it can highlight certain important features of the text and can make reading the text easier.

Justified Alignment
Notice that this text is flush (even) on both the left and right, like the text that is found in the columns of a newspaper. The alignment of text can enhance the look of your document. it can highlight certain important features of the text and can make reading the text easier.

FIGURE 2-21

Examples of text alignment available in ClarisWorks.

The set of four icons with horizontal lines in the shaded area of the text ruler allows you to control the way text is aligned. The first symbol is used to left justify the text, the next to center justify the text, the third to right justify the text, and the last to justify the text at both left and right margins. Notice the icons give you a small graphic image of what the lines of text will look like when that tool is selected.

Change the alignment for the word **Welcome** with the following steps. You want **Welcome** to be centered horizontally.

1. Move to the beginning of the document and select the word **Welcome**.

2. Click on the center align box (the second alignment icon) on the shaded area of the ruler. The text should now be centered on the first line.

3. Notice that only the selected text was changed. **Welcome** was the only word in that paragraph, so the rest of the document remained unchanged.

4. Click anywhere to deselect the text.

Find/Change

Many times when editing a document, it is helpful, or even necessary, to locate a particular word or phrase within the document. Other times a certain word or phrase needs to be changed everywhere it occurs in the document. These tasks can be accomplished easily by using the **Find/Change** option on the Edit menu. This option allows you to locate a particular word or phrase and, if you wish, to replace it with another.

Experiment with this example. The teacher who created the welcoming document has been transferred from East Elementary School to Bloom Elementary School. Rather than searching for the text by hand, highlighting each occurrence, and retyping the text, you can let the computer do it for you.

1. Point to the Edit menu and hold the mouse button down. Notice that the Find/Change option has an arrow at the right. This means that this option has a submenu.

2. Drag the mouse down to Find/Change and continue to hold the mouse button down to see the submenu.

3. Continue to hold the mouse button down and drag over to Find/Change... on the submenu, then release the mouse button. The Find/Change dialog box should be displayed on the screen.

4. Type **East** in the Find box, press the Tab key, and then type **Bloom** in the Change box as shown in Figure 2-22.

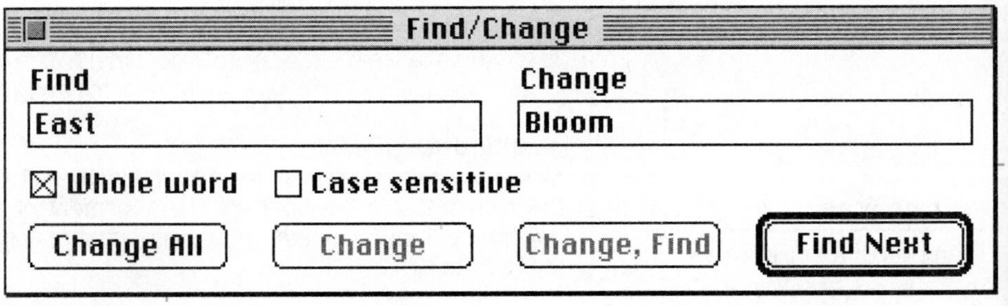

FIGURE 2-22

The Find/Change dialog box allows you to find particular text and, optionally, to replace the text found with other text.

5. Click on Whole word. This forces the computer to look for **East** as a complete word rather than a part of another word. Notice that east is a part of the word least. If whole word is not selected, the word least would be chosen, as well as east. Note that there is also an option to select Case sensitive. With this option selected East, east, and EAST would all be looked on as different words.

6. Click on Find Next. You will see displayed on the screen the first occurrence of the word **East**. If the Find/Change dialog box covers the first occurrence, place the mouse on the title bar of the dialog box and drag it so that the area of text with the highlighted word is visible.

7. Click on the Change, Find button. **East** will change to **Bloom** and the next occurrence of **East** will be found.

8. Click on the Change, Find button.

9. When the message East not found appears, the computer has not found any more occurrences of the word **East**.

10. Click on OK.

11. To close the Find/Change dialog box, click on the close box, the small square at the left end of the dialog box title bar.

CLASSROOM ◄──────► **CONNECTION**

To teach students to use the find and change feature of word processing, create a coded phrase using numerals in place of the alphabetic characters. Then have them replace the numerals with the appropriate letters to decode the message. Then have the students code their own messages using Find/Change to change the letters in their message to numerals or special characters. Use the file Coded Message from the Data Disk as an example. Use Find/Change to change the following characters: # to a, $ to e, 3 to l, 7 to u, @ to o, 1 to k, 4 to d, 6 to c, 9 to s.

Printing a Document

To print a document, your printer must be set up appropriately and turned on. You may need to select the printer. This selection is done in the Chooser option under the Apple (🍎) menu. Click on the icon that represents the type of printer that you have available. If you are not sure how to do this, please consult your Macintosh User Manual.

To print your document, follow the steps below:

1. While in the New Welcome document, choose **Print...** from the File menu. The Print dialog box displayed will be similar to Figure 2-23. This box will have different options for different printers.

2. Notice that default values have been chosen already. The entire document will print if no changes are made. (If you wished to print a portion of the document, you would type in the first and last page numbers in the From and To boxes.)

3. Click on Print. Your document should begin printing.

4. If you haven't saved all your changes, save the document again, then click the close box on the title bar to close New Welcome.

5. Choose Quit from the File menu to end the ClarisWorks program.

StyleWriter II   1.2   [**Print**]

Copies: `1`   Pages: ◉ All ○ From: [   ] To: [   ]   [Cancel]

Print Quality: ○ Best   ◉ Normal   ○ Draft   ┈┈┈┈┈┈

Paper Source: ◉ Sheet Feeder   ○ Manual   [Help]

Image: [Grayscale   ▼]   [Options]

Notification: [None   ▼]

FIGURE 2-23

The Print dialog box varies depending on your printer, but it always allows an option for the number of copies and for printing a portion of the document.

Launching ClarisWorks from the Desktop

When you began work with the A Welcome document, you launched ClarisWorks by opening the document. If you want to launch ClarisWorks to create a new document, as in the next set of exercises, you need to open the program itself.

1. Find the ClarisWorks program icon on the hard disk. It may be in a folder.

2. Double-click the program icon to launch the program. (Or, you could click the icon, then choose Open from the File menu.)

This launches the program and displays a New Document dialog box with options for choosing different document types, as shown in Figure 2-24. Follow the steps listed below in "Creating a New Document" to create a new document. If you wanted to open an existing document, rather than create a new one, you would click Cancel and then choose Open from the File menu to see a list of documents that could be opened.

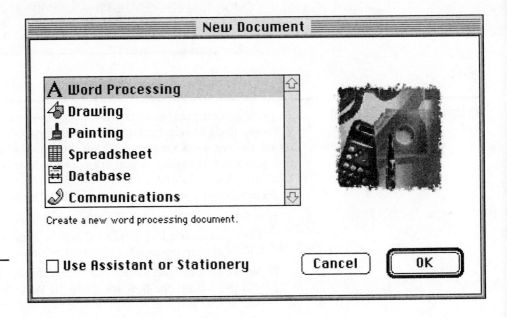

FIGURE 2-24

The New Document dialog box allows different types of documents to be created.

Creating a New Document

With the following steps you will create a new document, a test for social studies.

1. From launching ClarisWorks you should have the New Document dialog box on the screen, as shown in Figure 2-24.

2. If you did not quit ClarisWorks, you can choose **New...** from the File menu to display the New Document dialog box.

3. Word Processing is automatically selected when the New Document dialog box is displayed. When creating other types of documents, you will need to click the desired type.

4. Click on OK. A new, blank word processing document should be displayed on the screen with the name "Untitled 1" in the title bar.

5. You will see on the screen the menu bar, the title bar, and the text ruler as before—but this time there is no text on the screen. There is a blinking cursor at the top of the text area ready for you to begin typing.

Document Options

You may want to choose margins that are different from the default margins that are set when you open a new document. The margins and other options related to the whole document can be set with the **Document...** option on the Format menu.

1. From the Format menu choose Document.... Notice that, on a menu, the continuation marks (...) indicate that a dialog box will open. Here, the Document dialog box is displayed, as shown in Figure 2-25.

2. Look at the different choices available for a document. They include page display (how pages are displayed on the screen), footnotes, page numbering, and margins.

PAGE DISPLAY

The set of display options on the top right determine how pages are displayed on the screen. The default setting is one page above the next. Two pages can be viewed side-by-side by clicking in the circle in front of the second option to select it. This option can be useful if you are zooming out to see the general layout of your document. However, be aware that for larger zoom sizes you need to scroll horizontally to see successive pages on the screen when the display is set for two pages.

When the box next to **Show margins** is checked, the margins around the text are displayed on the screen, so that you can see what the entire page looks like. Clicking Show margins removes the X and hides the margins so they are not seen on the screen—only the working area is shown. **Show page guides** works in a similar manner to display, or not display, the page guide lines that show where margins are on the screen.

FOOTNOTES

The Footnotes option allows you to determine whether footnotes will be placed at the bottom of the page or at the end of the document. The default is set for the bottom of the page. This can be changed by clicking in the circle in front of At End of Document to select it. When you have a long document, you may want to divide it into two or more documents. When you do this, you generally want the footnotes in the second document to continue sequentially. This can be done by typing the appropriate number in the Start At box.

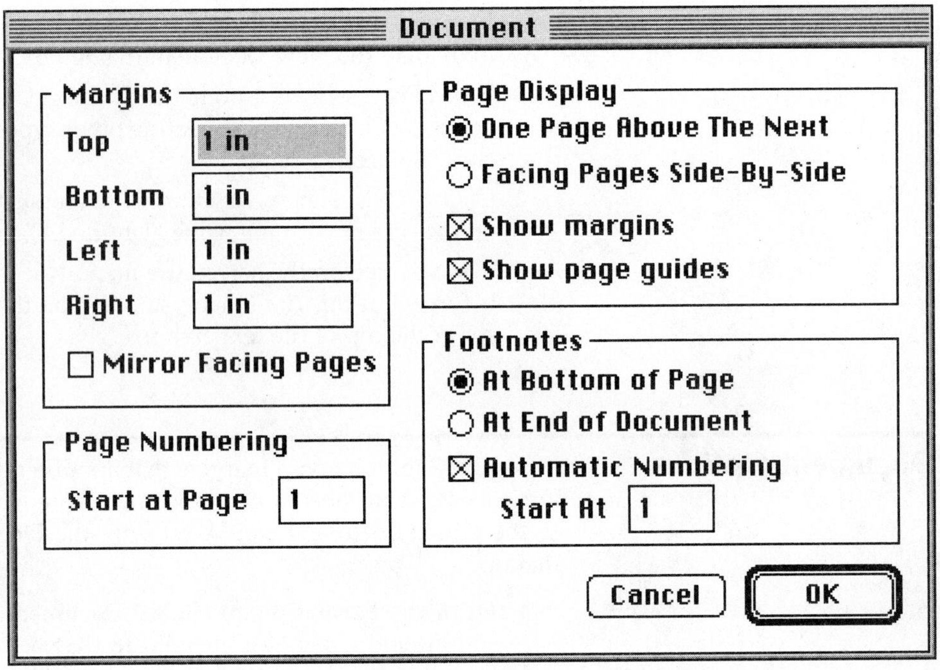

FIGURE 2-25

The Document dialog box allows you to change the margins, how pages are displayed, where page numbering starts, and how footnotes are to be numbered and displayed.

PAGE NUMBERING

If you divide a long document into two or more documents, you will generally want the page numbers of the second document to begin with the page number following the last page of the first document. This can be done by typing the appropriate number in the Start at Page box. Note, if you have a title page that you do not want to number and you wish the first page after the title page to be page one, set the starting page number to zero.

MARGINS

The default word processing margin settings in ClarisWorks place 1-inch margins around the edges of the paper. Changing the settings here causes the margins to be changed for the entire document. Margins are measured in inches (in), but the units can be changed to centimeters (cm), millimeters (mm), picas (p), or points (pt) by simply typing in the new unit of measure. If you plan to print your document on both sides of a page, select Mirror Facing so that the margins on the inside and outside of facing pages will match.

Changing Margins

Margins can be changed at any time. However, you may find it most convenient to set margins before you begin entering text. Change the margins of this document using the following steps. You should still be in the Document dialog box.

1. Press the Tab key to move the highlighted selection to the bottom margin value.
2. Type **.5 in** to set the bottom margin to .5 inch.
3. Tab to the left margin value and type **1.25 in** to set the left margin.
4. Tab to the right margin value and type **1.25 in** to set the right margin.

5. Click on OK to activate the margin changes you have made. (If you changed your mind and did not wish to make any changes, you would click Cancel to exit the Document dialog box.) Notice that the right and left page guides have moved in to the new specifications.

Entering Text

Your new document is going to be a social studies test. Begin by typing the information below. Press the Return key only at the end of paragraphs and short lines. Within paragraphs, the words will automatically wrap to the next line when you reach the end of the line. Edit your typing errors as you did earlier. Hold down the Shift key while pressing the Underline key to make the line for the name. Do not type the directions in parentheses.

Social Studies

Sample Test *(Press Tab 4 times)*

Name_____*(Press Return)*

(Press Return here to get a blank line, then do <u>not</u> press Return again until you get to the last word "once.")

I. Matching - Match the city described with its name. Place the letter of the best answer in the blank provided. Check your answers carefully before turning in your test. Each answer will be used only once.

(Press Return twice)

More Work with the Ruler

Often, typing text requires a standard paragraph format, with the first line of a paragraph indented. Other times, you may want to indent all lines of a paragraph, except the first one. By using the ruler, these and other paragraph format options can easily be set and changed. Occasionally, you may want to set tabs to line up columns of text or to indent lines of text more than the margin distance that has been set for the document. For instance, a paragraph that is a direct quote may need to be indented on both the left and the right sides. This can all be easily accomplished, once you are familiar with these uses of the ruler.

USING INDENT MARKERS

On the left-hand portion of the text ruler above the shaded area, notice a black triangular shape and the line under it. These shapes currently line up with the page guide that marks the left margin boundary. The triangle is the **left indent marker**, and the line under it (actually an upside-down T-shape) is the **first-line indent marker**, for indenting the first line of a paragraph. The black triangle at the right on the ruler is the **right indent marker**, which indents from the right margin of your text. These markers indent your text from the margins, that is, they control the distance between your text and the page guides.

Work through the next section to see how ruler changes affect the paragraph you've typed. Before you begin the steps, look at the samples in Figure 2-26. Remember that the text ruler applies to paragraphs. Any paragraph containing

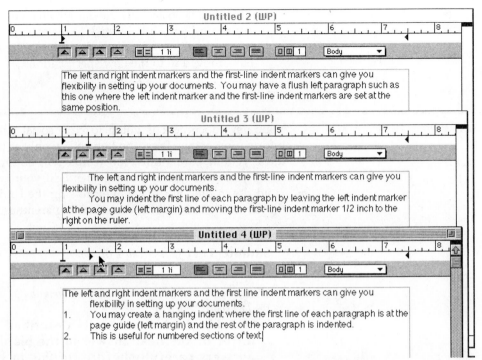

FIGURE 2-26

Examples of the type of indenting that can be done using the left and right indent markers and the first-line indent marker. Notice the placement of the indent markers on the ruler in relation to each other and the effect on the display of the text.

the insertion point or selected text is affected by ruler changes while the remainder of the document remains unchanged.

1. Position your insertion point anywhere in the paragraph beginning **I. Matching....**

2. Hold down the Option key and continue to hold it as you drag the left indent marker (the left triangle) to the 2.5-inch mark on the ruler.

3. Click to place the insertion point directly in front of the word "Match."

4. Press the Tab key. Your text should move to the right and line up neatly, as shown in Figure 2-27. This is called a hanging indent.

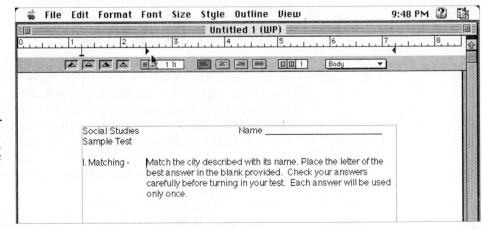

FIGURE 2-27

The first-line indent marker (the upside-down, T-shaped icon) sets the indentation for the first line of a paragraph. The triangular left indent marker indents the remainder of the paragraph's lines.

USING TABS

Tabs are used to position text in a particular location on a line without having to use the space bar. Tabs are most frequently used for lining up columns of text. When you typed the heading of the social studies test, you used the Tab key to move **Name** to the right on the line. You were able to do this even though no particular tabs had been set. ClarisWorks sets default tabs at half-inch intervals in new documents.

The tab positions can be changed. The four boxes on the left side of the shaded gray area of the ruler represent the four different types of tabs—left, center, right, and decimal. As shown in Figure 2-28, **left tab** aligns the left side of text with the tab, **center tab** aligns the center of text, **right tab** aligns the right side and **decimal tab** aligns text at the decimal (or at another character of your choice). By dragging tabs from the shaded area to the desired location on the ruler, a new tab can be set. When you do this, all default tabs to the left of the new tab are removed, whereas default tabs to the right of the new tab remain.

Setting Tabs

In this document, you will use tabs to line up test questions neatly. By placing the insertion point after a Return at the end of the text you have already typed, the changes you make to the ruler will not affect any of the existing paragraphs, but will apply only to further typing at the insertion point.

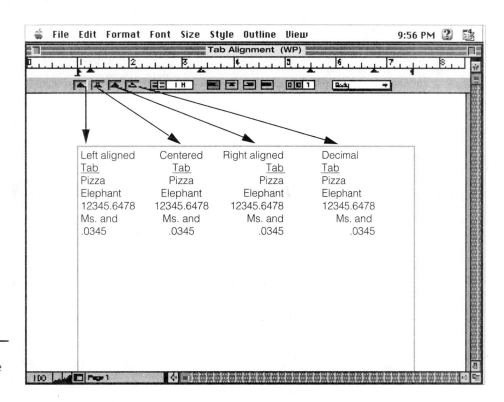

FIGURE 2-28

Examples of alignment for the four types of tabs shown on the text ruler.

1. To place the insertion point at the end of your document, move the I-beam to the lower right or left portion of the window and click the mouse. The insertion point should be positioned after the last thing you typed. (Remember, you typed two Returns at the end of the text.)

2. Make sure the left indent marker and the first-line indent marker are together on the left margin. If they aren't, move them there. The use of tabs is much less confusing if these markers are together when tabs are used.

3. Drag a decimal tab marker (the far right marker) from the shaded portion of the text ruler to below the 2-inch mark.

4. Drag a left tab marker (the far left marker) from the shaded portion of the ruler to below the 2.5-inch mark.

5. Drag a right tab marker to below the 5.25-inch mark and a left tab marker to below the 5.5-inch mark. The ruler should look like the one in Figure 2-29.

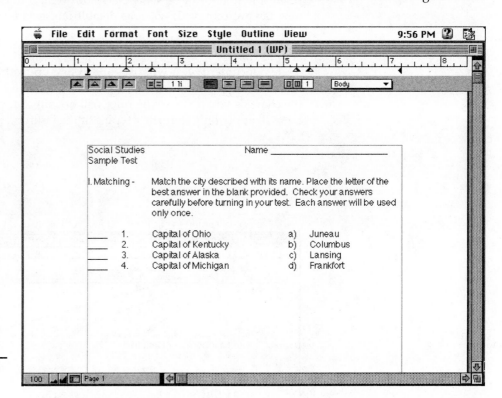

FIGURE 2-29

The text ruler has been set with tabs for typing test questions.

6. If you made a mistake and want to remove a tab, just drag it down to the shaded area of the ruler (anywhere). When you release the mouse button, the tab disappears.

The settings you just made will enable the matching questions and answers to be evenly spaced in columns. The tabs could be set differently depending on how long the questions and responses might be.

Typing Using Tabs

Once tabs have been set, text can be typed and spaced through the use of the Tab key. The **Tab key** moves text to line it up with the next **tab stop** that has been set on the line.

1. Type the following pressing the Tab key and Return key where indicated. While holding down the Shift key, press the Underline key four times to make the line for the answer.

____*(Tab)***1.***(Tab)***Capital of Ohio***(Tab)***a**)*(Tab)***Juneau***(Return)*

____*(Tab)***2.***(Tab)***Capital of Kentucky***(Tab)***b**)*(Tab)***Columbus***(Return)*

____*(Tab)***3.***(Tab)***Capital of Alaska***(Tab)***c**)*(Tab)***Lansing***(Return)*

____*(Tab)***4.***(Tab)***Capital of Michigan***(Tab)***c**)*(Tab)***Frankfort***(Return)*

2. When you finish typing, your document should be similar to Figure 2-29.

You may have noticed that as you type the question numbers, they move to the left. The reason for this is the decimal tab. It moves text to the left until you type a decimal. The decimal lines up with the tab and any continued typing appears to the right of the tab.

Using the right tab for the answer labels causes them to line up on the right at the ")" symbol. This helps to compensate for the fact that the letters are different widths. Some fonts are set up so that each letter takes up the same amount of space. New York is such a font. If you want the letters to line up evenly, you will need to use a font like New York.

Editing Tabs

The columns should be fairly well lined up, but they might look a little nicer if the questions were closer to the question number or if the answers were a little closer to the questions. Any time you set up tabs you may decide later that you wish to change them a little to make room for a longer item or to just make items more readable. In this section you will move the responses closer to the questions.

1. Select (highlight) all the questions and answers (but not the instructions), so tab changes will apply to only text in the columns.
2. Drag the tab marker at the 5.25-inch mark to the 4.5-inch mark to move the answer column left.
3. Drag the tab marker at the 5.5-inch mark down to the shaded area of the ruler to remove it. Notice that the answer columns moved to the 5-inch mark. When you remove a tab the default tabs present at half-inch intervals remain in effect on the ruler. (Remember, default tabs preset at half-inch intervals were deleted to the left of tabs you set, but not to the right.) Figure 2-30 shows how your document will look now.
4. Click anywhere to deselect the text.

COPYING A RULER

Next you need to type Section II of the test with the instructions first, as in Section I. This section will be multiple choice and as such will need some new tab settings.

1. Place the insertion point after Frankfort and press the Return key twice to space below question 4.
2. Type the following directions:

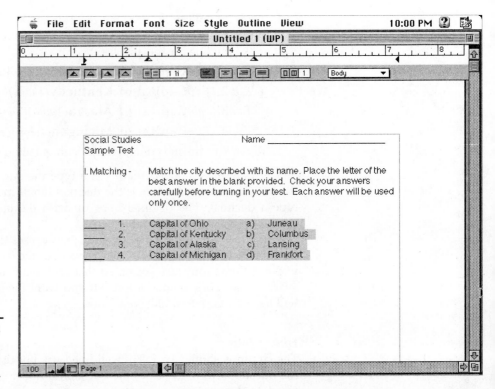

FIGURE 2-30

The first set of test questions has been typed using tabs to create columns. Note the placement of the tab markers on the text ruler.

II. Multiple Choice- *(Tab)***Choose the best answer to each question from the options given. Each answer will be used only once.** *(Press Return twice)*

Notice that the format for this paragraph is not the same as the paragraph containing instructions for the first section of the test. When you continue typing after the matching questions, the ruler has the same settings as the paragraph containing the questions. You could change the ruler settings so that they match those of the first set of instructions, but an easier way is to copy the first ruler settings and apply the copied ruler settings to the new paragraph.

3. Place the insertion point anywhere within the paragraph beginning **I. Matching ....** (or select any portion of that paragraph).

4. From the Format menu choose **Copy Ruler** (see Figure 2-31). This copies the ruler settings to an unseen memory area.

5. Move the text insertion point to any place within the paragraph beginning **II. Multiple Choice ....** Notice again that there are a variety of tab settings on the ruler that show on the screen for this paragraph.

6. From the Format menu choose **Apply Ruler**. Notice that there are no longer any additional tab settings and also that the left indent marker and the first-line indent marker are positioned as they were in the first instruction paragraph.

7. The original ruler you copied should still be stored. If you wished to format another section of the text with the same ruler settings, you could simply use Apply Ruler again.

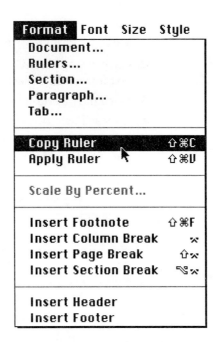

FIGURE 2-31

The Copy Ruler option on the Format menu saves a copy of the current ruler settings.

8. Because the heading of this section, Multiple Choice, is longer than Matching, you may wish to adjust the left indent marker.

9. Hold down the Option key and move the left indent marker (the triangle) to the 2.75-inch mark on the ruler. The second line of directions now lines up neatly under the first.

You need to add some multiple choice questions to your test. Follow the steps below to add questions.

1. To place the insertion point at the end of your document, move the I-beam to the lower right portion of the window and click the mouse. The insertion point should be positioned after the last thing you typed. (Remember, you typed two Returns at the end of the text.)

2. If any tabs appear on the ruler drag them one by one to the shaded area of the ruler to remove them.

3. Move the left indent marker (the triangle) to the 2.25-inch marker.

4. Drag a decimal tab marker under the 2-inch mark on the ruler.

5. Drag a left tab marker to below the 3.5-inch, 4.75-inch, and 6-inch marks on the ruler.

6. Type the following questions, pressing the Tab key and the Return key where indicated. While holding down the Shift key, press the Underline key four times to make the line for the answer.

__**5.** *(Tab)***Which of the following states borders on Lake Erie?***(Return)*

*(Tab)(Tab)***a. Michigan***(Tab)***b. Indiana***(Tab)***c. Kentucky***(Tab)***d. Illinois***(Return)*

The next question is very similar to the first. You can save the time it would take to type it by copying the question, pasting it into the text, and revising the items that need to be changed. Follow the steps below to see how this process works.

1. Select all of question 5 by highlighting the text ___ **5. Which of the following....d. Illinois**.

2. Choose Copy from the Edit menu. Remember that copy leaves the selected text intact while placing a copy on the Clipboard.

3. Place the insertion point below question 5.

4. Choose Paste from the Edit menu.

5. There should be two copies of question 5 on the test. Now edit the last question by changing the question number to 6 and the lake from Erie to Huron.

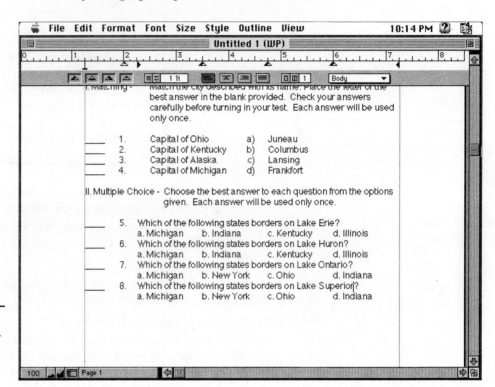

FIGURE 2-32

New tab settings have been set for the multiple choice questions. The tab settings on the text ruler apply to paragraphs not to the entire document.

6. Continue by adding the next two questions. When you finish, your text should look like Figure 2-32.

__**7.** *(Tab)***Which of the following states borders on Lake Ontario?***(Return)* *(Tab)(Tab)***a. Michigan***(Tab)***b. New York***(Tab)***c. Ohio***(Tab)***d. Indiana***(Return)*

__**8.** *(Tab)***Which of the following states borders on Lake Superior?***(Return)* *(Tab)(Tab)***a. Michigan***(Tab)***b. New York***(Tab)***c. Ohio***(Tab)***d. Indiana***(Return)*

You may have noticed that there is very little space for the students to write their responses. You can correct that by double spacing the questions, while leaving the directions as they are.

1. Select questions 1 through 4. Include the answer line and all the responses.

2. Click twice on the increase spacing tool (the one with 2 lines) on the text ruler.   The status box should indicate 2 li.

3. Select questions 5 through 8 and complete the same process. The questions on the test should now be double spaced.

More Practice Using the Text Ruler

One more section needs to be added to this test. Section III is a short essay portion of the test that requires the students to respond to a short quotation. If you have continued this portion of the directions from the beginning of this sample test, you have already copied the ruler setting from the directions for Section I. These ruler settings were used for Section II but still remain stored and can be used again to format other sections of the test. Complete the steps that follow to add Section III to the test.

1. From the Format menu choose Apply Ruler. Notice that there are no longer any additional tab settings and the left indent marker and the first-line indent marker are positioned as they were for the first set of directions. (If you haven't followed the text sequentially refer to the directions for Section II to copy the ruler settings.)

2. Type the following directions spaced two lines below question 8.

   III. Respond to the following quotation. Use full sentences to express your reaction. *(Press Return twice)*

3. Type the following quote after the Section III instructions. Edit your errors after you type the quote.

   The largest states contribute the most to our nation and as such should receive more votes in the Legislature and more Federal money for programs that they need.

4. Typically, long quotations are indented and single spaced rather than being put in quotes in double spaced format. Use the indent markers on the ruler to indent both the right and left edges of the text. Hold down the Option key to move the first-line indent marker to the 2.5-inch mark with the left indent marker. Move the right indent marker to the 5.5-inch marker.

5. Use the alignment tools on the ruler to justify the text of the quote so that both the right and left edges of the text line up evenly. Your text should look like Figure 2-33.

Inserting a Page Break

Generally, the directions for a section of a test should be on the same page as the questions. Sometimes, when there is an essay question, you may wish to have a large portion of the page free for the students' response. In either case, you may wish to start a page of text in a location other than where the text would usually break for a new page. To force the directions for Section III to be on the second page, do the following:

1. Place the insertion point at the beginning of the directions for Section III.

2. From the Format menu, choose **Insert Page Break**.

3. The text moves onto the next page. Placing a **page break** in the document will cause everything from the insertion point on to be moved to the next page.

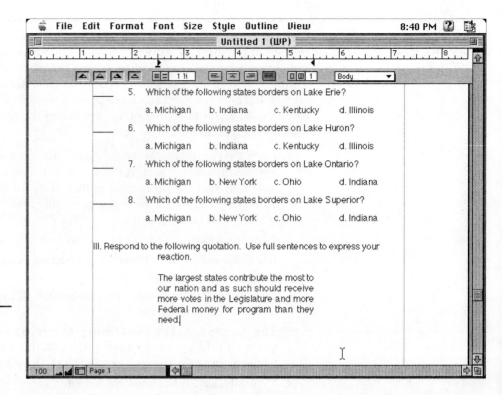

FIGURE 2-33

A long quotation has been entered in the test. Notice the changes in the left, right, and first-line indent markers in the text ruler.

The use of the Insert Page Break option forces the text onto the next page without waiting for the automatic page break to occur. Use of this option is also helpful at the end of a title page, which generally has limited text.

To take out a page break, simply place the cursor at the top of the new page and press the Delete key.

CLASSROOM ⟵⟶ CONNECTION

To give students practice with setting tabs in a document, have them type in basic information for a calendar or seating chart for the classroom. Have the students determine the approximate locations for the tabs and show them how they can be changed later if necessary.

Using Headers or Footers to Number Pages

You may want to number the pages of the test. This can be done with either a header or footer. A **header** prints at the top of each page, and a **footer** prints at the bottom of each page of a document, except the title page. Headers and footers may be extra blank lines or they may contain information such as page numbers, document titles, chapter titles, and so on.

1. From the Format menu choose **Insert Footer**. The insertion point moves to the bottom of the page and a dotted line marks the footer area. Note that the center alignment tool on the text ruler is selected. Because the insertion

point is in the footer area, the changes in the text ruler only apply to the footer. A footer can be one line or several lines, up to a maximum of one-third of the page. The same is true for headers.

2. Type the word **Page,** then press the space bar once. If the text font, style, or size is inappropriate, select it and change it using the Font, Style, and Size menus.

3. From the Edit menu, choose **Insert Page #**.

The Insert Page Number dialog box appears. Note that you have the option of printing the page number, the section number, the section page count, or the document page count. ClarisWorks 4.0 allows you to separate your document into sections and to number them as you wish.

4. Click on the arrow in the box beside Representation. Notice you have five different styles of representation available.

5. Click on OK. The page number should be displayed on the screen.

6. Scroll to the bottom of the second page to see that a page number is there also.

Creating a Title Page

A **title page** may be created by typing the information you wish to have on the first page of your document and then putting in a page break. If you are numbering pages and do not want to have the title page numbered, choose Section... from the Format menu. From the dialog box that appears, click on the box in front of Title Page to select it. To make sure that the first page of the actual document is labeled Page 1, select zero as the starting page in the Document options in the Format menu.

Checking Spelling in Your Document

You may want to check the spelling and typing in your test by using the spelling checker feature of the ClarisWorks Writing Tools. The **spell checker** will indicate whether it recognizes a word or not. Be aware that it does not check usage. If you type the word **them** when you actually meant to write the word **then,** it will not pick up that error. Also, the dictionary on a spell checker has limitations, so it will not always have every derivative of a word or special technical terms. Many proper names and abbreviations are also not found in the spell checking dictionary. You may work with these by adding a special user dictionary. See the ClarisWorks manual for directions if you wish to do this.

Check the spelling of this document. Note that your results may differ from those shown here because your typing may have additional errors.

1. From the Edit menu choose **Writing Tools** and from the submenu choose **Check Document Spelling...** as shown in Figure 2-34.

2. The spell checker will stop on at least the word **Frankfort.** As shown in Figure 2-35, the Spelling dialog box offers **Frankfurt** and **Frank fort** as possible options. When the spell checker does not find a word in its dictionary, it usually will give you one or more alternatives that you can choose from to replace the word. If the correct alternative is shown, simply select it and click on Replace.

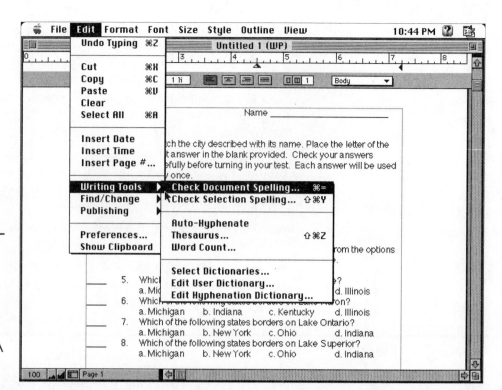

FIGURE 2-34

The Writing Tools option has a submenu. Drag the pointer to the desired submenu option to check the spelling in your document. Note that you also can check the spelling of a selected word or paragraph by using Check Selection Spelling. A Thesaurus is available to help you with word choices.

FIGURE 2-35

The spell checker did not find Frankfort in the dictionary. It suggests Frankfurt and Frank·fort as possible replacements. Clicking on the triangle in the lower right corner of the dialog box allows you to view the questionable word in the sentence or phrase in which it has been used in the text.

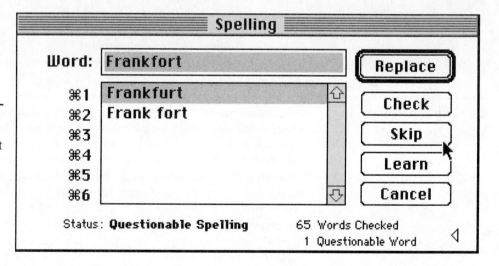

3. The word shown in the dialog box is also highlighted in the text. If you wish to see the selected word in the text, you can move the Spelling dialog box by dragging its title bar. You may also see the sentence or phrase that the word is used in by clicking on the triangle at the bottom right-hand corner of the Spelling dialog box.

4. **Frankfort** is the correct spelling of the capital of Kentucky. When this word is flagged by the spell checker, be sure you typed it correctly. If you made an error, correct it by editing the word in the box labeled Word: and click Replace.

5. If you did not have to make a correction, skip this word by clicking Skip.

6. Continue either replacing or skipping words the spell checker finds until the Done button appears as the only selectable button. Notice that the number of words in the document is shown in the bottom right portion of the dialog box. Click on Done to continue.

7. For more practice, open the document labeled Spelling Errors on your Data Disk and check it. Notice the types of errors the spell checker fails to catch. (Remember, don't save the document when you close it, unless you change the name.)

Saving a New Document

If you wish to save your document, follow these steps. You may also wish to refer back to "Saving Documents" for more information on saving.

1. Choose either Save or Save As… from the File menu. Both of these display the Save dialog box when a new document is saved for the first time.

2. Type the name of your new document. Any name will work, but it is best to choose names that will help you to remember the purpose of the document.

3. Be sure the disk name on the right of the dialog box is the disk you wish to use and that the disk or folder name at the top left of the dialog box is also the correct one.

4. Click Save.

5. Choose Close from the File menu to close this document.

Creating an Outline

Outlines are often useful in helping you to organize your thoughts. ClarisWorks offers an easy method of creating and labeling an outline. There are various styles available that can be used. As you type new text for the outline you can move the text left or right to create topic labels, topics, or subtopics for up to 16 levels. You may experiment with the outline features using the directions that follow.

1. Choose New from the File menu and click on OK to select a word processing document.

2. From the Style pop-up menu on the text ruler choose Harvard as shown in Figure 2-36.

3. Type the following text **Setting**. Notice there is a Roman numeral I preceeding the word Setting. Setting serves as a topic label in the outline.

4. With the cursor after the **g** in **Setting,** choose New Topic Right from the Outline menu. The cursor should move to the next line and indent.

5. Type **New York City** and press Return. Notice that New York City is labeled with a capital "A" and serves as a topic in the outline.

6. Type the following pressing Return where indicated.
Early 1960s *(Return)*
Small cafe downtown

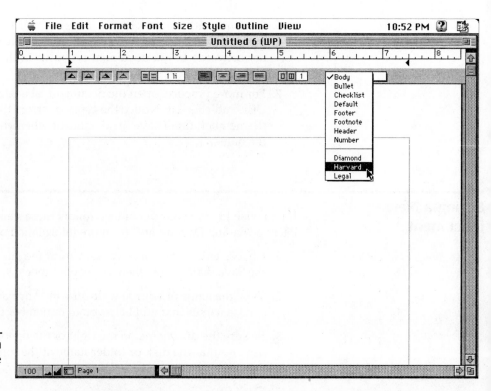

FIGURE 2-36

The Style pop-up menu gives you a quick way of changing the style of your text.

7. With the cursor still on the line with **Small cafe downtow**n, choose New Topic Left from the Outline menu.

8. Type **Characters**.

9. From the Outline menu choose New Topic Right and type the following:

   Sam, the cafe owner *(Return)*

   Jim, a daily customer*(Return)*

   Sally, the waitress*(Return)*

   Jason, a stranger

10. Complete the outline as shown in Figure 2-37 using New Topic Right and New Topic Left to place the items in the proper locations.

The items in an outline can be rearranged by simply moving them with the mouse. This enables you to put your ideas on the screen and then rearrange them without retyping the text. Try moving some of the topics as suggested in the steps that follow.

1. Move the mouse to place the pointer icon on the letter "C" preceeding the phrase **Jim wins the fight.**

2. Hold down the mouse button. The pointer icon should change to a plus sign with arrow on the top and bottom as show in Figure 2-38.

3. Move the mouse upward slowly until the bar is between topics A and B.

4. Release the mouse.

5. The topics should now be in the following order.

   A. **Sam tries to intervene**

   B. **Jim wins the fight**

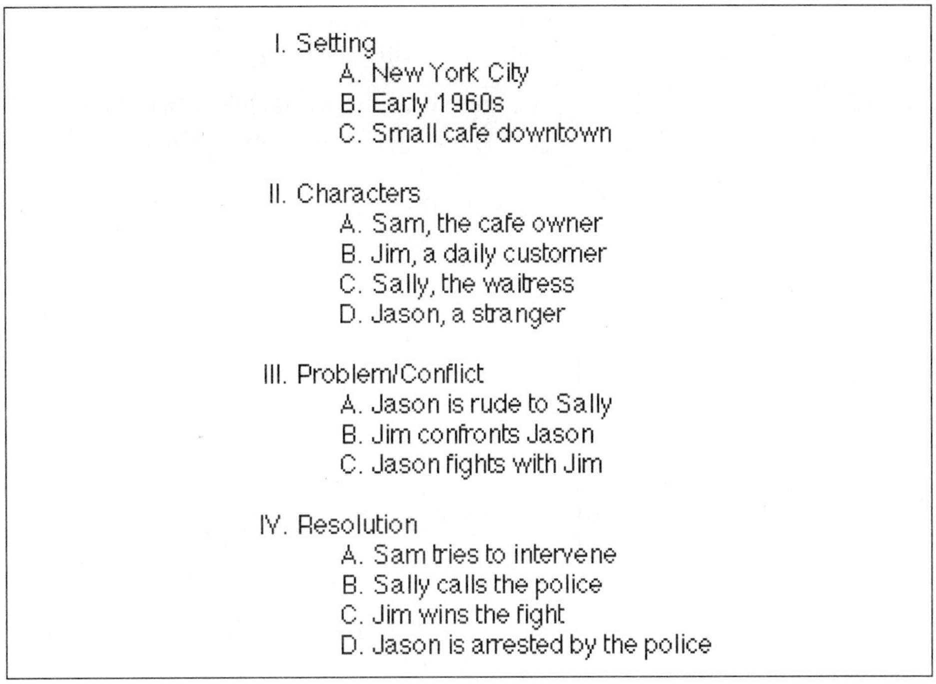

FIGURE 2-37

The outline is shown using the Harvard style.

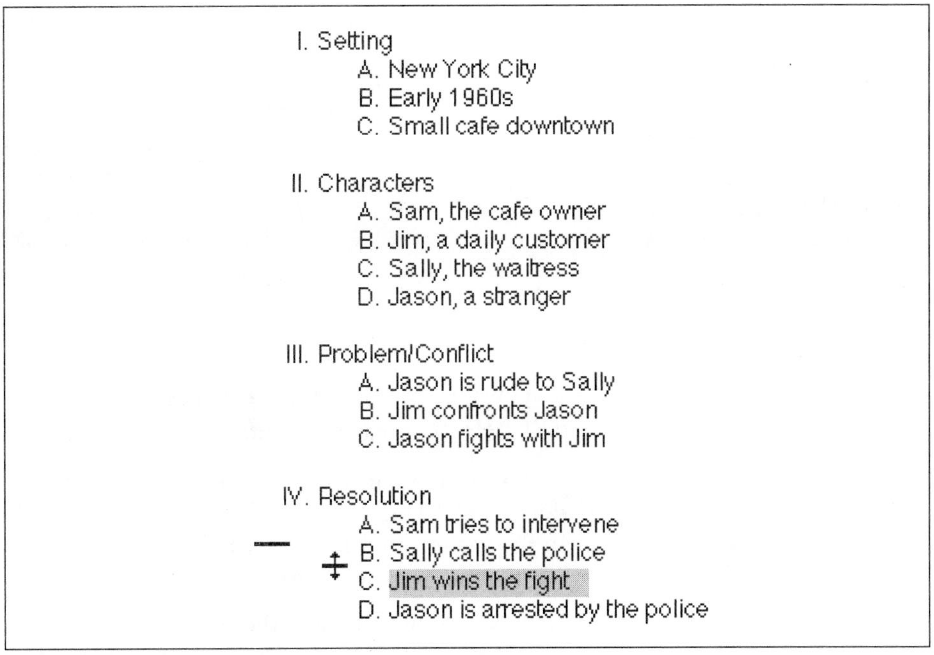

```
        I. Setting
            A. New York City
            B. Early 1960s
            C. Small cafe downtown

        II. Characters
            A. Sam, the cafe owner
            B. Jim, a daily customer
            C. Sally, the waitress
            D. Jason, a stranger

        III. Problem/Conflict
            A. Jason is rude to Sally
            B. Jim confronts Jason
            C. Jason fights with Jim

        IV. Resolution
            A. Sam tries to intervene
            B. Sally calls the police
            C. Jim wins the fight
            D. Jason is arrested by the police
```

FIGURE 2-38

When the pointer icon becomes a plus sign with an arrow on the top and bottom, you are able to move entries up and down in the outline.

```
        I. Setting
            A. New York City
            B. Early 1960s
            C. Small cafe downtown

        II. Characters
            A. Sam, the cafe owner
            B. Jim, a daily customer
            C. Sally, the waitress
            D. Jason, a stranger

        III. Problem/Conflict
            A. Jason is rude to Sally
            B. Jim confronts Jason
            C. Jason fights with Jim

        IV. Resolution
            A. Sam tries to intervene
          ‡ B. Sally calls the police
            C. Jim wins the fight
            D. Jason is arrested by the police
```

   C. Sally calls the police

   D. Jason is arrested by the police

6. Experiment moving other items by moving the topic label **Characters** above **Setting**. Notice that the topics under the topic label move also.

The outline is currently set up using the Harvard style. In this section you will examine some of the other styles available to you. Some of the styles available in the Style pop-up menu are more appropriate than others when working with an outline. You will look at legal, bullet, checklist, and diamond styles.

1. From the Edit menu choose Select All. The text you typed should be selected while the Roman numerals and capital letters labeling the topics are not selected.

2. From the Style pop-up menu choose Legal. The outline should look like the one shown in Figure 2-39.

1. Setting
    1.1. New York City
    1.2. Early 1960s
    1.3. Small cafe downtown

2. Characters
    2.1. Sam, the cafe owner
    2.2. Jim, a daily customer
    2.3. Sally, the waitress
    2.4. Jason, a stranger

3. Problem/Conflict
    3.1. Jason is rude to Sally
    3.2. Jim confronts Jason
    3.3. Jason fights with Jim

4. Resolution
    4.1. Sam tries to intervene
    4.2. Jim wins the fight
    4.3. Sally calls the police
    4.4. Jason is arrested by the police

FIGURE 2-39

The outline is shown in the Legal style.

3. While the text is still selected, choose other styles such as bullet, checklist, and diamond to see how the text is affected.

An outline can be combined with typical paragraph style text in the same document. This can be helpful in doing agendas and worksheets for students. In the section that follows you will add directions for a student to use with the outline that you have just created.

1. Move the cursor to the bottom right corner of the text and click the mouse button to place the cursor at the end of the text.

2. Press the Return key twice.

3. From the Style pop-up menu choose Body.

4. Press the Tab key and then type the following text.

   Using the information in the above outline, write a story. Use descriptive phrases to help the reader picture the setting, the characters, and the events taking place in the story.

Take some additional time to practice and experiment using outline features. The outline style can be useful in many situations. Students as well as teachers can use an outline to organize their thoughts before beginning to write.

ClarisWorks Help

You can explore additional features available in the word processing section of ClarisWorks by using the extensive Help function. Help contains information about all the tools and menu commands, as well as other definitions and explanations to assist you in your work. Help can be accessed at any time while you are using ClarisWorks, except when dialog boxes are open.

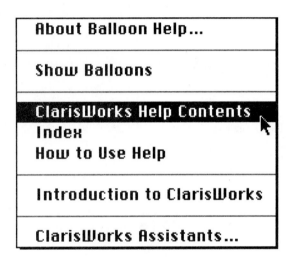

FIGURE 2-40

The Help menu, found at the ? icon at the right side of the menu bar, can be a useful source of information about additional features in ClarisWorks.

1. Choose ClarisWorks Help Contents from the ? menu, as shown in Figure 2-40. A list of Help topics will be shown.
2. Use the vertical scroll bar to see some of the additional topics.
3. Move the vertical scroll box back to the top of the bar to bring the beginning topics into view.
4. Click once on How to Use Help.
5. You should see displayed an expanded list of subtopics. Choose Navigate through Help by clicking on it once.
6. A screen like Figure 2-41 will be shown. Notice the buttons at the top of the screen.
7. Click on the Contents button. This takes you to the same ClarisWorks topics screen that you saw earlier.
8. Click on the Go Back button. This should take you back to the last topic viewed, Navigate through Help.
9. Notice the Forward and Backward buttons. Click on the Forward button. You should see the topic Browse topics one by one.
10. Notice the keyword text entry box located under the buttons. Slowly type in the first three letters of the word **outline**. You will see in gray the term that matches what you have typed. Notice how the term in gray changes as you type each character.

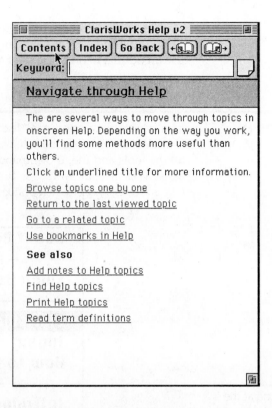

FIGURE 2-41

Navigate through Help provides
an explanation of the features
available within ClarisWorks Help
and how to use them.

11. When the term **outline Format command** appears, press Return. You should see the text associated with this topic. Using keywords can simplify searching for particular topics in Help.

12. Click on the Index button. You should see a list of significant words and phrases. You can scroll through these by using the vertical scroll bar. To view information about a topic, select the topic and choose Go To Topic. Selecting Go To Topic will go to the topic and close the Index window. View Topic will go to the topic and leave the Index window open.

13. Select a topic that interests you and then click on the Go To Topic button.

14. When you finish reading the topic, choose Quit from the File menu to quit Help.

Other aids available to you through the ? menu are Introduction to ClarisWorks and ClarisWorks Assistants. Introduction to ClarisWorks will give you an overview of the features available in ClarisWorks. ClarisWorks Assistants steps you through the process of creating certain types of documents such as calendars and newsletters. We will explore some of these later in the text.

Conclusion

At this point, you have worked with many of the word processing features available within ClarisWorks. You may have found portions of this work to be very easy, and you may have found portions to be confusing and difficult, depending on your prior experience. If you have found it difficult, rest assured that as you gain more practice you will become increasingly more comfortable and happy with ClarisWorks.

You have seen how powerful and helpful word processing can be. Many more word processing features are available, but those presented here should be a good start for learning and using a word processor. A few more options, such as graphics and mail merge, will be covered later in this book. For additional or more detailed help with your exploration of the ClarisWorks word processing application, consult your user manual, work with the Help screens, and consult with friends. Because ClarisWorks is a Macintosh application, it is similar in many ways to other Macintosh applications. Friends who have worked with other Macintosh word processors will recognize many of the ClarisWorks features, and once you master the ClarisWorks word processor you will find it easy to learn to use other Macintosh word processors.

You will also find what you have learned here to be extremely valuable in your teaching. You will be able to create lesson plans, handouts, and numerous other documents much more easily and efficiently than you could without a word processor. In addition, once you learn to merge documents with the database, to insert graphics in your documents, and to use other integrated software options covered later in this book, you'll have even more uses for the word processor.

KEY TERMS

alignment	Insert Page #	Show page guides
Apply Ruler	Insert Page Break	Show/Hide Tools
center tab	insertion point	control
Check Document	integrated software	Size menu
Spelling...	left indent marker	spacing
Close	left tab	spell checker
Copy	margin	spreadsheet
Copy Ruler	New...	Style menu
Cut	page break	tab
database	page guide	Tab key
decimal tab	page indicator	tab stop
Document...	Paste	title page
Edit menu	Preferences...	Undo
Find/Change	Print...	vertical scroll bar
first-line indent marker	Quit	word processing
font	right indent marker	wrap
Font menu	right tab	Writing Tools
footer	ruler	zoom-in control
header	Save	zoom-out control
Help	Save As...	zoom percentage
highlight	Select All	indicator
horizontal scroll bar	Show Invisibles	
Insert Footer	Show margins	

EXERCISES

1. Create a memo to be sent to parents for Open House. Include the date, times, location of important activities, and an agenda for the evening. Use a large type size and bold style for important parts of the communication.

2. Create a letter to be sent to parents that describes the events that have taken place in your classroom this month.

3. Make an assignment sheet for the week. Use Tabs to set up columns to report in a format similar to the one shown below.

ASSIGNMENT SHEET   ALGEBRA 1
WEEK OF JAN. 10

Mon.	1/10	p. 235	1-25 odd, 35, 39
Tues.	1/11	p. 237	1-10 all, 20-25 odd
Wed.	1/12	p. 240	1-20 even, 25, 26
Thu.	1/13	p. 245	Chapter Review
Fri.	1/14		Chapter Test

4. Create an agenda for a committee meeting using the outline feature.

5. Create a handout that looks like the one below for a science lab.

> **FUNGI LAB   NAME_____ HOUR_____**
>
> 1. **Look at the slide of Rhizopus. Draw what you see. Label sporangia, sporangiophore, stolon, rhizoid, and sponges. What class does Rhizopus belong to?**
>
> 2. **Look at the slide of yeast. Find cells that are budding and draw one. To what class do yeast cells belong?**

6. Have your students write short stories using ClarisWorks, then print them out to make a booklet of short stories for each of the students to keep.

7. Find two articles, one about how a teacher uses a word processor and the other about how students use a word processor. In ClarisWorks, write summaries of the articles. Share them with others.

8. Create a document that is at least two pages long. In that document you should have the following:

   a. pages numbered with a header or footer

   b. title of the document done in 18 pt bold

   c. use of underline, outline, and color to accentuate items in the text

   d. left margin set at 1.25 and right margin set at .75.

9. Create a three-page document that includes a title page. Make sure the title page is not numbered and begin numbering the page after the title page as 1. Include in the text of the document:

   a. an area with numbered items where the second line of each item indents under the first word of the item

   b. double spaced text

   c. a long quote that is single-spaced and has the margins indented

   d. two different sizes and two different styles of text within the document for emphasis.

3 ClarisWorks Graphics— Draw & Paint

Introduction to Graphics

The graphics components of the ClarisWorks program provide drawing and painting capabilities and more. The **Draw environment** can be used to draw simple shapes and to lay out pages for newsletters, posters, or flyers. Organizational charts, tournament bracket charts, furniture arrangements, other graphics-related documents, and simple diagrams that can be made with basic shapes can also be created or modified within the Draw environment. Slide shows can be created to present material to a class or to create a running slide show of information to be used at open house or parent conferences.

The **Paint environment** is used to produce artistic creations such as drawings or illustrations. Additional tools, not available in the Draw environment, can be used to create drawings with finer detail or to improve and enhance documents produced in the Draw environment. Fairly elaborate creative work can be done in the Paint environment.

Instructions in this chapter assume that you are familiar with the word processing functions of ClarisWorks presented in this text. In particular, you should already be familiar with using menus; opening, saving, and closing documents; scrolling; selecting, inserting, and deleting text; cutting and pasting; the ClarisWorks zoom icons; and font options. If you wish or need to stop working at any point in the chapter, simply save your document and return to it when you are ready. In most instances, it should be fairly easy to pick up from your stopping point.

The Draw Environment

When using the Draw feature of ClarisWorks, you will be creating graphic objects. These graphic objects can then be changed in a variety of ways. You can add color and patterns; change the width, color, and pattern of the outline of the object; and transform the object by flipping, rotating, or changing the size. Working with various draw objects is much like working with a collage. You are taking various forms and using them to create a drawing. Using the computer, you have the capability to rearrange and change the layering of objects quickly and easily. You select one object or a group of objects and perform various operations on them. In this section you will work with some of the basic **Draw tools** and features. Even if you don't believe that you are artistic, you will be surprised at the drawings you can create.

Using Draw Tools

A variety of Draw tools are available to create artwork and diagrams. The Draw tool palette and descriptions of each of the Draw icons are shown in Figure 3-1. The following steps will show you how to display and work with these tools.

1. Open the ClarisWorks program (double-click on the document icon) or choose New... from the File menu, if you are already in ClarisWorks.
2. On the New Document dialog box click Drawing for the type of document. A new drawing document appears.

   Notice that the **Pointer tool** (the arrow) at the top of the tool palette is selected. The menus at the top of the screen have some different options from those shown for other work you have done in ClarisWorks. In addition, on the screen you see a **grid** to help guide you in creating your graphics.
3. Choose **Hide Graphics Grid** from the **Options menu** to remove the grid.

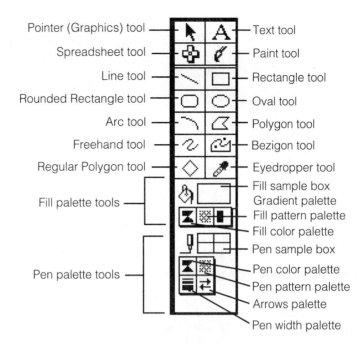

Pointer (Graphics) tool — Text tool
Spreadsheet tool — Paint tool
Line tool — Rectangle tool
Rounded Rectangle tool — Oval tool
Arc tool — Polygon tool
Freehand tool — Bezigon tool
Regular Polygon tool — Eyedropper tool
Fill palette tools — Fill sample box
Gradient palette
Fill pattern palette
Fill color palette
Pen sample box
Pen palette tools — Pen color palette
Pen pattern palette
Arrows palette
Pen width palette

FIGURE 3-1

The Draw tool palette. A tool is selected for a function by clicking its tool icon. The default tool is the Pointer tool.

4. Choose **Show Graphics Grid** from the Options menu to again display the grid. For now leave the grid on the screen.

USING THE RECTANGLE TOOL

Using the **Rectangle tool** is very similar to using several of the other tools on the Draw tool palette. After choosing the Rectangle tool, you will click the mouse and drag to create a rectangular shape.

1. Select the Rectangle tool by clicking on it once. As you move the mouse away from the tool box, notice that the pointer becomes a **crosshair**. This enables you to more easily position it. The center of the crosshair is the "hot spot" for the crosshair.

2. Place the crosshair on the corner of one of the grid squares and drag the mouse diagonally across two squares and down one to create a rectangle similar to the one shown in Figure 3-2.

3. Notice that as you release the mouse button the Pointer tool is automatically selected and small squares, or **handles**, appear at the edges of the rectangle. You can see the handles in Figure 3-2. These handles indicate that the graphic object is selected.

   The entire rectangle is called an **object** because it is treated as a whole unit. When selected, the entire graphic can be moved, copied, pasted, deleted, or duplicated—you do not have to work with any part of the rectangle individually. Graphics that are handled in this way are called **object-oriented** graphics—the ClarisWorks Draw environment is an object-oriented method of working with graphics.

4. Click outside the rectangle. The handles are no longer displayed; the object is no longer selected.

5. Click on the rectangle. The handles again appear; the object is now selected. Note that objects can be selected only with the Pointer tool.

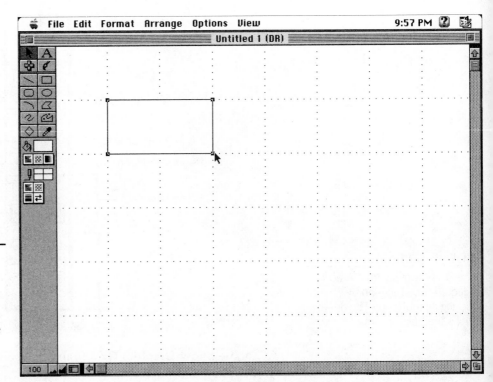

FIGURE 3-2

A rectangle has been drawn using the Rectangle tool. After completing use of the tool, the cursor changes back to the Pointer. The handles in the corners of the rectangle indicate that it is selected. While an object is selected, it can be changed or moved.

6. To move the object, place the pointer on any part of the object, except the handles, and drag it to a new location.

7. Drag the rectangle back to its original position.

Changing an Object's Appearance

When you have created an object using the Draw tools, you can easily make changes in its appearance. You can use the **Fill** and the **Pen tools** to change the color, pattern, and gradients of the object. You also can choose to make the object **transparent**; change the width, color, and pattern of the border; or even add arrows to some lines.

USING FILL AND PEN TOOLS

In the Draw application, you will be able to work with both Fill and Pen tools. Fill tools allow you to change the interior region of an object, whereas Pen tools will change the object's border. Experimentation with these tools will enable you to see the many possibilities that exist if you use your imagination. Refer to Figure 3-3 if you have difficulty finding any of the palettes used in the steps that follow.

1. Click on the rectangle you just drew to select it, if it is not already selected.

2. Click on the **Fill color palette**, the left icon found below the paint bucket on the Tool palette. From the Fill color palette choose a color such as dark blue or green. Notice that the rectangle fills with that color.

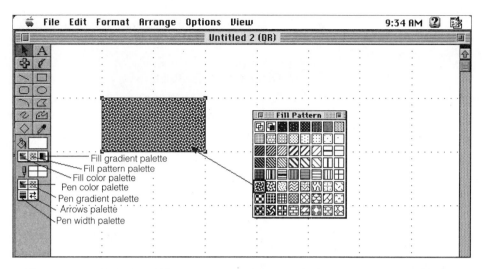

FIGURE 3-3

The Fill pattern palette with a
pattern selected for the
rectangle. If a color has been
chosen, the darker part of the
pattern appears in the chosen
color.

3. Click on the **Fill pattern palette**, the center icon found below the paint bucket on the Tool palette. From the Fill pattern palette choose a pattern similar to the one shown in Figure 3-3. Notice that the rectangle is filled with the pattern and the darker part of the pattern appears in the color you chose.

4. Click on the **Fill gradient palette**, the right icon found below the paint bucket on the Tool palette. Select a gradient from the Fill gradient palette. Notice that this erases both the color and the pattern chosen previously.

5. Click on the **Pen color palette**, the top left icon found under the pen on the Tool palette. From the Pen color palette choose a color different from the one you chose in Step 2.

6. From the **Pen width palette** choose 6 pt. line.

7. From the **Pen pattern palette** choose an angled striped pattern. Your rectangle should look similar to Figure 3-4.

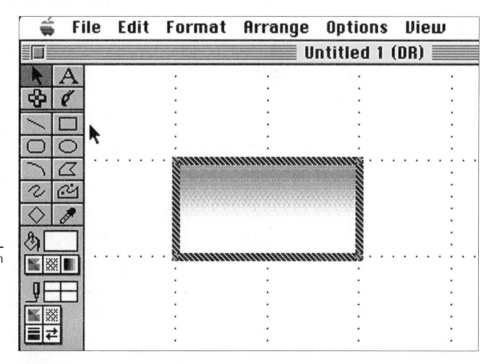

FIGURE 3-4

The rectangle has been filled with
a gradient. The border of the
rectangle has a pen width of 6
pt., and a pattern and color have
been chosen for the border that
complement the gradient
selected for the fill.

8. Practice changing the Fill palette and Pen palette selections until you feel comfortable with what is changed on each one.

DUPLICATING OBJECTS

Sometimes in a drawing you may wish to have multiple objects that are the same size. You could redraw them, but it is much easier to copy and paste them and still easier to duplicate them. When you have a selected graphic you can cut, copy, and paste the graphic as you would text. However, with ClarisWorks graphics you also have a duplicate option that essentially does the copy and paste in one step. Use it as follows:

1. With the rectangular object selected, choose **Duplicate** from the Edit menu. Duplicate displays another, overlapping rectangle just like the original rectangle. Only one rectangle is selected, the newly created one (see Figure 3-5).

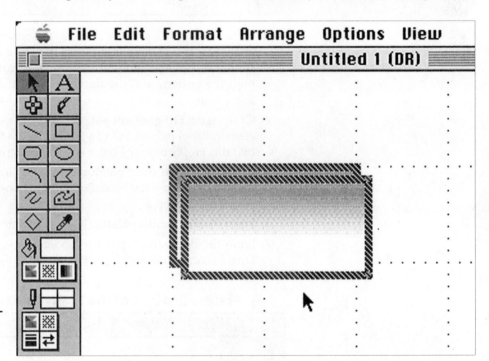

FIGURE 3-5

The original rectangle has been duplicated. Only the new rectangle is currently selected.

2. Place the Pointer anywhere on the selected rectangle, except on the handles, and drag it a little to the right of the other rectangle, but where it still overlaps. Notice that some of the lower rectangle is hidden by the one overlapping it.

3. While the top rectangle is selected, choose another color and pattern from the Fill palettes.

4. Choose Duplicate again from the Edit menu. You now have a third rectangle that may overlap the selected rectangle.

5. Drag the third rectangle to the right to arrange the three rectangles in a slightly overlapping manner.

6. While the last rectangle is still selected choose the transparent pattern from the Fill pattern palette as shown in Figure 3-6. Notice that the rectangle is now filled with white and you can see the rectangle immediately

below it. Notice that after you fill the object with the transparent pattern, you must place the mouse on its border to move it. Placing the mouse on the interior transparent portion of the rectangle to drag it will not cause it to move.

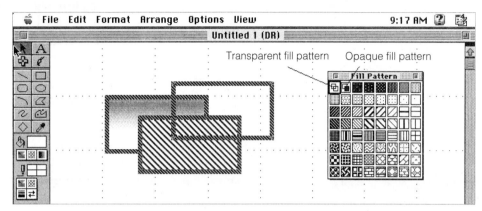

FIGURE 3-6

The selected rectangle has a transparent pattern chosen so the rectangles in layers beneath it are visible within the rectangle's border. The other rectangles are opaque so that overlapping regions are only visible on the object in the upper layer.

When objects are drawn, they are generally opaque unless you select transparent. The use of transparent objects can be particularly helpful when you wish to draw attention to select text or a special object and wish to frame it without covering it.

CLASSROOM ← → CONNECTION

Put several shapes in a template document for students to use to create a drawing. Have them duplicate the shapes and put them together with different colors, patterns, and gradients to form a design or a picture.

WORKING WITH LAYERS

Notice that the three rectangles appear to be in different **layers**. As you draw a new object, it creates a new layer. When an object is opaque, it hides the objects that are below it. This was illustrated in the drawing you did with the three rectangles. ClarisWorks gives you control of the various objects. You have the option of moving an object one layer forward (toward the top) or backward. You may also move an object to the front (top) or to the back (bottom) of the layers. Work through the steps that follow to see how you can move objects to different layers.

1. With the top rectangle selected, choose a pattern from the Fill pattern palette (not transparent) and a color from the Fill color palette that are different from the ones used in the other rectangles.

2. All three rectangles should be different colors and have different patterns. If they are not, select them one by one and make changes using the Fill palette tools.

3. Select the top rectangle. From the **Arrange menu** choose **Move Backward** as shown in Figure 3-7.

4. Notice how the rectangle is now below the second rectangle and yet still above the third.

5. With the same rectangle still selected, choose Move Backward again.

6. You should now see that the rectangle has moved below both other rectangles.

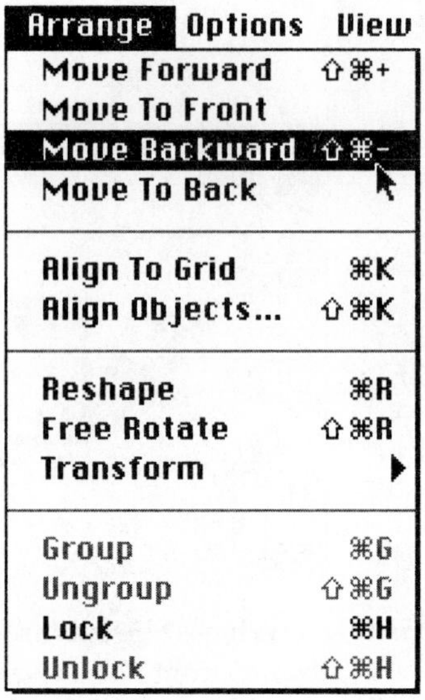

FIGURE 3-7

The Arrange menu with Move Backward chosen. There are also options to Move Forward as well as Move to Front and Move to Back. These options provide flexibility in moving objects from layer to layer in a Draw document.

7. With the same rectangle selected, choose **Move to Front**. Notice that the rectangle moves from behind both other rectangles to the top layer of the drawing.

8. Experiment selecting the different rectangles and moving them to different layers until you feel comfortable with the process.

C L A S S R O O M ⟷ C O N N E C T I O N

Have students create a mat for pictures they have cut out of magazines or newspapers relating to a topic of study. Create a large rectangle filled with the color, pattern, or gradient of their choice. Have them place different shapes filled with white onto the rectangle. The shapes will create regions where students can place their pictures. The borders of the shapes can be wide to create a frame for the picture. Access to a color printer would add some interest to the project for the students.

RESIZING OBJECTS

Sometimes after you draw an object you may want to change its size. There are several ways of doing this that will be demonstrated. The simplest method is to select the object and drag one of its handles to make it larger or smaller. If you wish to use the drag method and want the object to be resized proportionally, you must hold down the Shift key while dragging. The second method allows you to resize the object by scaling. You choose a percentage from 25 to 400, and the object will be resized by that percent. A percentage less than 100 makes the item smaller, whereas a percentage larger than 100 will increase the size of the object. The last method of resizing allows you to specify the dimensions of an object. This method will not necessarily keep the object proportional but will make sure that the object fits in a particular space. You will practice these methods on the three rectangles.

1. Click once on the top rectangle to select it.

2. Hold down the Shift key while dragging one of the handles to make the rectangle about half its original size.

3. Move the rectangle to the far right portion of the screen so that it no longer overlaps either of the other rectangles.

4. Click once on the next rectangle to select it.

5. From the Arrange menu choose Transform, and from the submenu that appears choose **Scale by Percent...**.

6. In the Scale by Percent dialog box, type 75 for the horizontal scale (the selected item). Press the Tab key and type 75 for the vertical scale. Note that you can also use different scales for horizontal and vertical scales if you wish. To make an item larger you would type a value over 100.

7. Click OK. The selected rectangle should now be 75 percent of its original size.

8. Drag the rectangle to the right so that it is not overlapping either of the other rectangles.

9. Click once on the last rectangle to select it.

10. From the Options menu choose **Object Info ....** You should see the **Info palette** as shown in Figure 3-8. The top portion of the Info palette indicates how far the top, left, right, and bottom of the object are from the top and left margins. This portion can be used to move an object to a specific location on the screen. The next portion indicates the width and height of the object. This allows you to change the width, height, or both. The last item on the Info palette is the angle of rotation. By typing a value for the angle of rotation you are able to rotate the object.

FIGURE 3-8

The Info palette indicates the position and size of the chosen object. The top portion indicates how far the left, top, right, and bottom edges of the object are from the top and left margins of the document, respectively. The bottom portion indicates the width and height of the object and the angle of rotation.

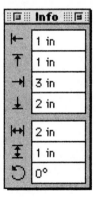

11. Select the width and change it to 3. Select the height and change it to 1.5. Your screen should look something like Figure 3-9. If your figures are not separated as shown in the figure, simply select them and move them until they are in an arrangement similar to Figure 3-9.

12. Close the Info window by clicking on the close box in the upper left corner of the window.

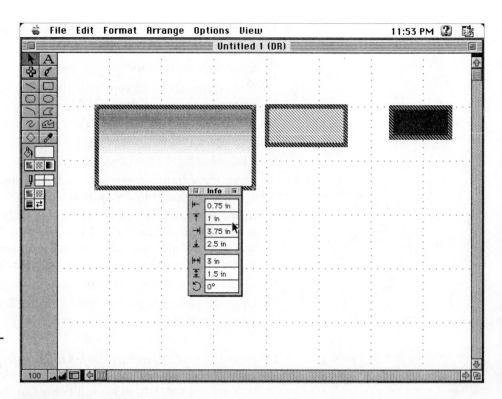

FIGURE 3-9

The three rectangles have been resized using the resizing options available in ClarisWorks.

ALIGNING OBJECTS

A variety of alignment options are available to help you place objects evenly within your design. Any selected items can be arranged. You can select all objects or only a few objects to **align** depending on what you are doing in your design. You could try to do that by hand but it is easier and more accurate to have the computer do it for you.

1. One rectangle should still be selected. If none are selected, click on any one of the rectangles to select it.

2. Shift-click (hold down the Shift key, then click the mouse) on each unselected rectangle to select all three rectangles. The handles should be displayed on each rectangle.

   Shift-clicking is for selecting multiple objects—it keeps any prior selection as it selects a new object. It will also deselect an already selected object, while still keeping all other selections.

3. From the Arrange menu choose **Align Objects...** to see the Align Objects dialog box.

4. In the Top to Bottom section, choose Align top edges as shown in Figure 3-10. You may have noticed that the objects in the sample box moved to demonstrate how the alignment would work. (If you didn't notice this, watch the sample box as you choose Align bottom edges, then choose Align top edges again.)

5. In the Left to Right section, choose Distribute space to indicate that you want the objects to be equally spaced, as shown in Figure 3-10.

6. Click OK. The three rectangles should now be arranged so that the top edges are lined up and the area between them is evenly spaced.

7. Choose Align Objects... from the Arrange menu again. This time select Align bottom edges in the Top to Bottom section and Align left edges in the Left to Right section. Notice how the arrangement of the rectangles changes.

8. Continue experimenting with the Align Objects dialog box selections until you feel comfortable with the variety of arrangements possible.

PRACTICE

Take some time to practice with the skills you have learned so far. Experiment with the Arc, Oval, and Rounded Rectangle tools. These tools work similarly to the Rectangle tool. Draw various objects and use the Fill palette and Pen palette tools to change their appearance. Resize the objects and then select two or more at a time to work in practicing alignment options.

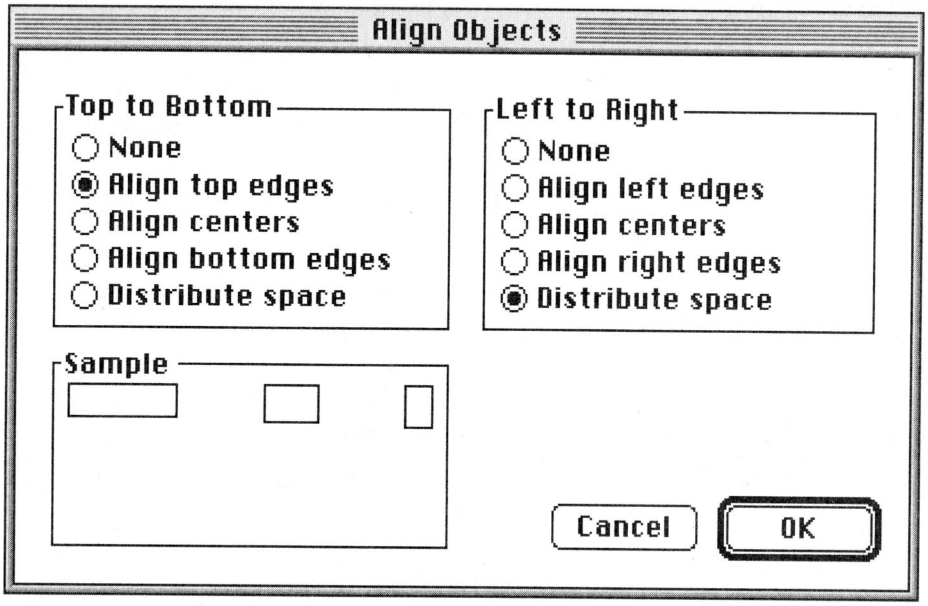

FIGURE 3-10

The Align Objects dialog box provides a means of aligning selected objects from top to bottom and from left to right. The results of choices made are displayed in the sample area.

Using Additional Tools

Some of the other Draw tools on the tool palette work a little differently from the Rectangle tool. In this section you will explore the use of some of those tools, setting Preferences, and what changes the Preference settings can make when working with the Draw tools. You will begin by using the Polygon tool.

USING THE POLYGON TOOL

The **Polygon tool** allows you to draw polygons that have as many sides as you wish. The polygon can be open (last point and first point are not connected) or closed. The sides of the polygon are straight lines. After choosing the Polygon tool, you will click the mouse once for each vertex of the polygon. When you get to the last point, you will double-click to signify that it is the last point.

1. Use the vertical scroll bar to move the rectangles out of view.

2. From the Draw tool palette, click once on the Polygon tool to select it.

3. Refer to Figure 3-11 for the shape of the irregular polygon you wish to draw. Starting at any point, click once to place the first point and then continue to click on consecutive points, finishing by double-clicking on the first point. If you are unhappy with your drawing, press the Delete key while it is selected and start again.

4. While the polygon is still selected, choose a color from the Fill color palette.

5. From the Edit menu choose Duplicate.

6. Drag the duplicated polygon below the first one so that they are not touching.

7. From the Arrange menu, choose Transform and then choose **Flip Horizontally**. Notice that when Flip Horizontally is chosen, the polygon is flipped horizontally around an imaginary vertical line passing through the center of the polygon.

8. Click on the original polygon to select it.

9. Choose Duplicate from the Edit menu.

10. Drag the duplicated polygon to the right of the original so that they are not touching.

11. From the Arrange menu, choose Transform and then choose **Flip Vertically**. Your screen should look similar to Figure 3-12. Notice the change in orientation when you flip horizontally and vertically. When Flip Vertically is chosen the polygon is flipped vertically around an imaginary horizontal line passing through the center of the polygon.

12. The last polygon you worked with (the one on the top right of the screen) should still be selected. If it isn't, select it by clicking on the polygon.

13. Choose Duplicate from the Edit menu.

14. Drag the duplicated polygon to the right and down into the open space on the screen.

15. From the Arrange menu, choose **Free Rotate**.

16. Place the cursor on the bottom right handle of the polygon and drag upward as shown in Figure 3-13. When Free Rotate is selected you may drag an outline of a selected object to any angle. When the outline is at the rotation you want, simply release the mouse.

17. From the Arrange menu, choose Free Rotate to deselect it.

GROUPING OBJECTS

Sometimes when you are trying to draw an object that is symmetrical, it is easier to draw half of the object, duplicate the object, and then flip it. You can then put the two objects together by using the **Group** command. In this section, you will create a primitive evergreen tree using this procedure.

1. To give yourself some room to draw, choose New from the File menu and create a new Draw document.

2. Select the Polygon tool.

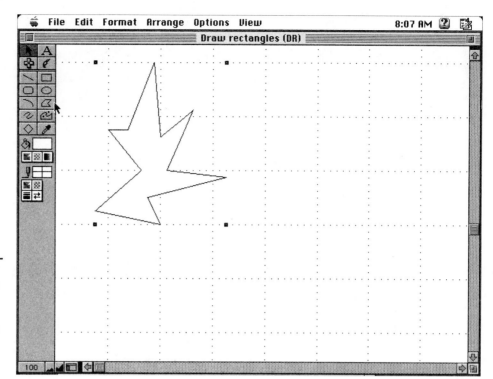

FIGURE 3-11

A variety of open or closed polygons may be drawn with the Polygon tool, indicated by the Pointer in the figure. Once the Polygon tool is selected, click the mouse for each point and double-click on the last point of the polygon.

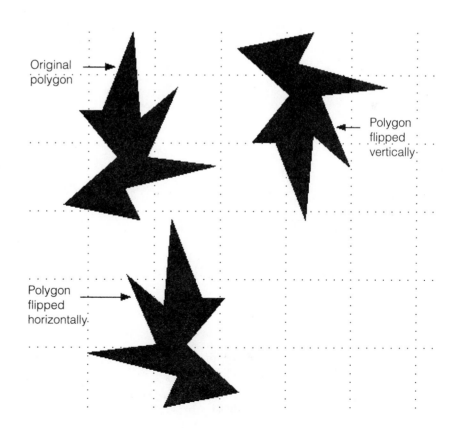

FIGURE 3-12

A polygon is shown as it was originally drawn and after it has been flipped horizontally and flipped vertically.

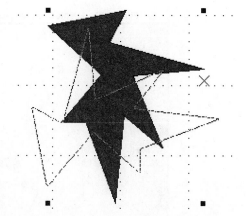

FIGURE 3-13

When using Free Rotate to
rotate an object, an outline of
the object shows the current
placement of object.

3. Draw the open shape shown in Figure 3-14, by clicking at each point
where an X has been marked and double-clicking at the double X. (The Xs
will not be displayed on the figure you draw. They are placed on the diagram to help you draw the figure.) If you are not pleased with the shape
you make, press the Delete key while the figure is selected to delete it and
begin again.

4. While the shape is still selected, choose dark green from the Fill color
palette.

5. While the shape is still selected, choose Duplicate from the Edit menu.

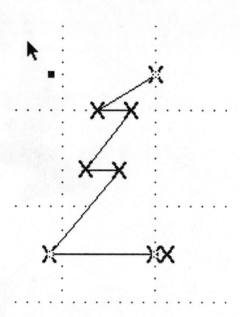

FIGURE 3-14

An open polygon created with
the Polygon tool. The Xs indicate
the points where the mouse
button has been clicked to
create the object. This shape will
be duplicated and flipped to form
a tree shape.

6. From the Arrange menu, choose Transform and then choose Flip
Horizontally.

7. Move the flipped object so that the top and bottom edges touch as shown
in Figure 3-15.

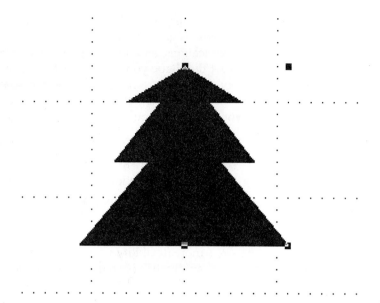

FIGURE 3-15

Two open shapes have been aligned to form this tree shaped object. Only the object on the right is currently selected.

8. While the right object is selected, shift-click (hold down the shift while clicking the mouse) on the left object to select it also. Both objects should be selected.

9. From the Arrange menu, choose Group. Both sides of the tree should now be grouped together. By grouping objects you can combine two or more objects and work with them as a single object.

10. Place the pointer on the interior of the tree and drag. Notice that the entire tree moves as one object.

This technique of Grouping can be done with many objects. You might draw a bell or a house or some other diagram made up of individual objects. To select the objects you may shift-click on each object as you did in the sample or you may use the pointer cursor to draw a dotted rectangle around all of the objects you wish to select. Each object enclosed within the rectangle should be selected. If any object appears to be unselected, you may simply use the shift-click method to select it also. Once all of the objects you wish to group are selected, you may Group the objects together. This allows you to treat all of the objects as one. If you need to revise an individual portion of the Grouped object, you may choose Ungroup to work with any individual object.

CLASSROOM ⟷ CONNECTION

Have students create a map of a region of study—a state, a country, or another local area. Either draw or paste the outer border of the regions, then fill in the details using the Draw tools.

RESHAPING AN OBJECT

In an earlier section you transformed an object by flipping it and rotating it. In each case the original shape of the object remained intact while its position on the screen changed. In this section you will learn ways to actually reshape an object. Sometimes an object is almost the way you want it but just needs minor modifications, and other times it is easier to draw a basic shape and then modify it to get the shape you want. In either of these situations, reshaping can be a useful tool. You may reshape polygons and some other objects that we haven't worked with yet, such as freehand objects, bezigons, and arcs. In the sample that follows, you will use a regular pentagon to form a star.

1. Use the vertical scroll bar to move the tree out of view.
2. Select the **Regular Polygon tool**.
3. From the Options menu, choose **Polygon Sides....**
4. In the dialog box that appears, type **5** since you want a pentagon, a five-sided figure. Click OK.
5. From the Options menu, choose **Turn Autogrid Off**. This will allow you more flexibility when reshaping the object. When **Autogrid** is on, the points automatically snap to the graphics grid as set in the graphics ruler settings. Sometimes this can be helpful, and other times it can be frustrating when you cannot move to the exact point you want.
6. Draw a medium size pentagon by clicking on the screen and moving the mouse outward to make it larger and inward to make it smaller. Your pentagon should look similar to the one in Figure 3-16.

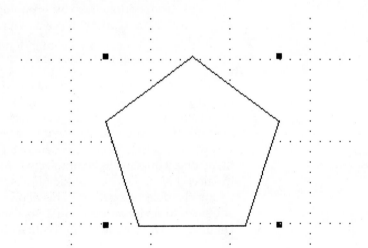

FIGURE 3-16

A pentagon has been drawn using the Regular Polygon tool. The number of sides in the polygon is chosen from Polygon Sides... in the Options menu after the Regular Polygon tool has been selected.

7. From the Arrange menu, choose **Reshape**. You now see anchor points on each of the vertices of the pentagon. (If you do not see the anchor points, click on the figure to select it—the anchor points will then appear.) By dragging these anchor points you could reshape the regular pentagon and make it into some other shape. The pointer tool changes to a reshape pointer as shown in Figure 3-17.
8. In this case, instead of changing these anchor points, you will add other anchor points to reshape the pentagon.

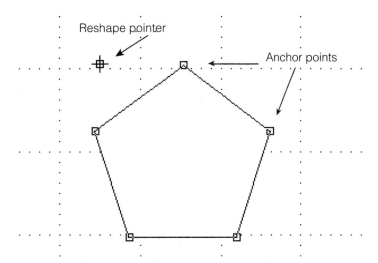

FIGURE 3-17

Choosing Reshape from the Arrange menu causes the selected object to display anchor points that can be used to reshape the object. The Pointer tool changes to a Reshape pointer, which is used to drag the existing anchor points or create new ones.

9. Position the cursor on the middle of one of the sides of the pentagon and click. A new anchor point should be formed.

10. Drag the new anchor point in toward the center of the pentagon as shown in Figure 3-18. If you did not like the position of the new anchor point, continue moving it until you are satisfied with its position.

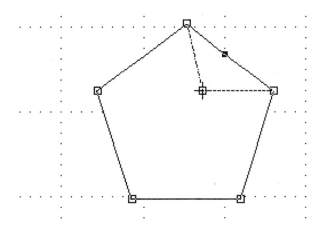

FIGURE 3-18

A new anchor point has been created on a side of the pentagon. Dragging the new anchor point reshapes the object.

11. Continue making new anchor points in the middle of each side of the pentagon and dragging them toward the center of the pentagon until your figure looks similar to Figure 3-19.

12. From the Arrange menu, choose Reshape again to deselect it. The reshape cursor returns to the pointer cursor, and the anchor points are no longer displayed on the screen.

SMOOTHING

Another technique that can be useful is smoothing. You may create a rough pointed image of an object and then have the computer "smooth out" the edges. You can even do that with the star.

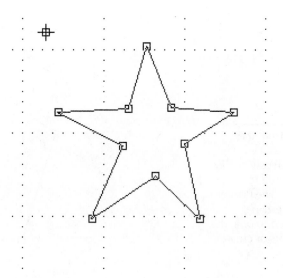

FIGURE 3-19

The pentagon has been reshaped into a star-shaped figure through the use of the Reshape feature found on the Arrange menu.

1. While the star is still selected, choose Transform from the Arrange menu and then choose **Smooth** from the submenu that appears.

2. The star image should now appear similar to Figure 3-20.

3. To change the image back to the original star, you may simply choose Unsmooth from the Transform submenu in the Arrange menu. The object should be back to its original shape.

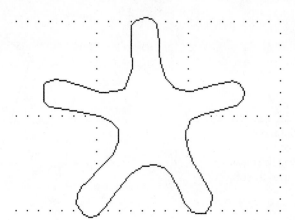

FIGURE 3-20

The star-shaped figure has been "smoothed" through the use of the Smooth feature on the Transform submenu found in the Arrange menu. To change the image back to its original form, Unsmooth can be selected from the same menu.

PRACTICE

Take time now to practice using the new tools you have learned. Try drawing another polygon shape. Flip it, rotate it, and reshape it using the tools you have used in this section. When you feel comfortable with the use of these various tools, continue with the next section.

Other Drawing Tools

In the previous sections you have used some of the Drawing tools. In this section you will spend some time working with the Line tool, the Arc tool, the

Freehand tool, and the Bezigon tool. By the time you finish learning to use these tools, you should be ready to create many interesting and helpful objects using Drawing tools.

USING THE LINE TOOL

The **Line tool** allows you to draw lines. By using the Pen tools you can change the appearance of a line to fit almost any need you may have. Lines may be drawn individually and then grouped together to form an object. Lines may also be used with arrows to highlight or label a specific piece of information in a drawing.

1. Choose New from the File menu and create a new Draw document.

2. Double-click the Line tool from the Draw tools. By double-clicking on a tool you may use that tool repeatedly without reselecting it from the tool palette. The tool icon background should appear black to indicate it has been selected for repeated use. To deselect the tool, you simply select another tool from the tool palette.

3. Place the crosshair where you want the first endpoint of the line.

4. Click the mouse button and drag across the screen to draw a horizontal line about three squares long. Then release the mouse button.

5. Click and drag to create another line that is not horizontal or vertical and does not cross the first line.

6. Hold down the Shift key while dragging the Line tool on the screen at an angle that is not horizontal or vertical. If you move the mouse from side to side, you will notice that the line is restrained to multiples of 45°. When you hold down the Shift key, you will always draw lines whose angles are multiples of 45°. This can be especially helpful when you wish to draw horizontal or vertical lines.

7. Click on the Pointer tool to select it.

8. Click on the horizontal line to select it. Select 4 pt. from the Pen width palette.

9. Click on the Pen pattern palette and drag the palette to the right onto the screen as shown in Figure 3-21. By dragging the Pen pattern palette on to the screen, it is available for you to use repeatedly. Any of the Fill or Pen palettes may be opened for repeated use in this manner.

10. Click on the wide vertical line pattern shown in Figure 3-21. Notice the line now looks like a wide dotted line.

11. With the horizontal line still selected, choose the wavy line pattern shown in Figure 3-21.

12. Continue choosing other Pen patterns to see the effect on the horizontal line. Note that by making changes in the Pen width you increase the number of different types of lines that can be formed. When you are finished, click on the close box on the top left corner of the Pen patterns palette to close it. The box on the top right corner of the palettes allows you to "collapse" it so that only the title bar shows. This allows you to keep multiple palettes on the screen without taking up too much room. To use the palette, click on the same box to "expand" it (see Figure 3-21).

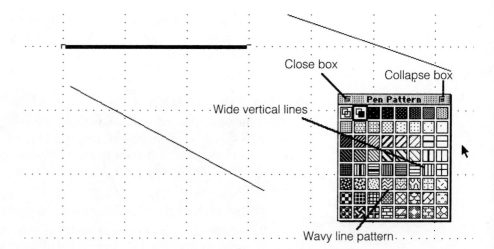

FIGURE 3-21

The Pen pattern palette allows the choice of various patterns to be applied to lines to create dotted, wavy, and other shaped lines. Some patterns are labeled on the figure.

13. Using the Pointer tool, click on one of the diagonal lines to select it.

14. Drag the **Arrow palette** onto the screen.

15. Choose Arrow at Start. Notice that an arrow now appears at the point at which the line starts.

16. Choose each of the other arrow options to see the effect on the line. Try changing the Pen width to see how this changes the look of the line and the arrow. When you finish, close the Arrow palette by clicking on the close box on the top left corner of the palette.

Colors may also be chosen from the Pen color palette to form lines of different colors. Continue experimenting with the various Pen palettes until you feel comfortable using them.

USING THE ARC TOOL

The **Arc tool** provides an easy way to make smooth curves. Options within ClarisWorks allow you to specify the number of degrees the arc forms or to move the curve to an arc that is pleasing to you. Arcs may be filled or formed into wedges.

1. Use the vertical scroll bar to move the lines out of view. Select the Arc tool.

2. Click on the screen and drag downward to form an arc similar to the arc shown in Figure 3-22.

3. Double-click on the arc or choose **Modify Arc...** from the Options menu. The Modify Arc dialog box should appear as shown in Figure 3-23.

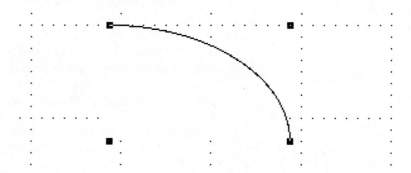

FIGURE 3-22

An arc created with the Arc tool. The handles indicate the arc is selected.

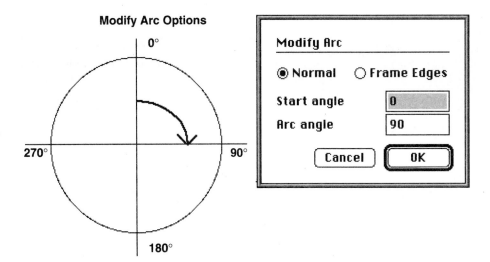

FIGURE 3-23

The Modify Arc dialog box is shown with a diagram indicating the various Start angle positions and the direction of measure for the Arc angle. When normal is selected only the arc is displayed. To create a wedge, select Frame Edges.

4. There are various options available. To form a wedge, you click on the button in front of Frame Edges. Click OK to see the change in the arc.

5. Double-click on the arc again to see the Modify Arc dialog box. Click on Normal to return to a normal arc.

6. Currently the Start angle is 0° and the Arc angle is 90°. Notice the diagram in Figure 3-23. The Start angle positions are noted on the figure. The Arc angle is measured in a clockwise rotation from the Start angle.

7. Change the Start angle to 45. Click OK. Notice the change in the arc.

8. Double-click on the arc to display the Modify Arc dialog box again. Change the Start angle to 90 and the Arc angle to 180. Click OK. Notice the change in appearance of the arc.

9. Continue making changes in the arc until you feel comfortable with the various options available within the Modify Arc dialog box. The range for the value must be 0 to 359.

10. While the arc is selected, choose Reshape from the Arrange menu. The cursor changes to a reshape cursor and anchor points are shown on the ends of the arc.

11. Place the Reshape cursor on either of the anchor points and drag to reshape the arc.

12. Continue reshaping the arc until you feel comfortable using this technique to reshape an arc.

13. When you are finished reshaping, choose Reshape again from the Arrange menu to deselect it.

USING MULTIPLE ARCS TO CREATE SHAPES

Combining use of the Fill and Pen tool palettes with the ability to change the arc angles gives you the ability to create interesting curves that may be used in drawings. The sample that follows shows how you may use a second curve to block out and therefore reshape the image of an existing curve.

1. Double-click on the arc once more to display the Modify Arc dialog box. Choose Normal if it is not already selected. Change the Start angle to 0 and the Arc angle to 180. Click OK.

2. From the Fill gradients palette, choose the yellow/gold gradient.
3. While the arc is still selected, choose Duplicate from the Edit menu.
4. Drag the bottom handle on rounded portion of the duplicated arc to the left to make the arc smaller, as shown in Figure 3-24.

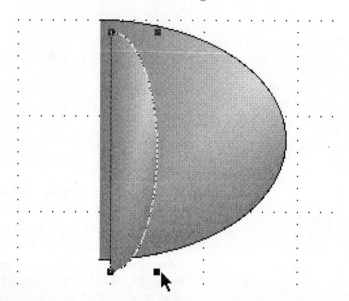

FIGURE 3-24

The outline shows the new shape as the selected arc is made smaller. Dragging the handles allows the arc to be made smaller or larger.

5. While the smaller arc is still selected, choose White from the Fill color palette.
6. Drag the smaller arc into position over the left portion of the larger arc as shown in Figure 3-25. Notice the interesting fish-tail look. This technique of covering a portion of an object with another white object can also be used with other objects to create interesting and unusual shapes.

USING THE FREEHAND TOOL

The **Freehand tool** is used to draw curved or irregular lines. It is used in the same way that you would use a pencil to draw or doodle. You have the same Fill and Pen tools available with the Freehand tool that you had with the other tools we have used.

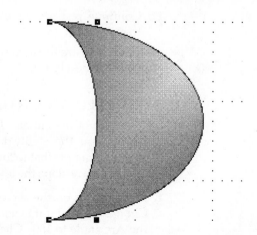

FIGURE 3-25

The fish-tail look has been achieved by placing an arc filled with white over the end of the original arc. Layering different objects provides a means of creating interesting and unusual shapes. These objects may then be grouped in order to move or resize them as one object.

1. Use the vertical scroll bar to move down the screen a little.
2. From the Draw tools, choose the Freehand tool.
3. Drag the mouse to draw an irregular shape that is not connected, as shown in Figure 3-26.

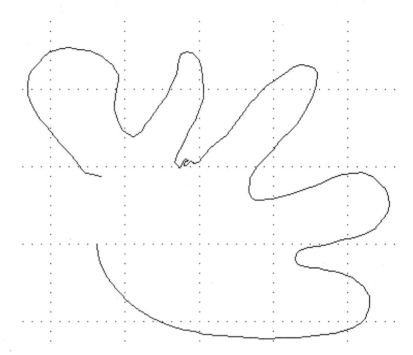

FIGURE 3-26

The Freehand tool can be used to create irregular shapes in much the way a pencil or pen would be used. In general, curves are rather jagged.

4. While the shape is still selected, select dark blue from the Pen color palette.
5. Select gold from the Fill color palette. Notice how the color fills the shape.
6. Continue experimenting by changing the Pen width and Fill pattern.
7. When you finish experimenting, go on to the next section.

USING THE BEZIGON TOOL

The **Bezigon tool** allows you to draw shapes with precise curves. When you were using the Freehand tool, you drew curves and shapes by moving the mouse through the actual path of the curve. Using the Bezigon tool you will click to specify the points that define each curve. When you finish the drawing, you can reshape the curve if necessary by moving individual points that define the curve. Using the Bezigon tool you can create smoother curves in irregular shapes than you can with the Freehand tool.

1. Use the vertical scroll bar to move down the screen a little or choose New from the File menu to create a new Draw document if there isn't enough room on the screen.
2. Click on the Bezigon tool.
3. Click on the screen. Move the cursor and click again for the next point. Continue clicking until you have a bezigon curve similar to the one shown

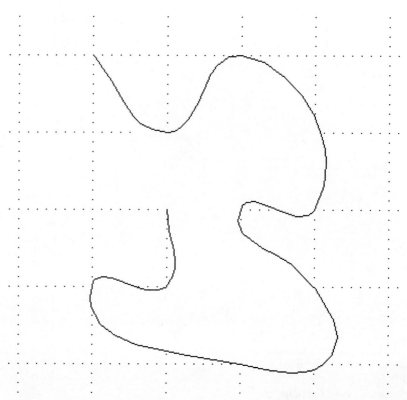

FIGURE 3-27

The Bezigon tool has been used to create the irregular shape shown. In general, curves created with the Bezigon tool are more smooth than those created with the Freehand tool.

in Figure 3-27. Double-click to indicate where you want the last point. (Don't worry if your bezigon curve looks different from the one shown. All of the steps should still work.)

4. While the bezigon is still selected, choose Reshape from the Arrange menu.

5. The cursor changes to the Reshape cursor, and the bezigon should now display anchor points.

6. Click on one of the anchor points. You should now see control handles in addition to the anchor points, as shown in Figure 3-28.

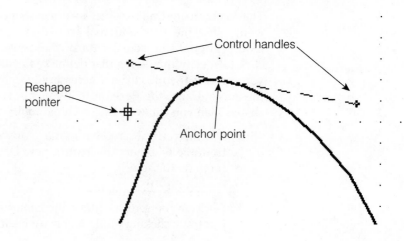

FIGURE 3-28

Anchor points and control handles on bezigon curves provide an easy means to reshape a curve when Reshape has been chosen from the Arrange menu.

The anchor points are the points you originally clicked to form the figure. A control handle is a line that intersects an anchor point. The ends of this line can be dragged to reshape the curve or angle.

7. Drag one of the end points of the control handle. Notice how the curve changes.

8. Drag an anchor point. Notice how the shape of the figure changes.

9. Continue selecting anchor points or control handles to reshape the bezigon.

    Note: You may add new anchor points by clicking on any spot on the bezigon border. To add a new control handle, click an anchor point to select it, then hold down the Option key while dragging away from the anchor point.

10. Select Reshape from the Arrange menu to deselect it.

The Fill and Pen tools may also be used with a bezigon, as they were with the other figures you have used. Practice using these tools until you feel comfortable with them.

CLASSROOM ←——→ CONNECTION

Create a chart explaining an historical event such as a battle, pioneer settlement, or an Indian village. Use a legend to explain the meaning of symbols used in the chart.

USING TEXT WITH GRAPHICS

Text can be typed over graphic objects or used to label objects, or the graphic objects may be used to accent the text. Text font, size, style, and color may be changed by using the menus.

1. Double-click on the **Text tool** (the A icon beside the Pointer tool). The background of the icon should be black.

2. Choose font from the Format menu and choose Helvetica or another font you like from the submenu.

3. Choose Size from the Format menu and choose 18 Point from the submenu. Choosing the font and size now, before any text or text box is selected, will enable it to stay the same for each text box until you change it. (Setting the size when something is selected will apply the size only to that selection and not to future selections.)

4. Click inside the bezigon. A small rectangle, called a text box, should appear on the screen with an insertion point.

5. Type **Bezigon**, as shown in Figure 3-29.

6. Click on the Pointer tool to select it.

7. Click on the word **Bezigon** to select the text box. Handles should appear as shown in Figure 3-29.

8. Drag the handles to resize the text box used to hold the word. You may make it longer or shorter by dragging any of the handles. A text box can be as large as a newspaper column or as small as a single letter. The height of a text box is controlled by the amount of text in it and by the size of the font.

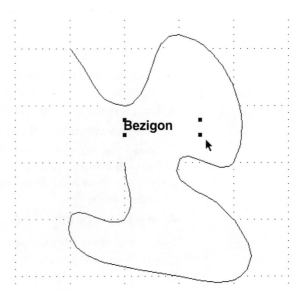

FIGURE 3-29

A text box has been placed inside the bezigon to label it. The handles indicate that the text box is selected and can be resized or moved.

9. Move the text box containing the word by putting the pointer anywhere in the rectangle, except on the handles, then dragging the box. Position it so the word is contained completely within the bezigon.

10. Create other text boxes and place them inside or outside of existing graphic objects that you have created. Move and resize the boxes until you are pleased with the way they look. Try drawing an arrowed line from a text box to an object that it labels.

CLASSROOM ◄———► CONNECTION

Create a drawing of an invention or a diagram related to a science experiment or project. Items in the drawing can be labeled with text boxes and arrows used to show movement or change.

PRACTICE WITH DRAWING

You have now worked a little with some of the Draw environment graphics tools. If you are artistically inclined or just like to draw, you may want to take the time to experiment with the various tools and options you have used and also with others that have not been covered here. The following may give you some ideas for practicing the skills you have learned so far. When you finish, save any documents you wish to keep and close all of the Draw documents.

1. Create any of the graphics that follow.

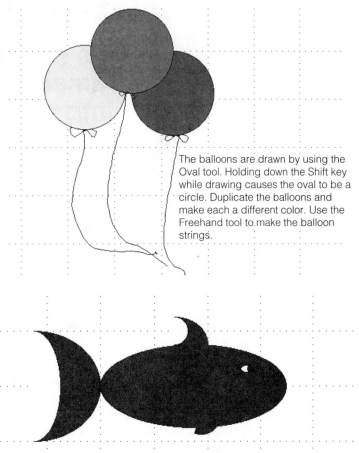

The balloons are drawn by using the Oval tool. Holding down the Shift key while drawing causes the oval to be a circle. Duplicate the balloons and make each a different color. Use the Freehand tool to make the balloon strings.

Draw a fish similar to the one shown here. Use the Arc tool and the Oval tool. The top and back fins are created with a white arc blocking out some of the colored arc. The eye is created by placing a black oval inside a white oval.

This television or monitor has been created using the Rectangle tool filled with gray then overlaying a Rounded Rectangle filled with white. The controls were created with the Oval tool (using the Shift key to make a circle). The outer circle is filled with a pattern and the inner circle with black. The two circles are selected and grouped. The grouped circles are then duplicated to get a second control of the same size.

This is a title that is framed and placed into a document.

2. Use graphics tools to draw coins. Use Duplicate to make stacks of coins. Try using various patterns on some of the coins to shade and add interest to the stacks.

3. Design a logo for the class store, the Pencil Place.

4. Design a header for the school computer club stationery.

5. Draw a seating chart of your class.

6. Create a map of your school.

Creating a Slide Show

The Draw application is a perfect place to create a **slide show** that can be used for a presentation, or even a message center. The slide show can then be set up to run independently or can be controlled by a click of the mouse. Using an LCD projector or a large screen monitor can make a slide show into a presentation that can be seen by a large group. All of the Draw tools are available within the screens that make up a slide show.

CREATING A MASTER PAGE

A **master page** can be created that will enable you to place items on a page that should appear on each screen of the presentation. Placing the items on a master page will give a consistent look to each screen. First you will begin by setting up the Document... options and Page Setup... for the slide show document. Then you will add a background, a graphic image, and text on the master page that will appear on every screen.

To begin, choose New from the File menu and select a new Draw document.

1. From the File menu choose Page Setup....

2. For the orientation choice, click on Landscape (the horizontal icon on the right) to choose that view. Click OK.

3. From the Format menu choose Document....

4. In the Document dialog box... change the top, bottom, left, and right margins to 1.25. (Use the Tab key to move the selection to the next margin item.) Change the Pages down to 4. Click OK. This creates a four-page slide show. The number of screens in the slide show is controlled here.

5. Use the Zoom control indicator at the bottom left side of the screen to change the zoom to 75.

6. Select Page View from the View menu. Use the horizontal and vertical scroll bars to center the page on the screen.

7. From the Options menu, choose **Edit Master Page**. Notice that the bottom of the screen now displays "Master Page" instead of the page number.

8. From the File menu choose **Library**, and then choose Education. Notice that there are various libraries of images that come with ClarisWorks. At another time you may wish to explore them further.

9. The Education Library palette should appear on the screen. Select Blackboard and click on Use. The blackboard image should appear on the screen.

10. From the Arrange menu, choose Transform and then choose Scale by Percent.... The horizontal and vertical scales should be at 50; if they are not, type **50** for each and then click OK. This makes the blackboard image smaller.

11. Drag the blackboard to the upper right corner of the screen.

12. Click on the close box on the upper left corner of the Education Library palette to close it.

13. Click on the Text tool to select it.

14. From the Format menu, choose Size and then choose 36 point.

15. From the Format menu, choose Style and then choose bold.

16. From the Format menu, choose Text Color. Choose a color that will be distinct when displayed.

17. Click in the upper left region of the screen and type **Central City Schools**. Your screen should look like Figure 3-30.

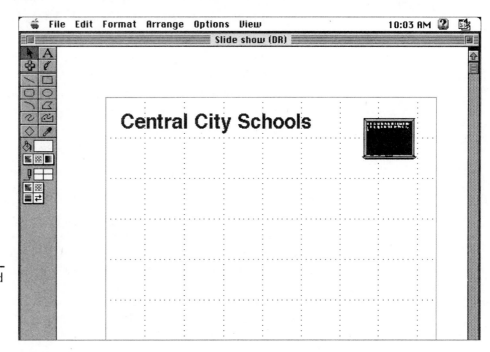

FIGURE 3-30

A master page has been created in order for the text and graphic to be placed consistently from one slide to another in the slide show.

18. Click on a blank area of the screen to deselect the text box.

19. From the Options menu, choose Edit Master Page to deselect it. The display at the bottom of the screen should now indicate Page 1.

CREATING THE SLIDES

You have now created a master page. The background, blackboard, and text will appear on each screen of the slide show. You will now add the information needed for each additional slide.

1. Click on the Text tool (the letter A on the Tool palette).

2. Draw a text box in the center of the page that stretches across five squares and down two squares.

3. From the Style menu, choose Color and choose a different color that will display well.

4. Type:

   Welcome to

   Open

   House

5. Click on the Pointer tool.

6. Click on the text box to select it.

7. Draw the handles on the text box until they are positioned similar to Figure 3-31.

8. From the Format menu choose Alignment. From the submenu, choose Center to center the text in the text box.

9. Use the vertical scroll bar to move to the next screen.

10. Follow the steps above to create a text box and enter the following:

    Please find your child's seat. There should be a folder on your child's desk with papers for you to review.

11. Move to each of the next two screens, create a text box, then add your own text.

12. You should now have four slides in your slide show.

13. To view your slide show, choose Slide Show… from the View menu. (Note: The Pointer cursor must be selected for this menu to be available.)

14. The Slide Show dialog box should appear as shown in Figure 3-32.

Notice that the Order area allows you to change the order and appearance of the slides. Each slide is listed by its page number. To change the order, select a slide and drag it up to view it earlier and down to view it later in the slide show. The page number will not change but the order in which the slide will be viewed will change. The icon in front of the page number indicates how the slide will be displayed. The options are opaque (the default), transparent, or hidden and are identified by the key found below the Order area. To choose a different option, click on the icon that precedes the page number. Transparent allows you to layer items in different slides on top of each other. This can be used to view bullets one at a time or to add items to a chart or graph one at a time. Hidden allows you to hide a slide from view without removing it from the document.

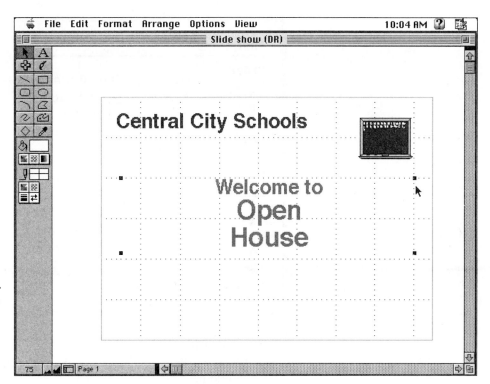

FIGURE 3-31

The text box on the first slide has been selected and the handles moved to widen the area. The text boxes on the slides that follow should be placed in the same position.

Slide Options allow you to choose how the slides will appear on the screen. In Figure 3-32, the selected options will cause the slides to fit within the screen and to be centered on the screen. The cursor will also be displayed and can be used to point to items of interest on the screen during a presentation. The slide show will loop on its own and advance every 5 seconds. You could also select Fade, which would cause each slide to fade out of view and the new slide to gradually appear. Fade is called a transition. Certain other programs offer many different transition options. In this example you also have the option to change the background and the border of the slides. There are also QuickTime Options, which would allow you to control the use of QuickTime movies within a slide show. QuickTime movies will not be dealt with in this text.

Notice at the bottom of the dialog box there is a message indicating that you must press q to quit the slide show.

1. Click on the boxes in front of the Slide Options that are selected in Figure 3-32.

2. Choose a color for the background that is complementary to the other colors you have chosen.

3. Choose a different color for the border. (This will allow you to see just where each area is located on the screen.)

4. Click on Start to begin viewing the slide show.

5. When you finish viewing the slide show, type **q** to quit.

6. Click on the check box in front of Loop and Advance every 5 seconds to deselect them.

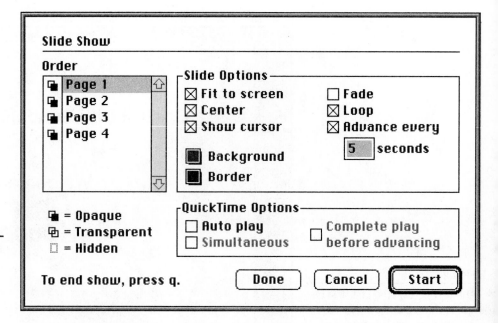

FIGURE 3-32

The Slide Show dialog box offers
many options for the slide show.
It is here that slides may be
reordered and various slide
options may be set.

7. Click on Start.

8. When you finish viewing the first slide, click the mouse. The slide show
   should go on to the next screen.

9. Continue by clicking on the mouse or pressing the spacebar, right arrow,
   down arrow, or tab keys. Notice that when you reach the last slide, the
   slide show stops; it no longer loops back to the beginning.

10. When you reach the last slide, type **q** to quit the slide show.

11. Click on Done to quit viewing the slide show and return to the Draw doc-
    ument.

12. Save the document and call it Slide Sample. Close the document.

You may continue revising the slides in the slide show and experimenting
with the various options in the Slide Show dialog box until you feel comfortable
with them. When you finish, close the document.

CLASSROOM ←——→ CONNECTION

Have students create a slide show to present material to the class for a project or
report. Text, charts, and graphics may be added to the slide show to enhance and
explain sections of the project.

The Paint Environment

The Paint environment is somewhat different from the Draw environment even
though some of the tools look very much the same. In the Paint environment the
images created are **bit-mapped** instead of object-oriented. This means that the
graphic is created by placing small dots, or pixels, next to each other to form the
desired shape or pattern and any part of the shape can be edited. For instance, a
line would be created by drawing a series of pixels side by side so close to each

other that they look like a solid line, as shown in Figure 3-33, and any part of the line could be erased. In object-oriented graphics, only the whole line could be erased. As a result, the Paint environment is one layer rather than the many layers that are created with each object in the Draw environment. If you move one object so that it covers part of a second object, the pixels or dots from the first object will replace those of the second.

FIGURE 3-33

The line at the right has been enlarged to show the pixels that form the line.

In comparison with the Draw environment, the Paint environment allows greater flexibility for some types of work and more restrictions for other types of work. For instance, because it is bit-mapped, text created in the Paint mode is more jagged than that created in the Word Processing or Draw environment. Also, once text is created it cannot be edited as word processing text can. However, you can alter the letters themselves in many ways that you cannot in the Draw environment. You can resize them, distort them, add fancy curls on the tails or designs in the circles, or any number of other changes to create special effects.

As you work in the Paint environment, keep in mind that you can undo changes that you find are not pleasing, but this must be done immediately after the action is taken. For this reason it is usually wise to save your work often so that if you make a mistake you can revert back to the last image that was saved. This can eliminate a great deal of work in recreating a graphic that has been destroyed by an accidental move of the mouse.

USING THE POLYGON TOOLS

1. Open a new paint document (choose New… from the File menu). Notice that the **Pencil tool** is selected.

2. Look at the Paint tool palette. Many of the tools are similar to those in the Draw environment, but there are a few additional tools. These are labeled in Figure 3-34.

3. Double-click the Regular Polygon tool, the diamond-shaped icon (◇). You will see a dialog box appear asking for the number of sides. Type **5** and click OK.

   Notice that selected **Paint tools** remain selected until another tool is clicked. Unlike the Draw tools where you must double-click to maintain a selection after using the tool, double-clicking on a tool provides other options on many of the Paint tools.

4. In the Fill sample box, the box next to the pouring paint bucket, you now see black. Use the Fill color palette, the left icon below the paint bucket, to choose white.

Selection Rectrangle tool   Lasso tool
Magic wand tool   Brush tool
Pencil tool   Fill tool
Spray tool   Eraser tool

FIGURE 3-34

The tool palette in the Paint environment with the "new" Paint tools labeled.

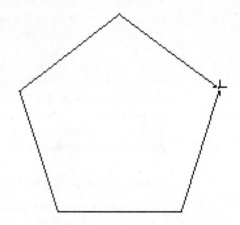

FIGURE 3-35

A pentagon drawn in the Paint environment with the Regular Polygon tool. Double-clicking on the tool provides a means of choosing the number of sides for the regular polygon.

5. With the Regular Polygon tool still selected, move the crosshair onto the page. Hold down the mouse button and drag until the polygon looks like Figure 3-35. (If it is not quite like you want it, choose Undo Paint from the Edit menu and try again.)

6. Click on the Polygon tool (below the Oval tool).

7. Draw a star, as in Figure 3-36, by using the points of the polygon you just completed as a guide:

   a.   Click on one point.

   b.   Click on an opposite point.

   c.   Repeat until a star shape is drawn.

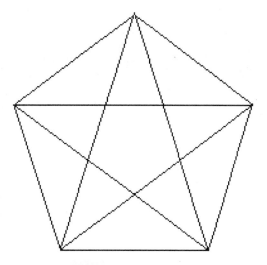

FIGURE 3-36

A star has been created with the Polygon tool using the points of the pentagon as a guide.

USING THE PENCIL TOOL

The Pencil tool will draw one pixel at a time. It will draw in black if you click or start dragging on a white area; it will draw in white if you click or start dragging on a black area.

1. Zoom in to 400 percent so that you can look at your work. You can see that the figure is made up of dots or pixels.

2. Click the Pencil tool. If black is not the current fill selection in the box beside the paint bucket, choose black from the Fill color palette to select it. If black (or the color you are drawing in) is not selected, the changes you make will not be viewed as a part of the diagram. If white is selected when the background is white, you will not be able to see any changes.

3. Use the horizontal and vertical scroll bars to scroll to the corners of the polygons. Make sure that all lines are solid, with no holes or gaps, as shown in Figure 3-37.

4. If there is a gap, you can close it by clicking the Pencil tool on the gap to create a new dot to fill in the area. The pencil can also be used to create additional pixels for accent or interest. If you add too many dots you may remove extra dots by clicking or dragging the pencil on each dot you wish to remove.

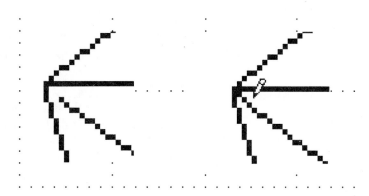

FIGURE 3-37

On the left, a gap in the figure near a vertex. On the right, the gap has been closed using the Pencil tool.

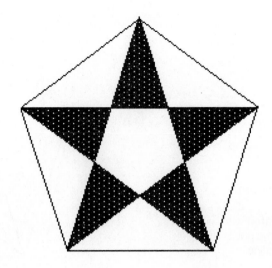

FIGURE 3-38

The Fill tool (paint bucket) has been used to fill the points of the star with a pattern.

USING THE FILL TOOLS

1. Change the zoom percentage back to 100 percent.

2. Change the Fill pattern to a dark background with white dots. (You may also change the color if you wish.)

3. Click the Fill tool (the paint bucket). Note that the tip of the pouring paint is the "hot spot" for this tool, the point that determines where the pattern will go. Make sure that this is the part you position for filling sections of the diagram.

4. You will be filling the points of the star with the pattern, as shown in Figure 3-38. With the paint bucket positioned inside a point of the star, click the mouse to fill the point. (Remember to choose Undo Paint from the Edit menu immediately if it doesn't fill correctly.)

5. If the paint spilled over into other sections of the star, check again for gaps in the lines. If there is even a one pixel gap, the paint will "spill" out into other regions of the graphic.

USING THE ERASER TOOL

Now it might be nice to get rid of the original pentagon that was used to help you draw the star. In the Draw environment, you can select the polygon and delete it. In the Paint environment, you cannot do that, but you can use the **Eraser tool**.

1. Zoom to 200 percent. It is easier to control the erasure when the diagram is enlarged so that individual pixels can be seen more easily.

2. Click the Eraser tool, the icon above the Fill sample box that looks like a blackboard eraser. (Beware: Double-clicking on the eraser will erase the entire screen.)

3. Drag the eraser over the lines of the pentagon around the outside of the star. Move slowly, clicking and dragging small sections at a time. If you accidently erase too much, choose Undo Paint from the Edit menu to put back the last section that was erased.

4. You have now created a star that could be used as a logo.

SELECTING PAINTED GRAPHICS

Part or all of a Paint image can be chosen to be moved, copied, or modified by using the **Selection Rectangle tool** or the **Lasso tool**. The Selection Rectangle tool selects the image plus the white space surrounding the image within a rectangular selection area. Holding down the Command key while using the Selection Rectangle tool causes it to include only the graphic and not the white space. The Lasso tool is used to select irregularly shaped graphics. Selection made by the Lasso tool includes only the graphic and not the white space around it.

1. Change the zoom percentage to 100 percent.
2. Select the Selection Rectangle tool (next to the Lasso tool).
3. Starting above and left of the star, drag until a rectangle surrounds the star.
4. When you release the mouse button, everything inside the rectangle, including the white space, is selected. This is indicated by the flashing rectangle.
5. Click outside the rectangle to deselect the graphic.
6. Drag over the star again while holding down the Command key (right of the Option key on the bottom row of the keyboard). This selects the star without including the white space around it.
7. Click the Lasso tool. The pointer changes to a lasso shape.
8. Drag the lasso around the star. When you release the button, only the graphic is selected. The Lasso tool is especially useful for selecting details in graphics and parts of graphics.
9. Any selection can be deselected in any of the following ways:
   a. Click outside the selection.
   b. Make another selection.
   c. Select another tool.

CLASSROOM ←——→ CONNECTION

Using Draw and Paint tools, have students create business cards with a logo that represents something of interest to them.

OTHER OPTIONS

1. Use one of the selection tools to select the star without the white space.
2. From the **Transform menu** choose Scale by Percent.... This changes the size of the graphic. The current size is 100 percent. Less than 100 percent makes the graphic smaller, more makes it bigger. Selecting equal percentages for length and width makes the graphic change in size, but not in shape. Differing percentages will change the proportions of the graphic.
3. Change the selection to 75 percent for each dimension.
4. Click OK. The star should be the same shape, but smaller. The pattern in the star may look different. Some distortion of patterns and shape can occur when a selection of a bit-mapped graphic is resized, rotated, or otherwise changed.

5. Zoom to 50 percent.

6. Drag the selected star to center it equally between the right and left sides of the page, if it is not already centered.

7. From the Edit menu choose Duplicate to make a copy of the selected star. The copy may be on top of the original star.

8. Drag the new star down to a position similar to the position of the leftmost star in Figure 3-39. Be sure the crosshair becomes an arrow pointer over the star before you drag it, or the star will be deselected.

9. Duplicate the star again and drag it down to the position of the rightmost star in Figure 3-39.

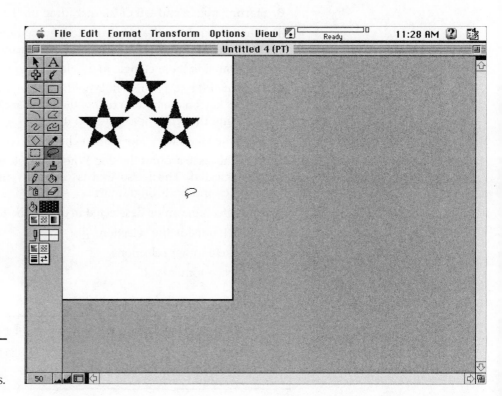

FIGURE 3-39

A logo can be created by copying and arranging a design such as the star in different ways.

Text can also be created in a text box and then manipulated as a graphic. This enables the creation of interesting and eye-catching text for titles and logos. Try the following.

1. Click the Text tool.

2. Drag to create a text box below the three stars that now make up your logo. You must drag the I-beam in the Paint environment if you need a long text box. When you finish typing and click anywhere on the screen, the text box disappears—it cannot be resized or otherwise treated as an object, as it would be in the Draw environment.

3. Change the Size of the type to 48 Point and the Style to Outline.

4. Type **Three Star.**

5. Click the Selection Rectangle tool.

6. Hold down the Command key while dragging to select just the text.

7. From the Transform menu choose **Distort**.

8. Use the pointer to drag the top left handle upward. When the mouse button is released, this will enlarge the first letters of the words, as shown in Figure 3-40.

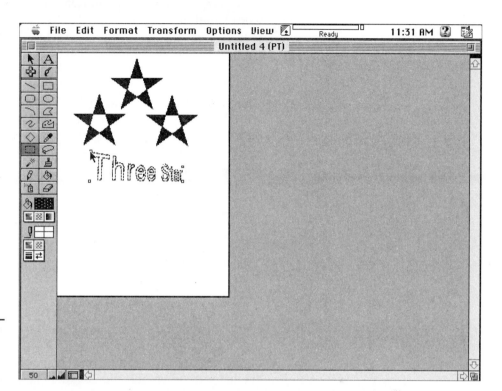

FIGURE 3-40

Three Star has been distorted by using Distort on the Transform menu and dragging the top left handle.

9. If you don't like the way that looks, choose Undo Distort from the Edit menu.

10. Click anywhere outside the handles to exit the Distort option and keep the graphic selected.

11. While the text is still selected, experiment with some of the other options available on the Transform menu, such as Shear, Perspective, and Rotate. Each time you choose one of the options, if you are unhappy with the result, you can undo it. Keep in mind that you can only undo the last action that you have performed. You may wish to Save the document first, so that you have the option of reverting back to the last saved version if you make changes that you don't like.

CLASSROOM ←——→ CONNECTION

Have students use Draw or Paint tools to illustrate a story they have written or a book they have read for a book report.

PRACTICE WITH PAINTING

You have now created a simple logo using some of the Paint tools. Experiment using some of the other tools. You will find that working in a Paint document can be a little tricky. If you move an object so it overlaps another or so that part of it moves off the screen and you don't immediately undo the move, you will lose some of your image.

1. Use the Paint environment to experiment with a headline for a flyer for the school's Ice Cream Social. Try using Outline for the text style and filling the letters with a pattern or color. Distort the word(s). If you are feeling comfortable using the tools you have learned, try others as well.

2. Use the Paint environment to draw a cloud. Duplicate the cloud and fill it with different patterns (or colors) to make a thunderstorm, or draw other types of clouds to demonstrate the variations for a science class.

3. Draw a triangle similar to the one shown below. Experiment using some of the Transform menu options. Then duplicate the triangle several times, fill it, and create a design.

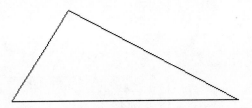

4. Create a logo for the school track team, the bicycle club, the chess club, or another team or organization of your choice to use on their announcements and fund-raiser advertisements.

5. If you are feeling really brave, draw a self-portrait for your students to use as a story starter. Try some of the tools you haven't used yet, such as the Spray Can or Brush tools, as well as others you would like to practice more.

Conclusion

You have learned the basics of using both the Draw and the Paint environments. Each of these has its advantages and disadvantages. Using the many layers created in a Draw document can be a little less restrictive in some ways than using the one layer of the Paint environment. However using the pencil, spray can, and brush tool give some special visual detail to a graphic that cannot be done within a Draw document.

There are many more features of the Paint and Draw environments that could not be covered in this book. You can learn more about these by using Claris-Works Help and documentation.

Keep in mind that because ClarisWorks is an integrated package, images can be created in the Draw environment, then copied and pasted into the Paint environment for the addition of special details or created in the Paint environment and copied into the Draw environment to be labeled with the smoother text characters. As you experiment with the graphics tools available in the Paint and Draw environments, you will find them increasingly easy to use and you will recognize more and more uses for them. You are likely to discover that they will become an indispensable part of your toolbox of teaching aids.

KEY TERMS

align
Align Objects
Arc tool
Arrange menu
Arrow palette
Autogrid
Bezigon tool
bit-mapped
crosshair
Distort
Draw environment
Draw tools
Duplicate
Edit Master Page
Eraser tool
Fill color palette
Fill gradient palette
Fill pattern palette
Fill tools
Flip Horizontally
Flip Vertically

Free Rotate
Freehand tool
grid
Group
handles
Hide Graphics Grid
Info palette
Lasso tool
layers
Library
Line tool
master page
Modify Arc
Move Backward
Move to Front
object
Object Info...
object-oriented
Options menu
Paint environment
Paint tools

Pen color palette
Pen pattern palette
Pen width palette
Pen tools
Pencil tool
Pointer tool
Polygon Sides...
Polygon tool
Rectangle tool
Regular Polygon tool
Reshape
Scale by Percent...
Selection Rectangle tool
Show Graphics Grid
slide show
Smooth
Text tool
Transform menu
transparent
Turn Autogrid Off

EXERCISES

1. Create a book cover for a book written by the second grade class, titled *When I was Little....*

2. In the Paint environment draw a panoramic scene with buildings to use on a bulletin board for a social studies unit on cities. Use Transform menu options to change the look of the scene.

3. Create a layout for a class newspaper. Use text boxes up to a full column in size for articles. Put a header at the top for the name, date, and class.

4. Draw a seating chart for your classroom. First create it from your perspective, then create a second by copying and modifying the original to view it from the students' perspective. Any who are new to the school or who do not know each other yet can use the chart to learn each other's names more easily.

5. Create and label a diagram of something in your subject area. You may need to teach your students about the parts of a flower or the parts of a sentence, the gears in a machine, the differences between maple leaves and oak leaves, or the meaning of a fraction.

6. Create a header for your monthly newsletter to parents. (Yes! You can send it every month with these new computer skills you are learning!)

4

ClarisWorks— Database

OUTLINE

Introduction

A **database** is a collection of **data**. Electronic databases are collections of data that are stored and accessed electronically—information is stored on a disk rather than in a file cabinet. Electronic databases provide easy manipulation and retrieval of information. Data can be quickly sorted, selected, and formatted into meaningful reports, making it readily usable and quite valuable to the user.

Different kinds of information can be stored on databases, which can have a wide range of uses. For teachers, databases can be useful for classroom management. For students, they can provide information resources and opportunities to explore subject areas and ideas. Database files with information on American presidents, national parks, inventors, historic events, and many other topics can be purchased for classroom use. Databases can also be created by students, based on research they have done on current topics of study in their classroom. Databases with information about students, equipment inventory, books, and other data pertinent to teachers can be created and used by the teacher.

You will explore the use of databases by first learning to manipulate a database that has already been created. Then you will create a new database of information that could be used for instructional purposes. If you are not confident of your skills in working with windows, editing text, and saving documents, you may want to review the sections of Chapters 1 and 2 that deal with these as you work.

Data Basics

Knowing some database terminology and being able to move around in a database are important first steps in learning to use a database effectively. You will be learning these as you work with the Class Data database on the Data Disk that accompanies this book. This is a database document containing information about a fictional class of students.

To begin, open the database named Class Data on the Data Disk. Opening this database (by double-clicking on the document icon labeled Class Data) should start, or launch, the ClarisWorks program at the same time, because the Class Data file was created with the ClarisWorks program. If you need additional instruction on opening the document, refer to "Beginning ClarisWorks" in Chapter 2. You should see the database on the screen as shown in Figure 4-1.

DATABASE TERMS

In the Class Data database window you see all the information in the file about John M. Anderson—his name, guardian, address, city, state, zip, phone number, and other facts or notes about the student. Each type of information in a database, such as the student's name or the guardian, is called a **field**, or a category. The boxes located to the right of the field names are the actual fields where the data is stored. Every field has a field name. The **field names**—Student, Guardian, Address, City, State, Zip—are displayed here beside each field. Each piece of specific information you see—John M. Anderson, John & Elaine Anderson, 1147 Sylvania Avenue, Toledo—is called an entry or value. An **entry** is composed of text, numbers, dates, times, or formulas.

All the fields you see in the window make up a **record**—a set of related information. In summary, a database is a collection of records, records are sets of related fields, and fields contain data or entries. As an analogy, you could think

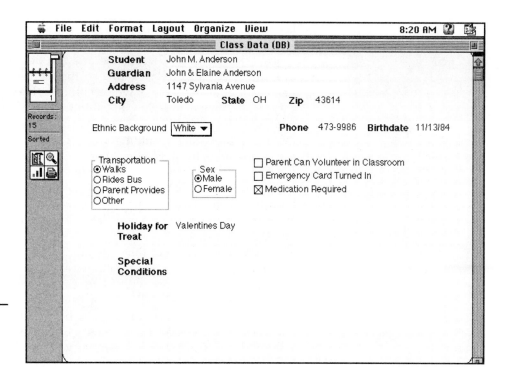

FIGURE 4-1

One record in the Class Data database in standard layout. A variety of types of fields are represented in this database.

Database Terms

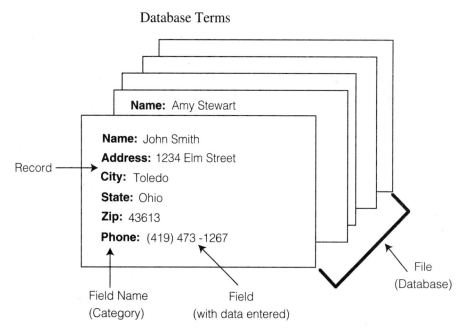

FIGURE 4-2

A database can be compared to file index cards, with information for each record stored on a different card. Each card holds various types of information called fields or categories, which contain data specific to that record.

of this database as a set of index cards, with each record as an individual card. Each card would contain the same categories of information, but the data on each card would vary. This is illustrated in Figure 4-2.

The fields in Figure 4-1 and on your screen reveal the variety of fields available within the ClarisWorks database. The fields Student and Guardian are of type Name. In these fields, names can be typed in first name, middle name, last name order but when sorted will be arranged by the last name, the last set of characters in the field. If the last name has a title such as Jr. or III, you must type Option-space (hold down the Option key while you press the spacebar) between the last name and the title. Use of the Option-space will link the title with the last name so the name will be sorted correctly. Text fields can hold numeric as well as alphabetic characters. The fields Address, City, State, Phone, and Special Conditions are examples of text fields. If the data in each field will be the same for each record, you can set up the field so that the proper data is automatically filled in for each record. For example, if each student is from Toledo, Ohio, you can preset the value and it will be filled in as each new record is created. The Zip field is a number field. This type of field can hold numbers. Options available for this field allow you to limit the range of values that can be used for the field. Ethnic Background is an example of a pop-up menu field. The values for this field are set up in a pop-up menu that allows for easy selection. Birthdate is a date field. In this field you may type dates that can later be sorted chronologically or in reverse chronological order. Date functions are available that allow you to do a variety of calculations with date fields. Radio button fields, such as Transportation and Sex, allow choices to be selected by clicking the mouse in the appropriate radio button. Check box fields can be used for information that is either selected or not selected. Examples of this are seen in Parent Can Volunteer in Classroom, Emergency Card Turned In, and Medication Required. A value list field allows you to select the value from a scrolling list. Holiday for Treat is an example of this type of field.

CLASSROOM ←——————→ CONNECTION

Print sets of large cards with several fields of data with about ten records in each set. Duplicate and laminate the cards. Use the cards to explain fields, field names, records, and files. Have students work with the cards in small groups during the explanation. Use the Parks database on the Data Disk with the report Cards.

When setting up a database, you must determine what "type" of field you wish to use for each field that you enter. The type could be any of those mentioned above. You will look at field types in more detail later in the chapter.

STANDARD LAYOUT

In ClarisWorks, when all the information about one single record is displayed on the screen, as it is in Figure 4-1, the database is in standard layout, or single-record format. The **status panel** on the left side of the screen indicates that there are a total of 15 records. Under the number of records notice that there is a status of Sorted. This indicates that the file is sorted in some manner, in this case alphabetically by the student names. Sorting will be discussed later in the chapter. Above the number of records notice the number 1. That indicates that the record you are viewing is Record 1, the first record on the database. At this point you are in the **Browse mode**. Click on the Layout menu to notice that Browse is checked. Here you may add new records, change values in records, or delete records that are no longer needed.

MOVING IN THE DATABASE

When you use a database, you must be able to move to view various records. The icon with the 1 on it (which looks like a stack of index cards in a three-ring binder) is called the **File icon**. It is one of the options you have for moving through the database.

1. Click on the lower "page" of the File icon as shown in Figure 4-3. This moves to the next record in the file, which should be Julie Baker.

2. Click again on the lower page of the File icon. Record 3, Christopher Campbell, should be displayed on the screen.

3. To move back to the previous record, click on the top page of the File icon. Record 2 should be displayed again on the screen.

4. There is a **bookmark** at the side of the File icon. Using the bookmark allows for quicker movement through the database. Drag the bookmark about half way down the icon, as shown in Figure 4-4. Notice that the record number changes as you do this. If you move to Record 8, you should see information about Samuel Johnson.

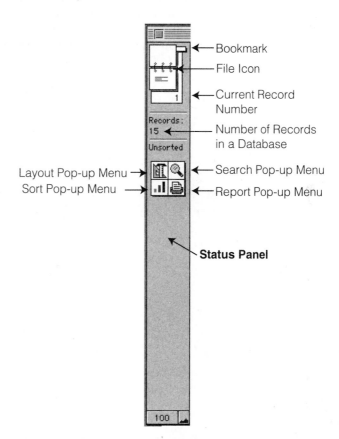

FIGURE 4-3

The status panel assists you in moving through the database and determining its status. Click on the bottom page of the File icon to move to the next record in the Class Data database. A number of objects are labeled that will be dealt with later in this chapter.

5. Practice using the pages and bookmark on the File icon to move around in the database until you feel comfortable with these steps.

6. Use the bookmark to move back to Record 1.

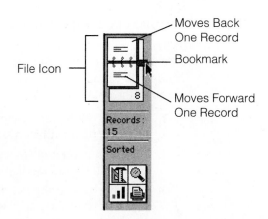

File Icon
Moves Back One Record
Bookmark
Moves Forward One Record

Records: 15

Sorted

FIGURE 4-4

Using the bookmark to move quickly to Record 8 in the Class Data database. The upper and lower pages of the File icon allow you to move back or forward one record, respectively.

LIST MODE

The information in the database can be viewed in other ways. In the previous example you saw all the fields in one record. Sometimes you may want to see multiple records at one time. This allows for easy comparison of information from one record to another—to look for similarities and differences. One way to accomplish this is through the **List mode**. The steps that follow explain how you change the view of the Class Data database from Browse to List mode.

File Edit Format Layout Organize View   10:43 PM

Class Data (DB)

Student	Guardian	Address	City	State	Zip	Ethnic Backg	Phone
John M.	John &	1147	Toledo	OH	43614	White	473-9986
Julie Baker	Richard & Jill	8473	Toledo	OH	43606	White	473-6598
Christopher	William &	9976	Toledo	OH	43623	White	478-6627
Jim	Yellow Horse	5576	Toledo	OH	43612	Ameri...	478-5696
Emilio A.	Carlos &	1259 Elm	Toledo	OH	43613	Hispanic	472-5586
Ginger M.	Mark &	2254 Walnut	Toledo	OH	43615	White	478/5522
Beau	William &	4599	Toledo	OH	43612	Black	478-5698
Samuel A.	Eric and	1234	Toledo	OH	43612	White	474-6698
Mathew R.	James &	3354	Toledo	OH	43623	Black	478-6653
Sandra	Joshua &	8934	Toledo	OH	43606	Black	473-6592
Yuka	Hiroma &	7845	Toledo	OH	43613	Asian	473-8252
Renee	Thomas &	8844	Toledo	OH	43623	Black	473-6576
Carrie	John & Karen	9873	Toledo	OH	43606	Mixed	473-6652
Carlos	Juan & Maria	1983	Toledo	OH	43606	White	473-8652
Elizabeth	David &	9376	Toledo	OH	43615	White	473-9662

Records: 15

Sorted

100   Page 1

FIGURE 4-5

The Class Data database in the List mode. To see additional information click on the right arrow on the horizontal scroll bar at the bottom of the screen. Records may be changed or added while in the List mode or the Browse mode.

1. From the Layout menu, choose List.
2. The display should change to what is shown in Figure 4-5. You will notice that not all of the information fits on the screen. To view additional information, click on the right arrow of the horizontal scroll bar, found at the bottom of the screen.

The information in the Ethnic Background, Transportation, Sex, and Holiday for Treat fields is displayed in List form in pop-up menus. The check box fields—Parent Can Volunteer in Classroom, Emergency Card Turned In, and Medication Required—have check marks if they are selected and are blank if not.

Changing the Column Size

All the fields are displayed but not all the information can be seen in many of the fields. You may change the size of the columns and rows displayed to allow for more ease in reading the values. To widen the column containing the student name, follow the steps below.

1. Move the mouse to the line separating the field name Student and the field name Guardian at the top of the columns.

2. The mouse icon should change from an arrow into a crossbar with arrows on the left and right. The crossbar is positioned on the line between the field names.

3. While the crossbar has left and right arrows, drag it to the right to widen the column. Widen the column until John M. Anderson's entire name is displayed. Then release the mouse button. If you drag the crossbar to the left, you make the column more narrow.

Changing the Row Size

In a similar manner rows may also be resized so that more information may be displayed. The steps that follow explain how to increase the size of the row containing Christopher Campbell's information.

1. Make sure the horizontal scroll box is at the left of the horizontal scroll bar. Place the cursor on the bottom of the row header by Christopher Campbell's information, as shown in Figure 4-6. (Note: Only Christopher is displayed in the Student field.)

2. The cursor should change to crossbar with arrows on the top and bottom. The crossbar is positioned on the bottom line of the row header.

3. While the crossbar has up and down arrows, drag it down to enlarge the row so that Christopher's last name, Campbell, appears on the screen. Release the mouse button.

FIGURE 4-6

In the List mode rows may be resized by placing the mouse on the row header. The cursor changes to a crossbar with arrows on the top and bottom as shown. While the cursor is a crossbar with arrows, you may drag down to make the row larger or drag up to make the row smaller.

Row Header   Crossbar Cursor

Student	Guardian
John M. Anderson	John &
Julie Baker	Richard & Jill
Christopher	William &
Jim Crowfoot	Yellow Horse
Emilio A. Garza	Carlos &
Ginger M. Jackson	Mark &
Beau Johnson	William &
Samuel A. Johnson	Eric and
Mathew R. Lawson	James &
Sandra Longfellow	Joshua &

Records: 15

Sorted

Experiment widening and narrowing various columns and rows in the List layout until you feel comfortable making these changes.

Rearranging the Column Order

You may also reorder the columns while you are in the List layout. This will allow you to arrange the data so that the columns you wish to compare are located adjacent to each other. The directions that follow will walk you through the steps needed to move the Birthdate field adjacent to the Student field.

1. Use the horizontal scroll bar at the bottom of the screen to bring the Birthdate field into view.

2. Place the mouse on the field name Birthdate at the top of the column. The mouse icon should change from an arrow to a hollow double arrow icon as shown in Figure 4-7.

FIGURE 4-7

Placing the mouse on the field name Birthdate causes the cursor to change to a hollow double arrow as shown. While the cursor is a hollow double arrow, the Birthdate column may be moved to another location by dragging it to the left or the right.

Ethnic Backg	Phone	Birthdate	
White ▼	473-9986	11/13/84	
White ▼	473-6598	1/13/85	
White ▼	478-6627	10/5/84	

3. While the pointer is a hollow double arrow, hold down the mouse button and drag the column to the left until it is on top of the Guardian field.

4. Release the mouse button. The Birthdate field replaces the Guardian field, which moves to the right. The fields should be in the order Student, Birthdate, Guardian....

Data may be viewed, added, changed, and deleted in the List layout as in the Browse layout. Rows and columns can be resized and reordered so that the values contained in the records can be displayed in any manner you wish.

Moving through the database can be accomplished by using the File icon located in the status panel. The File icon can be used in both the Browse and List layouts. In the List layout you may select a column by clicking the mouse on the field name at the top of the column. You may select a row (record) by clicking on the row header found at the left of the row, as shown in Figure 4-8. Multiple rows can be selected by first selecting one row and then holding down the Shift key while clicking the mouse on other rows to select them. The same procedure works with columns. The font, size, style, and color of the values in the fields can be changed after they are selected by changing the settings in the Font, Size, Style, or Color submenus under the Format menu.

FIGURE 4-8

Clicking on the row header selects the entire row. To select multiple rows, select one row, then hold down the Shift key while clicking on the row header of the additional rows.

Student	Guardian	Address	City	State	Zip	Ethnic Back
John M. Anderson	John &	1147	Toledo	OH	43614	White ▼
Julie Baker	Richard & Jill	8473	Toledo	OH	43606	White ▼
Christopher Campbell	William & Susan	9976 Winterhaven	Toledo	OH	43623	White ▼
Jim Crowfoot	Yellow Horse	5576	Toledo	OH	43612	Ameri... ▼
Emilio A. Garza	Carlos &	1259 Elm	Toledo	OH	43613	Hispanic ▼
Ginger M. Jackson	Mark &	2254 Walnut	Toledo	OH	43615	White ▼
Beau Johnson	William &	4599	Toledo	OH	43612	Black ▼
Samuel A. Johnson	Eric and	1234	Toledo	OH	43612	White ▼
Mathew R. Lawson	James &	3354	Toledo	OH	43623	Black ▼

USING OTHER LAYOUTS

Additional layouts are available in the Class Data database. These are available while in the Browse mode. The **layouts** are listed at the bottom of the **Layout menu**. Although the system default names for layouts are Layout 1, Layout 2, and so on, it is generally helpful to give the layouts meaningful names as has been done in this database. You may have many fields in a database but only need to view certain fields at certain times. Layouts may be created that display only the data needed at any given time. Also the order of the data may be changed from the original layout. Sometimes eliminating extraneous information from view can allow you to more easily see relationships between certain fields and records. The following will step you through examination of several different layouts that have been created for the Class Data database.

1. Choose Browse from the Layout menu. You should see displayed on the screen the Class Data database in the original layout that you saw when you opened the database. That layout is named Full Record.

2. From the Layout menu choose Names & Addresses from the layouts listed at the bottom of the menu, as shown in Figure 4-9. In this layout you see displayed the fields Student, Guardian, Address, City, State, and Zip. Notice that the name given to this layout clearly conveys the type of information found in the layout. Most of the values would not fit on one line so the layout has been modified so that two lines can be used to display values in several of the fields.

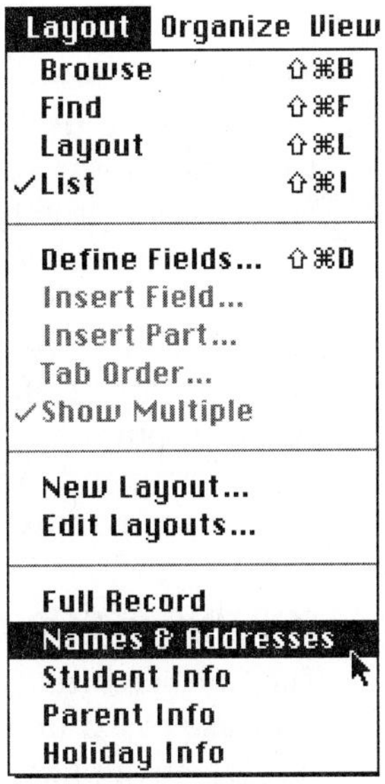

FIGURE 4-9

Layouts that have been created for a database are listed at the bottom of the Layout menu. A layout may be chosen by selecting it from the menu, as Names & Addresses has been done here.

Layout	Organize View
Browse	⇧⌘B
Find	⇧⌘F
Layout	⇧⌘L
✓**List**	⇧⌘I
Define Fields...	⇧⌘D
Insert Field...	
Insert Part...	
Tab Order...	
✓**Show Multiple**	
New Layout...	
Edit Layouts...	
Full Record	
Names & Addresses	
Student Info	
Parent Info	
Holiday Info	

3. From the Layout menu choose Student Info from the layouts listed at the bottom of the Layout menu. The fields Student, Birthdate, Phone, and Sex are the only fields that are listed on this layout. Again notice that extra space has been allotted to accommodate the values in the field Sex.

CLASSROOM ←——————→ CONNECTION

Using the large set of cards developed earlier, have students work in small groups with each group having a set of cards. Have each group use their cards to "sort" or "search" for information in the database. Have them find the following: (1) The largest national park, (2) The smallest national park, (3) The oldest national park, (4) The state with the most national parks. After the students complete this activity, use a computer with large display capability to demonstrate finding the same information with the entire database using the computer.

4. From the Layout menu choose the layout Parent Info. Notice that this layout is similar to the Student Info layout but has the fields listed in a different order and also includes the phone number field to provide data needed for calling parents.

5. From the Layout menu choose Holiday Info. This layout contains all the information needed to call parents about bringing treats for the holiday they have chosen. It includes the student's name, parents' names, phone number, and the holiday chosen.

The layouts that you have examined were all created as what is called columnar type, where the fields are displayed in columns with multiple records displayed. Other options are available when creating new layouts. Later in the chapter you will explore some of those options when you create new layouts.

Retrieving Information

Databases are used to store large amounts of information. That information is worthless unless you can organize and retrieve it in ways that make it usable. Sorting and searching records are two primary techniques used to extract information from a database. ClarisWorks' Sort Records... arranges records in order, and the Find mode and Match Records... command help you search for particular records. You will learn to use these commands as you answer questions about our fictional classroom. Sometimes one of the commands will suit your purpose; sometimes a combination works best. Generally, determining which command to use will be a problem-solving situation in which there may be more than one way to manipulate the database to find the information you seek.

SORTING RECORDS

The **Sort Records...** command can be used to arrange or sort the records in the database based on the values in certain fields. You may choose to arrange the records in alphabetical order based on the student's name or possibly in numerical order by zip code. Multiple sorts can be created in which you sort the records numerically by zip code and then alphabetically within each zip code. Another possibility is sorting chronologically by date for a birthday list. In the example below, you will sort the list chronologically by birthdate using the Student Info layout.

1. From the Layout menu choose the layout Student Info. You should see displayed on the screen the fields Student, Birthdate, Phone, and Sex.

2. From the **Organize menu** choose Sort Records.... The Sort Records dialog box shown in Figure 4-10 should appear. You see the database is already sorted by Student, because Student appears in the Sort Order box.

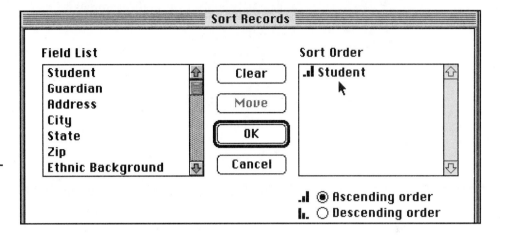

FIGURE 4-10

The Sort Records dialog box is set up to sort the database in ascending order using the Student field.

3. Click on Clear to remove Student from the Sort Order box.

4. Use the vertical scroll bar to scroll through the fields until Birthdate is in view. Click on Birthdate, because you want to sort by each student's birthdate.

5. Click on Move to move Birthdate into the Sort Order box.

6. The current selection, ascending, should sort in chronological order, so you will not have to change it.

7. Click OK.

8. The display should show the list of students sorted with the first birthdate first. Notice that the first few names are: Christopher Campbell, Elizabeth Yeager, and Samuel A. Johnson.

Practice now by choosing the Holiday Info layout and sorting by the field Holiday for Treat. Birthdate was sorted last, so you must clear that before selecting Holiday for Treat. Notice that the holidays are sorted alphabetically, rather than chronologically as they occur through the school year. Christmas is first with five students' parents agreeing to bring treats. The students are Carlos Vargas, Carrie Sample, Samuel Johnson, Christopher Campbell, and Elizabeth Yeager. There are many ways that sorting can be helpful when using a database. This same database could be sorted in zip code order, by sex, or even by ethnic background. Sorting can give you additional information about the database that could be time consuming to determine by hand.

SEARCHING FOR SPECIFIC INFORMATION

You just sorted the database to put the data in a specific order. Sometimes you may want to look at only records that have a common characteristic. You might want to create a list of the students who have not turned in emergency cards so that you can contact them or their parents individually. You might want a list of the students who walk to school so you could recommend students to patrol cross walks at school. You might want to prepare a list of the students whose parents indicated they would volunteer in the classroom so that you could send each of them a letter indicating the assistance you need. All of these needs and many more can be met using a database. ClarisWorks has two primary search tools: Find and Match Records.... The sections that follow will examine these tools and step you through examples to help you see how they can be used.

Finding Records

The **Find** option can be used to search for information in a database. When you are in the **Find mode,** you see a layout displayed with all the field boxes blank. You type in the data you wish to find in the field boxes to create a find request. Begin by finding all the students who have not turned in an emergency card.

1. From the Layout menu choose the layout Full Record. Because you will be working with the Emergency Card Turned In field, you need to be working with a layout that contains that field.

2. From the Layout menu, choose Find. You should see a screen like the one in Figure 4-11. On this screen the criterion for searching the records is entered.

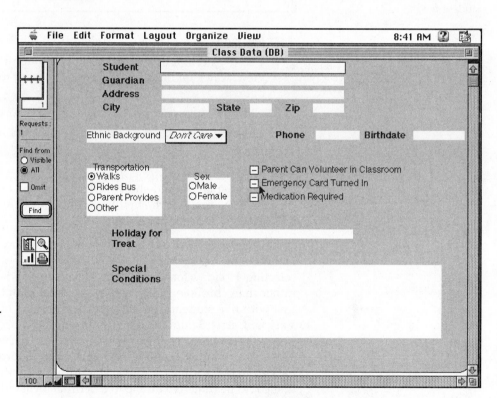

FIGURE 4-11

The Find Request screen before the find criterion has been set. The find criterion is set by typing values in the blanks beside the fields.

3. You will notice a hyphen in the check boxes in front of all the check box fields. This means that they are currently excluded from the find request. To change that, click once in the box in front of the field Emergency Card Turned In. The check box should be blank. Because the field is blank it means that the field has not been checked—in other words, the emergency card has not been turned in.

4. In the status panel on the left side of the screen, you should see the words Find from, with options below. Use All, the selected option, to search through all records on the database.

5. Click on the Find button in the status panel.

6. The display on the left side of the screen changes. Under the File icon, Records: is now displayed with the values 3(15) below. This means that 3 records of the 15 total records have the criteria you are looking for. In this case there are 3 students who have not turned in emergency cards. You may use the File icon to move to see the other two selected records.

Using Multiple Find Requests   In the first example you created a Find request based on only one criterion. You may also find records based on more than one selection criterion. You may find all the students who walk to school that live in zip codes 43612, 43613, or 43614. This will be a two-step process. You will first find all the students who walk that live in zip codes less than or equal to 43614. From the **visible records**, the ones chosen in the first step, you will find all records with zip codes greater than or equal to 43612. These two steps yield all students who walk who live in zip codes 43612 through 43614. When you select records from one Find request, then create another and select from "visible" records, you are selecting records that satisfy both request conditions, which is equivalent to the logical AND statement.

1. From the Layout menu choose Find.

2. Click in the radio button in front of Walks until a dot appears in it. This will select all students who walk to school.

3. Click in the box beside the field Zip, then type ≤**43614**. (Use the Option key with the Less than key to type ≤. You could also type this as <= if you forget about using the Option key.) This will select all records that have zip codes less than or equal to 43614.

4. In the status panel, make sure that All is the selected Find from option. Note that this Find request will find all records that have both characteristics. So it will find all student who walk to school and live in a zip code less than or equal to 43614.

5. Click on the Find button. Notice that 4 of the 15 records are selected.

6. Use the File icon in the status panel to look at the four records. Notice that they are in zip codes 43606, 43612, 43613, and 43614. All zip codes in the selected records are less than or equal to 43614 and all have walk as the selected mode of transportation.

7. To find only the zip codes in the range 43612 to 43614, you need an additional find request.

8. Choose Find from the Layout menu.

9. In the box beside Zip type: ≥**43612**. (Use the Option key with the Greater than key to type ≥.)

10. At the left of the screen select Visible as the Find from option. This will select only from the four visible records rather than from the entire file.

11. Click on the Find button. You should now have only 3 records of the 15 selected. These are the individuals who walk to school and live in the specified zip code areas.

Using New Request   Notice changing the Find from selection from All to Visible allows you to use multiple find requests to extract the data that you want. Sometimes you may wish to select all the records that contain one or the other set of values. This can also be accomplished using a Find request. In the example that follows you will find all the records in which the zip code is either 43612 or 43613. This can be accomplished by creating one Find request and then choosing New Request from the Edit menu to create the second request. When you have multiple requests, records are selected that satisfy either of the options, which is equivalent to the logical OR statement.

1. From the Layout menu choose the layout Names & Addresses. Using this layout will enable you to more easily view the records selected.

2. Select Find from the Layout menu.

3. In the box next to the field name Zip, type **43612**. (Note: By not typing another operator such as < or >, the program assumes equality or "=".)

4. From the Edit menu choose **New Request**. A new set of field boxes appears in which to type the new find request.

5. In the box next to the field Zip, type **43613**.

6. With All as the Find from selection, click on the Find button. There should be 5 records from the 15 selected. There are 3 from zip code 43612 and 2 from zip code 43613.

These examples should acquaint you with how the Find command works. Notice that you have dealt with selections that include only one field, a range of values, and also one value or another. You can also select all records that do not contain a specific value. This can be done by typing <> (Less than and Greater than, which also means "not equal to") before the value in the field box. Typing <> 43612 in a Find request would give you all records except those with zip code 43612. Practice creating find requests by trying the samples that follow or by creating your own. Keep in mind that you need to choose a layout that contains the field or fields that you wish to use in making your find request.

1. Find all the male students in the class.

2. Find all the female students whose parents can volunteer in the classroom.

3. Find all the students whose birthdays are in November 1984. (Hint: Find all birthdates ≤11/30/84 from All records and then find all birthdates ≥11/1/84 from Visible records.)

Matching Records

Another way in which records with certain characteristics can be extracted is by using the **Match Records...** command in the Organize menu. Generally the Match Records feature is used for searches that are more complex.

The Match Records feature works a little differently than the Find feature. You remember that when you used a Find request you saw the records that were found and the rest were hidden. When you use the Match Records feature, the records are selected (highlighted), but all the other records are visible on the screen also. If you wish to work with only the matching records, you may hide the others by choosing **Hide Unselected** from the Organize menu. Similarly if you only wish to view the records that do not match the selection criterion, you may hide the selected records and view the others by choosing **Hide Selected** from the Organize menu. Sometimes this is a bit tedious at first, but this setup gives you additional ease in creating complex selection criterion.

You will begin working with the Match Records feature by searching for all records with a specific value similar to some of the Find requests you did earlier. In this case you will find all the students who live in zip code 43612.

1. From the Layout menu choose Names & Addresses if that Layout is not already chosen.

2. From the Organize menu choose Match Records....

3. You should see the Enter Match Records Condition dialog box as shown in Figure 4-12. Notice the top portion of the dialog box contains Fields, Operators, and Function areas. The Fields area contains the fields in the database. Comparison symbols are found in the Operators area, and some built-in functions are found in the Function area. A Formula box is used to specify the matching conditions. In creating the **formula** you may choose items from the top boxes or simply type in the conditions that you want.

4. From the list of fields, click on Zip. Zip should then be displayed within single quotes in the Formula box.

5. From the Operators, click on =.

6. Now type **43612,** and your formula should look like the one displayed in Figure 4-12.

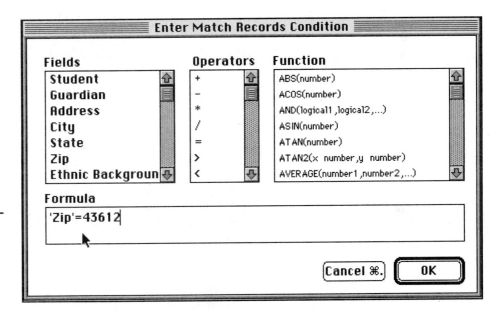

FIGURE 4-12

Using Match Records to find all of the students who live in zip code 43612. Note that the field name Zip is enclosed in single quotes (apostrophes) in the formula.

7. Click OK. You will see all the records displayed with the ones with zip codes 43612 selected (highlighted). You can use the File icon or vertical scroll bar to view the records. The status panel indicates that 3 records have been selected of the 15 displayed records.

8. To view only the selected records choose Hide Unselected from the Organize menu. You should see only the 3 selected records on the screen. The status panel now indicates that 3 of 15 records are displayed and 3 are selected.

9. To again see all the records choose **Show All Records** from the Organize menu. Again you see all the records with the three selected records highlighted.

10. To display all records except the selected records choose Hide Selected from the Organize menu. You will now see the other 12 records with none of the records highlighted. Notice the status panel indicates that 12 of the 15 records are displayed.

Using Functions in Formulas   In this first example you created a simple formula to select records. More complicated formulas can also be created using the various **functions** available. In the previous practice section you found all the students whose birthdays ranged from November 1, 1984 to November 31, 1984. In this example the database was being used to create a November birthday list. However, some students in the class could have November birthdays but were not born in 1984. The Match Records feature using a date function allows for easily choosing a November birthday date range. In this example you will be using the MONTH function. The MONTH function takes the serial value of a date field and returns the number of its month, for example, January = 1 and February = 2. For this to work, the field must be of type date. Follow the steps below to create a selection rule for November birthdays.

1. From the Organize menu choose Show All Records.

2. From the Layout menu choose Student Info. This layout will display student information including birthdays in a columnar format that will be easier to view. (Note: The Full Record layout could also be used but would require you to move from screen to screen to view each record.)

3. Choose Match Records... from the Organize Menu.

4. Notice that the last formula you used is displayed and highlighted. When you begin typing your new formula, it will replace the previous one. If the formula is not selected, you need to select (highlight) it before you begin typing your new formula.

5. While the old formula is selected, use the vertical scroll bar in the Function list to locate the function MONTH. Click once on MONTH(serial number) from the list of functions.

6. The function MONTH should be visible in the formula box with the serial number portion highlighted. Click on Birthdate in the Field list to replace "serial number," the selected value, with 'Birthdate'.

   In ClarisWorks when a field is defined to be of type date, the values stored in that field are stored as serial numbers reflecting the number of days since January 1, 1904 (an arbitrary date that was chosen by the developers of ClarisWorks). Using a date field value as the value for the serial number, the MONTH function returns the number of the month for that date.

7. The cursor should be within the parenthesis to the right of 'Birthdate'. To move it outside the parenthesis, click the mouse anywhere to the right of the parenthesis within the Formula box.

8. Click on the operator "=" from the Operators list.

9. Type the number **11** to choose November, the eleventh month. Your formula should look like the formula displayed in Figure 4-13. If it does not, edit and correct it until it does.

10. When your function is correct, click on OK to select the appropriate records.

11. From the Organize menu choose Hide Unselected to view only the selected records, the students whose birthdays are in November. There are three students, Elizabeth Yeager, Samuel A. Johnson, and John M. Anderson.

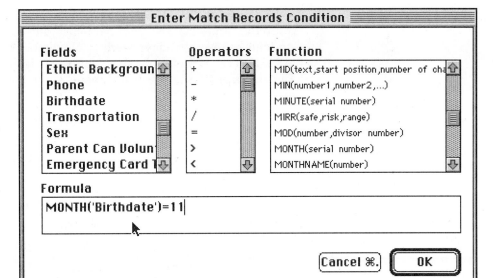

FIGURE 4-13

The Match Records formula includes a special date field function, MONTH. The MONTH function provides a means of determining the month of a particular date when the field is a date field. The result is the number of the actual month. This formula determines if the date is in November, the eleventh month.

ClarisWorks has functions available that allow you to use AND and OR logic with various conditions. These functions give you the capability of creating even more complex selection rules. You used simple AND logic in the Find request when you entered values in two different fields and when you created a second request from "visible" records. Finding all the students who were female and whose parent can volunteer is an example of using AND logic. You would be finding all records in which the students were female AND the parents could volunteer in the classroom. In this case you have two criteria that you wish to have met for the student to be included in the list. First the student should be female and second the student's parent must be able to volunteer. Both criteria must be met for the student to be included in the list. When AND logic is used, all criteria set must be met for a record to be selected.

OR logic is different. When OR logic is used, a record is selected if any of the criteria are met. Only one of the criteria needs to be met for the record to be selected. The Find request for all students with zip codes 43612 or 43613 in which you created a New Request is an example of OR logic. Another example would be looking for students whose birthdays are in June or July or August. In this case if a student had a birthday in any of these months, the student would be included in the selection.

The format for the function is a little different than one might expect and bears a little explanation. The functions AND and OR have the formats that follows:

AND(logical1, logical2,...)

OR(logical1, logical2,...)

In these functions, logical1, logical2, and any other logical statements represent the various conditions that you wish to check. Each of these conditions is separated by a comma. Taking the example of finding the students whose birthdays are in June, July, or August and writing a description of what goes in the function for each logical statement follows.

OR(BIRTHDATE is June, BIRTHDATE is July, BIRTHDATE is August)

Of course, BIRTHDATE is June must be translated into a formula that the computer understands. But you just did a similar example to find the students whose birthdays were in November using the MONTH function. BIRTHDATE is June translates into the formula MONTH('Birthdate')=6. The descriptive sample from above should be written with formulas as follows:

OR(MONTH('Birthdate')=6,MONTH('Birthdate')=7,MONTH('Birthdate')=8)

Notice that this is a rather complicated formula. It is composed of a number of parentheses. It is very important that the parentheses are entered correctly. If you get errors when trying to enter a function like this, look first at the parentheses and check closely to make sure that each item is in the correct order. To set up the selection rule to find all students whose birthdays are in either June, July, or August, follow the steps below.

1. From the Organize menu choose Show All Records.
2. From the Layout menu choose Student Info if it is not already selected.
3. Choose Match Records... from the Organize Menu.
4. While the old formula is highlighted, click once on OR(logical1,logical2,...) from the Function selections.
5. The function should appear in the formula box with logical1 highlighted. Click once on MONTH(serial number) from the Function selections to use it in creating the first logical condition.
6. The function MONTH should be visible in the formula box with the serial number portion highlighted. Click on Birthdate in the Fields box to replace serial number with 'Birthdate'.
7. The cursor should be within the parenthesis to the right of 'Birthdate'. To move it outside the parenthesis, press the right-arrow key once.
8. Click on the operator "=" from the Operators list.
9. Type the number **6** to choose June, the sixth month.
10. Double click on logical2 to select it.
11. Click once on MONTH(serial number) from the Function list.
12. Again click on Birthdate to select it for the serial number.
13. Press the right-arrow key once to move the cursor outside the parenthesis and select "=" from the Operators list and type **7** to choose the seventh month.
14. Drag the mouse to highlight ... to add a third condition to the formula.
15. Click once on MONTH(serial number) from the Function list.
16. Click on Birthdate to select it for the serial number.
17. Press the right-arrow key once to move the cursor outside the parenthesis, select "=" from the Operators list, and type **8** to choose the eighth month. There should be a **)** following the 8. If it is not there, type it now.
18. Your function should be complete and look like Figure 4-14. Click on OK to select the appropriate records. If you see an error message displayed on the screen, double check your formula to make certain that it looks exactly like the one displayed in the figure. Edit your errors until it does, then click OK to continue.

19. From the Organize menu choose Hide Unselected to view only the selected records, the students whose birthdays are in June, July, or August. They are Jim Crowfoot, Sandra Longfellow, and Carrie Sample.

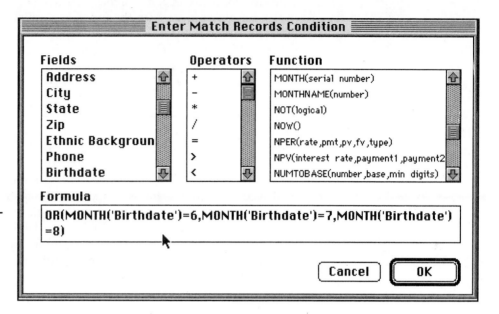

FIGURE 4-14

The Match Records formula determines if the value in the field Birthdate is in the months June, July, or August. The OR function allows the use of OR logic in setting up the formula.

Note that if you only have two logical formulas to enter, you would simply delete the "..." at the end of the function. If you had a fourth logical formula to enter you would separate it from the third with a comma.

Using Functions for Special Field Types When using the Match Records feature to create a selection rule with pop-up menu or radio button fields, the use of a function is required. The values used in each of these types of fields are actually stored in tables that are numbered. To make comparisons, you must actually compare values within those numbered tables.

To be more specific, using a selection rule within the Match Records feature to find all the students who walk to school requires the following formula:

NUMTOTEXT('Transportation')="Walks"

A similar formula for finding all the students who are female would be:

NUMTOTEXT('Sex')="Female"

The NUMTOTEXT function translates a number to its textual representation within the table. This allows you to work with the values in pop-up menus or radio boxes.

Checking for a selected or deselected check box is done by determining if the value for the field is true or false. If it is selected, it is true; if it is not selected, it is false. A formula for finding students with parents who can volunteer in class would be:

'Parent Can Volunteer in Classroom'=true

Using the Find and Match Records features enables you to search for records that meet simple or complex rules. It may take a little time to become accustomed to the logic required to create these rules but with a little practice you will be able to create searches to identify records that contain almost any combination of characteristics. If you feel a little confused by using functions, don't worry, many of the searches you will use only require the Find request.

For more assistance with the functions available within ClarisWorks, choose Index from the Help menu. Find the topic Functions and within it, Alphabetical listing of functions. From there you may choose individual functions and examine what they do.

Creating New Layouts

When a database is created using ClarisWorks, it is automatically put in standard layout in which all the fields for each record are displayed. When you are looking for a birthday list, you would probably want the students' names and birthdates immediately visible—and you might not want other information displayed that could be unnecessary and even distracting.

The information in a database may be used for a variety of purposes. As the purpose changes, the fields required often change also. To meet these varying uses, ClarisWorks allows you to create a variety of layouts to view the same database in different ways. The same information is used, it is just displayed in different formats in the window. A large database of information might have many layouts to display the data in a format best suited to a particular use of the database. When you work in **Layout mode**, you have the ability to add or delete fields from view, change the format of the data in fields, add or delete layout parts, and add pictures or graphics enhancements to the layout. The colored background on the Class Data Full Record layout is an example of a graphics enhancement that was added in the Layout mode. There are also several layout parts available that will be discussed later in this chapter.

COLUMNAR LAYOUT

In this section you will create a new layout to be used for a birthday list. In this layout you will need only the students' names and their birthdays so you will include only those fields. Follow the steps below to create the new layout.

1. From the Organize menu choose Show All Records.
2. From the Layout menu choose, **New Layout**....
3. You should see the New Layout dialog box. The default title, Layout 6, is highlighted.
4. Type **Birthdays,** the new layout name, to change the title. Naming your layouts helps you remember what each one contains.

Notice there are several options for the type of layout that you can create. In this text you will be working with only one or two of the layout types available. A brief discussion here of the types of layouts should help you when you begin to experiment with them. The layout types available are standard, duplicate, blank, columnar report, and labels. The standard layout displays all the fields in the record stacked vertically with the field name to the left of each field data box. When you wish to make a layout very similar to one you are currently using, you would choose duplicate for the type and then edit to make the necessary changes. A blank layout gives you only one layout part, a body. This is the main section of the layout and allows you to then add any fields or other objects that you wish. To

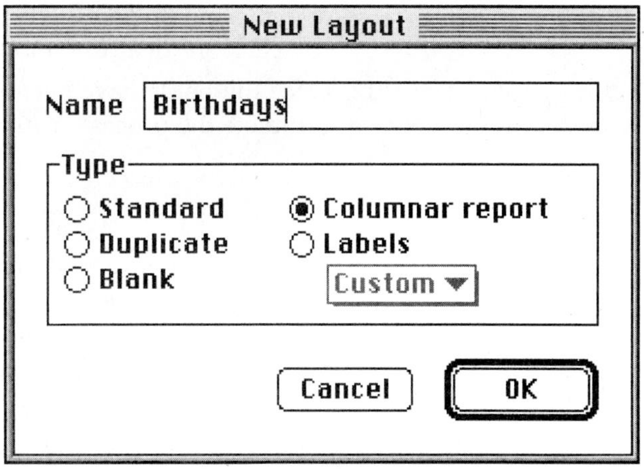

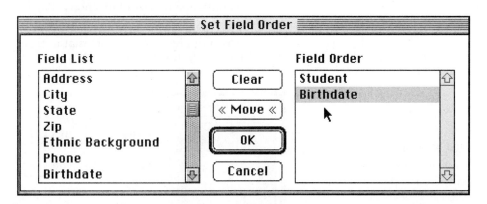

FIGURE 4-15

The New Layout dialog box with Birthdays typed for the name of the layout and Columnar report chosen as the type.

have the fields appear in columns with multiple records displayed on one screen, choose a **columnar layout**. The label type allows you to put fields from the database in a mailing label format. These can be used for more than mailing labels, however; they can be used for name tags, Rolodex cards, or other similar purposes.

5. Click on Columnar report. Figure 4-15 displays the New Layout dialog box after the title of the layout has been changed.

6. Click OK or press Return to select OK, the highlighted button.

7. You now see displayed the **Set Field Order** dialog box, as shown in Figure 4-16. This dialog box allows you to set the order in which the fields will be displayed in this layout.

8. At this point you must choose the order in which you wish the fields to appear in the columnar layout. Place the fields in the order shown in Figure 4-16 by following the steps below.

9. Select Student from the Field List by clicking once. Notice that Move is no longer gray and that small arrows point in the direction of the Field Order box.

10. Click on Move to move the category into the Field Order box. Notice that the small arrows now point to the Field List box

11. Double-click on Birthdate. This is a shortcut to move the field into the Field Order box.

FIGURE 4-16

The Set Field Order dialog box with the fields Student and Birthdate chosen.

If you accidentally select the wrong field or get the fields in the wrong order, you can move any field out of the Field Order box by selecting it and clicking on Move when the arrows point to the Field List box, or you can click on Clear to remove all the fields and begin entering again.

12. Once the fields have been selected in the indicated order, click on OK to complete the process. Your screen should look like that in Figure 4-17.

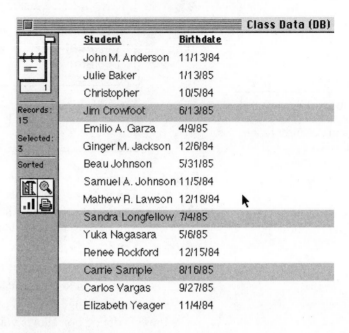

FIGURE 4-17

The Birthdays columnar layout with records selected from the last search.

PRINTING THE COLUMNAR DATA

Once you have created the columnar layout you may wish to do more than simply display it on the screen. You may wish to print it. In general printing is very similar to printing using word processing. There are some considerations in getting the data to print as you want it. First you need to consider if the number of fields you have chosen will print with the paper in the normal orientation. If it will not print, you need to change the orientation from portrait to landscape mode in the Page Setup. Also, you need to check the margins to see whether the data will fit within the margins for your printer.

1. If you wish to change the orientation of the paper from portrait (vertical) to landscape (horizontal), choose Page Setup... from the File menu.

2. From the Page Setup dialog box, click on the landscape orientation icon as shown in Figure 4-18. Note that in this case portrait or landscape orientation would be okay. Click OK.

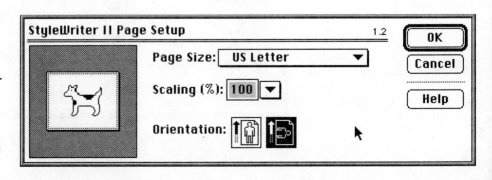

FIGURE 4-18

The Page Setup dialog box allows you to choose portrait (vertical) or landscape (horizontal) orientation for the paper. In this example landscape orientation has been chosen.

3. To check the margins, choose Document... from the Format menu. Many printers need to have margins that are at least 0.5 inch. If yours is such a printer, you will need to adjust the margins accordingly. When you finish, click on OK. Figure 4-19 shows the Document dialog box.

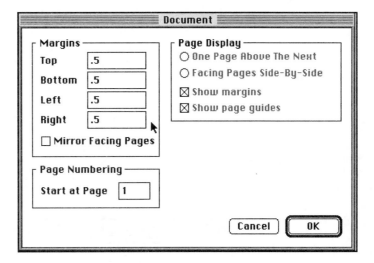

FIGURE 4-19

The Document dialog box with the margins for the document all set a 0.5 inch. Page Numbering and Page Display can also be changed using this dialog box.

4. From the Layout menu, choose Layout. You should see a screen like Figure 4-20.

FIGURE 4-20

The Birthdays layout displayed in Layout mode with Show Rulers selected. Notice the Header and Body parts with field names in the Header part and fields in the Body part.

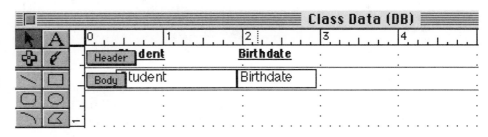

This is a graphics type format with a toolbox and a grid showing 1-inch squares. This is the mode used to change the way fields are laid out on the screen or for a report. There are two layout parts displayed in this layout, the header and the body. The header contains the field names, the text that contains the name of the field. The field names are underlined and in bold type. The body contains the actual fields, the container or box where the data is stored. The fields are shown as boxes indicating that data is stored there.

5. From the **View menu** choose Show Rulers. The vertical and horizontal rulers are then displayed on the top and left portions of the screen. This allows you to determine whether the fields that are chosen will print appropriately.

6. In this case, with half-inch margins, as you compare the layout with the ruler, it appears that the fields will not print without clipping off some of the titles and the student's name. To correct this you will need to adjust the size and placement of the fields using the Layout mode.

7. Click on the Header and drag it down so the line is on the 1-inch vertical ruler.

8. Click on the field name Student, in the Header section. Four handles should appear at the corners of the box surrounding the field name. Handles are small squares marking the corners of the box. This indicates that the field has been selected.

9. Hold down the Shift key and click on the field name Birthdate. Holding down the Shift key while clicking on a second object allows you to select multiple objects. Release the Shift key. The field names Student and Birthdate should both be selected as shown in Figure 4-21. Notice that the field names are selected when handles appear around the field names.

FIGURE 4-21

The Birthdays layout in Layout mode after the Header part has been moved to accommodate the top margin. Note that the field names Student and Birthdate are both selected so that they may be moved down within the margins of the document. When in the Layout mode the fields and field names are objects and so when selected have handles that enable them to be moved, be resized, or have their format changed.

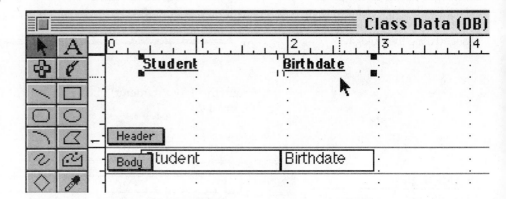

10. Drag both label names down and to the right until the left end of Student is at the 1-inch horizontal ruler mark and both field names are just above the header line, as shown in Figure 4-22.

11. Click on the field Student in the Body part of the layout. It should have handles to show it is selected. The handles on the field names that were selected before should disappear. (If the handles are still on the field names as well as the field Student, you held down the Shift key while you clicked on the field. Click anywhere away from the field names and fields to deselect them, then again click on the field Student.) If you click on the line for the Body part, the field will not be selected. Click more in the middle of the box surrounding the field and the field will be selected.

12. Hold down the Shift key and click on the field Birthdate. Both the Student and Birthdate fields should be selected.

13. When both fields are selected drag them to the right until they are directly below the field names (see Figure 4-22). Now the labels and the data in the fields should be well within the margins.

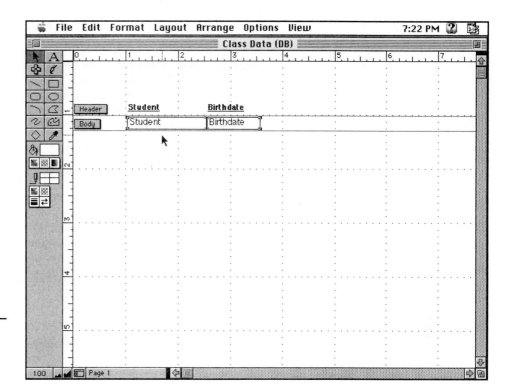

FIGURE 4-22

The Birthday layout in Layout mode after the field names and fields have been moved within the margins.

14. Choose Browse from the Layout menu to see how the changes you have made will look. If you would like to space the data in the fields farther apart, go back into Layout mode and move the Birthdate field name and field more to the right. When you are satisfied with the layout, go on to the next step.

15. Choose Print from the File menu. If you have a very large database, you may want to just print one page to see how it will look before printing the entire document. Do this by filling in the From and To areas in the Print dialog box. When you finish, click on Print.

Creating Labels

Often you may wish to create labels either to mail information home or to label folders or file cards. Using ClarisWorks you can easily create labels of any type including any fields of data that you choose.

LABEL LAYOUT

In this section you will create mailing labels that will include the parents' names and the address information. Follow the steps below to create the label layout.

1. From the Layout menu choose, New Layout….

2. You should see the New Layout dialog box. Notice that the title, Layout 7, is highlighted.

3. Type **Mailing,** the new layout name, to change the title. Naming your layouts helps you remember what each layout contains.

4. Click on Labels for the type of layout.

5. Choose Avery 5161, 5261 label from the Label pop-up menu. If you have another type of Avery label, choose it or leave the default at Custom if you do not have an Avery label. (Note: Avery is a brand of label supported by this program.) If you choose Avery 5161, 5261, your display should look like Figure 4-23. (If you choose custom, select the number of labels across and the size from the dialog box that appears.)

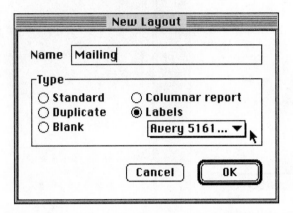

FIGURE 4-23

The New Layout dialog box for the layout Mailing. Notice that Avery 5161... labels have been chosen for the type.

6. Click OK or press Return to select OK, the highlighted button.

7. You now see displayed the Set Field Order dialog box.

8. Select these fields in order: Guardian, Address, City, State, and Zip by either double-clicking on each field in succession or by selecting the field and clicking on the Move button.

9. When the fields are in the correct order, click OK to continue. If the fields are not in the correct order, either select the field name from the Field Order box and move it back to the Field List box or click on Clear to clear the Field Order box and begin again.

10. Notice that the information is displayed with each field on a separate line as is shown in Figure 4-24. (Your screen may be slightly different.) Most mailing labels have the city, state, and zip on the same line, so you will need to adjust this.

11. From the Layout menu, choose Layout. The database will be displayed as shown in Figure 4-25.

ADJUSTING A LABEL LAYOUT

Sometimes when working on the layout of a database it is helpful to view the changes in Browse mode so the effect of each change can be viewed immediately. In ClarisWorks you can see multiple views of any document. In a ClarisWorks database, for example, you can see both the Browse mode and the Layout mode of one database at the same time. A second view of the same database can be opened on the screen as follows.

1. From the View menu, choose New View. Another window is opened for viewing the database.

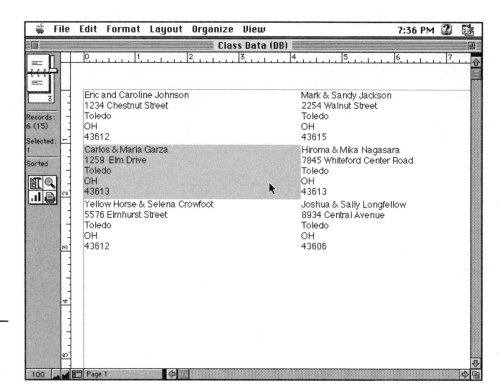

FIGURE 4-24

The Class Data database in the Mailing layout in Browse mode. Notice that the City, State, and Zip fields are on separate lines.

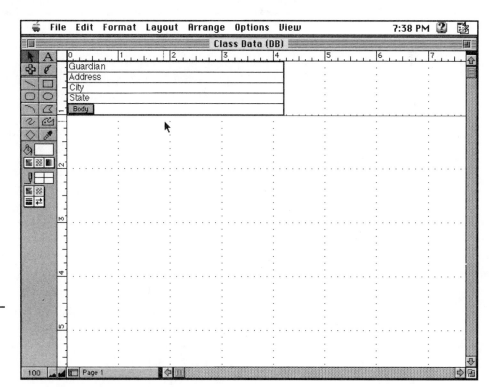

FIGURE 4-25

The Class Data Mailing layout in the Layout mode. Notice that the mailing layout only has a Body part and that each field is on a separate line.

2. To see both views at once on the screen, choose **Tile Windows** from the View menu. Tile Windows creates equally sized windows that fill the screen. Here, the windows display one above the other, as shown in Figure 4-26.

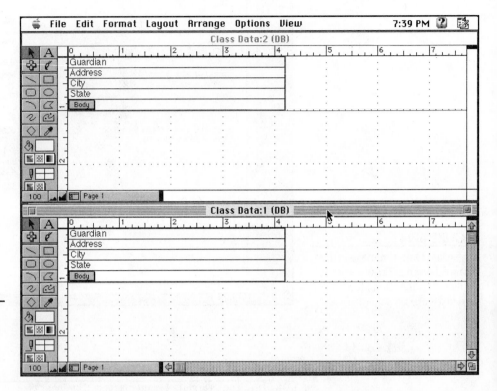

FIGURE 4-26

The database displayed in two views, both in the Layout mode. The bottom view is currently selected because there are lines in the title bar of that view.

3. Click on the Graphic tool (the arrow pointer on the tool palette), unless it is already selected. With it you can select graphic objects.

4. Click anywhere in the lower window on the screen to select that window. (The title bar will have lines on it when the view is selected.)

5. Choose Browse from the Layout menu. Your screen should look like the one in Figure 4-27. At the top of the screen, the database is a window displayed in Layout mode, and at the bottom, a window displayed in Browse mode.

6. Click on the top window to make it active.

7. Click on the field City to select it. You should see handles apear.

8. Place the pointer on the handles on the right end of the box and drag to the left to make the box smaller. If you watch the lower view, you can estimate when it is approximately the right size for the name of the city to fit properly on the label. In Figure 4-28 the field City has been resized.

9. Click on the field State. Handles should appear. Drag the handles on the right end of the box to the left to make the box smaller.

10. Place the pointer anywhere on the inside of the State field (except on the handles.) Hold down the mouse and drag the State field on the line beside the City field. Notice the effect of the change in the Browse mode.

11. Click on the Zip field. (Note: The word Zip is hidden under the word Body.) Handles should appear. Again drag the right handles to the left to make the

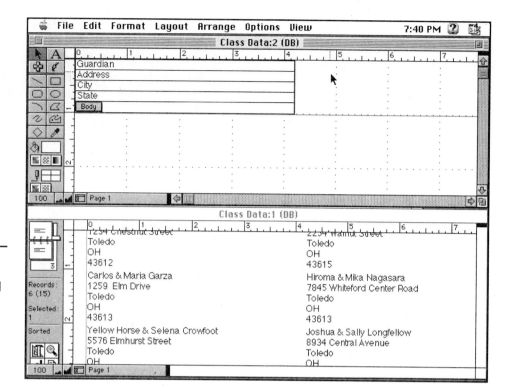

FIGURE 4-27

The database displayed in two views with the views tiled. The top view is in Layout mode, and the bottom view is in Browse mode. Note, the top view is currently selected. As changes are made in the Layout mode, the effects can be seen in the lower view in Browse mode.

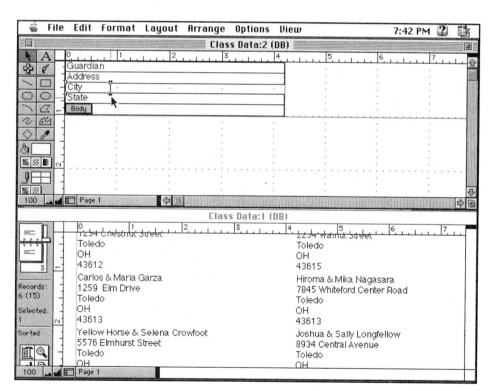

FIGURE 4-28

The City field in the top view has been resized. Examining the data shown in the bottom view determines whether the field is large enough to accommodate the data in the field.

box smaller. (If you place the mouse on the Body part line, you can't select or drag the Zip field. Move the pointer a little higher and try again.)

12. Place the pointer anywhere on the Zip field except on the handles. Hold down the mouse and drag the Zip field on the line beside the State field. Notice the effects of the change in the Browse view.

13. The City, State, and Zip fields may not line up horizontally. ClarisWorks allows you to easily align them properly. While the Zip field is still selected, hold down the Shift key and click once on the City field and once on the State field. All three fields should be selected.

14. From the Arrange menu choose Align Objects.... You will see a dialog box as shown in Figure 4-29.

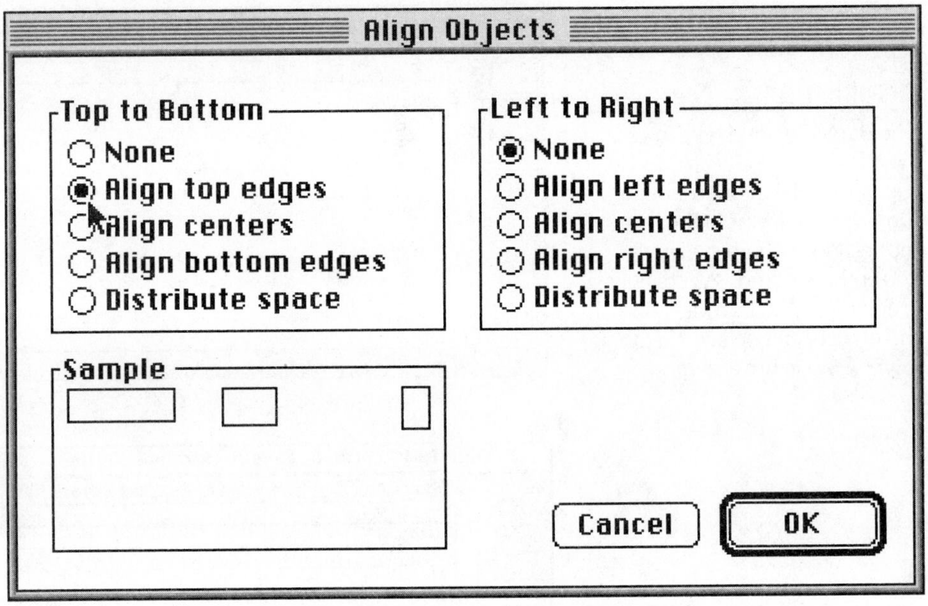

FIGURE 4-29

The Align Objects dialog box allows for easy alignment of selected objects. The results of the choices made are displayed in the sample area.

15. From the Top to Bottom area choose Align top edges. Notice how the boxes in the sample change. You have a variety of options available to align selected items Top to Bottom and Left to Right. Any changes that you make in the alignment are reflected in the Sample display shown at the bottom of the dialog box. Click on OK to continue.

16. From the View menu choose **Stack Windows** to return the screen to a larger display of only one window at a time. The windows are displayed as if one were on top of, and slightly lower than and to the right of, the other, as shown in Figure 4-30.

17. The view displayed is in the Layout mode. Either click on the window that is partially hidden or from the View menu choose Class Data:1 (DB) to see the other view, which is in Browse mode.

PRINTING LABELS

Sometimes getting labels to print correctly can be a little tricky depending on the type of label and the type of printer that you are using. The steps below should help you get your labels printed. Labels may be purchased in individual sheets or continuous forms. Individual sheets of labels can be stacked in your printer's

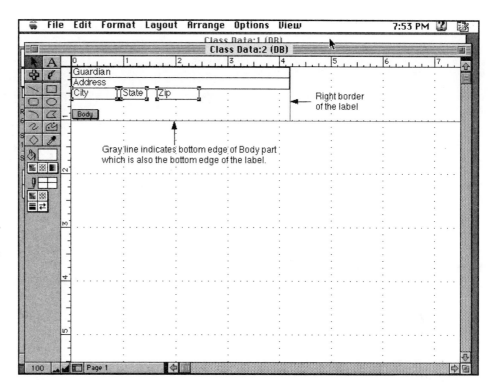

FIGURE 4-30

The two views of the database are currently stacked one on top of the other for a larger display of only one view at a time. Notice that the fields City, State, and Zip are selected and aligned by the top edges. Notice the gray lines that indicate the bottom and right borders of the label.

tray. If you are using an ImageWriter, you may have success using continuous form single width labels. You also have the option of manually feeding the labels through the printer if you wish. If you have difficulty, choose Index from the ? menu to get help. From the Index select Labels or Database Layout to get additional information.

1. With the Mailing layout still selected, choose Class Data:2(DB) from the View menu to see the label in Layout mode. Make sure that the Body part for the label equals the actual distance from the top of one label to the top of the next label. If it does not, adjust the size of the Body part. Figure 4-30 shows the gray line that indicates the lower border of the Body part of the label. The right edge of the label is also indicated by a gray line.

2. If you are using a LaserWriter or ImageWriter printer, choose Page Setup from the File menu, otherwise skip to Step 4.

3. If you are using a LaserWriter, click on the Options button and then click on Larger Print Area. If you are using an ImageWriter, click on No Gaps Between Pages. Click OK when you are finished.

4. Using your actual labels, measure the distance from the top of the page to the first label; this should be your top margin. Then measure the distance from the left of the page to the left edge of the first label; this should be your left margin. Generally these distances are 0.5 inch.

5. From the Format menu, choose Document.... Enter the values for the Top Margin and the Left Margin that you found by measuring the actual labels.

6. Choose Print from the File menu. If you wish to hand-feed the labels choose Manual Feed for LaserWriter, Hand Feed for ImageWriter, or Manual for a StyleWriter.

7. Click on Print to begin printing. If you are hand-feeding, have your label sheets ready and follow the prompts on the screen or printer as to when to load each sheet.

You have a great deal of flexibility in how you arrange the layout of the field names and actual fields on the page. You can put them almost anywhere you want. In addition, by using the tools in the tool palette at the left you can paint and draw on the page, as you did in Chapter 3. By selecting field names and fields, you can also use options on the Format menu to change fonts, font sizes, and styles of the text in the fields. This book cannot be large enough to deal with all these options (and more) for layouts, but you can experiment, use the Help options, and refer to the manual when you are ready to apply them in your layouts. Do take time, though, to be sure you are comfortable with these basics before you try the extras.

If you do not feel comfortable as yet with some of the work you have done with the database, you may wish to practice creating new layouts, sorts, and searches.

Using Reports

ClarisWorks has a feature that allows you to easily create and name a report that you may wish to use repeatedly. A report includes a named layout, a named sort, and/or a named search. You may wish to create a report that prints a list of students in alphabetical order or chooses all the students whose parents have agreed to bring treats for Christmas. Once a report has been created you may return to it simply by choosing it from the Reports pop-up menu on the status panel. You may then review the information on the screen or print it. We will begin this section by viewing some reports that have already been created for you.

1. Close Class Date:2 (DB) by clicking in the Close box on the title bar or by choosing Close from the File menu.

2. Click on the Report icon on the status panel. You should see a pop-up menu like the one shown in Figure 4-31.

3. Choose the first report Student Alpha from the list of reports in the bottom half of the menu. Notice that the database appearance changes to an alphabetical list of students with name, birthday, phone number, and sex information displayed.

4. Choose the report Street in the same manner. You should now see displayed student name, guardian, address, city, state, and zip in alphabetical order for all students who live on Central Avenue.

5. View the other reports, Christmas treats and Walkers, in a similar manner. Note the fields and records in each report.

REPORT PARTS

Each of the reports created uses a particular layout and a named search, a named sort, or both. To understand a little more about the reports, you will now edit a report to see how it is set up.

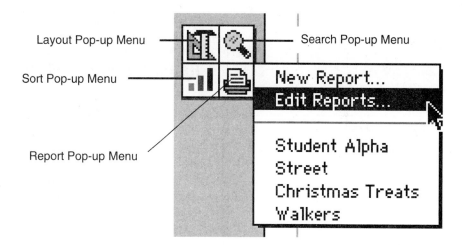

Layout Pop-up Menu

Search Pop-up Menu

Sort Pop-up Menu

Report Pop-up Menu

FIGURE 4-31

Edit Reports has been chosen from the Reports pop-up menu. Note labels on each of the pop-up menus.

1. Click on the Report icon in the status panel and choose Edit Reports... from the pop-up menu that appears.
2. An Edit Reports dialog box appears as shown in Figure 4-32.
3. Click on the report Student Alpha to select it.
4. Then click on the Modify button.

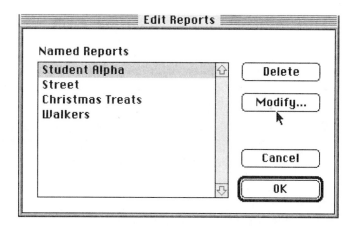

FIGURE 4-32

The Edit Reports dialog box is selected from the Reports pop-up menu. Here you can modify or delete existing reports.

5. You should now see the Modify Report dialog box as shown in Figure 4-33. You should see the report name, Student Alpha, followed by the layout, the search, and then the sort. In this case Student Info is the selected layout, Student Alpha is the selected sort, and no search is selected.
6. Click on the triangle beside Student Info to open the pop-up window displaying the other named layouts available. Look at the Search and Sort pop-up menus as well.
7. Notice the box beside Print the Report. If that box is selected (checked), the report will automatically be printed when you choose the report. This option can be very handy for weekly or monthly reports that are routine. In general when creating a new report you may wish to display it on the screen to make sure that you are getting what you want before choosing to automatically print the report.

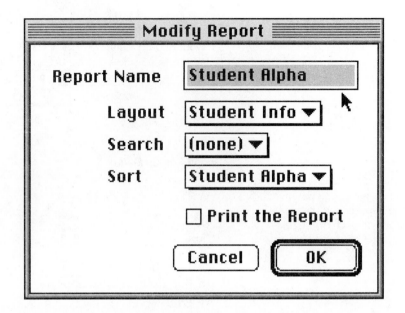

FIGURE 4-33

The Modify Report dialog box provides a means of changing the Layout, Search, or Sort that is used in a named Report. Note that checking Print the Report will cause a report to be printed automatically when the report is selected. When Print the Report is not selected, the report is displayed on the screen and can be printed by choosing Print from the File menu.

8. Click OK on the Modify Report dialog box.

9. You should then see the Edit Reports dialog box. Click OK.

CREATING A NEW REPORT

A report is needed that will print the guardian name and address of each student who has not turned in his/her emergency medical card. It would be helpful if this information could be printed in zip code order. Follow the steps below to create the report.

1. Click on the Report icon and from the pop-up menu choose New Report... to get the New Report dialog box.

2. For the report name type Emergency Card Out.

3. Click on the arrow in the Layout box to display the available layouts. Choose Parent Info.

4. Click on the arrow in the Search box to display the available searches. Choose Emergency Info Out.

5. Click on the arrow in the Sort box to display the available sorts. Choose Zip Order.

6. Click on OK.

7. Click on the Report icon and note that the report Emergency Card Out now appears on the list of available reports. Although the report has been created, the database display doesn't reflect the settings in the report until it is selected. Select the report Emergency Card Out now.

8. You should see displayed on the screen information about five students who have not turned in their emergency cards.

9. Note that at this point you may also choose another layout by selecting it from the Layout icon in the status panel. Choose Full Record from the layout choices. You should now see the full record of information displayed

on the screen for one of the five students. You may click on the upper or lower page of the File icon to display other records.

10. You may also choose other searches or sorts. From the Sort icon in the status panel choose Student Alpha. The data should now be in alphabetical order by student name.

CREATING A NEW LAYOUT

You may create new layouts as well as named searches and sorts using the icons. Creating a layout using the Layout icon is essentially the same procedure used with New Layout... on the Layout menu. A named search is created just as you did the Find request earlier in this chapter. Keep in mind that you need to choose a layout that contains the field(s) that you wish to use to create the find request before choosing New Search from the Search icon pop-up menu. Creating a named sort is a very similar procedure to using Sort Records... from the Organize menu. To practice you will create a new layout, search, and sort that will allow you to create a report that finds all the students whose parents provide their transportation. Sort the resulting records in alphabetical order by the student name. Include the following fields: Student, Guardian, Address, and Transportation.

1. To create a new layout choose New Layout... from the Layout icon pop-up menu in the status panel as shown in Figure 4-34.

FIGURE 4-34

A new layout can be created by choosing New Layout... from the Layout pop-up menu.

2. Name the layout Parent Transports and choose Columnar for the type. Click OK.

3. From the Set Field Order dialog box that appears select and move the fields Student, Guardian, Address, and Transportation into the Field Order box in that order.

4. Create the new layout by clicking on OK when you have the fields in the correct order. You should see the new layout displayed on the screen as shown in Figure 4-35.

5. Notice that the data in the Student, Guardian, and Transportation fields is not displayed completely and the field name Transportation wraps to the next line. To view more of the data and make it more visually pleasing, you must adjust the size of the fields and field names.

6. From the Layout menu choose Layout. To edit the size of the fields, you must be in the Layout mode.

7. Use the mouse to move the layout part Body down about seven grid spaces (dots). See Figure 4-36 for placement of the Body part.

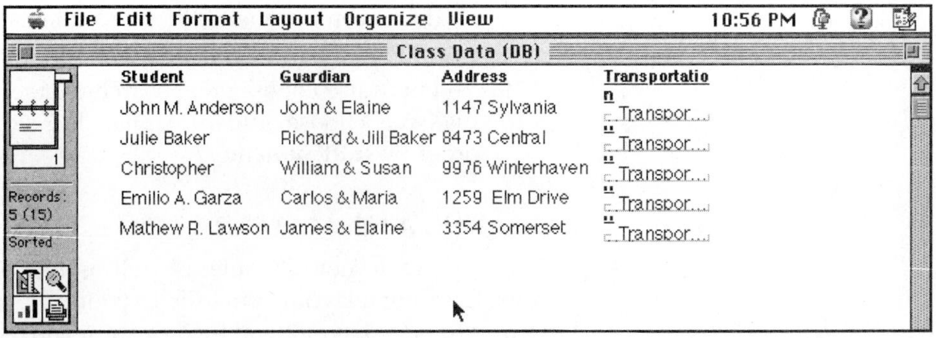

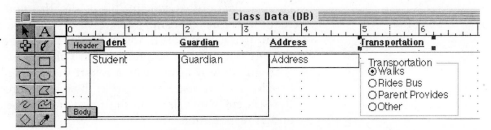

FIGURE 4-35

The Parent Transports layout shown in Browse mode.

FIGURE 4-36

The Parent Transports layout displayed in Layout mode. Notice the Body part marker has been moved down to allow enlarging the fields Student, Guardian, and Transportation.

8. Click on the field Student in the Body part to select it. Drag the bottom right handle down to just above the Body part line.

9. Click on the field Guardian to select it. Drag one of the bottom handles down to just above the Body part line.

10. Click on the field Transportation to select it. Drag one of the bottom handles down and to the right until all of the radio boxes for this field are displayed.

11. Click on the field name Transportation in the Header part to select it. Drag one of the right handles to the right enough so that the name Transportation fits on one line. See Figure 4-36 for the final look of the layout.

12. From the Layout menu, choose Browse to view the data in the fields.

CREATING A NEW NAMED SEARCH

The next step in creating the report to find all students whose parents transport them is to create a named search that will select only records that have Parent Provides as the selected option in the Transportation field. This will be done by using the Search icon on the status panel. The resulting search will be done much as a Find request was created earlier in this chapter.

1. Select New Search from the Search icon pop-up menu found on the status panel.

2. In the dialog box that appears, type **Parent Transports** to give the new search a meaningful name.

3. Notice that under the name, the directions indicate that you will press the Enter key when you finish defining the search. Click on OK to go on to define the search.

4. You will now see a screen displayed similar to the screen shown in Figure 4-37. Because the search is to find all records in which the parents transport the student, click on the radio box in front of Parent Provides to select it.

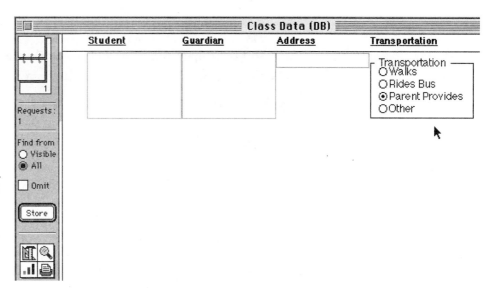

FIGURE 4-37

After selecting New Search from the Search pop-up menu, this screen appears to permit entering the search request data. Note that in this search Parent Provides Transportation is the criterion for selection.

5. Note in the status panel the search will Find from all records. Press Return.

6. At this point you will see the database displayed again on the screen. You have created a new search but you have not chosen it so records will be displayed for students other than those whose parents provide the transportation. To select only records for students whose parents provide the transportation, select Parent Transports from the Search icon pop-up menu as shown in Figure 4-38.

7. You should see two records displayed.

FIGURE 4-38

The named search Parent Transports is selected from the list of named searches. When selected the search operates on the database and the resulting records are displayed.

EDITING A NAMED SORT

Because an alphabetical sort by student name already exists, you will not need to create one. Instead you will step through the Edit Sort section to view how the sort was created and to see how you could edit a sort. The edit process works in a similar manner for editing a layout, a search, or a report.

1. From the Sort icon pop-up menu in the status panel, choose Edit Sorts.

2. From the Edit Sorts dialog box, select Student Alpha and click on the Modify button.

3. You will now see the Sort Records dialog box. You used the same dialog box earlier in the chapter when you created sorts from the Organize menu. Notice that the only field selected in the Sort Order box is Student and that the sort chosen is ascending. If you wanted to modify the sort, you would

add or remove fields from the Sort Order box or select fields in the Sort Order box and change the sort from ascending to descending. Because the sort is set up to sort alphabetically by student name, click on OK.

4. The Edit Sorts dialog box will be displayed. Click on OK to continue.

CREATING THE REPORT

Now you have the layout, search, and sort defined that you need to create the report for students who are transported by their parents. You will now create the report.

1. From the Reports icon pop-up menu in the status panel choose New Report.
2. In the New Report dialog box that appears, type **Parent Transports** for the report name.
3. Select Parent Transports for both the layout and the search.
4. Select Student Alpha for the sort. The dialog box should look like the one displayed in Figure 4-39. When it does, click on OK.

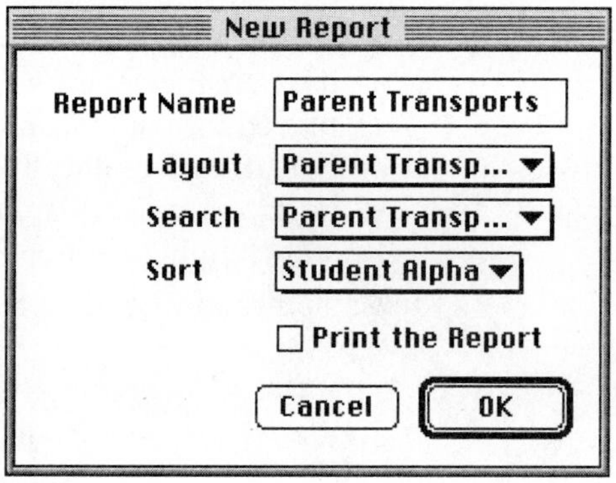

FIGURE 4-39

The New Report dialog box as chosen from the Reports pop-up menu. Notice the Layout, Search, and Sort used can be chosen from the pop-up menus.

5. You have now created the Report but have not selected it.
6. From the Organize menu choose Show All Records. If the beginning of the list is not displayed, use the vertical scroll box to move to the beginning.
7. From the Reports icon pop-up menu choose Parent Transports. You should see just two of the records displayed, those of Samuel A. Johnson and Yuka Nagasara.

Mail Merge

You have now completed the process of creating layouts, named searches, sorts, and reports. There is another tool that can be helpful in making use of a database, and that is creating a mail merged letter.

Being able to place information from a database into a word processing document to produce a personalized document is very useful. For instance, database fields with grades and personalized comments could be included within a progress report to each student. Advertisers use mail merge to send thousands of form letters to people with personal names and information included in each letter. Merging is useful for such tasks as personalizing notices to committee members, other staff, and parents and for creating specialized reports on database information.

CREATING A MAIL MERGE LETTER

In this section you will be using information from your database to fill in information in a letter. This allows you to create one form letter and fill in information for every student in the class or for selected students in the class. If you wish to create the letter for all the students, all records must be selected. If you wish to create a letter for just certain students, then you need to create selection criteria using a Find request, Match Records... , or named search so that only those students are selected. You will create a mail merge letter for each student in the class that will explain some of the activities available in the next month.

1. Note that the database must be open to use mail merge. In this case it is already open. If it were not open, you would have to open it.

2. From the File menu choose New... to see the New Document dialog box.

3. Click OK. Because Word Processing is already selected, this creates a new word processing document. A blank document appears on the screen with the insertion point in the top left corner of the document.

4. From the Edit menu, choose Insert Date. This is another way of typing the current date in a document. The advantage of this method is that each time you print the document, the current date will be printed. This eliminates the need for editing the date on future printing of the document.

5. In a letter, the date looks best if it is written in long form, such as November 29, 1994. If the date is not in that form, choose Preferences... from the Edit menu to see the Preferences dialog box, as shown in Figure 4-40. This controls many of the ClarisWorks defaults, the choices that are automatically made when ClarisWorks is used.

6. Click on the circle in front of November 29, 1994, in the Date Format region, then click OK to accept the change in preferences. The date in your letter should now be in the long format.

FIGURE 4-40

The Preferences dialog box allows for the selection of a format for dates. Notice in this case the format November 29, 1994, has been chosen.

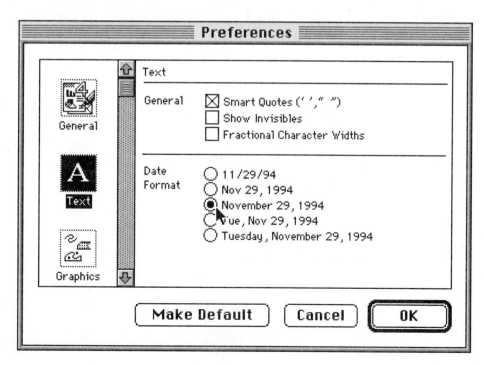

7. Press Return four times to move the cursor down the page a little.

8. From the File menu, choose **Mail Merge**.... A dialog box should appear as in Figure 4-41 listing available databases. This dialog box appears automatically the first time Mail Merge is used in a document. For subsequent merges, ClarisWorks assumes that the same database is to be used unless you choose Switch Databases on the Mail Merge window.

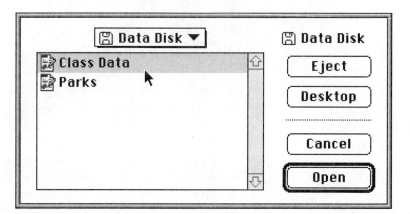

FIGURE 4-41

When selecting Mail Merge you must choose the database you wish to use. Notice that you have the option of clicking on Desktop to choose another disk or ejecting this disk in order to get the correct database.

9. Select Class Data, if it is not already selected, then click Open. The Mail Merge window should then appear as shown in Figure 4-42.

10. If necessary, drag the title bar of the Mail Merge window to move the window to the right so that the text is visible. Because this is a window rather than a dialog box, it can be moved and kept on the screen, rather than having to be reopened each time it is needed.

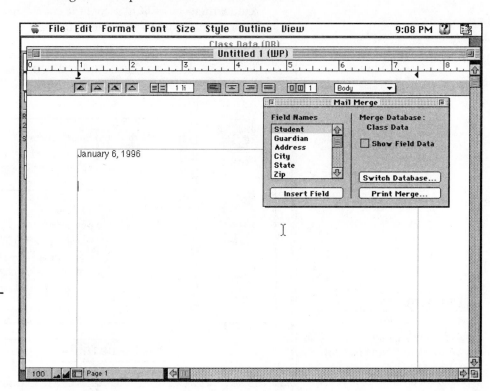

FIGURE 4-42

The Mail Merge window is displayed. Because it is a window and not a dialog box, it can be moved around on the screen and can remain open to make additional selections.

11. Click on Guardian to choose the Guardian field.

12. Click on the Insert Field button to insert the field into the word processing document. Notice that <<Guardian>> was inserted at the insertion point in the document. This means that when the document is printed, data from the Guardian field will be inserted in that location.

13. Press Return to move the cursor to the next line.

14. Double-click on the Address field to select it and insert it into the word processing document. Double-clicking is a short cut that allows you to select and insert the field in one step.

15. Press Return to move the cursor to the next line.

16. Double-click on the City field to select it and insert it into the word processing document.

17. Type a comma and press the spacebar once.

18. Double-click on the State field to select it and insert it into the document.

19. Press the spacebar twice.

20. Double-click on the Zip field to select it and insert it into the document.

21. Press Return twice.

22. Type **Dear Parent,** then press Return twice.

23. Type the following: **I am pleased to inform you that your child,**

24. Press the spacebar once, then double-click on Student in the Mail Merge window to insert that field into the sentence.

25. Type a comma and then press the spacebar.

26. Type the following pressing Return where indicated.

will have the opportunity to participate in the following activities at school.

(Press Return twice.)

First, there will be a school spelling bee for each grade level. The winner from each class will compete at the school level. There will be a district level competition for the winners from each school. District winners will have an opportunity to compete at the county level. Please help your child practice with the review words in the back of the spelling book.

(Press Return twice.)

Our class will be working on a unit on Explorers. Each child will choose an explorer and then use classroom and library resources to find some specific data on that explorer. That data will then be entered by the student into an explorers database. When the database is complete, the students will use it to search and investigate similarities and differences in the explorers.

(Press Return twice.)

Sincerely

(Press Return four times.)

(Type your name here.)

27. Use the zoom control at the bottom of the screen to change the view to 75 percent.

28. The body of your document should look like Figure 4-43.

29. Save the document and call it Class Letter.

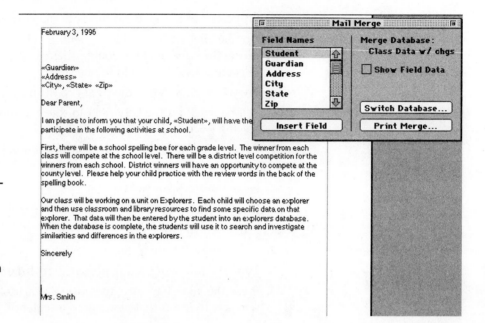

FIGURE 4-43

A mail merge letter has been created using fields from the Class Data database. Fields are inserted into the letter by using the Mail Merge window. When the letters are printed, data from selected records in the database will be automatically inserted into the letter.

PRINTING A MAIL MERGE LETTER

The merged letter has been created but still needs to be printed. Keep in mind that one letter will be printed for each selected record in the database. If all records are selected, there will be 15 letters. You could also select only certain records by creating a Find request, using Match Records..., or selecting a named search. To eliminate printing 15 letters, you will choose a named search in which only 3 records are selected. This will result in only 3 letters printing.

1. From the View menu, choose Class Data.

2. From the Search icon pop-up menu, choose Medication Required. Three of the 15 records are now selected. When printing the merged letter, only the selected records will have a letter printed.

3. From the View menu, choose Class Letter.

4. The Mail Merge window should still be displayed on the screen. If it is not, choose Mail Merge from the File menu.

5. Click on the **Print Merge**... button.

6. The printer dialog box should appear. Press Return to begin printing.

Notice that you also have an option to view the actual data within the letters by selecting Show Field Data on the Mail Merge window. The letters should be printed with records for students John M. Anderson, Mathew R. Lawson, and Ginger M. Jackson.

Saving and Closing the Database

Unless you accidently changed some field entries in the database, you have not edited data in this file. However, you did create a new layout, search, and report. If you save the database, the new layout is saved right along with it. As described in Chapter 2, "Saving Documents," you may want to save your edited database with a new document name, so that the original Class Data file is available in the future. If you wish to do this, choose Save As... from the File menu. Refer to Chapter 2 if you need to review this. The Class Data database will not be used in the next set of exercises. Follow the steps below to save the database and close the letter and the database.

1. Close the letter by choosing Close from the File menu.
2. The Class Data database should now be displayed on the screen. Save the database by choosing Save As... from the File menu.
3. Give the database the name New Class Data and make certain you are saving to your Data Disk.
4. Close the database by clicking the close box on the top left corner of the title bar.

Creating a New Database

You will now create your own database—one with a variety of information about the provinces of Canada. As you create this database, you should see similarities in the type of information used for the provinces and the type of information that students could enter into a database to study a particular unit in your curriculum. The fields used can either be chosen by the teacher or selected by the students based on the data that they wish to study. As you go through the process of creating your own database, reflect on the types of databases that you might wish to use for management as well as instructional purposes.

1. If you are continuing from the previous section and have not quit ClarisWorks, do the following. Otherwise skip to Step 2.
   a. From the File menu choose New.... You should see a New Document dialog box with options for types of documents.
   b. Skip to Step 3.
2. If you are not in ClarisWorks, launch ClarisWorks by double-clicking on the ClarisWorks program icon. You should see a New Document dialog box.
3. In the New Document dialog box, click on Database, the type of document you want to create.
4. Click OK. The **Define Fields** dialog box appears, as shown in Figure 4-44. To create a database, you need to tell ClarisWorks what fields you want to have in your database.

DEFINING FIELDS

Using the Define Database Fields dialog box, you will create each field, giving each field a name and defining the type of data that will be in the field. There are a number of different field types available. The field type determines the

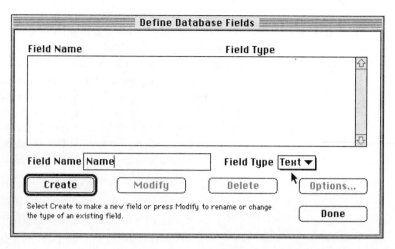

FIGURE 4-44

The Define Database Fields dialog box. The first field, Name has been entered and the Field Type Text chosen. Clicking on Create would actually create the field and move it into the upper area of the dialog box.

kind of data that can be put in a field and what you can do with the data. The field types are text, number, date, time, name, pop-up menu, radio buttons, check box, serial number, value list, record info, calculation, and summary. You looked at many of these types when you began working with the Class Data database at the beginning of this chapter. The field types that were discussed in the Class Data database were text, number, name, data, pop-up menu, radio buttons, check boxes, and value list. The time type allows a time to be entered in hours, minutes, and seconds using either 12-hour or 24-hour format. To use numbers that automatically increment as a new record is added, you will use field type Serial. When a field of type Record info is used in a database, an automatically generated date, time, or name is entered in the field. A **Calculation field** can be used to set up a formula from which values are calculated and entered into the field. A field of type Summary can be added to summarize data within the database. You will be working with summaries later in the chapter.

1. Type **Name** in the box beside Field Name in the lower part of the Define Database Fields dialog box. This is the name of the first field you are creating.

2. Note that the Field Type currently selected is Text. You do not need to change it. (If you were creating a field of another type, you would select it.)

3. Click Create, or press Return. (Because Create is the highlighted button, pressing Return will have the same effect as clicking Create.) Now Name and Text appear in the upper portion of the dialog box while still remaining as selected text in the field name box. As you type the new field, it will replace the previous one.

4. Type **Capital** to replace the highlighted previous field name (Name) in the lower part of the dialog box.

5. Because the type is Text, click on Create.

6. Type **Entered Confed** (for Entered Confederation) to replace the highlighted previous field name (Capital).

7. Select Date from the Field Type pop-up menu, and then click Create.

8. Type **Population**, choose Number for the Field Type, then click on Create.

9. Type **Area** then click Create. Note that this field is also of type Number and Number was already selected.

10. Type **Country**, choose Text for the Field Type, then click on Create.

11. The Options button should now be highlighted. Click on it to select additional options for this field.

12. In this database, the country will be Canada for all the provinces. Rather than entering the data for each record ClarisWorks allows you to choose to automatically fill in data for such a field. In the box under Default Text Automatically Fill In, type **Canada** then click OK.

13. The Define Database Fields dialog box should now look like the one shown in Figure 4-45.   If not, select the incorrect field and correct it by clicking on Modify and changing the incorrect item. When your database looks the same as the figure, then click on Done.

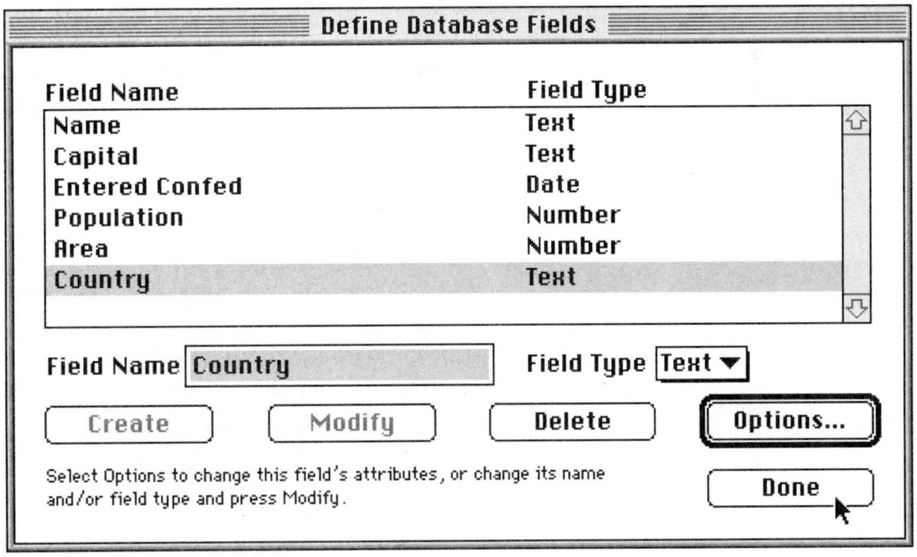

FIGURE 4-45

The Define Database Fields dialog box after the fields Name, Capital, Entered Confed, Population, Area, and Country have been created. Note that the last field created, Country, is still selected and displayed in the Field Name box. If another field were entered, it would replace the entry in the Field Name box and once created would be placed in the upper box below Country.

Define Database Fields

Field Name	Field Type
Name	Text
Capital	Text
Entered Confed	Date
Population	Number
Area	Number
Country	Text

Field Name Country   Field Type Text ▼

[Create]   [Modify]   [Delete]   [Options...]

Select Options to change this field's attributes, or change its name and/or field type and press Modify.   [Done]

Other options are also available for fields but will not be covered in this text. These allow serial numbers to be created, input to be checked from a pre-defined list, ranges to be set for numbers and verification of the data in a field. See the ClarisWorks manual or the Help screens for more information when you are ready to use these.

CLASSROOM ◄────► CONNECTION

Use a database to introduce students to each other. Create an "All About Me" database with fields for name, number of siblings, pets, favorite food, etc. Have students enter their own record of data, then use the database to find similarities.

CHANGING FIELD NAMES

The fields are arranged in the order in which they were typed. If you have made any errors typing the field names or types, you can correct them. To change the name of the field or the type:

1. From the Layout menu choose Define Fields....
2. Click on the field to be corrected.
3. If the field name is in error, retype or edit the name.
4. If the field type is incorrect, select the correct type.
5. Click on Modify when you have made your corrections. If you do not do this, the corrections will be ignored.
6. Click on Done to exit the Define Fields dialog box.

If the order of your fields is incorrect, it can only be changed by going back into Define Fields and deleting field names and reentering them. If you notice something out of order after the database has been created and data entered, it might be better to simply define a new layout with fields in the desired order. **Deleting fields can cause you to lose all the data in the fields, potentially a major problem if the database is large.**

CHANGING THE FIELD FORMAT

Before you type data into the fields that you created, you may want to look at the field format. The field **format** allows you to determine how the data in each field is displayed. The default display for data of type date is MM/DD/YY so September 1, 1905, would be displayed as 9/1/5. Because there are dates in the 1800s and 1900s, the default format would be confusing. Also it might be helpful to put commas in the data for the fields Population and Area so that it will be easier to read. To change the field format, the database must be in the Layout mode.

1. With the first record of the database displayed with no data yet entered, choose Layout from the Layout menu.

2. You should see displayed the field names, in bold type, and next to them the fields enclosed by boxes. Click on the Entered Confed field to select it. Handles should appear on the corners of the box as shown in Figure 4-46.

3. From the Options menu choose Field Format.... (If Field Format... is not shown in the Options menu, make sure that you have selected the field Entered Confed.)

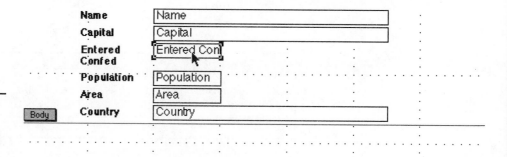

FIGURE 4-46

The newly created fields in Layout mode. Notice the field Entered Confed is selected and has been made smaller.

4. From the Date Format dialog box click on the circle in front of Nov 29, 1994, then click OK.

5. Double-click on the Population field data box. The **Number Format** dialog box should appear.

6. Click in the box in front of Commas to select it. Click OK to continue.

7. Double-click on the Area field data box. Click on the box in front of Commas, then click OK.

8. From the Layout menu choose Browse to move back into the Browse mode. Remember data can only be added or changed when in the Browse or List modes.

ADDING DATA TO THE DATABASE

There are ten provinces in Canada. Follow these steps to put data for each province into the database.

1. Outlined boxes, called **data boxes**, should appear to the right of each field name. These boxes are where you will type the data. The cursor should be in the data box beside the field Name. (If the data boxes aren't displayed next to the field names, position the pointer in the white area to the right of the field name, Name, then click. If the entire record becomes highlighted, click the mouse a little further to the right of the field name.)

2. Type the following information in the fields. Press the Tab key after each entry. If you make an error, fields can be edited (text inserted, cut, pasted, etc.) in the same way as in the word processor. If you tab to the wrong field,

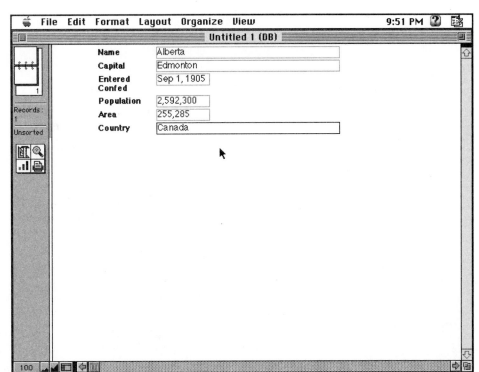

FIGURE 4-47

The first record of the Canada database with data entered for the one province. Note that the entry for the field Country, "Canada" was automatically entered by the computer.

use the mouse to click on the field you want to edit. Your screen should look like Figure 4-47 when you are finished. You will have added the first record to your database.

Name	**Alberta**
Capital	**Edmonton**
Entered Confederation	**Sep 1, 1905**
Population	**2592300**
Area	**255285**
Country	Canada (Already entered by the computer.)

3. From the Edit menu choose **New Record** to get a blank form in which to add the next record.

4. Continue adding the following records to the database, pressing the Tab key after each entry and choosing New Record from the Edit menu to start entering each new record of data. After entering the last record, you should have ten records in your database.

British Columbia	**Manitoba**	**New Brunswick**
Victoria	**Winnipeg**	**Fredericton**
Jul 20, 1871	**Jul 15, 1870**	**Jul 1, 1867**
3376700	**1100700**	**731000**
366255	**251000**	**28354**
Newfoundland	**Nova Scotia**	**Ontario**
St. John's	**Halifax**	**Toronto**
Mar 31, 1949	**Jul 1, 1867**	**Jul 1, 1873**
577300	**909800**	**10259200**
156185	**21425**	**412582**
Prince Edward Island	**Quebec**	**Saskatchewan**
Charlottetown	**Quebec City**	**Regina**
Jul 1, 1873	**Jul 1, 1867**	**Sep 1, 1905**
131700	**6985400**	**992400**
2184	**594860**	**251700**

5. Use the File icon in the status panel to move back through the records to look at the data entered. (Remember, click on the top page of the File icon or drag the bookmark up to move back to previous records in the file.) If you find errors, they can be corrected by clicking in the data box and editing the entry.

Notice that more than one record is displayed on the screen at a time. The database is being viewed with multiple records displayed on the screen. To change the view so that one record is displayed at a time, do the following.

1. Look at the Layout menu by positioning the pointer on Layout and holding the mouse button down.

2. Notice that **Show Multiple** is selected with a checkmark. This indicates that multiple records are being viewed at once.

3. From the Layout menu choose Show Multiple. This deactivates the option. You should now see each record displayed separately on the screen.

```
C L A S S R O O M  ←——————→  C O N N E C T I O N
```

Use a database for students to review books they have read. Include fields for book title, author, type of book, number of pages, rating, summary of book, comments. When students are trying to find a book they would like to read, have them use the database to find other students' opinions about certain books. Search for books by type, rating, or other fields to find the books of interest.

DEFINING A NEW CALCULATION FIELD

Sometimes after a database has been created a need arises to use it in a way that was not anticipated. When this happens, new fields may be added to the database. For this database, you will define a field that will calculate the population per square mile. Here you will be not only adding a new field, but also using a calculated field for the first time.

1. From the Layout menu choose Define Fields….
2. Type **Pop/Sq Mile** for the field name.
3. Select Calculation for the Type.
4. Click Create. The Enter Formula dialog box should appear. Figure 4-48 shows the Enter Formula dialog box with the formula entered. (If the Enter Formula dialog box did not appear, you probably forgot to select Calculation for the type. Return to Define Fields in the Layout menu and modify the selection.)

Now you must enter a formula so ClarisWorks will know how to calculate the value for the field. To calculate the population per square mile, you will divide the data in the field Population by the data in the field Area. There are regions in the dialog box for Fields, Operators, and Function. Many of the operators may be familiar to you. If you are inexperienced using a computer, you may not be familiar with the computer's symbols for multiplication (*) and division (/).

1. On the left portion of the Enter Formula dialog box is a list of the fields in the database.
2. Click on Population in the Fields listing. It should appear in the Formula box in single quotes.

FIGURE 4-48

The Enter Formula for Field dialog box with the formula for "Pop/Sq Mile" entered.

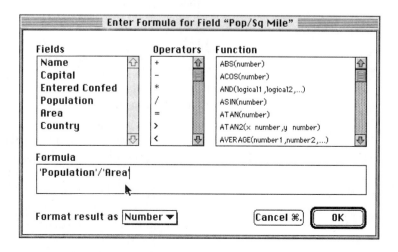

3. Click on the / in the Operators box to select it. (Note: / means division and * means multiplication. Addition and subtraction are the usual + and – .)

4. Click on Area in the Fields listing. Your screen should look like Figure 4-48. (Note: You could also have simply typed the formula. The method that is most efficient for you depends on your typing skills. If you type the formula, you must include the single quotes around the field names as shown.)

5. Click OK to return to the Define Fields dialog box.

6. Click Done to return to the database. Notice that the values are calculated and placed in the field for you.

SAVING THE DATABASE

Periodically you need to save your database to make sure you don't lose it. You should save often when creating your database or adding to it.

1. Save your document by choosing Save or Save As... from the File menu. Because this document has never been saved, both options will display the Save dialog box.

2. Name the document **Canada.**

3. Make sure that the disk icon and name Data Disk appear above the Eject button. If not, click on the Desktop button and select Data Disk from the list that appears by double-clicking on it. When you have the correct disk, click Save.

Refer to Chapter 2, "Saving Documents," if you need more assistance.

PRACTICE

1. A database can be used by teachers at the beginning of a school year to help them and their students become acquainted with each other. Students could enter data about themselves and browse through data about others. They can sort and search to find what they have in common and what is unique about each of them. For such a database, possible fields are number of sisters and brothers, hobbies, or favorite sports, toys, pets, foods, books, or television shows. You might want to have fields for what makes your students most happy or angry, where they study best, or what their goals are. Create a new class database that would serve one of these purposes.

2. If you collect stamps, baseball cards, thimbles, train sets, old records, books, or anything else, a database can help you keep an inventory. Create a database for your favorite collection. You might want to include the item, where you got it, its original cost, its current value, where it is stored, or other important details. Once you have created the database, enter data into it.

3. The Canada database could be improved to be more useful. Do some research on information available about Canada and organize the information into fields that you would like to have in the database. Edit the Canada database or create a new one to suit the ways you would want to use the database. Enter data into it and see how well your organization works.

4. Create a database inventory of lesson plans, ideas, and/or materials that you have on file. Include such fields as grade level, prerequisite skills, sub-

ject area(s), objectives, where the plans are filed (or if you created them with a word processor, what disk and document name), and summary description. You may even want to give yourself a field for a quality rating. Then when you need a math lesson on multiplication of compound fractions or a set of English, math, and social studies lessons related to your current science lesson on animal habitats, you can use the Find or Match Records commands to find related lessons.

Preparing More Complex Reports

You will invariably want printed reports from a database. To prepare a report, first determine what information you want. Often, you will need only particular fields, or a selection of records, rather than everything on the database. You may also want summarized or calculated information of some kind, such as the totals or averages for a field. When you know what you want, you must then decide how you want to see it organized on a page. Finally, you will need to create a new layout for printing.

For the following exercises the information, decisions, and organization have been done for you—you just need to create the layout. You will prepare a report similar to the one in Figure 4-49. Notice that the report is in columnar format. Also, there are totals fields that have the total of the population and area fields—you can have ClarisWorks automatically do these calculations for you.

To set up a report layout, follow the steps below.

1. The Canada database should be open on your Desktop.

2. From the Layout menu choose New Layout....

3. Choose Columnar report.

4. Type **Totals** for the layout name.

FIGURE 4-49

A database report in columnar format with totals calculated for the fields Population and Area. Note that numbers have been formatted to include commas and decimals rounded to the nearest hundredth.

Name	Population	Area	Pop/Sq Mile
Alberta	2,592,300	255,285	10.15
British Columbia	3,376,700	366,255	9.22
Manitoba	1,100,700	251,000	4.39
New Brunswick	731,000	28,354	25.78
Newfoundland	577,300	156,185	3.70
Nova Scotia	909,800	21,425	42.46
Ontario	102,595,200	412,582	248.67
Prince Edward	131,700	2,184	60.30
Quebec	6,985,400	594,860	11.74
Saskatchewan	992,400	251,700	3.94
	119,992,500	2,339,830	

File Edit Format Layout Organize View   3:07 AM

Canada:1 (DB)

Records: 10
Unsorted

5. Click OK. The Set Field Order dialog box should appear to allow you to select the fields you want in the report.

6. From the Set Field Order dialog box select the following fields by double-clicking on each one in the order listed. (If necessary, refer back to "Creating New Layouts," earlier in this chapter.)

   Name

   Population

   Area

   Pop/Sq Mile

7. The fields should appear in the Field Order box on the right side of the screen. (If you have made a mistake, select the field name in the Field Order box and click on Move to take it out of the box.)

8. Click OK when finished. This returns you to the database and creates a new layout, but it is not yet organized in the way you want to see it. You need to make more changes in the layout.

BROWSE, FIND, LAYOUT, AND LIST MODES

Figure 4-50 shows the Layout menu. There are four options at the top of the menu, Browse, Find, Layout, and List. These are all different modes, or types of screen formats. When you use a ClarisWorks database, you are always looking at a screen in one of these modes. In Figure 4-50 the current mode is Browse, as can be seen by the checkmark beside Browse.

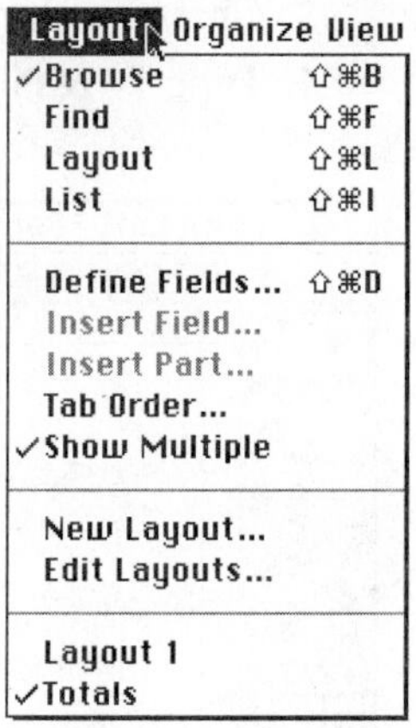

FIGURE 4-50

The Layout menu with the Browse, Find, Layout, and List modes shown.

Try switching between the different modes to see what their differences are by using the following steps. (You will need to be able to do this easily when you change the layout of your report.)

1. From the Layout menu, choose Find. You may remember the screen looking like this when you were finding records in the Class Data database.

2. From the Layout menu, choose Layout. The screen should look like Figure 4-51.

3. From the Layout menu, choose List. Notice that all the fields from the database are displayed in columns with grid lines separating them, similar to a spreadsheet. The List mode provides a good means of viewing all the data

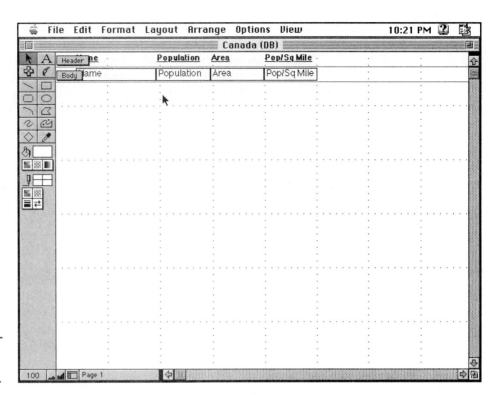

FIGURE 4-51

The database in Layout mode where changes can be made in the way the file will be displayed.

in the database. You have the ability to enter or edit values in the List mode, as well as sort and match records.

4. From the Layout menu, choose Layout 1, the original layout of the Canada database.

5. Repeat Steps 2, 3, 4, and 5, observing differences between the screens. Keep in mind that this layout is not a columnar format, so the screens appear a little different from the Totals layout.

6. Continue to change between the four modes and the two layouts until you are confident that you know what you are looking at when you see a screen.

CHANGING THE LAYOUT

Now you are ready to change the Totals layout to the way you want it for your report.

1. From the Layout menu, choose Totals to be sure you are looking at the Totals layout.

2. From the Layout menu, choose Layout to view in the Layout mode. In this mode, you will be arranging the items on your page.

Refer again to Figure 4-51. Header and Body refer to two parts of your report, the heading and the data from the records, respectively. A horizontal line separates each part of the report. Notice that the field names are underlined and in bold type in the Header part. Boxes for field data are displayed in the Body part of the layout.

Sometimes when working on the layout of a database it is helpful to view the changes in Browse mode so the effect of each change can be viewed immediately. You did this when editing the mailing labels layout earlier in the chapter. In ClarisWorks you can see multiple views of any document—such as the Browse mode and the Layout mode—at the same time. A second view of the same database can be opened on the screen as follows:

1. From the View menu, choose New View. Another window is opened for viewing the database.

2. To see both views at once on the screen, choose Tile Windows from the View menu. Tile Windows creates equally sized windows that fill the screen. Here, the windows display one above the other.

3. Click on the Graphic tool (the arrow pointer on the tool palette), unless it is already selected. With it you can select graphic objects.

4. Click anywhere in the lower window on the screen to select that window. (The title bar will have lines on it when the view is selected.)

5. Choose Browse from the Layout menu. At the top of the screen, the database window is displayed in Layout mode, and at the bottom, the window is displayed in Browse mode.

6. Click anywhere on the top window to make it active. The title bar will have lines on it when it is active.

7. Double-click on the field Population (in the Body part of the layout). You should see the Number Format dialog box appear. Click on the box in front of commas to have commas displayed in the number. Click OK.

8. While the field Population is still selected, choose Right from the Alignment submenu under the Format menu. This will cause the data to be aligned to the right so the numbers will be more readable.

9. Repeat Steps 7 and 8 with the field Area.

10. Double-click on the field Pop/Sq Mile. In the Number Format dialog box choose Fixed and leave 2 as the Precision choice. This will cause the data to be rounded to two decimal places.

11. While the Pop/Sq Mile is still selected, change the alignment to right as you did in Step 8.

12. Change the alignment to right for the field names Population, Area, and Pop/Sq Mile in the Header part of the layout.

13. From the View menu choose Stack Windows to return the screen to a larger display of only one window at a time. The windows are displayed as if one were on top of, and slightly lower than and to the right of, the other.

14. The view displayed is in the Layout mode. Either click on the window that is partially hidden or from the View menu choose Canada:1 (DB) to see the other view, which is in Browse mode.

You have a great deal of flexibility in how you arrange the layout of the field names and fields on the page. You can put them almost anywhere you want as you did earlier when you created mailing labels. In addition, by using the tools in the tool palette at the left you can paint and draw on the page, as you did in Chapter 3. By selecting field names and fields, you can use options on the Format menu to change fonts, font sizes, and styles of the text in the fields. This book cannot be long enough to deal with all these options (and more) for layouts, but you can experiment, use the Help options, and refer to the manual when you are ready to apply them in your layouts. Do take time, though, to be sure you are comfortable with these basics before you try the extras.

SUMMARY PARTS

As indicated earlier, the report should include the total population and area for all the provinces. You can get ClarisWorks to calculate this total for you by using **summary parts**. The term part is used because there are "parts" to the report. So far you have worked with the Header part, which contains the titles for columns, and the Body part, which contains the data in the records. The Summary part will contain a summary of the data. You will create a grand summary that is a grand total for all of the data. (There are also sub-summaries that will not be dealt with here.)

The steps for creating a Summary part include (1) defining a field or fields to contain the summary information, (2) adding the Summary part of the report to the layout, and (3) telling ClarisWorks what summary field(s) to use in the Summary part of the report. It may sound a bit complicated, but follow the steps below and you will see how to set it up.

Defining a Summary Field
First, define a field to contain the summary information.

1. With the database layout in Browse mode choose Define Fields… from the Layout menu.
2. Type **Total Population** for the field name.
3. Select Summary for the Field Type.
4. Click on Create. An Enter Formula dialog box will appear.
5. In the Enter Formula dialog box type the formula:
   SUM('Population')
   This tells the computer to add (sum) the values in the Population field of all the records.
6. Click OK to return to the Define Fields dialog box.
7. To create a similar field to sum the area, type **Total Area** for the field name and again choose Summary for the Field Type. Click on Create.
8. In the Enter Formula dialog box type the formula:
   SUM('Area')
9. Click on OK to return to the Define Fields dialog box.
10. Click on Done.

Adding a Summary Part
Next you must add a Summary part to the layout.

1. Display the window that is still in Layout mode, either by clicking on the partially hidden window or by choosing Class List:2 (DB) from the View menu.
2. From the Layout menu choose **Insert Part…**.
3. Select Trailing grand summary as shown in Figure 4-52, then click OK. (Trailing means that the summary will print after the data in the records.)

4. The Grand Summary part of the report should now be visible in the window. The layout now has three parts, Header, Body, and Grand Summary.

```
╔══════════════════════════════════════════════════════════════╗
║                        Insert Part                           ║
╠══════════════════════════════════════════════════════════════╣
║  ○ Header                          ┌─────────────────────┐   ║
║  ○ Leading grand summary           │ Name                │   ║
║  ○ Sub-summary when sorted by      │ Capital             │   ║
║  ◉ Trailing grand summary          │ Entered Confed      │   ║
║  ○ Footer                          │ Population          │   ║
║    ▶                               │ Area                │   ║
║                                    │ Country             │   ║
║                                    └─────────────────────┘   ║
║                              ┌──────────┐  ┌──────────┐      ║
║                              │  Cancel  │  │   OK     │      ║
║                              └──────────┘  └──────────┘      ║
╚══════════════════════════════════════════════════════════════╝
```

FIGURE 4-52

The Insert Part dialog box with Trailing grand summary chosen.

Inserting a Summary Field

The Grand Summary part of the report has nothing in it yet. To make the Total Population and the Total Area fields display in this part, you need to insert the fields into the layout and place them in the Grand Summary part of the report.

1. Choose Insert Field... from the Layout menu.

2. Click on Total Population to select it.

3. Click Insert. The Total Population field name and Total Population field appear in the Body of the layout.

4. Drag the Total Population field into the Grand Summary area and place it directly under the Population field. (Make sure you get the field and not the field name.)

5. Click on the Total Population field name to select it. (The field name is boldfaced and underlined.) Then press the Delete key to delete it. The way this layout is set up you will not need the Total Population field name.

6. Repeat Steps 1 through 5 to place the field Total Area in the Grand Summary area directly under the Area field. (See Figure 4-53 for positioning.)

7. Look at the view of the database that is in Browse mode. Notice that there is extra space between each record. This can be fixed.

8. Click on the zoom-out control at the bottom of the screen. The zoom percentage indicator should show 66.7. (Zoom is explained in detail in Chapter 2, "Zoom Controls.")

9. Return to the Layout mode.

10. Position the pointer on the line under the Body part of the layout. The pointer should change to a crossbar with arrows pointing up and down.

11. Drag the line up until there is only a very small space below the fields. Any extra space left here is space that will print after every record in the Body of the layout. The layout should now look like Figure 4-53.

12. Double-click on the Total Population field. From the Number dialog box that appears, select the number format with commas. Click OK. Change the alignment to right by changing the value in the Alignment submenu in the Format menu.

13. Repeat Step 12 for the Total Area field.

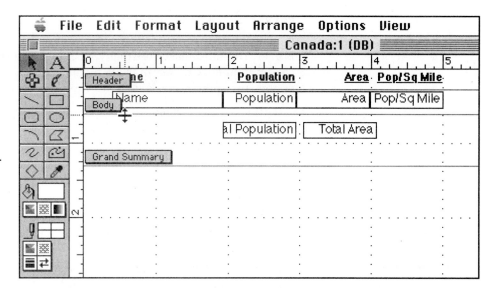

FIGURE 4-53

The database in Layout mode after the Grand Summary part has been added. The summary fields Total Population and Total Area have been moved to the Grand Summary part. The Total Population and Total Area field names have been deleted.

14. View the layout in the Browse mode to see what effect this has had on the display. Notice that the records are closer together, but nothing else has changed. The totals that you have created are not displayed.

15. From the View menu choose **Page View**. Totals are only shown when Page View is selected from the View menu. Figure 4-54 shows what the display should look like.

16. After making all these changes, save your file again by choosing Save from the File menu.

Name	Population	Area	Pop/Sq Mile
Alberta	2,592,300	255,285	10.15
British Columbia	3,376,700	366,255	9.22
Manitoba	1,100,700	251,000	4.39
New Brunswick	731,000	28,354	25.78
Newfoundland	577,300	156,185	3.70
Nova Scotia	909,800	21,425	42.46
Ontario	102,595,200	412,582	248.67
Prince Edward	131,700	2,184	60.30
Quebec	6,985,400	594,860	11.74
Saskatchewan	992,400	251,700	3.94
	119,992,500	2,339,830	

FIGURE 4-54

The database with summary information in Browse mode after Page View has been selected from the View menu.

PRINTING THE DATABASE

Now that you have your report ready, you probably will want to print it out on the printer. You must make sure that your printer is turned on, that you have a printer chosen from the Chooser in the menu, and that your Page Setup and Document options are appropriate. Follow the directions below.

1. If you wish to change the orientation of the paper, choose Page Setup... from the File menu and choose the appropriate orientation.

2. To check the margins, choose Document... from the Format menu. Many printers need to have margins that are at least 0.5 inch. If yours is such a printer, you will need to adjust the margins accordingly. When you finish, click OK.

3. From the View menu choose Show Rulers. The vertical and horizontal rulers are then displayed on the top and left portions of the screen when in the Layout mode or in Page View. This allows you to determine whether the fields chosen will print appropriately.

4. If it appears that they will not, adjust the size and placement of the fields using the Layout mode.

5. If you wish to add a header to the page, choose Insert Header from the Format menu. You may change the font or size of the characters if you wish. Type the following header:

Canada's Province Population and Area

6. Choose Print from the File menu. In this case you may simply click on Print to print your report. You may want to notice the print options that are available. Current Record prints only the selected record, or the first selected record if more than one is selected. Visible Records prints all records except those that are hidden from a Find search, a Hide Selected command, or a Hide Unselected command. If you had a very large database, you might want to print just one page to see how it will look before printing the entire document. Do this by filling in the From and To areas in the Print dialog box. When you finish, click on Print.

PRACTICE WITH REPORTS

1. Add an additional summary field to your report to average the population per square mile. Use the formula AVERAGE('Pop/Sq Mile') when creating your new summary field.

2. Add another summary field to display how many provinces are included in the report. (Hint: Use the Count function to count how many entries there are. The formula could be COUNT('Name'), but other fields could also be used.)

3. Use the Sort Records... and Match Records... options (on the Organize menu) and the Find option (on the Layout menu) to select only particular records for your report. Create a report that displays in alphabetical order only the provinces that have a population per square mile greater than 20.

4. If you have added additional fields to your database, or created other databases, use them to create reports you might be able to use.

Conclusion

You have learned to sort and search through a database for specific records, to add records, to create a new database, to change layouts, and to print particular items from specific records in a database. Take some time to practice these skills. You will find that the more you learn about how to use databases, the more useful they will become to you. For a teacher, databases can be valuable for management and record keeping as well as an excellent instructional tool. Databases can help you keep track of grades, materials, books, resources, and any number of other facts, objects, or ideas.

Databases can be sources of information for students, or they can be a means for students to organize and demonstrate their knowledge. Students could research a topic, organize the information they find, and enter the information into a database. After each student or group entered information for individual topics, the entire class could use the database created to explore the information about all topics. An example of this would be use of a database to gather information about the states in the United States. Each student or group could be assigned to look up information such as the size of the state, its population, the date that it entered the union, birth rate, unemployment rate, major industries, major agriculture, geographic and historic landmarks, natural resources, and so on. For extra credit students could also research aspects such as current problems, budget priorities, crime rates, poverty rates, cost of living, ethnic composition, and political tendencies. Once the information has been entered into the database, all students could use the database to learn about the similarities and differences among states. They could explore relationships within the data by generating hypotheses and trying to prove them. For example, higher-order thinking skills can be stimulated as they try to determine what, if any, relationships exist among population, birth rate, crime rate, poverty rate, and budget priorities or among natural resources, population, and types of industry.

Once you can perform the operations in this chapter easily, you will then be able to experiment and explore other useful ClarisWorks database options that could not be covered here. Feel free to try new things. You will find many other options available that can make your life easier and more productive. And don't forget that the ClarisWorks Help function and the ClarisWorks manuals can be valuable in your explorations.

KEY TERMS

bookmark	Hide Selected	Set Field Order
Browse mode	Hide Unselected	Show All Records
calculation field	Insert Part...	Show Multiple
columnar layout	layout	Sort Records...
data	Layout menu	Stack Windows
data box	Layout mode	status panel
database	List mode	Summary part
Define Fields...	Mail Merge…	Tile Windows
entry	Match Records...	View menu
field	New Layout...	visible records
field name	New Record	
File icon	New Request	
Find	Number Format	
Find mode	Organize menu	
format	Page View	
formula	Print Merge…	
function	record	

EXERCISES

1. Create a database to keep records on audiovisual aids available for various units in a particular subject. Before beginning, determine some category codes for the different types of audiovisuals and the different units of subjects. Once the database is complete, create a report to list all the aids that are available for a particular unit.

2. Create a database Roster that includes the following fields: Last Name, First Name, Class, Address, Phone Number, Jersey Number, Position, Height, Weight. Use the database to do the following:

   a. Create a telephone listing using only the fields Last Name, First Name, Class, Address, and Phone Number. Print the listing with the names in alphabetical order by last name.

   b. Create a roster for the athletic program using only the fields Jersey Number, Last Name, First Name, Position, Height, Weight, and Class. Print the listing in numerical order with the smallest number first.

3. Develop a database on facts about famous scientists. Some fields could be Name, Date of Birth, Date of Death, Primary Residence, Scientific Discoveries or Inventions, Area of Study, Observations, and Other Information. Choose fields that would be of interest to you or your students. Try to answer the following questions using the database.

   a. Which scientists lived during approximately the same time periods?

   b. Which scientists lived in the same state (country)?

   c. Which scientists had discoveries in the same general area of science?

4. Create a database about the states in the United States. Include fields such as State Name, Capital, Population, Area, Birth Rate, Death Rate, Unemployment Rate. Use the database to find the following information.

a. Find the five states with the largest population.

b. Find the five states with the largest area.

c. Find the five states with the highest birth rate.

d. Find the five states with the lowest death rate.

e. Find the five states with the highest unemployment rate.

f. Is there any correlation among the answers to questions c, d, and e? Write questions for your students that would help them to explore relationships among fields and to stimulate ideas.

5. Set up a database to organize observational data on students. Include at least the following fields: Date, Name, Behavior, Relationship to IEP Goals, Consequence. You may add other fields if you wish. Enter data and then create reports by date and by student. Explain how these reports could be beneficial at parent conferences and IEP conferences.

5 ClarisWorks— Spreadsheet

OUTLINE

Introduction

An electronic spreadsheet can be used to do all types of calculations. You can think of it as making the computer become a "super calculator." A teacher might use a spreadsheet to calculate grades, to keep club or department accounting records, to keep athletic team statistics, and even to determine income tax figures. Students can use spreadsheets to keep budget information for a school store, to enter hours worked on school-related jobs, to keep track of the number of meals and proceeds for dinners or banquets that are sponsored by school organizations, and even to aid in learning mathematics.

The spreadsheet, like the calculator, can allow students the opportunity to break through the rigor of tedious calculations and gain a greater understanding of basic mathematics concepts. Students studying the area of figures, for example, can work with basic formulas for the area of squares, rectangles, circles, trapezoids, and parallelograms on a spreadsheet. When given more complicated shapes that are part of one of the basic figures or a combination of them, students can modify the spreadsheet formulas to do the calculations. Many believe that a spreadsheet is "math" and therefore not for them. In reality, the reverse is true. The spreadsheet is a tool of great practical value that requires minimal math skills.

You begin in this chapter by looking at the different features of a spreadsheet that has already been created. Then you continue by modifying an existing spreadsheet. Finally, you create a spreadsheet of your own.

If you are not confident of your skills in working with text, windows, and saving documents, you may want to review the sections of Chapters 1 and 2 that deal with these as you work.

This chapter will not be divided into lessons. When you wish to take a break, you can save your document and simply return to it, and this text, later at the point where you stopped. As in Chapters 2 and 4, it is recommended that when you first save a document from the Data Disk you save it with a new document name (using Save As...) and continue to work with that document, leaving the original Data Disk document unchanged for future reference.

Spreadsheet Basics

Some basic vocabulary and information about spreadsheets will help you to understand how they work and what they can accomplish.

OPENING A SPREADSHEET DOCUMENT FROM THE DESKTOP

1. Double-click on the Data Disk icon to open the Data Disk.
2. Double-click on the document icon labeled Pizza Sale to open the spreadsheet document. Because the Pizza Sale file was created with the ClarisWorks program, when you open the file the ClarisWorks program should be launched at the same time.
3. Now the spreadsheet is on your screen. It should look like Figure 5-1.

BASIC SPREADSHEET INFORMATION

An electronic spreadsheet is very similar to an accountant's worksheet. It is composed of rows and columns used to create areas for information. Notice the **columns** (going down) are labeled with letters (across the top) and the **rows** (going

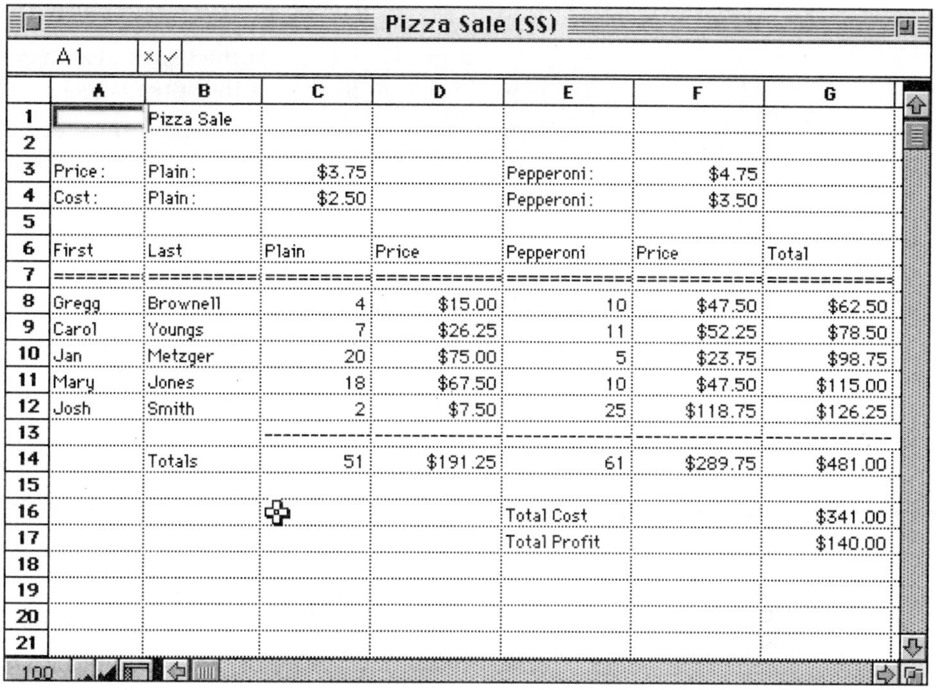

	A	B	C	D	E	F	G
1		Pizza Sale					
2							
3	Price:	Plain:	$3.75		Pepperoni:	$4.75	
4	Cost:	Plain:	$2.50		Pepperoni:	$3.50	
5							
6	First	Last	Plain	Price	Pepperoni	Price	Total
7	========	==========	==========	============	============	============	============
8	Gregg	Brownell	4	$15.00	10	$47.50	$62.50
9	Carol	Youngs	7	$26.25	11	$52.25	$78.50
10	Jan	Metzger	20	$75.00	5	$23.75	$98.75
11	Mary	Jones	18	$67.50	10	$47.50	$115.00
12	Josh	Smith	2	$7.50	25	$118.75	$126.25
13			----------	------------	------------	------------	------------
14		Totals	51	$191.25	61	$289.75	$481.00
15							
16					Total Cost		$341.00
17					Total Profit		$140.00
18							
19							
20							
21							

FIGURE 5-1

The Pizza Sale spreadsheet. Notice there are columns labeled with letters at the top and rows labeled with numbers on the left side. Each region formed by the intersection of a row and column is a cell. Cells are named by their column and row. Currently Cell A1 is selected. The spreadsheet cursor is a plus sign located in Cell C16 in this figure.

across) are labeled with numbers (down the left side). Each rectangular region formed by the intersection of one row and one column of the spreadsheet is called a **cell**. The **cell name** tells you its location. Cell A1 is in Column A and Row 1. In Figure 5-1 the Cell A1 is selected, as indicated by the highlighted outline of the cell.

Explore the size of a ClarisWorks spreadsheet:

1. Using the horizontal scroll bar at the bottom of the screen, move the scroll box to the far right of the scroll bar. The label on the column of the spreadsheet farthest to the right is AN. (Note that ClarisWorks labels the columns using the letters A, B, C, … Z, and then uses AA, AB, AC, … AN.)
2. Use the horizontal scroll bar to move the viewing area back to Cell A1.
3. Move the vertical scroll box to the bottom of the vertical scroll bar; the last row displayed should be 501. The amount of area available for use in a spreadsheet is definitely more than the ordinary application requires.

Notice that as you move the pointer across the spreadsheet the arrow becomes a plus sign. This indicates that you are working in the spreadsheet application. Notice also that when the pointer is on the scroll bars and title bar, the plus sign reverts back to the arrow.

1. Use the vertical scroll bar to move the viewing area back to the beginning of the spreadsheet.
2. Click the pointer on Cell A1.
3. Look at the upper left corner of the spreadsheet, just under the title bar. You should see the letters A1. This is the **address box**, which tells the **cell address**—the name or location—of the selected cell.
4. Press the right arrow key to move the selection to the right two cells. Watch the cell name in the address box change. This is an easy way to always know where you are.

5. Use the arrow keys or the mouse to select Cell B3. The text **Plain**: is located there. Notice that the text is also displayed in the **entry bar**, below the title bar at the top of the spreadsheet.

6. Select Cell C8 and look at the entry in that cell. This is a number that has been typed into the cell. It can be seen both in the entry bar and in the cell.

7. Select Cell D8. This time the cell contains **$15.00**, but the entry bar contains =**3.75∗4**. This is a formula that tells the computer to multiply 3.75 times 4 and to put the result in Cell D8.

   ClarisWorks spreadsheets use four types of data: text, dates and times, numbers, and formulas. Text is information that cannot be used for calculations, such as titles for rows or columns of data. Dates and times may be entered into a spreadsheet and displayed in various formats. Cells containing dates and times may be sorted. Numbers are values that have been typed into the spreadsheet. A **formula** is a value that is calculated by ClarisWorks. A formula can be almost any math calculation that you define using addition, subtraction, multiplication, division, square roots, and other operations. A formula can include information in other cells in the calculations. The formula is displayed in the entry bar, and the value calculated by the formula is found in the spreadsheet cell.

8. The actual display of the value in Cell D8 is in currency format, using a $ to indicate a monetary value. This is not typed in but is obtained by setting the format for the cell display through the Format menu. You will be doing this in later exercises.

9. Select Cell C11. Edit the data in the cell as follows:

   a. Notice that the total number of plain pizzas sold is 51, the price of Mary's plain pizzas is $67.50, and the total for Mary is $115.00.

   b. Type **8**. Mary sold 8 pizzas, rather than 18.

   c. Press Return. Now notice that the total number of plain pizzas sold is 41, the price of Mary's plain pizzas is $30.00, and the total for Mary is $77.50. All these amounts changed automatically, as did the grand total, the total cost, and the total profit.

10. Now, click on Cell C14 and look at the entry bar. The formula =**C8+C9+C10+C11+C12** is composed of cell names rather than actual numbers. These are called **cell references**; they refer to the numbers or values in the named cell.

This ability to refer to other cells is what makes the electronic spreadsheet such a valuable tool. You can change data in one cell and see immediately how the change affects the other cells. In this case, when fewer pizzas were sold, the totals and the profit were decreased. By using cell references in formulas you have the ability to make "what if" projections: What if the cost of pizza went down to $2.00, or what if everybody sells two more plain pizzas? This is one way managers make projections and do planning, and it can be just as useful in a school.

For instance, when working with a school budget, a spreadsheet allows you to experiment with different ways of using the budget, while staying within it. By simply changing numbers of items or prices you can change the budget to meet your needs! A spreadsheet can also be useful in helping students to see relationships when learning math, science, or even social studies—How does the area of a circle change if the radius doubles or triples? What would the world population be in 10, 15, or 20 years if it were doubling every 2, 4, or 10 years? As you work with spreadsheets more, you will gain increasing understanding of this capability and its potential.

CLASSROOM ←——→ CONNECTION

To begin explaining spreadsheets to your class, give each student a small bag of M&M's (or other similar multi-color candy). Have students count the number of candies of each color. Record the number of each color. Use the spreadsheet functions to determine which color generally is more prevalent in each bag, the total number of M&M's in each student's bag, the average number of M&M's in each bag, the average number of each color in a bag, and so on. Use the candy to demonstrate spreadsheet functions, then let the students eat the candy! See M&M's spreadsheet on the Data Disk for a sample spreadsheet.

Sometimes you may need to look at the formulas carefully to determine whether the calculations are correct or just to find out how they were done. You can see all the formulas in a spreadsheet by doing the following:

1. From the **Options menu**, select **Display...** to see the Display dialog box as shown in Figure 5-2.

2. In the Display dialog box click on Formulas.

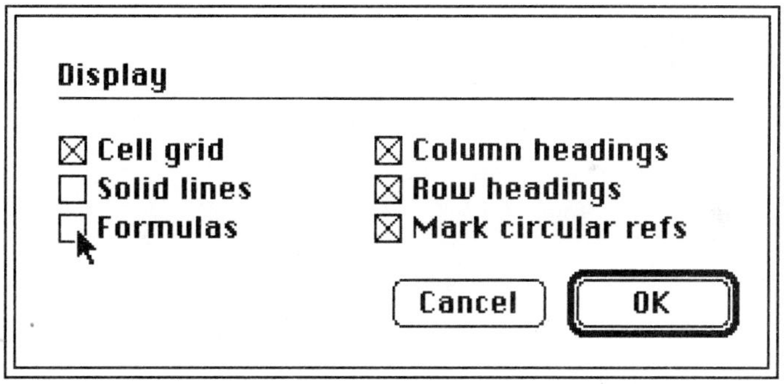

FIGURE 5-2

The Display dialog box allows you to choose which parts of a spreadsheet are displayed on the screen and printed. When the box in front of Formulas is blank, values will display in the cells of the spreadsheet; if it is checked, formulas will appear in the cells of the spreadsheet.

Display

☒ **Cell grid**   ☒ **Column headings**
☐ **Solid lines**   ☒ **Row headings**
☐ **Formulas**   ☒ **Mark circular refs**

[Cancel]   [**OK**]

3. Click OK. The formulas for the spreadsheet are displayed as shown in Figure 5-3.

4. Click on Cell C14. As shown in Figure 5-3, you can see the entire formula in the entry bar, but not in the cell.

You can click on a particular cell to see the entire formula for that cell in the entry bar, or you can widen the column of a spreadsheet to see the entire formula within the cell when formulas are displayed. You may also want to change column width for other reasons—to make data easier to read or to make cell size appropriate for the size of the contents. To change the column width:

1. Place the pointer on one of the vertical lines separating the columns in the heading area. The plus sign should change to a crossbar with left and right arrows on it. In Figure 5-3, the crossbar is positioned on the line between the titles of Column C and Column D. While the crossbar looks like this, (✛), drag it to the right to widen and to the left to narrow the column on its left (Column C).

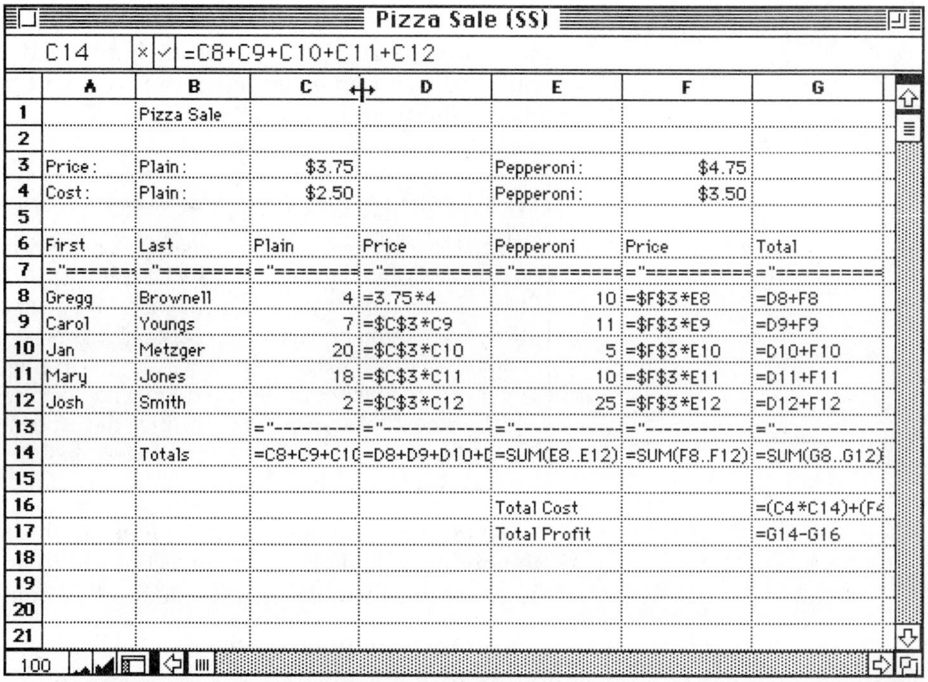

Pizza Sale (SS)

C14 =C8+C9+C10+C11+C12

	A	B	C	D	E	F	G
1		Pizza Sale					
2							
3	Price:	Plain:	$3.75		Pepperoni:	$4.75	
4	Cost:	Plain:	$2.50		Pepperoni:	$3.50	
5							
6	First	Last	Plain	Price	Pepperoni	Price	Total
7	="======	="========	="=======	="==========	="==========	="==========	="==========
8	Gregg	Brownell	4	=3.75*4	10	=$F$3*E8	=D8+F8
9	Carol	Youngs	7	=$C$3*C9	11	=$F$3*E9	=D9+F9
10	Jan	Metzger	20	=$C$3*C10	5	=$F$3*E10	=D10+F10
11	Mary	Jones	18	=$C$3*C11	10	=$F$3*E11	=D11+F11
12	Josh	Smith	2	=$C$3*C12	25	=$F$3*E12	=D12+F12
13			="---------	="-----------	="-----------	="-----------	="-----------
14		Totals	=C8+C9+C1(	=D8+D9+D10+[	=SUM(E8..E12)	=SUM(F8..F12)	=SUM(G8..G12)
15							
16					Total Cost		=(C4*C14)+(F4
17					Total Profit		=G14-G16
18							
19							
20							
21							

FIGURE 5-3
The Pizza Sale spreadsheet with the formulas displayed. Using this option allows you to look carefully at formulas to determine whether they are correct.

2. The spreadsheet also utilizes several special functions that are not established math functions. Move to Cell E14 and look at the formula: **=Sum(E8..E12)**. SUM is a **function**, a predefined operation. The operation in this case is to add the values of all the cells in parentheses. E8..E12 means the **range** of cells from E8 through E12, all cells from E8 to E12. This function tells the computer to find the sum of the values in Cells E8, E9, E10, E11, and E12. The functions available for ClarisWorks are listed under **Paste Function...** in the Edit menu.
3. From the Options menu, choose Display…,
4. Click on Formulas to deselect it, then click OK. The spreadsheet should again display values rather than formulas.

Now you know some of the basic features of the spreadsheet. Next, you will begin to work with one.

Cells

ClarisWorks provides a variety of ways to select cells and enter data. Knowing these will enable you to work more efficiently and will simplify your work with spreadsheets.

To develop these skills, you will work with the Gradebook spreadsheet on your Data Disk.

1. You may close the current document, Pizza Sale, without saving it. (Use the close box, or choose Close from the File menu.)
2. From the File menu choose Open… to view the Open dialog box.
3. Open the Gradebook document on the Data Disk by double-clicking on its name in the list of documents. (If the Data Disk is not shown, click on the Desktop button and double-click on Data Disk when it appears as a choice.

Then open the Gradebook file.) The Gradebook spreadsheet should look as shown in Figure 5-4.

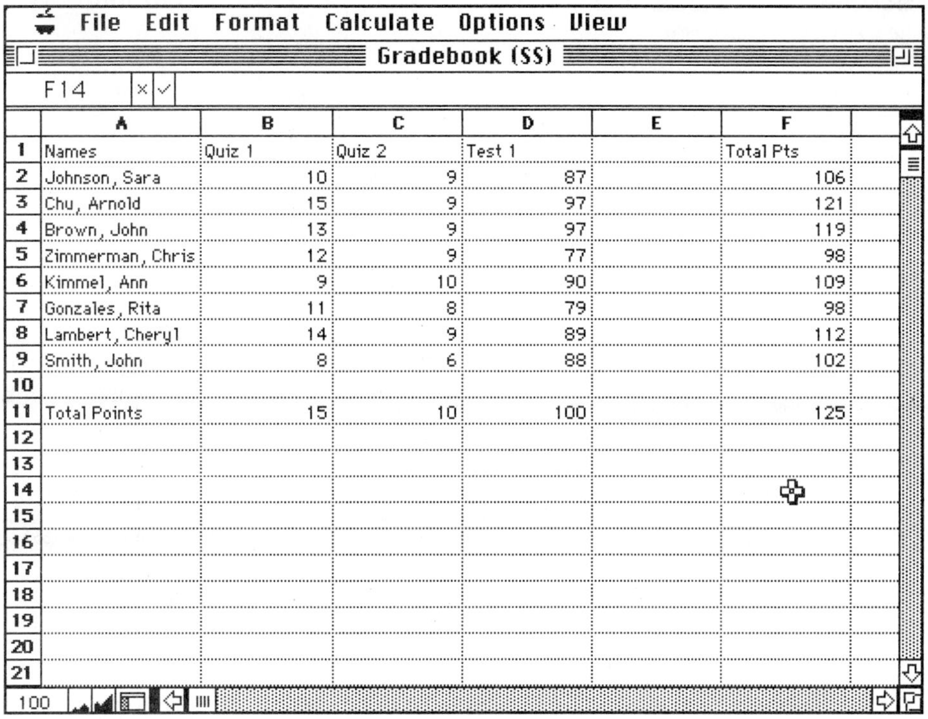

	A	B	C	D	E	F	
1	Names	Quiz 1	Quiz 2	Test 1		Total Pts	
2	Johnson, Sara	10	9	87		106	
3	Chu, Arnold	15	9	97		121	
4	Brown, John	13	9	97		119	
5	Zimmerman, Chris	12	9	77		98	
6	Kimmel, Ann	9	10	90		109	
7	Gonzales, Rita	11	8	79		98	
8	Lambert, Cheryl	14	9	89		112	
9	Smith, John	8	6	88		102	
10							
11	Total Points	15	10	100		125	

FIGURE 5-4

The Gradebook spreadsheet shows various grades earned by students in a class.

SELECTING CELLS

So far you have selected particular cells in the spreadsheet by clicking a cell or using the arrow keys—arrow keys move the selection in the indicated direction cell by cell. You may also use the Tab key to move to the right. If you have a large spreadsheet, the vertical and horizontal scroll bars quickly change your view to a different location in the spreadsheet, but do not change the selected cell; you must click a cell to select it in the new location. The **Go To Cell...** command on the Options menu will take you to any location on the spreadsheet and select the indicated cell.

1. Use the arrow keys to move to Cell B6. The address box shows that you are at Cell B6 and the entry there is the number 9.
2. Now use the Tab key to move to Cell F6. The address box shows that you are at Cell F6 and the entry bar displays a formula containing the **Sum function**. The value calculated from the formula is displayed in the cell.
3. From the Options menu, select Go To Cell.... A dialog box such as the one shown in Figure 5-5 appears on the screen.
4. Type **W45** for the cell address.
5. Press Return or click on OK. Cell W45 should be selected.
6. From the Options menu, select Go To Cell....
7. Type **N17** for the cell address.
8. Click OK.

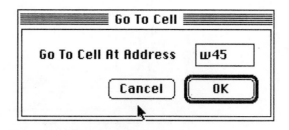

FIGURE 5-5

The Go To Cell dialog box allows you to move to any cell in the spreadsheet by typing the cell location.

9. Select Cells N17 through R17 by dragging from N17 to R17. As you drag to the right end of the screen, it will automatically scroll, if necessary.

10. If you go too far, continue to drag back to Cell R17 or just repeat the selection process.

11. Notice that N17 has a border around it and the remaining four cells selected are highlighted, as shown in Figure 5-6. This is because N17 is the top left cell of the selection, the beginning of the selected range of cells. It is the address used for the address box.

FIGURE 5-6

In this spreadsheet the range of cells from N17 to R17 has been selected. By selecting a range of cells, changes can be made to the spreadsheet more easily.

	M	N	O	P	Q	R	S	T
6								
7								
8								
9								
10								
11								
12								
13								
14								
15								
16								
17		1	2	3	4	5		
18		11	22	33	44	55		
19		111	222	333	444	555		
20		1111	2222	3333	4444	5555		
21								
22								
23								
24								
25								
26								
27								
28								
29								
30								
31								
32								
33								

Menu bar: File Edit Format Calculate Options View   7:27 PM
Title: Gradebook (SS)
Cell: N17   1

12. Select all the cells on the screen with numbers in them by dragging from Cell N17 through R20. This is the range of Cells N17 through R20.

13. Selection of ranges of cells is usually used for clearing, cutting, copying, or pasting data in the cells. From the Edit menu, select Clear to clear the data from the cells.

14. Go to Cell W45 and clear it.

15. Go to Cell A1.

EDITING CELL DATA

John Smith found an error was made in the grading of his test. You need to change his score for Test 1 from 88 to 95. Note that John currently has 102 total points.

1. Select Cell D9.

2. Type **95**. Notice that this changes the data only in the entry bar. It does not change the data in the cell until you confirm the entry.

3. Click the **Accept button**, the check mark at the left of the entry bar. The Accept button is shown in Figure 5-7. Now the entry in Cell D9 changes to 95 and also the value in Cell F9 changes from 102 to 109.

4. Select Cell C4.

5. Type **xyz.**

6. This is a mistake. You do not want this entered in the cell. Click the **Cancel button**, the X at the left of the entry bar. Your entry will be ignored. (Note: It is also possible to Undo Enter, if you have already accepted an entry, as long as you undo it right away.)

FIGURE 5-7

The Cancel (X) and Accept (check mark) buttons are used to ignore or enter data that has been typed into the entry bar.

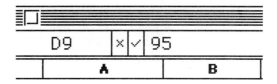

Using either the check mark or the X keeps you at the selected cell. To confirm your entry and then move to another cell, you may press Return or the Tab key. Return confirms or accepts the entry and moves the selection down to the cell below. The Tab key accepts an entry and moves the selection one cell to the right. Pressing the Enter key, on the numeric keypad, accepts the entry and keeps the cursor in the same cell. The arrow keys will not accept an entry but will move the cursor around in the spreadsheet when no new entries have been made.

Adding Data in a Blank Column

For a spreadsheet to be useful, you must be able to add new data as well as make changes. With the gradebook example you may get new students or have new grades to enter, which would require creating new rows or columns of data. You will now continue by adding more information to the spreadsheet. You have just given Test 2 and want to record the results.

1. Move to Cell E1.

2. Type **Test 2.**

3. Press Return. This accepts the entry and moves the selection down in position to enter the first grade.

4. Type **93.**

5. Press Return.

6. Type **100.**

7. Continue in the same manner entering the scores listed below, pressing Return after each entry. Notice as you add values in Column E, the sum in Column F changes also.

Brown	**80**
Zimmerman	**73**
Kimmel	**91**
Gonzales	**78**
Lambert	**85**
Smith	**90**
Total Points	**100**

Most of the time you will not have blank columns or rows available in which to add new data to your spreadsheet. You will need to add the columns or rows needed for the new data.

Columns and Rows

INSERTING COLUMNS

Column E was left blank in the spreadsheet so you could add these values. Also, the formulas for Column F were set up to include Column E in the sum. However, you do not need to have a blank row or column in the spreadsheet in order to add more grades. You can insert or delete rows or columns within the spreadsheet whenever you need them. Insert another column to enter values for Quiz 3:

1. Click on the label D at the top of Column D to select the entire column. The whole column will be highlighted except Cell D1, the first cell in the column.

2. From the **Calculate menu,** choose **Insert Cells...** as shown in Figure 5-8.

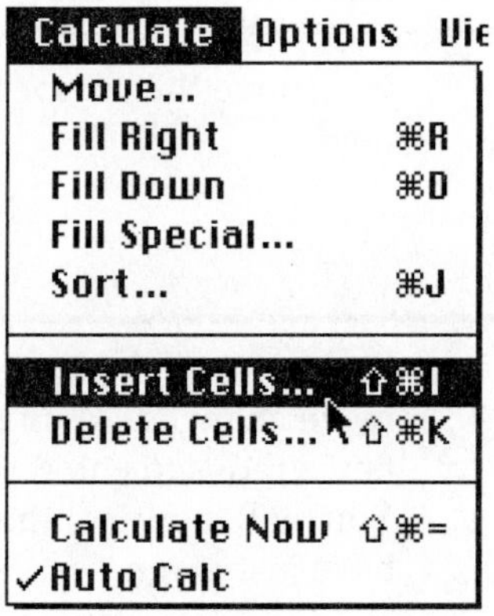

FIGURE 5-8

The Calculate menu provides a variety of options, including the ability to insert or delete cells. It also provides a means of copying formulas or other data by "filling" an area with the selected cell formula or value. You can also sort selected cells in the spreadsheet.

3. You should have a blank column in Column D and the values from the former Column D should have moved to Column E. The values in Column E moved to F and those in F to G.

ClarisWorks will move the highlighted column to the right and insert the blank column at the selected position. If you had picked a row, it would have moved the selected row down and made a blank row where the selected row was located. All columns to the right are relettered, or all rows below are renumbered. In addition, all formulas that referred to these lettered columns, or numbered rows, are updated to reflect the changes.

4. Select Cell G2. Notice that the formula is **=Sum(B2..F2).** Previously, the formula was **=Sum(B2..E2)**. Because the column was inserted within the B2 to E2 range, the formula was automatically adjusted. In the original spreadsheet, if Column F had been highlighted and the Quiz 3 column added after Test 2, the new column would have been Column F, outside the range of cells in the formula, and the formula would not have changed to include the new column.

5. Select Cell D1.

6. Type **Quiz 3**.

7. Press Return.

8. Type the additional data as listed below for each person and for Total Points, pressing Return after each entry.

Johnson	9
Chu	8
Brown	7
Zimmerman	10
Kimmel	9
Gonzales	9
Lambert	8
Smith	7
Total Points	10

INSERTING ROWS

As mentioned earlier, rows can be inserted with the same procedure used for inserting columns. You need to insert two students into the spreadsheet after Row 4, John Brown.

1. If necessary, use the horizontal scroll bar to bring the the names into view.

2. Select Rows 5 and 6, the two entire rows below John Brown, by dragging the arrow pointer over the labels 5 and 6 (at the left of the rows).

3. From the Calculate menu choose Insert Cells....

4. Because two rows are selected, two rows are inserted, starting at the beginning of the selection. The number of rows (or columns) selected is the number of rows (or columns) inserted. In this way, you can insert as many rows (or columns) as you need.

5. Add the following data for the two additional students:

Castle, Sandy	12	8	7	84	95
Getful, For	5	3	2	56	61

Formulas are entered into a spreadsheet to do calculations. If you know the operations required to do a calculation, you can create a formula and have the spreadsheet do it for you.

Formulas

ENTERING A FORMULA

You may want to know the average number of points for each quiz and test.

1. Select Cell A14.
2. Type **Average Points.**
3. Press the Tab key. Make sure Cell B14 is selected.

   Because an average is the sum of all the values divided by the number of values, to calculate the average you could type any one of the following formulas. Keep in mind that the slash indicates division:

   =(B2+B3+B4+B5+B6+B7+B8+B9+B10+B11)/10

   =SUM(B2..B11)/10

   =AVERAGE(B2..B11)

   Like SUM, AVERAGE is a ClarisWorks spreadsheet function. There are advantages to using the **Average function**, but for the time being use the first formula.

4. Type =(, that is, the equal sign and the left parenthesis. At this point you could continue typing the rest of the formula, but ClarisWorks offers a shortcut.
5. Click Cell B2. Notice that **B2** is inserted into the entry bar at the insertion point.
6. Click Cell B3. At the insertion point **+B3** is entered. If no sign is typed between cell names, ClarisWorks includes a plus sign along with the name of the cell clicked.
7. Click each of the remaining cells through B11.
8. Type the rest of the formula: **)/10.** (Don't forget to type the ")".)
9. If the formula is not correct, edit it in the entry bar as any other text—select the incorrect portion and retype it correctly, or click to get an insertion point at the position where you need to insert text.
10. When the formula is correct, accept it with the Accept button, the Return key, the Tab key, or the Enter key.

COPYING A FORMULA TO OTHER CELLS

To find the averages for the remaining quizzes and tests, you can type in each formula. However, an easier way is to copy the formula into the other cells. This can be done by copying and pasting the formula or by filling the remaining cells in the row with the same formula. You will use both of these methods now to see how they work.

Pasting Cell Contents

The copy and paste procedures in the spreadsheet are similar to the copy and paste word processing procedures. Select the cell or cells to be copied, then paste the cell or cells in the desired new location as follows:

1. Select Cell B14.
2. From the Edit menu choose Copy.
3. Select Cell C14.
4. From the Edit menu choose Paste. The formula is now pasted into Cell C14.

Take a good look at the formula in Cell C14. Notice that it refers to different cells from the original formula in Cell B14. In C14, the formula is **=(C2+C3+C4+C5+C6+C7+C8+C9+C10+C11)/10.** All the cell references are one cell to the right of the original references. This is because when you paste, cell addresses are automatically changed to reflect the difference between the address you are pasting from and the address you are pasting to. You pasted in Cell C14, one cell to the right of the copied cell, B14, so references in the formula are also one cell to the right of references in the copied formula.

Filling Cells

Another way to copy data into cells is to select a row or column of cells and fill all cells in the row or column with the data in the first cell. To do this you use the **Fill Right** or **Fill Down** commands, as follows:

1. Select Cells C14 through G14 by dragging the mouse across them.
2. Choose Fill Right from the Calculate menu. The formula in Cell C14 should be copied into each of the other cells, D14 through G14.
3. Click Cell D14. Notice that in the entry bar for D14, the formula adds cells in the D column, and in E14 cells in the E column are summed. Similar changes are reflected in the rest of the row.
4. The spreadsheet should now be similar to that in Figure 5-9.

The total points for the two new students have not yet been calculated. Fill Cells G5 and G6 with the formula from G4 as follows:

1. Select the range of Cells G4 through G6.
2. From the Calculate menu select Fill Down. The values should be entered in Cells G5 and G6.

FIGURE 5-9

The Gradebook spreadsheet after edits have been made. Notice that Cell C14 contains the value 8, whereas the entry bar contains the formula that was used to calculate the value in the cell.

	A	B	C	D	E	F	G	H
1	Names	Quiz 1	Quiz 2	Quiz 3	Test 1	Test 2	Total Pts	
2	Johnson, Sara	10	9	9	87	93	208	
3	Chu, Arnold	15	9	8	97	100	229	
4	Brown, John	13	9	7	97	80	206	
5	Castle, Sandy	12	8	7	84	95		
6	Getful, For	5	3	2	56	61		
7	Zimmerman, Chris	12	9	10	77	73	181	
8	Kimmel, Ann	9	10	9	90	91	209	
9	Gonzales, Rita	11	8	9	79	78	185	
10	Lambert, Cheryl	14	9	8	89	85	205	
11	Smith, John	8	6	7	95	90	206	
12								
13	Total Points	15	10	10	100	100	235	
14	Average Points	10.9	8	7.6	85.1	84.6	162.9	

C14 =(C2+C3+C4+C5+C6+C7+C8+C9+C10+C11)/10

Cell References

There are two ways of referencing other cells within spreadsheet formulas, relative and absolute references. What you have seen so far have been relative cell references.

RELATIVE CELL REFERENCE

A **relative cell reference** indicates the position of a cell in relation to (relative to) the cell in which the reference is made. The cell references in the formulas you just copied are relative references. In Cell E14 the formula adds cells that are in the same column and 12, 11, 10, ..., 4, and 3 cells above E14. In Cell F14 the formula adds cells that are in the same relative position—in the same column and 12, 11, 10, ..., 4, and 3 cells above F14. Take a look at another example of a relative cell reference. Click on Cell G2. Here the formula is =**SUM(B2..F2)** and the result is placed in Cell G2. This relative reference tells ClarisWorks to find the sum of the range of five cells immediately to the left of Cell G2 and in the same row, Row 2. If this formula were copied and pasted to a new address, the formula would change so that the range of cells would be in the same position relative to the address containing the formula—immediately to the left of, and in the same row as, the new address. If you copied the formula to Cell G3 the range would be (B3..F3); if you copied it to Cell H2, the range in the formula would be (C2..G2); or if you copied it Cell P243, the range in the formula would be (K243..O243). In every instance the cell references would be in the same position, relative to the cell containing the formula, as they were originally relative to the position of the copied formula.

ABSOLUTE CELL REFERENCE

The other type of reference is an **absolute cell reference**. This is a reference that always refers to the same cell address, no matter where the formula might be pasted. For instance, in Column H there could be a percentage score for each student. For Sara Johnson, this would be calculated by dividing Sara's total points, in Cell G2, by the total points possible, in Cell G13. As a formula, this could be expressed as: H2=G2/G13. For Arnold Chu, it would be calculated by dividing his points in Cell G3 by the total possible in Cell G13 or the formula: H3=G3/G13. In fact, for every student you would need to divide by the value in Cell G13. This means Cell G13 would be an absolute reference, a reference that does not change location. In ClarisWorks this is indicated by typing the cell reference as $G$13. The $ indicates that the column or row named with the $ will not be changed if the formula is copied or pasted. It tells ClarisWorks to look for the value in Cell G13 regardless of the current cell position.

Another example of absolute references is in the Pizza Sale spreadsheet used earlier in this chapter. Figure 5-10 shows that the prices in Column F were all calculated using the price of the pepperoni pizza in Cell F3. Using absolute cell references in a separate area of the spreadsheet in this way enables you to cut and paste formulas referring to the specific cell. With this technique, costs or other current values need to be edited in only one location when they change. Increasing or decreasing the one sale price in F3 would change all the pepperoni pizza prices, the totals, and the total profit.

USING AN ABSOLUTE REFERENCE

Now it's time to create a column in the Gradebook spreadsheet to calculate each student's percentage of the total points possible. To calculate this value for each student, the student's total points need to be divided by the value in Cell G13, the total points possible.

1. Move to Cell H1.
2. Type **Average** to label the column.

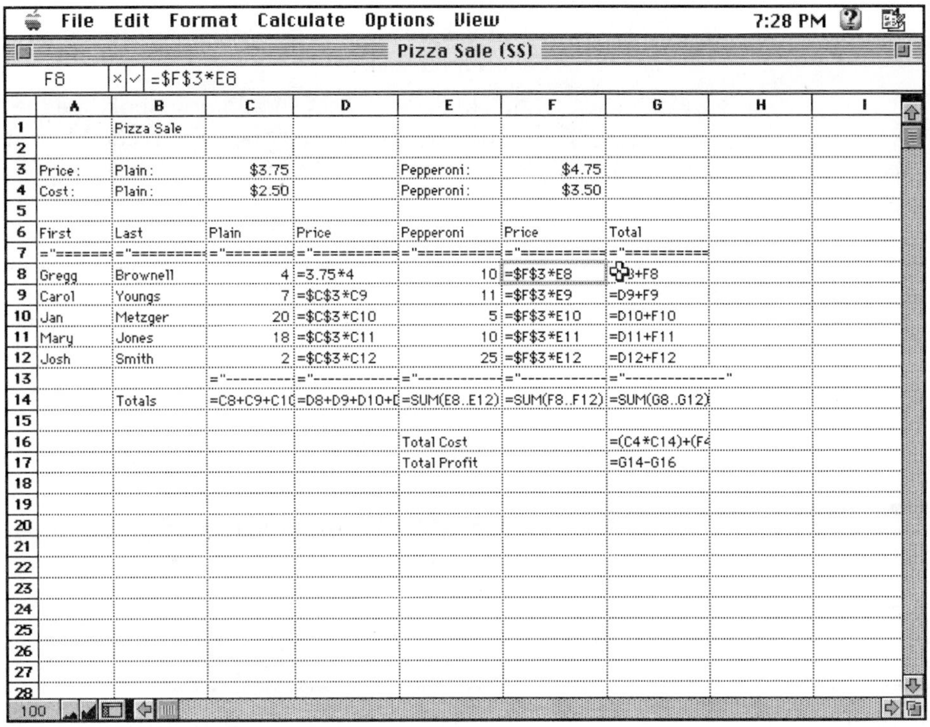

	A	B	C	D	E	F	G	H	I
1		Pizza Sale							
2									
3	Price:	Plain:	$3.75		Pepperoni:	$4.75			
4	Cost:	Plain:	$2.50		Pepperoni:	$3.50			
5									
6	First	Last	Plain	Price	Pepperoni	Price	Total		
7	="======	="========	="=======	="==========	="==========	="==========	="==========		
8	Gregg	Brownell	4	=3.75*4	10	=$F$3*E8	[illegible]+F8		
9	Carol	Youngs	7	=$C$3*C9	11	=$F$3*E9	=D9+F9		
10	Jan	Metzger	20	=$C$3*C10	5	=$F$3*E10	=D10+F10		
11	Mary	Jones	18	=$C$3*C11	10	=$F$3*E11	=D11+F11		
12	Josh	Smith	2	=$C$3*C12	25	=$F$3*E12	=D12+F12		
13			="---------	="-----------	="-----------	="-----------	="-------------"		
14		Totals	=C8+C9+C1(	=D8+D9+D10+[	=SUM(E8..E12)	=SUM(F8..F12)	=SUM(G8..G12)		
15									
16					Total Cost		=(C4*C14)+(F4		
17					Total Profit		=G14-G16		

FIGURE 5-10

In Column F of the Pizza Sale spreadsheet, references to Cell F3 are absolute references. This is denoted by $F$3 in the formula shown in the entry bar.

3. Press Return to accept the entry and select Cell H2.
4. Type =**G2/$G$13** and press Return. Notice that ClarisWorks displays the value in exponential form.
5. Select the range of cells from H2 through H14.
6. Choose Fill Down from the Calculate menu. The formula should be copied down into the other cells.
7. Click Cell H3. Notice that in the entry bar for H3 the formula reads =**G3/$G$13.** The values in the rest of the column are similarly calculated. The first value in the formula changed relative to the formula's location in

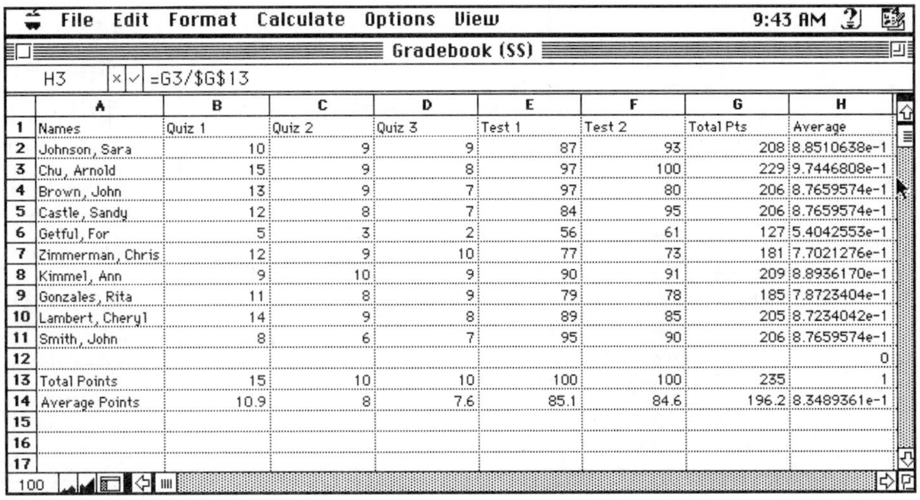

	A	B	C	D	E	F	G	H
1	Names	Quiz 1	Quiz 2	Quiz 3	Test 1	Test 2	Total Pts	Average
2	Johnson, Sara	10	9	9	87	93	208	8.8510638e-1
3	Chu, Arnold	15	9	8	97	100	229	9.7446808e-1
4	Brown, John	13	9	7	97	80	206	8.7659574e-1
5	Castle, Sandy	12	8	7	84	95	206	8.7659574e-1
6	Getful, For	5	3	2	56	61	127	5.4042553e-1
7	Zimmerman, Chris	12	9	10	77	73	181	7.7021276e-1
8	Kimmel, Ann	9	10	9	90	91	209	8.8936170e-1
9	Gonzales, Rita	11	8	9	79	78	185	7.8723404e-1
10	Lambert, Cheryl	14	9	8	89	85	205	8.7234042e-1
11	Smith, John	8	6	7	95	90	206	8.7659574e-1
12								0
13	Total Points	15	10	10	100	100	235	1
14	Average Points	10.9	8	7.6	85.1	84.6	196.2	8.3489361e-1
15								
16								
17								

FIGURE 5-11

The Gradebook spreadsheet with Averages expressed in exponential format. Notice that an absolute reference is made to Cell G13, which contains the total points possible.

the spreadsheet, the second value stayed the same because it is an absolute cell reference.

8. The spreadsheet should now look like the one in Figure 5-11. The averages on your screen may be expressed either in exponential notation or as decimal values. Later you will change this to percent format.

Erasing an Entry

Averages do not need to be calculated for Cells H12 and H13. Data in these cells can be deleted using the standard editing procedures. However, it is easier to clear the cells as follows.

1. Select Cells H12 and H13.

2. From the Edit menu, choose Clear. The entries should be erased.

This can also be accomplished by pressing the Delete key when cells are selected or by choosing Cut. Cut puts a copy of the entry on the Clipboard, whereas Clear and Delete do not. Cut also removes cell formats, such as the percent format that you will create next.

Changing Number Format

Averages for each student are displayed in Column H in exponential format, or perhaps in decimal format, depending on what value is calculated. Most teachers would prefer to see them displayed as percentages. This can be accomplished by changing the **cell format** for Column H.

1. Select Cells H2 through H14.

2. From the Format menu, select **Number...**. The Format Number, Date, and Time dialog box is displayed, as shown in Figure 5-12. Note the format options available for numbers, dates, and times.

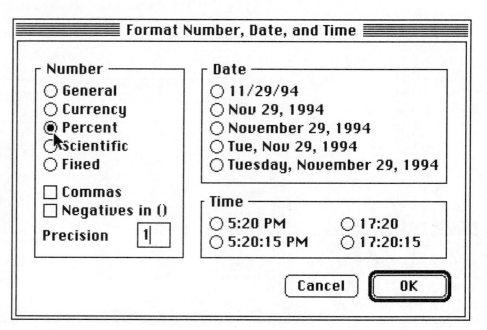

FIGURE 5-12

The Format Number, Date, and Time dialog box provides a means of changing the format of a cell. In this example, Percent is the selected number format with a Precision of 1. This means numbers in selected cells will be displayed as percents rounded to the nearest tenth. There are also several formats available for cells containing dates or times.

3. Click Percent.

4. Type **1** for Precision. This will round the value to one place after the decimal point.

5. Press Return or click OK. The values in Column H are now rounded off to the nearest tenth of a percent.

You should now see the averages displayed in percent format, rounded to the nearest tenth. You could have rounded the values to the nearest whole percent, by typing **0** for Precision.

Note that the percent format does not just add a percent sign. When the format is changed to Percent, the value in the cell is multiplied by 100 (the decimal is moved two places to the right) and the % sign is inserted. For instance, a value such as .87 is converted to 87% and 87 is converted to 8700%. Sometimes the value in a cell is already a percent, displayed without the percent sign, as when test scores are percentages entered as integers—87, 92, 76. Choosing the percent format for cells with these values would display 8700%, 9200%, and 7600% respectively, unless the values were divided by 100 first.

CLASSROOM ← → CONNECTION

Use a spreadsheet to simplify a problem-solving situation. An example: George has 36 feet of fencing to use to fence his garden. What dimensions would give him the most area? Create a spreadsheet in which students enter the perimeter and a length of a side and the other values (second side and area) are calculated. The student can try whole and decimal values. Have students try a similar problem with other lengths of fencing. Can they determine any pattern? See the spreadsheet FENCE on the Data Disk for a sample.

Practice

At this point you will use this spreadsheet a little and make some improvements. This spreadsheet is quite small, with too few students for the typical class and only a few tests and quizzes. Using the spreadsheet and improving it will provide practice with the skills that have been covered.

1. Change some of the students' grades. (Click a cell and type the new grade.) As you do, notice what differences there are in totals and percentages. How does a high quiz grade affect a student's average as compared with a high test grade? Does a particularly high or low grade have a greater effect on the average of a poorer student than on that of a better student, or is there no difference? How would grades be affected if one test or quiz were dropped from the average? (Remember, if you make a mistake, the Undo command is on the Edit menu.)

2. Insert five rows after row 2. (Select rows 3 through 7. From the Calculate menu choose Insert Cells....)

   a. Add data for five more students.

   b. Fill Down (Calculate menu) to enter data for the new students' Total Points and Average cells. (Notice how the average formula has changed. Because the cell with the absolute reference was pushed down, the references to that cell were changed accordingly.)

    c. Look at the Average Points at the bottom of the columns to see how the formulas were affected. Edit the formula for Column B to correct it. (Add the extra cells to the formula by positioning the insertion point in the formula, then typing the cell names or clicking the cells.) Then Fill Right to correct other Average Points formulas.

3. Insert a column for another test. Check to see if any formulas need to be changed.

4. Select cells containing the average formula and change the format displayed in the cells. (Choose Number… from the Format menu.) Try each of the choices, other than date and time, to see how the formats are displayed.

5. In Cell A21, or another blank cell at the bottom of the spreadsheet, type **Last Update:,** then type the date in the next cell and the time in the following cell. Change the time and date formats and edit the time and date in different ways to see how the formats are affected.

CLASSROOM ⟷ CONNECTION

Create a spreadsheet to help determine patterns. As the radius of a circle doubles how do the area and the circumference of the circle change? How do the area and circumference change when the radius is tripled? Have students assist in setting up the spreadsheet. Prior to entering any data, have students predict how they think the area and circumference will change. Enter data in the spreadsheet as a class or in small groups to "discover" how the area and circumference will change. Have students generalize their answers.

Entering a Function in a Formula

When rows are inserted in this Gradebook spreadsheet, the formula used to calculate the Average Points has to be edited to include the new rows. Also, if one or more students have not taken the test, the average will be incorrect, because the divisor in the formula will not reflect the appropriate number of students to divide by.

Using the ClarisWorks function AVERAGE would solve these problems. This function will calculate the average of scores in specified cells by adding the scores and dividing by the total number of scores. If a cell is blank or contains non-numeric data, the cell is ignored, and the total number of scores does not include that cell. The cells to be averaged can be specified as a range, so that when columns or rows are inserted within the range, the new cells will be automatically included.

1. Select cell B14. (If you inserted the five rows in Exercise 2, this is probably B19, the cell at the right of the cell labeled Average Points.)

2. Type **=Average(B2..B11).** (If you added more students, use the cell corresponding to the last student, rather than B11.)

3. Press the Return key. The average is displayed in the cell.

4. Select this cell and the remaining cells in the row containing Average Points formulas.

5. From the Calculate menu, choose Fill Right. The averages should be displayed.

Many other functions are available in ClarisWorks. By using the option Paste Function… on the Edit menu you can see a list of these functions and can enter a function in a cell without having to type it.

1. Select a blank cell in Column A below the student names.

2. From the Edit menu choose Paste Function… to see the Paste Function dialog box as shown in Figure 5-13.

3. Choose COUNT(number1,number2,…). The function is placed in the entry bar, with **number1** highlighted.

4. Select the range of cells in Column A that contains student names. This replaces the highlighted text, **number1**, with the range of cells, such as **A2..A11**. (Or the range from A2 to the cell of the last student if you added students.)

5. Delete **,number2,**… in the entry bar by selecting it and pressing the Delete key.

6. Now the formula should be similar to: **COUNT(A2..A11)**. It is also possible to simply type the function, as you did with the average function, or to use a combination of typing and selection to create the formula.

7. Click the Accept button (check mark) to accept the entry. The cell should display a count of the number of entries in the selected cells.

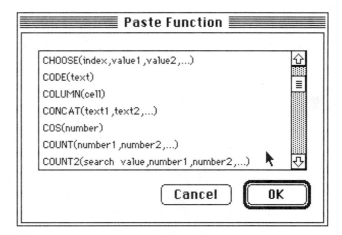

FIGURE 5-13

The Paste Function dialog box lists available ClarisWorks functions. These functions may be pasted into formulas or simply typed.

Right-Justifying Cell Data

The headings for tests and quizzes are aligned with the left sides of the columns, whereas the data in these columns is aligned on the right. To align the headings with the data, use the following steps.

1. Select Cells B1 through H1.

2. From the Format menu, choose Alignment. A submenu appears, as shown in Figure 5-14.

3. From the Alignment submenu choose Right. The column headings for the numeric columns are now right-justified.

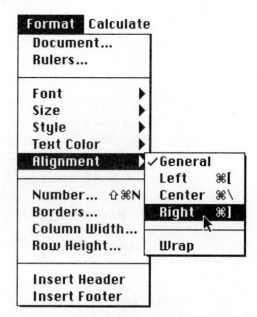

FIGURE 5-14

The Format menu with the Alignment submenu. Notice that cell entries may be aligned left, right, or center within the cell.

Locking Titles on the Spreadsheet

When a spreadsheet is larger than the screen, it can become difficult to use because column and row headings scroll off the screen. In this Gradebook spreadsheet, when the student averages are on the screen, student names cannot be seen. It is difficult to tell whose average is being viewed. Using **Lock Title Position** can solve this problem by locking the titles so they are always in view as you move around in the spreadsheet. Lock the titles by following the steps below.

1. Click on Cell A1 to select it.
2. Choose Lock Title Position from the Options menu.
3. Click several times on the arrow at the right end of the horizontal scroll bar. Notice that as the columns move, Column A is locked in view.
4. Move to the upper left section of the spreadsheet so that cell A1 is in view.
5. Click several times on the arrow at the bottom of the vertical scroll bar. As the rows move up, Row 1 remains in view.
6. Choose Lock Title Position again to deselect this option.

Note that by clicking on Cell A1 prior to choosing Lock Title Position, you were locking Column A and Row 1. If you were to select Cell A2 instead, you would be locking Column A and Rows 1 and 2. Any row or column preceeding the selected cell position is locked as a title. To lock only Column A and not Row 1, select the column by clicking on the column heading A. Then choose Lock Title Position. This procedure works similarly for rows.

Splitting the Spreadsheet Window

If your spreadsheet is very large, you may want to view two different, non-adjacent sections at one time. Splitting the spreadsheet window into separate window panes resolves this problem.

1. Scroll so that Column A is displayed on the screen.

2. Without pressing the mouse button, move the pointer slowly over the vertical pane control, the black rectangle between the tool box icon and the left horizontal scroll arrow at the bottom of the window. In Figure 5-15, the vertical pane control is below the crossbar.

3. The pointer should change to a crossbar with arrows on each side. This crossbar is the Split Pane tool.

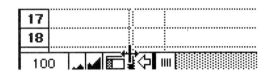

4. Press and hold the mouse button when you see the **Split Pane tool**, the crossbar with the left and right arrows. Double vertical lines extend up the screen from the tool.

5. Drag, releasing the mouse button when the Split Pane tool is on the line that separates the columns Quiz 1 and Quiz 2. This splits the spreadsheet window into two panes. Notice that each pane has its own horizontal scroll bar.

6. Scroll the right pane by using the horizontal scroll bar. The portion of the spreadsheet on the right moves while the left pane stays in place.

7. Use the two scroll bars to see how views of the spreadsheet can change.

8. Now, drag the horizontal pane control, the black rectangle beneath the title bar on the right, down about seven rows. This splits the screen horizontally into two panes. Now there are four panes on the screen, as in Figure 5-16. Various sections of the spreadsheet can be viewed by using the horizontal and vertical scroll bars for the panes.

9. Use the four scroll bars to change the views of the spreadsheet in different ways.

10. Remove the split panes by dragging each double line to an edge of the spreadsheet and releasing the mouse button.

FIGURE 5-15

The vertical pane control is the solid black bar beside the scroll arrow at the bottom of the screen. The double vertical lines and the crossbar indicate where the screen will be split.

FIGURE 5-16

The spreadsheet is split vertically and horizontally. There are a total of four panes on the screen, each of which are controlled by a vertical and horizontal scroll bar.

	A	B	C	D	E	F	G	H
1	Names	Quiz 1	Quiz 2	Quiz 3	Test 1	Test 2	Total Pts	Average
2	Johnson, Sara	10	9	9	87	93	208	88.5%
3	Chu, Arnold	15	9	8	97	100	229	97.4%
4	Brown, John	13	9	7	97	80	206	87.7%
5	Castle, Sandy	12	8	7	84	95	206	87.7%
6	Getful, For	5	3	2	56	61	127	54.0%
7	Zimmerman, Chris	12	9	10	77	73	181	77.0%
8	Kimmel, Ann	9	10	9	90	91	209	88.9%
9	Gonzales, Rita	11	8	9	79	78	185	78.7%
10	Lambert, Cheryl	14	9	8	89	85	205	87.2%
11	Smith, John	8	6	7	95	90	206	87.7%
12								
13	Total Points	15	10	10	100	100	235	
14	Average Points	10.9	8	7.6	85.1	84.6	196.2	83.5%
15								
16		10						
17								
18								

File Edit Format Calculate Options View   10:15 AM

Gradebook (SS)

B1   Quiz 1

ClarisWorks allows you to have up to three horizontal and three vertical panes for a total of nine possible panes. For a very large spreadsheet this would allow you to vew various related data at one time. The option of creating panes is also available in other types of documents.

Sorting

Sometimes you may want to sort information in a spreadsheet much as you did in the database. The class in the Gradebook spreadsheet can be sorted alphabetically by name or numerically by any one of the grades.

1. Make sure all panes have been removed and Lock Title Position is deselected. Select the range of cells from Cell A2 through Cell H11, or through the last cell containing a student average. Do not include the Total Points or Average Points at the bottom of the spreadsheet.

2. From the Calculate menu choose **Sort...** to see the Sort dialog box, as shown in Figure 5-17.

   The Sort dialog box displays the range of cells selected. In Figure 5-17 the Order Keys indicate that the sort will be made in ascending order, meaning from smaller to larger or from A to Z, starting with Cell A2. Vertical indicates that items in a column are to be sorted, in this case Column A. A's will be at the top and Z's will be at the bottom.

   Notice that more than one column can be used in the sort. This is useful if cell contents are not unique. For instance, if two columns are used, items that are identical in the first column are arranged in the order of the items in the second sort column.

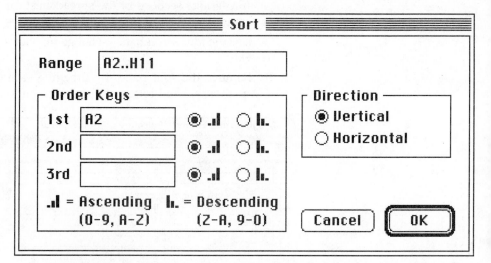

FIGURE 5-17

The Sort dialog box. You may choose up to three levels of sorting with options of ascending or descending order for each. You may also change the direction of the sort from vertical to horizontal.

3. Click OK or press Return to accept the sort. The names are rearranged in alphabetical order. (Scroll, if necessary, to see them.)

4. While the cells are still selected, choose Sort... from the Calculate menu again.

5. Double-click **A2** in the first Order Keys box to select it.

6. Type **H2**. The sort order will now be based on Column H.

7. Click on the button for descending order.

8. Click OK. The class should now be sorted by their averages.

9. To change the class back to alphabetical order, sort again or select Undo Sort from the Edit menu. Undo Sort should place the spreadsheet back in alphabetical order. Remember, only the most recent change can be undone.

10. Click any cell to deselect the range of cells that are highlighted.

Keep in mind that only selected cells will be included in the sort process. If you select only cells in Column A, the names will be sorted, but the scores in other columns will remain unchanged—students will have each other's scores. If this happens, try to undo the sort immediately, or close the document without saving and reopen the document to return to the last saved version.

Printing a Spreadsheet

Several options are available for printing your spreadsheet. Print… from the File menu will print the portion of the spreadsheet that has data. Set Print Range… from the Options menu will allow you to select a range of the spreadsheet cells to be printed. Before printing, it might be useful to change the way the spreadsheet is displayed.

CHANGING THE DISPLAY

Earlier in this chapter the display of the spreadsheet was changed to show formulas. Other options are also available from the Display… command on the Options menu. The spreadsheet grid can be solid lines rather than dotted lines or it can be completely hidden. Column and row headings (A, B, C, … and 1, 2, 3, …) can be removed and circular references (references that refer back to the same cell) can be identified. For printing purposes, hide the cell grid with the following steps:

1. From the Options menu select Display… to see the Display dialog box, as shown in Figure 5-18.

2. Click Cell grid to remove the X from the Cell grid box.

3. Click OK. The cell grid should no longer be displayed on the screen. It also will not be printed.

FIGURE 5-18

The Display dialog box controls what is displayed and printed with the spreadsheet. Notice you may remove the cell grid, column headings, and row headings if you wish.

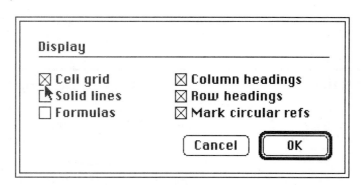

USING PAGE SETUP AND PRINTING

Depending on your system, you may need to turn on your printer, to use Chooser to select your printer, or to otherwise prepare for printing. Once your printer is ready to print, these steps will print your spreadsheet.

1. From the File menu select Page Setup… to see the Page Setup dialog box.

2. Click the landscape (horizontal) orientation of the paper, as shown in Figure 5-19. This prints the spreadsheet sideways on the paper.

3. Click OK.

FIGURE 5-19

The Page Setup dialog box with the landscape (horizontal) orientation chosen. This will vary depending on your printer.

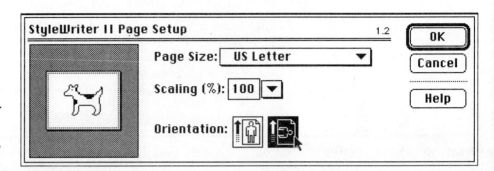

4. Select Print... from the File menu to print the entire spreadsheet. (Caution: If you did not clear Cell W45 and the range of Cells N17 through R20 in the "Selecting Cells" section of this chapter, these cells will also print, along with all the empty cells to the left of, and above, them. You will have pages of empty cells. In this case, you should select the cells to be printed and choose Print Range... from the Options menu.)

5. Click OK or press Return. The spreadsheet should be printed.

6. The spreadsheet can be closed when you are finished. Do not save it, or if you wish to save it, cancel and use Save As... from the Edit menu to save the document with a new name before closing it.

Creating a New Spreadsheet

After working with two spreadsheets, you should now be ready to create your own. In this section you will create a spreadsheet to keep track of students' progress during a special Reading Month promotion and use it to practice some of the skills you learned in the previous sections.

1. Choose New... from the File menu.

2. Click on Spreadsheet.

3. Click OK. A blank spreadsheet grid should appear on the screen.

More Practice

Practice the skills you have learned so far by entering data into the new spreadsheet.

1. Enter headings and values like the ones listed in Figure 5-20. Use the Tab and arrow keys to move around in the spreadsheet.

2. In Cell F3, type **Total** as the heading for this column.

3. In Cell F4, type **=SUM(B4..E4)** and press Return. This formula will add the total number of books read during the four weeks of the promotion to get a final total for Joe.

4. Copy the formula in F4 to Cells F5 through F7. (Hint: Highlight the cells from F4 to F7 then use the Fill Down command on the Calculate menu.)

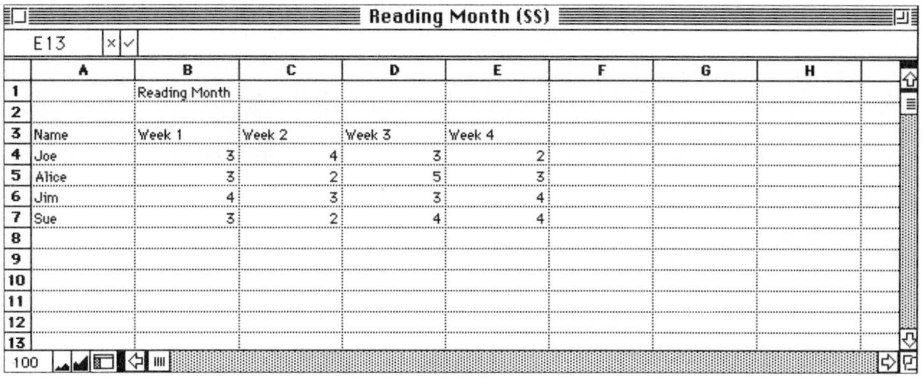

Reading Month (SS)

E13

	A	B	C	D	E	F	G	H
1		Reading Month						
2								
3	Name	Week 1	Week 2	Week 3	Week 4			
4	Joe	3	4	3	2			
5	Alice	3	2	5	3			
6	Jim	4	3	3	4			
7	Sue	3	2	4	4			
8								
9								
10								
11								
12								
13								

100

FIGURE 5-20

The Reading Month spreadsheet with the number of books read per week listed for four students in the class.

5. In Column G calculate each individual's weekly average. Use the Average function.
6. Change the format for the average to Fixed with a precision of one decimal place. (Hint: Use Number... on the Format menu.)
7. Calculate a weekly class average and put it in Row 9.
8. Sort the class alphabetically by name and then by total number of books read.
9. Expand the spreadsheet to include more students and the number of books read for additional weeks.
10. Change the way the spreadsheet is displayed and print it.
11. When you are finished, save your spreadsheet as Reading Month and keep it open.

Using Chart Options

The **chart** feature of ClarisWorks provides a means of graphing the values on a spreadsheet. When you create a chart it becomes a part of the spreadsheet document—a graphic object that can be moved to any position in the document, can be cut or copied, and can be pasted within the same document or into another document. To save a chart you simply save the spreadsheet document that it is in.

There are 12 different types of charts to choose from within ClarisWorks, as shown in Figure 5-21. The choice of a chart type depends on the data being represented and the audience who will view the chart. In the following exercises, a bar chart and a stacked bar chart will be created from the Reading Month spreadsheet created in the previous practice session. Your chart may vary from the ones pictured in the figures depending on the order of the data in your spreadsheet when you finished the previous section.

CREATING A BAR CHART

1. Select Cells A3 through E7.
2. Choose **Make Chart...** from the Options menu to view the Chart Options dialog box, as shown in Figure 5-21. Notice that currently the gallery of chart types is being displayed.
3. Select the Bar icon to create a bar chart, if it is not already selected.
4. Click OK. The chart displayed should be similar to the chart in Figure 5-22.

FIGURE 5-21

The Chart Options dialog box with Gallery options chosen. Notice that you may choose a variety of charts and also whether to display in color, horizontally, shadow, or 3-dimensional. Buttons on the left portion of the dialog box provide easy access to modify other sections of the chart.

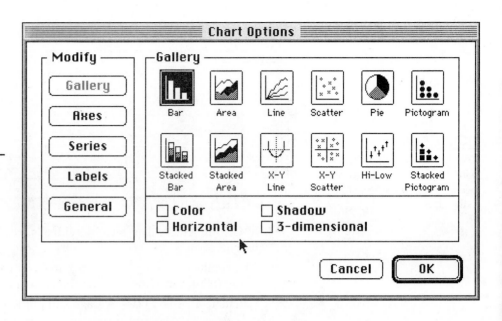

FIGURE 5-22

A bar chart representing the Reading Month data. The diagram indicates the spreadsheet data used for the different parts of the chart.

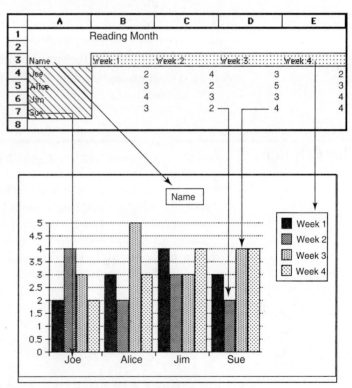

MODIFYING A CHART TITLE AND LEGEND

In the chart, each student's book totals are graphed for each week. Figure 5-22 illustrates how the spreadsheet information is used in the chart. Labels on the chart are appropriately placed. However, the title of the chart itself is Name and the chart covers part of the spreadsheet. You can change the title and move the position of the title and the legend by using the **Modify Chart...** command on the Options menu.

1. From the Options menu, select Modify Chart... to view the Chart Options menu.
2. Click Labels to see the chart options for labels. Figure 5-23 shows the dialog box with edited label information.
3. Type **Weekly Book Total** for the title.
4. The position of the title and the legend are indicated in diagrams. The title is in the center above the chart. On the legend placement icon, click on the middle right circle, as shown in Figure 5-23, to move the legend down.
5. Click OK. The legend has been moved and the title has changed.

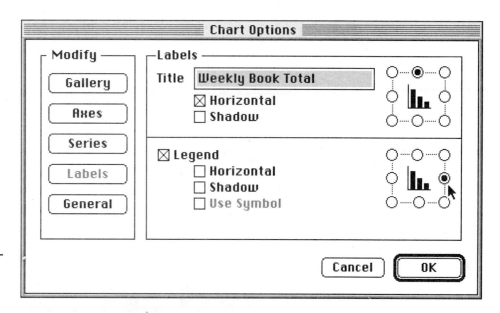

FIGURE 5-23

The Chart Options dialog box displaying options for chart labels.

6. Click on the chart title to select it.
7. From the Format menu, change the size of type to 12 and the style to Bold.
8. Click anywhere off the title. This selects the entire chart.

CHANGING CHART SIZE AND LOCATION

You can also resize the chart and move it to a new location.

1. With the chart selected, drag one of the handles (the small black boxes in the corners) with the arrow pointer to make the chart smaller. Scale Selection... and Object Size... on the Options menu can also be used to change the chart size. (See Chapter 3 for further reference.)
2. Drag the chart to an area of the spreadsheet where there is no data by placing the arrow pointer anywhere except on the handles and dragging.
3. Change one of the numbers on the spreadsheet. The chart should also change.

A chart may be cut, copied, duplicated, or pasted in the same document or another document. However, on the pasted or duplicated copies the values are no longer linked to the spreadsheet, so changes in the spreadsheet will not be reflected in the chart.

CREATING A STACKED BAR CHART

Multiple charts can be made using the same spreadsheet. Make a stacked bar chart using the following steps.

1. Click anywhere on the spreadsheet (not the chart) to select the spreadsheet.
2. Select the the range of Cells A3 to E7 in the Reading Month spreadsheet.
3. Choose Make Chart… from the Options menu.
4. Select Stacked Bar.
5. Click Labels.
6. Type **Reading Totals** for the title.
7. Click OK. Figure 5-24 shows the stacked bar chart. Information is displayed for each week with each student in a different color or pattern. Notice that data from each row is in each stack.

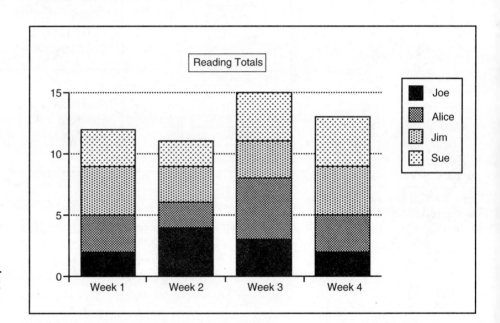

FIGURE 5-24

The stacked bar chart displaying reading totals for each student by week.

MODIFYING CHART SERIES

The chart can be modified to display a stack for each student with weekly totals in different colors or patterns. It can also be modified to label the number of books read in each piece of the stack.

1. With the Reading Totals chart still selected, from the Options menu choose Modify Chart… to see the Chart Options dialog box.
2. Click General to see the General options for a stacked bar chart displayed in the Chart Options dialog box. The chart shown in Figure 5-25 was made with Series in Rows. This means a value from each of the rows of the spreadsheet is in each stack. The Series names also show that Joe, Alice, Jim, and Sue are in each stack.
3. Click on Series in Columns.
4. Click OK. The data should now be displayed with a stack for each student. Data from each column is in every stack.

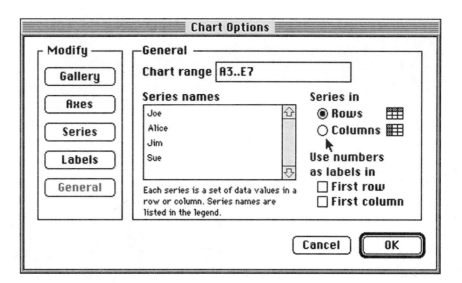

FIGURE 5-25

The Chart Options dialog box with General Options chosen. Options are given to change the chart range, the series from rows to columns and to use the first row or column as labels in the chart.

5. Now choose Modify Chart… from the Options menu to see the Chart Options dialog box.

6. Click Series to see the Series options displayed in the Chart Options dialog box, as shown in Figure 5-26.

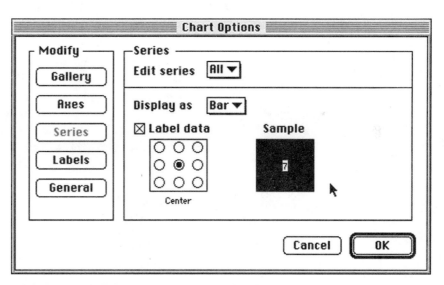

FIGURE 5-26

The Chart Options dialog box with Series Options chosen. Notice that there is an option here to label the data in the bar chart and to choose where the label will be located.

7. Click on Label data. This indicates that labels will be placed in each pat-terned area of the stack in the diagrammed position.

8. Click OK. The chart should now have the numbers printed within the chart areas, as shown in Figure 5-27.

PRACTICE WITH CHARTS

Although the charts are relatively simple, they do give you a means of easily graphing the data from your spreadsheet. Practice what you have learned here by making bar charts from other spreadsheets and making other charts from the Reading Month spreadsheet. There are too many charting possibilities to be covered in this book, but they all use similar dialog boxes for chart options and modifications.

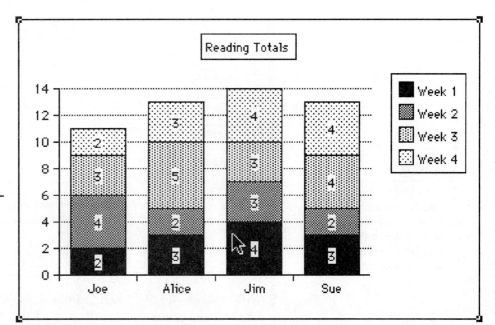

FIGURE 5-27

The stacked bar chart displayed with each student's total for each week in a different shade of gray and labeled. This was done by choosing Series in Columns from the GeneralOptions and choosing Label Data in the Series Options.

Drag the current chart off to the side of the spreadsheet and do the exercises below. Remember to select the range of cells you wish to chart with the spreadsheet tool before selecting Make Chart....

1. Create the bar chart for the Reading Month spreadsheet again. Modify it to display a series by week rather than by student. (Hint: Use the General option of the Chart Options dialog box to put the series in rows.)

2. Some charts will be more meaningful and useful than others, depending on what information is being used and why it is being used. Modify the Reading Month chart to make it an area chart, then a line chart. Try each of these with the series in rows and the series in columns. Which of the four types—bar, stacked bar, area, or line—with which series would be most useful for looking at the individual performance of each student? Which for the performance of the class as a whole?

3. Try making a pie chart of the same data. What happens? Do whatever is necessary to make the pie chart. Would this be a useful chart? What could the chart best be used for?

4. Select a different range of cells, B3 through F7. Make a bar chart of this data. Does it work? Is it meaningful data?

5. Select other ranges, such as the totals for the week or the totals for the students, or use data from other spreadsheets. Try making charts of various kinds for these. What purposes might you have for the various charts?

CLASSROOM ◄————► CONNECTION

Use a spreadsheet to record data for a class project—keeping track of the high and low temperature each day, each student's height in inches, or even the results of a science experiment. Use formulas to calculate appropriate information about the data such as the average high temperature and average low temperature for the week. Sort the data to determine largest or smallest values. Chart the data. Experiment with different types of charts. Have students help determine which charts most effectively present a graphical picture of the data.

Creating a Grid Form

There are many occasions when a form needs to be created that has grid-type lines for individuals to fill in various items of information, as in Figure 5-28. Although this entire form could be created in a word processing document with draw tools, you will have more flexibility if you create the heading in word processing and then add a spreadsheet frame to make the various regions for data. Creating a frame is a way of setting up an area within a document to use tools from another type of ClarisWorks application. This method can also be used to create a table of contents at the beginning of a book or paper.

Follow the steps below to create a form on which book information can be written, as shown in Figure 5-28.

SETTING UP A HEADING

1. Choose New… from the File Menu.
2. Click OK to choose Word Processing when the New Document dialog box appears.

Race to Read

Name _____

Book Title	Author	Type	Pages

FIGURE 5-28

A form has been created for listing books read using the spreadsheet to create the grid of lines.

3. Click on the Center Alignment icon in the shaded portion of the ruler.
4. From the Size menu choose 24 Point.
5. From the Style menu choose Bold.
6. Type the following with two Returns at the end:

   Race to Read
7. Click on the Left alignment icon. Change the type size to 18 point.
8. Type the following with one Return at the end:

   Name _____

CREATING A SPREADSHEET FRAME

A **frame** is a section of a document in which another ClarisWorks application is used. On the screen it looks almost like a separate window, but it has no title bar or close box. Like a graphic object, a frame can be selected, moved, resized, or deleted. Inside the frame, the tools for the application work just as they would in a document for that application. For instance, in a paint frame, the Paint tools are used exactly as they are in a paint document. (See Chapter 3 for further reference.) By using the appropriate tools, a frame for any application can be placed in any other application. In this case an area of the word processing document is going to be used for a spreadsheet frame.

1. Click on the Show Tools control at the bottom of the screen or from the View menu choose Show Tools.

2. Click on the **Spreadsheet tool** (the plus sign) in the tool palette as shown in Figure 5-29.

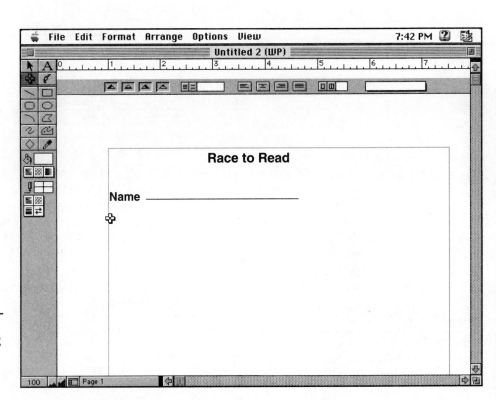

FIGURE 5-29

The Spreadsheet tool has been chosen within a word processing document to create a spreadsheet frame that will provide the grid for the form.

3. Position the plus sign pointer about a half inch below the name at the left edge of the paper.

4. Drag across to the right edge of the paper and down to the bottom of the page. This creates a **spreadsheet frame**. Notice that the menu bar now contains spreadsheet menu items.

5. Use the vertical and horizontal scroll bars to move to the upper left area of the frame. The screen should look similar to Figure 5-30.

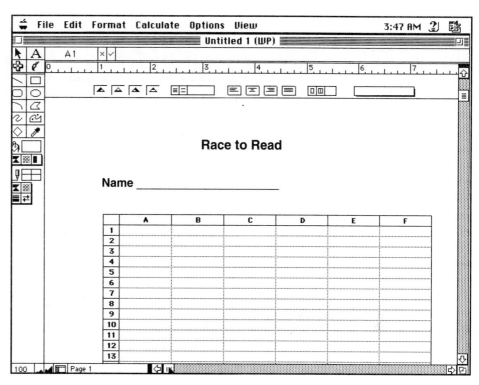

FIGURE 5-30

A spreadsheet frame has been created within a word processing document using the Spreadsheet tool.

EDITING IN A SPREADSHEET FRAME

1. Select Column A by clicking on A at the top of the column.
2. From the Format Menu choose Column Width…. As shown in Figure 5-31, the present width of Column A is 72 points or 1 inch.
3. Type **200** and click OK.

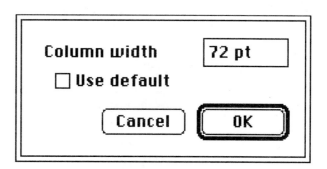

FIGURE 5-31

The Column width dialog box provides a means of changing the width of selected columns.

4. Select Column B by clicking on B at the top of the column.
5. From the Format Menu choose Column Width….
6. Type **120** and click OK.
7. Repeat Steps 4 and 5 to set the width of Column C to 90 points.
8. Select Columns A, B, C, and D by dragging across all their column headers. (Even though you can't see the D in Column D, you can drag onto the header space to select the column.)
9. From the Format menu choose Row Height… to see a Row height dialog box similar to the Column width dialog box.

10. Type **18** and click OK.

11. While Columns A, B, C, and D are still selected, from the Format Menu choose Size and 14 Point.

12. Click on Cell A1 and type **Book Title**.

13. Press the Tab key to move to Cell B1.

14. Type **Author**.

15. Press the Tab key to move to Cell C1.

16. Type the word **Type**.

17. Press the Tab key to move to Cell D1.

18. Type **Pages**.

19. Press Return. Note that the whole word Pages isn't displayed now; it will be displayed when all of the steps are completed.

20. From the Options menu choose Display... to see the spreadsheet Display dialog box, as shown in Figure 5-30.

21. Click on Column headings and Row headings to deselect them. This keeps the row and column labels from being displayed (or printed). Notice that other options are available at this point as well, if they are desired.

22. Click OK to accept the changes and continue.

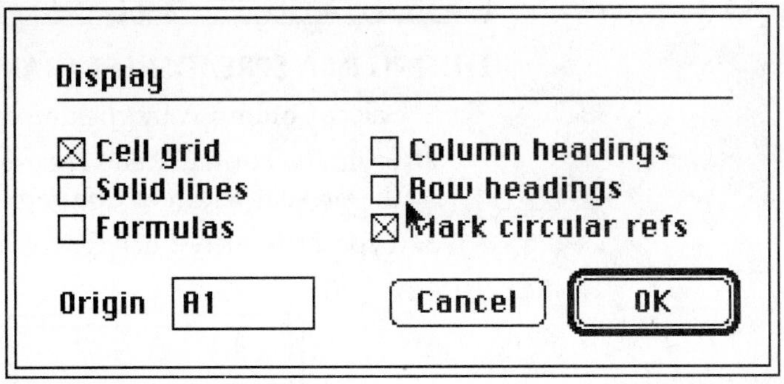

FIGURE 5-32

The Display dialog box with display of column headings and row headings deselected. This will print the grid without the labels at the top and the sides. Selecting solid lines would give solid lines rather than dashed lines for the grid.

```
┌─────────────────────────────────────────────┐
│  ┌───────────────────────────────────────┐  │
│  │ Display                               │  │
│  │ ─────────────────────────────────────│  │
│  │ ⊠ Cell grid      □ Column headings    │  │
│  │ □ Solid lines    □ Row headings       │  │
│  │ □ Formulas       ⊠ Mark circular refs │  │
│  │                                       │  │
│  │ Origin  [ A1    ]   (Cancel)  ( OK )  │  │
│  └───────────────────────────────────────┘  │
└─────────────────────────────────────────────┘
```

REMOVING A FRAME OUTLINE

Currently the frame is outlined with a fine solid line. This can be removed with the following steps.

1. Use the horizontal scroll box to move to the left margin of the sheet so that the Book Title area is in view.

2. Click on the Graphics tool (the arrow) in the tool palette.

3. Click on the edge of the spreadsheet. A handle, a small black square, should appear in the corner above **Book Title** to indicate that the spreadsheet is selected.

4. From the Pen tools hold down the Line width tool, as shown in Figure 5-33.

5. Select None. This eliminates the box drawn around the entire spreadsheet.

6. Zoom out to 50 percent. Your form should look like Figure 5-34.

7. You are now ready to print your form. Choose Print... from the File menu. When the printer dialog box appears click OK to print your document.

8. The document may now be saved and closed.

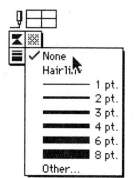

FIGURE 5-33

The size of the line around the frame of the spreadsheet is controlled by the Line width tool. When none is selected, there is no line around the frame.

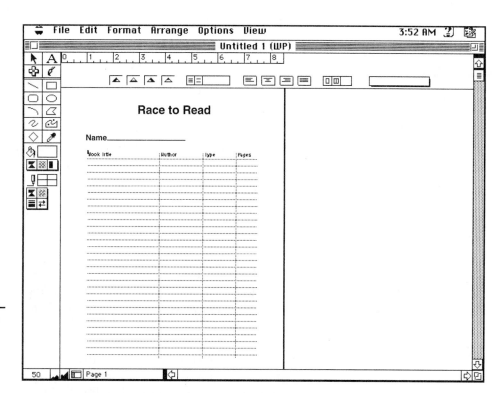

FIGURE 5-34

The finished Race to Read form at 50 percent of its normal size. Notice the zoom percentage box in the lower left corner of the screen indicates 50.

Using a spreadsheet frame can make creating a list-type of form easy. No longer is it necessary to use a ruler to create horizontal and vertical lines within a form. A spreadsheet makes it simple to change column width and row height to create any size grid on a form.

CLASSROOM ←——→ CONNECTION

Use a spreadsheet to make a seating chart for your class or to divide them into groups. Make the rows about 70 points high and the columns about 116 points wide. Make the font size 16 points and use a landscape (horizontal) orientation for the page. Simply type the names in each cell. Use the top cells for group names if you are using groups. When you wish to make a change, simply retype the names. Experiment with row, column, and font sizes that work for the size of class that you have.

Conclusion

There are many things you can do with spreadsheets beyond those you have experimented with in this chapter. Using a spreadsheet can ease the drudgery of keeping up with various budgeting and record keeping that is required in school classrooms and clubs, and even in personal finances. Because changes in cell information are reflected in any related cells, a spreadsheet makes it easy to do recalculations when a figure or a formula changes in some way. The number or formula can be changed and everything else will reflect those changes automatically. Practice and experiment using a spreadsheet—as you become more comfortable with it you will wonder how you ever got along without it.

KEY TERMS

absolute cell reference
Accept button
address box
Average function
Calculate menu
Cancel button
cell
cell address
cell format
cell name
cell reference
chart

column
Display…
entry bar
Fill Down
Fill Right
formula
frame
function
Go to Cell…
Insert Cells…
Lock Title Position
Make Chart…

Modify Chart…
Number…
Options menu
Paste Function…
range
relative cell reference
row
Sort…
Split Pane tool
spreadsheet frame
Spreadsheet tool
Sum function

EXERCISES

1. Create a spreadsheet that will calculate the average yards per carry for the football team, given the number of yards gained by each individual on each play. Include the players' names, number of yards gained, number of carries, and average number of yards per carry.

2. Create a spreadsheet to use as a demonstration tool for calculating the area of a rectangle. Use one column for the length and one for the width. Use the formula to calculate the area. Use this tool to show what happens to the area if only the length is doubled, if only the width is doubled, and if both length and width are doubled. Do the same with tripling the dimensions. (Note: This could be done with any similar type of shape or formula.)

3. Create a spreadsheet that will maintain a small school supply budget. Begin with the yearly allocation of money and subtract as each item is purchased. Include the order number, date, item(s) ordered, company, and total for each entry.

4. Create a spreadsheet that either students or a teacher can use to keep track of the number of books each student has read for a report period. Have the students type in the number of books at the end of each week. The spreadsheet should be set up so that it automatically calculates the total.

5. Create a spreadsheet as a tool in a probability demonstration in which groups of students throw one or two dice a given number of times (50 or more) and record the results. Set up the spreadsheet to sum the results within each group and calculate the percentages when students enter the results. (This could also be done with coin tosses.)

6

ClarisWorks— Additional Features

Introduction

In this chapter you will see some of the additional features that are available in ClarisWorks. First, you will be introduced to ClarisWorks Stationery and ClarisWorks Assistants. These tools permit the novice user to create impressive documents with little or no instruction.

ClarisWorks Stationery is simply a collection of templates that have been preset for you to add your own information. You may select text and retype the text you wish to use. After doing one sample, you should be able to work with any of the stationery instruments to create interesting and complex documents. These may be used for personal as well as educational use. There are stationery instruments for creating a home budget, tracking investments, and even analyzing a mortgage. All the formulas are already set; you simply type in the values you wish to use. You may also create your own stationery documents.

ClarisWorks Assistants guide you through the steps of performing certain tasks. For the novice, creating an envelope can be simplified by answering questions within the Assistant. Assistants can be used when creating a new document or from the ? (Guide) menu within an existing document.

The following sections will step you through the process of using stationery to create a certificate and an assistant to create a calendar. Once you have tried using these features, you will find it very easy to work with the other types of documents available.

The second part of this chapter deals with creating communications documents. Using a computer, modem, and telephone line, teachers can communicate with each other and with experts in various fields throughout the world. The communications portion of this chapter will introduce you to not only the creation of communications documents but also the various other ways that telecommunications can be used.

Telecommunications has become a new buzzword in education. In reality, telecommunications is affecting the business and social segments of our world. In many areas telecommunications is also affecting the education of our children. In the future, telecommunications may make a profound difference in the way our children learn. Children will be able to view themselves as a part of a global society rather than merely a member of their classroom or their community. They will be able to see how events in different areas of the world affect them and their future.

Using ClarisWorks Stationery

You can automate your work by using ClarisWorks **Stationery** when creating certain kinds of documents. These documents, sometimes called **templates**, are already set up with standard text, graphic images, and formatting. You simply use the stationery and customize the text to suit your needs. A variety of stationery documents is available with ClarisWorks. Some examples include certificates, a newsletter, an expense report, invitations, a letterhead, a meeting agenda, resumes, and a to-do list.

You also have the option to create your own stationery documents. Stationery can be a standard letter, your own stationery, a flyer, or any other similar document. You can create stationery documents as templates for students to use when working on a particular assignment. When a stationery document is opened, it opens as an untitled document. This leaves the original stationery document intact, ready to be opened again at some other time. Stationery can be used to create a story starter, a lab report spreadsheet, or even a database format for students to use in reporting data. When students open a stationery document, they may make modifications and then save the document with a new name. This allows other students to begin with the same document and modify it to create their own interpretation of the assignment.

In this section you will create a certificate for an Outstanding Student Award using ClarisWorks Stationery. After going through this lesson, you may wish to try some other stationery options.

1. Launch the ClarisWorks program if it is not already open.

2. Choose New from the File menu. The New Document dialog box should appear on the screen.

3. Click on the check box in front of Use Assistant or Stationery. You should see a category list above the list box as shown in Figure 6-1.

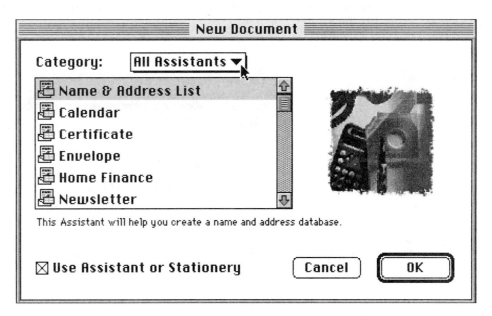

FIGURE 6-1

When Use Assistant or Stationery is checked in the New Document dialog box, a listing of available Assistant or Stationery documents appears. In this example, the category is All Assistants so there are Assistants documents listed. Other categories may be selected to display a different set of documents.

4. The Category currently is All Assistants. Click on the triangle to the right of All Assistants to see your other choices. Choose All Stationery. Notice that you also have the option of choosing by selective categories such as Business, Home, and Internet (see Figure 6-2).

5. From the stationery names that appear choose Certificate A. You should see a document that looks similar to Figure 6-3.

   Notice that the document name is Untitled 1 (or some other number if you have continued working from another section). You will now make the changes necessary to create an Outstanding Student Award.

6. Click on the text tool (the letter A) on the tool palette. (If the tool palette is not visible, click on the Show/Hide Tools icon at the bottom of the page or choose Show Tools from the View menu.)

7. Click to the left of the "C" and drag to select the words "Community Service." Type the words **Outstanding Student** to replace the selected words.

FIGURE 6-2

Several categories are available when Use Assistant or Stationery is checked in the New Document dialog box. In this example, All Stationery has been chosen and the stationery documents are displayed in the window.

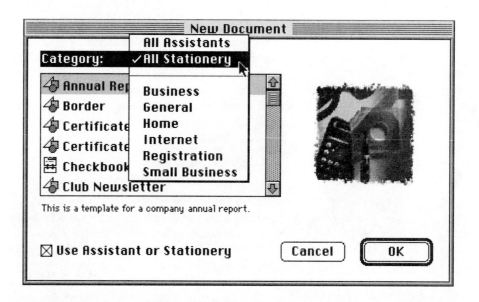

FIGURE 6-3

The stationery document Certificate A opens to display the document shown here. Because this is a stationery document, it opens as Untitled 1.

8. Click and drag to select the name "Vincent Powell" and replace it with your name or the name of a student in your class.

9. Click and drag to select the words "volunteer work" and replace them with the word **service.**

10. Replace "the Fourth Street Shelter" with your school name.

11. Change the date to today's date.

12. You may now save or print the certificate you have created.

There are endless possibilities for creating certificates. You may wish to take a look at the Certificate B stationery document for another type of certificate. Working with other stationery documents is very similar to creating this document. You will open the document, select and change the portions of the document that are unique to your situation, then save the document with your own name and print it if you wish.

You may also create your own stationery documents that include your own particular settings, text, graphics, and formats. When you open the document as a stationery document, you are opening a copy of the document while the original remains unchanged.

1. Create a document you wish to use as stationery. If you do not have a specific document in mind, try a general form letter for a field trip or an awards assembly.

2. Choose Save from the File menu.

3. Click in the radio button in front of Stationery as shown in Figure 6-4. Notice that the folder the document is to be saved in is the ClarisWorks Stationery folder. The document must be stored in this folder in order to pull it up automatically from the New Document dialog box. (If the document is stored somewhere else, you will have to choose Open from the File menu to open the document. It will still open Untitled and leave the original document intact.)

FIGURE 6-4

The Save dialog box with stationery chosen. Notice that when stationery is chosen, the ClarisWorks Stationery folder is chosen for the Save location. If you change to another folder, the stationery document will be available through an Open command rather than through the New Document dialog box. In this example the stationery document has been named Memo.

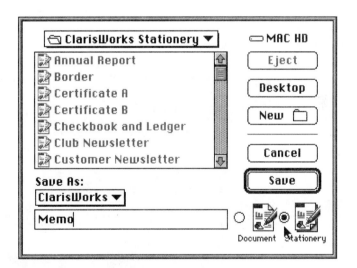

4. Click Save to save your stationery document.

5. A Document Summary dialog box should appear as shown in Figure 6-5. Here you may enter information about the document, especially its name, description, and category. If you do not use a category, ClarisWorks automatically assigns it to the General category. You may use the existing categories or you may create your own.

6. Click OK after completing the Document Summary dialog box.

You may wish to take the time now to try a few other ClarisWorks stationery options. A variety of documents is available for personal or school uses.

Document Summary

Title:

Author: | Carol Youngs

Version:

Keywords:

Category: | Business

Description:

Cancel   OK

FIGURE 6-5

The Document Summary dialog box with the author and category information entered. This dialog box allows you to enter information about a stationery document.

Using ClarisWorks Assistants

Although stationery can be a big help to you in creating documents, so can Assistants. ClarisWorks **Assistants** guide you through the steps of creating a document or a feature within a document. By simply answering the questions posed, you create the feature or document of your choice. ClarisWorks Assistants are available for several features, including a Name and Address List, Calendar, Certificate, and Envelope. Assistants can be called on from within an existing document by choosing ClarisWorks Assistants... from the ? or Guide menu.

One item many teachers like to use is a calendar. Various programs are available to create calendars, but ClarisWorks has an Assistant that will guide you through the process.

    1. From the File menu, choose New.

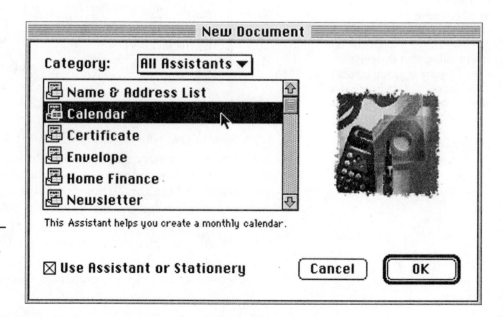

New Document

Category: [All Assistants ▼]

- Name & Address List
- **Calendar**
- Certificate
- Envelope
- Home Finance
- Newsletter

This Assistant helps you create a monthly calendar.

☒ **Use Assistant or Stationery**   Cancel   OK

FIGURE 6-6

The New Document dialog box with Use Assistant or Stationery checked. From the list of All Assistants, Calendar has been chosen.

2. Click on the check box in front of Use Assistant or Stationery. You should see a category list above the dialog box.

3. The Category currently is All Stationery. Click on the triangle to the right of All Stationery to see your other choices. Choose All Assistants.

4. You should see a list of Assistants. Choose Calendar as shown in Figure 6-6 and click OK.

5. The Calendar Assistant screen should appear. Click Next to continue.

   The next screen allows you to choose the month, year, and the number of months to display. You may also choose the font, how the weekends display, and whether the year is printed on the calendar.

6. Click on the triangle beside the current month to bring all the months into view. Choose March of the current year.

7. Click Create.

8. You should see a calendar displayed similar to Figure 6-7.

   If you have completed Chapter 5, you will probably recognize this document as a spreadsheet. The spreadsheet features are all available in this document as they were in the spreadsheet exercises in Chapter 5.

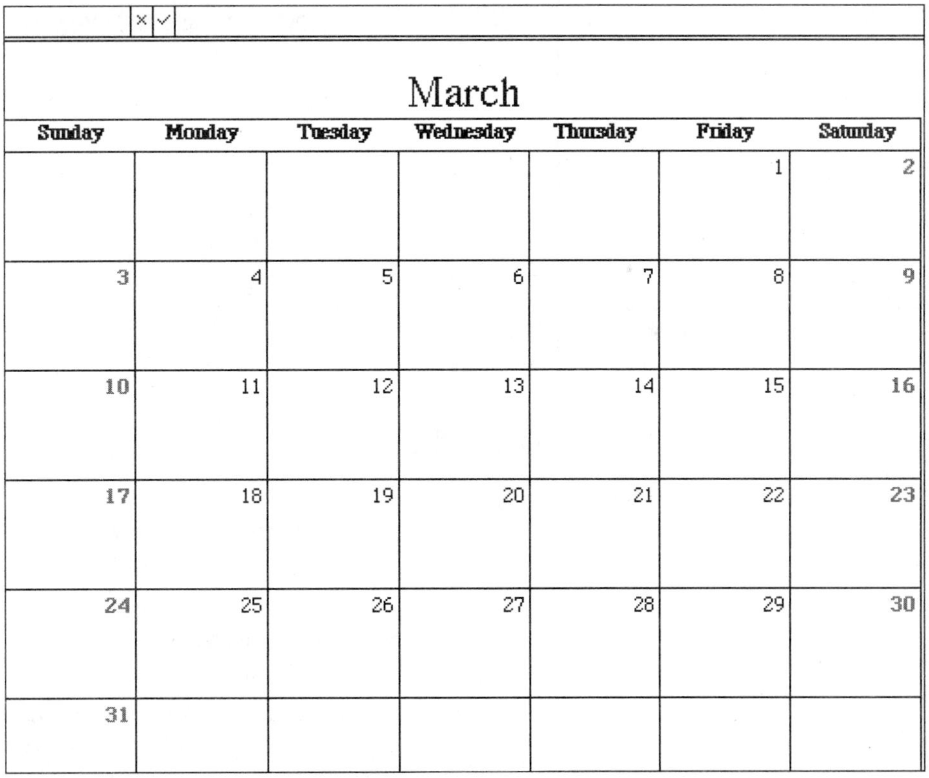

March						
Sunday	Monday	Tuesday	Wednesday	Thursday	Friday	Saturday
					1	2
3	4	5	6	7	8	9
10	11	12	13	14	15	16
17	18	19	20	21	22	23
24	25	26	27	28	29	30
31						

FIGURE 6-7

The March calendar has been created using Assistants. Additional details can be added by clicking in the lower portion of any date.

9. Click in the bottom portion of the date March 17 and type **St. Patrick's Day.**

10. Press the Return key to enter the text in the cell. Text can be entered in the bottom portion of any date in the same manner.

11. You may also wish to add a graphic image to the calendar. From the File menu choose Library and from the submenu that appears choose Events & Holidays.

12. The Events & Holidays palette should appear on the screen. Place the pointer on the title bar of the palette and drag it to the right so it will be out of the way.

13. Use the vertical scroll bar on the Events & Holidays palette to bring St. Patrick's Day into view.

14. Click once on St. Patrick's Day to select it, then click Use.

15. A shamrock should appear on the screen with handles to indicate that it is selected. However, the shamrock appears to be too large to use in the calendar. To make it smaller, from the Arrange menu choose Transform and from the submenu that appears, choose Scale by Percent... as shown in Figure 6-8.

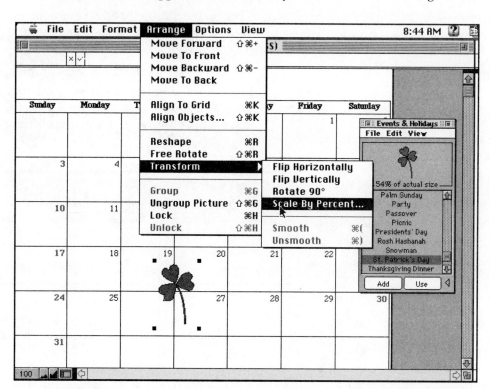

FIGURE 6-8

The size of the selected shamrock is being changed by using the Scale by Percent... option. It could also be resized by dragging the selection handles.

16. The Scale by Percent dialog box should appear. Type **35** for the horizontal percentage, press the Tab key, then type **35** for the vertical percentage.

17. Click OK. The shamrock should now appear much smaller.

18. Click on the shamrock (but not on the handles) and drag it to the March 17 cell. Place it where is does not cover the text or the date. Your calendar should look similar to Figure 6-9.

19. You may now practice adding text or graphics to the other dates on the calendar. You may add field trips, conferences, special assemblies, or other items of interest such as students' birthdays. Check the other graphic images available in the various Library palettes or add images that you have created by cutting and pasting.

20. When you finish, you may save your calendar on your Data Disk and print it by choosing Print from the File menu.

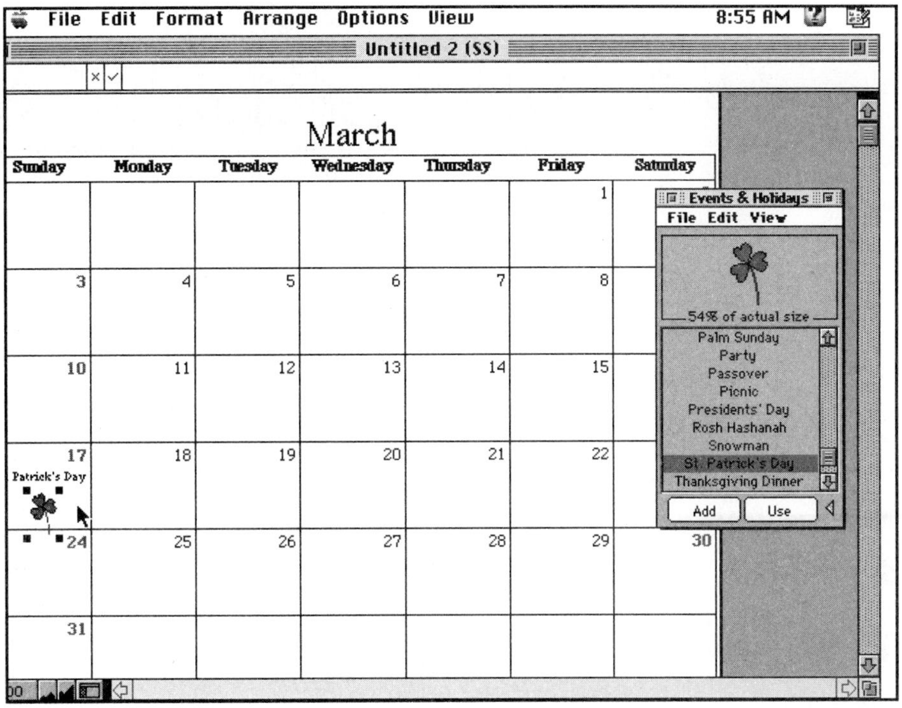

FIGURE 6-9

The March calendar has St. Patrick's Day labeled with text and a shamrock graphic.

The ClarisWorks Assistants provide an easy method of creating specific kinds of documents or features. Not only do they help guide you through the steps, they also allow you to see how versatile the ClarisWorks program actually is. Assistants may also give you ideas for other documents that you may wish to create for yourself using the various ClarisWorks applications.

Introduction to Communications

Teachers have long been isolated from each other and the "real world," confined to a classroom in which communication occurs primarily between the teachers and students. Most teachers want and need increased communication with their colleagues. However, time constraints and outside commitments limit the opportunity to share ideas and interests with peers to chance encounters. With a computer, a telephone line, and a small item of hardware called a modem, many obstacles that have prevented this exchange in the past can be removed. The teacher, and the classroom, are no longer isolated.

The **modem** is the key to this communication. It is a small device through which a computer is connected to a telephone line. A modem takes the data from the computer and translates it into a form that can be transmitted across telephone lines. A modem on a receiving computer translates the signal sent across the phone line into data the computer understands. This ability to communicate computer to computer is one of a host of communication options called **telecommunications**. Bulletin boards can also be a part of the services offered by a larger network.

Systems of computers that are connected to each other so that messages can be sent back and forth are called **networks**. A network may connect one computer to another, or there may be many computers connected together. Often there are many personal computers connected to a large computer. Messages can be sent individually in a network such as this, but also, great amounts of information can be stored on the large computer, providing access for each of the connected smaller computers to many files and programs. In general, telecommunications refers to parceling data, voice, and video across distance. This is generally accomplished using telephones, computers and video conferencing equipment.

Many public and private networks of all types and sizes have been created for innumerable purposes. A network may be in a small area, such as a classroom or a school. These small networks are usually called **local area networks,** or LANs. Generally, they have one larger computer on which programs and files are stored, providing common access for all the other computers. Some other networks are called **bulletin boards**. Generally organized by topic, these allow groups of people who have common interests to express their ideas, opinions, and experiences related to the topic. On bulletin boards people usually leave messages that are comments and questions in their area of interest. Others in the group can read the comments and questions and add their own responses.

There are also very large commercial networks that are subscription services. These charge either for the time that the computer is connected to the service or a flat monthly fee, or both. Fees vary with the service. A normal flat monthly fee might be $5 to $12 per month for a specified amount of time ranging from 2 to 5 hours. Such computer services are usually maintained by a private organization or company, and they provide access to vast amounts of database information, including services and items that can be purchased. These networks—such as America Online, CompuServe, the Microsoft Network, and Prodigy—offer everything from airline schedules, fees, and reservations to encyclopedias and stock market reports to sales items ranging from special chocolates to major appliances. Some services are included in the monthly fee and others require an additional charge. Many commercial services provide supporting instructional materials and technical assistance.

For teachers, telecommunications offers a wealth of opportunities. A teacher can use the computer to connect to discussion groups or special interest groups on either local bulletin boards or on national or international services. Some bulletin boards are specifically organized for educators. In addition, a number of states now have networks set up specifically for teachers that offer lesson plans, ideas, bulletin boards, references, and much more. Generally, the local networks and bulletin boards and the state teacher networks are free or have a minimal fee. Sometimes universities offer special subject-related services, such as in science or engineering, that are free. Telecommunications can also be used to look up references that would relate to a classroom project or assignment. Encyclopedias, ERIC references, journals, library books, and other materials are available through your own computer. In addition, technical information on setting up hardware for specific computer projects can be obtained.

Classroom projects can also be designed to use telecommunications. Students can communicate with other students in different parts of the country—or the world! Many foreign language teachers are beginning to use telecommunications as an integral part of their courses. For stimulating student interest in language arts, history, and geography, communications with students from other locations can be a prime motivator. Students can share information about local customs, weather, history, and topics of personal interest. Also, in particular curriculum areas students in a classroom can work with other groups of students through

through networks to gather information for meaningful projects that extend beyond the classroom walls. These projects can be set up with other interested teachers or through specific services that design the projects and provide consultation. National Geographic Kids Network and The JASON Project are examples of structured networks that involve groups of classrooms from different locations in specific learning curricula. This will be covered in more detail later.

One of the networks that seems to offer great possibilities for the future, both in and out of the field of education, is the Internet. The Internet is the world's largest computer network. Created for government, military, and educational purposes, it is a network of networks that are connected together, funded by various government agencies such as the National Science Foundation and NASA. Educational use of the Internet may be free or may require a monthly or yearly fee. Access can usually be obtained through a local university, state teacher's network, or a local Internet service provider. Internet will be discussed in greater detail later.

There are many uses for telecommunications for the teacher as an educator, but there are also uses for the teacher as an individual. The uses of telecommunications are increasing in our society. By taking advantage of the information available and becoming familiar with telecommunications, a teacher can maintain a broader picture of what is happening in society in general, can access tools such as banking services, and can expand and explore personal interests with available resources in the many, many networks available.

GETTING STARTED

To get started, you must know the telephone number of a service and what is required to make connection with that service. There are several ways to obtain information about available networks. The local Macintosh users group can usually be helpful. Chances are the group has a bulletin board and may also have information on other free or inexpensive services that might be available. To find a Mac users group, check with a local Macintosh dealer, the public library, or the Education Department or Computer Science Department of a local university. In addition, check to see if the local library and university have any dial-in services available to educators. Check with a school district's computer coordinator to determine whether the district subscribes to any network services described earlier. Once a source of network information is found, get details on exactly what is needed to access a specific network.

To get started, you must also have a computer—for the purposes of this book, a Macintosh—a modem, a telephone line, and communications software. As described earlier, a modem translates computer data to data that can be carried via telephone signals and translates telephone signals to computer data. Communications software is a program that sets up the computer to work appropriately with the modem and sends data to and receives data from the modem. One of the ClarisWorks applications is communications. For many situations, the ClarisWorks communications application will work fine. For certain services, connection and navigation are only available when using the software that was provided with the subscription to the service.

Most communications software comes with certain settings, related to the sending and receiving of data, already in place. These preset values are called defaults. For some networks, the defaults may need to be changed to other settings. You may have to contact the service provider for specific details about the connection.

When using a modem to make connection to another computer, your computer will be acting as a terminal. A terminal is a computer screen and keyboard that are used to communicate with a separate computer. Part of the ClarisWorks communications software is a terminal emulation package that allows the Macintosh and the connected computer with which it must communicate to "speak the same language." When connections are made with a larger computer that serves many smaller computers or terminals, the larger machine is often referred to as the host or as a host computer.

Usually a connection with a host computer requires a special identification code. This identification code indicates to the host computer that you are authorized to access information on that computer. The identification code usually consists of a user name or number and a password. Often the first time a connection is made with "free" services a generic ID is used, such as newuser, public, or guest. In some cases after connection, a specific code is assigned or you may choose one. Many times, your identification is some form of your name, such as last name and first initial (YoungsC). The password is generally a specific set of characters that you choose. User IDs and passwords need to be guarded carefully so that others do not obtain access to a computer system that they are not authorized to use.

Each time a connection from a computer to a host computer is made, a communications **session** is initiated. To end a communications session, you must sign off or log off of the host computer. This is usually accomplished by typing a keyword such as exit, logoff, or signoff. The time from the initial log on to the log off is called the connect time. Some subscription services bill for connect time, but there are also many excellent free services available.

CREATING A NEW COMMUNICATIONS DOCUMENT

Setting up a **communications document** is similar to setting up a new document in the other application areas. To try this you must know the telephone number of a computer service and also a user name and password that will allow access to the host system. To make the connection, you must also know what values to use for the modem and port settings. The following steps assume these settings on the communications software: Modem = Hayes-Compatible, Baud Rate = 19200, Parity = None, Data Bits = 8, Stop Bits = 1, Handshake = None, and Current Port = Modem Port; but your requirements may vary. Specifics of these will be explained below.

Once you have the necessary information, follow the steps below to log on to the service or network you will be using. Familiarity with the Macintosh interface and basic ClarisWorks skills is assumed for the following exercises.

1. Launch ClarisWorks, if you have not already done so.

2. Create a new communications document by double-clicking Communications in the New Document dialog box. The communications document window should look similar to Figure 6-10.

3. From the **Settings menu**, choose Connection.... The Connection Settings dialog box should appear similar to the one in Figure 6-11, although your display may vary somewhat.

4. Type the telephone number of the service you wish to connect to. If you are in a school or university, the phone line may be part of a telephone system that requires dialing a specific number and then waiting for a dial tone before continuing to dial. That wait can be built into the dialing of the phone number by using a comma to indicate a delay. Each comma is approximately a 2-second delay. Begin with one comma and add more if you need a longer delay.

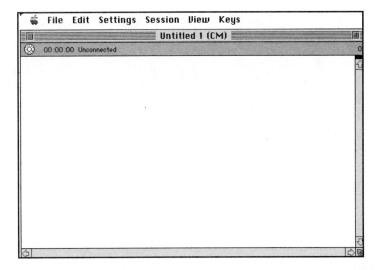

FIGURE 6-10

A new communications document. Notice that some of the menus are different from the menus used in the other applications.

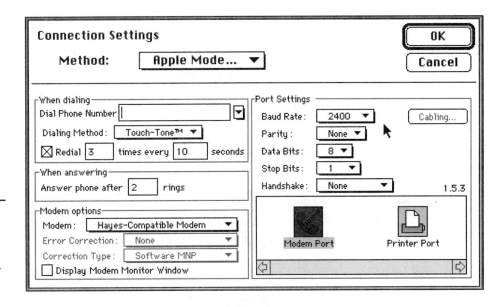

FIGURE 6-11

The Connection Settings dialog box permits you to enter the phone number you wish to dial. You may also indicate the type of modem used and settings for the modem.

The phone number may be typed with or without hyphens, but hyphens make it easier to read. For example:

9,5551234	dials 9, pauses, then dials 555-1234
9,555-1234	dials 9, pauses, then dials 555-1234
9,1-419-555-1234	dials 9, pauses, then dials 1 (for long distance), the area code, and phone number

5. Choose the type of modem you have from the Modem pop-up menu. If your specific brand is not listed, try Hayes-Compatible.

6. Change the baud rate, if you need a baud rate other than 2400, the default rate. The **baud rate** is the speed at which the modem sends and receives data. This rate must match with the modem's capability and the baud rate of the computer to which you are connecting. Most modems today are much faster than 2400.

7. Other port settings may or may not need to be changed. Consult with the set-up instructions or the manager of the service to which you are connecting for specific settings.

    a. Parity is a means of checking to determine whether the data being transmitted is garbled. The possible settings are None, Odd, or Even. The default setting is None.

    b. Data Bits specifies the number of bits, or binary digits, that make up a character. The values usually range from 5 to 8. The default value is 8.

    c. Stop Bits marks the end of a character. The setting can be 1, 1.5, or 2. The default setting is 1.

    d. Handshake is a way of regulating the flow of data between the two computers. Several handshake methods are available, including XON/XOFF, DTR & CTS, DTR only, CTS only, or None. The default setting is None.

8. The current port setting indicates which port the modem cable is in on the computer. Usually the setting will be Modem Port, but it can be Printer Port if that is where you have connected the cable.

9. You may also change settings for other items in the dialog box, such as Redial or Method. When you have finished all changes in the settings, click OK.

10. From the Settings menu, choose Terminal.... When you use your computer as a terminal, there are several types that you may choose. ClarisWorks supports VT102, TTY, and VT320.

11. The default setting is VT102 terminal emulation, which also works for VT100 terminals. Other choices, TTY and VT320, are also available if your service requires it. You can choose one of them from the pop-up menu if you need to change. Do not change the setting unless you know your service requires it.

12. Click on the Keyboard icon on the lower left portion of the window. You should see a dialog box like the one in Figure 6-12.

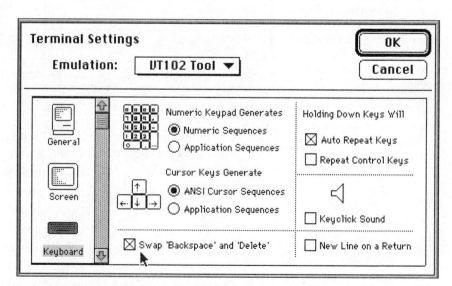

FIGURE 6-12

The Terminal Settings dialog box with keyboard setting selected. Checking Swap 'Backspace' and 'Delete' allows the backspace key to be used to delete typing errors.

13. Click on the box in front of Swap 'Backspace' and 'Delete'. This will allow you to backspace and delete characters that you type incorrectly. Click OK to exit Terminal Settings.

14. Turn on the modem. (Make sure it is connected to a working telephone line and that it is plugged into an outlet and also into a port on the computer.)

15. From the Session menu, choose **Open Connection**. The computer will dial the number you have selected. You may be able to hear it dial on a Touch-Tone phone.

16. Once you are connected, you will generally need to log on to the computer system by typing your user identification and password when requested.

17. Use the commands that are required by the service to obtain the information that you want.

18. If you are not able to get a connection to a subscription service, check with the technical support people. If you are unsuccessful in trying to connect to a local bulletin board or other local service, you may wish to contact them directly or check with someone who uses the service to determine what the correct connection settings are.

SETTING THE SCROLLBACK AND CAPTURING DATA

While you are connected to the host computer, various pieces of information will be displayed on the screen. Sometimes you may wish to view information that was previously displayed on the screen but is no longer in view. This data is stored in an area called the scrollback if the **Save Lines Off Top** command is selected on the Session menu (this is the default setting). You can show the scrollback area in either of two ways.

1. Position the mouse on the pane control, the small black box at the top of the vertical scroll bar. Drag the horizontal pane control down to display the scrollback area as shown in Figure 6-13.

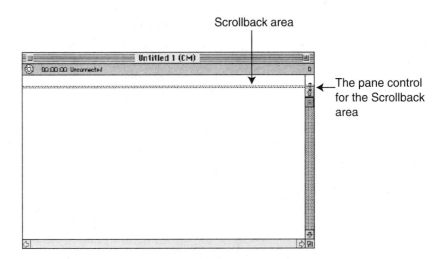

Scrollback area

The pane control for the Scrollback area

FIGURE 6-13

The pane control can be moved so that the scrollback area can be viewed. This can also be done by choosing Show Scrollback from the Settings menu.

2. Or, choose **Show Scrollback** from the Settings menu.

You may change the size of the scrollback pane by dragging the pane control up or down until you find the size satisfactory. If you do not wish to see the scrollback area, you can hide it from view in either of two ways.

1. Drag the pane control back to the top of the vertical scroll bar.

2. Or, from the Settings menu, choose **Hide Scrollback**.

Depending on the amount of memory you have, the hard disk space you have available, and your need for the information, you may wish to capture and save all incoming data. When you capture the data, it is saved in a text file that you may review later. Capturing data may be started before you connect to another computer or it may be started sometime after the connection has been made. To capture data follow the steps below.

1. From the Session menu, choose **Capture to File...** to see the Capture dialog box. This dialog box is similar to a Save dialog box.

2. In the Capture dialog box, choose the place you wish to have the data stored and give the file an appropriate name.

3. Click Save.

4. To stop capturing data, choose Stop Capture from the Session menu.

There are also communications preferences that can be set within ClarisWorks communications documents. The Preferences... command on the Edit menu controls such things as how much memory to allow for the scrollback and where to place files that you may import. Importing a file means that you are bringing a copy of a file from another computer to your computer. There are other settings here that you may deal with as you become a more experienced user of telecommunications.

ENDING A COMMUNICATIONS SESSION

Eventually you will need to end your communications session. You may or may not be saving information from the session, but you will want to exit it appropriately.

1. Type in the command that your service uses to disconnect. Some examples are exit, logoff, signoff, and quit. You will need to check with the service to find out the exact term used.

2. Choose **Close Connection** from the Session menu. At this point your modem connection is off. Depending on the type of modem you have, it may have lights that signal when you are connected and using the phone line and when you are not.

Telecommunications in the Classroom

Telecommunications can open new sources of information to the classroom teacher. It can also provide new means of instruction for students. Gone are the days of living in isolation in the classroom. The walls have come down to allow students and teachers to have access to information and resources never before possible. Various collaboration efforts between schools and agencies such as NASA or universities allow students to have access to scientists and professors who have a great deal of knowledge about areas of interest. In addition teachers from various classrooms can work on projects together to enhance the educational experience for all.

COMMERCIAL COLLABORATIVE LEARNING SERVICES

If you have never used telecommunications before, a good way to start classroom use might be through a learning network such as National Geographic Kids

Network. This is a service offered by NGS Educational Services to assist class-room teachers in planning and completing telecommunications projects with their students. Students in various locations conduct research under the guidance of a scientist and then exchange and compare their research with other classes. Topics include water supply, weather, pollution, nutrition, and solar energy. A specific learning program lasts about 8 weeks and is supported through text and on-line help. The program is focused and represents "real science." The kit includes material necessary to perform the required experiments, and kits are reuseable.

The JASON Project is another collaborative learning service. Each year there is a new interactive field trip. The 1995 project was Planet Earth, with students and scientists exploring the volcanoes of Hawaii, and the 1996 project is Adapting to a Changing Sea, an expedition in the Florida Keys. The project centers around the scientific method and focuses on hands-on learning, an interdisciplinary approach, teaching about technology, and connecting with current research. Professional development programs designed to engage and excite teachers who use the program in their classrooms are available.

COMMUNITY RESOURCES

A variety of community resources are available in some areas. You can access information from many public libraries electronically. You may call into the library system, use its resources, reserve or order books, and then simply pick them up at your local branch. Free-Nets are being developed in many cities. Through the Free-Net, individuals have access to a variety of community resources such as government offices, museums, zoos, educational services, and libraries. To determine what local resources may be available, check in your local newspaper, public library, or with computer retailers.

ELECTRONIC MAIL

Electronic mail or E-mail as it is often called is another way that teachers and students can work together on a project. An interested teacher often organizes the project and supervises the information flow. A variety of projects can be accomplished by simply using electronic mail. Weather conditions can be compared from one geographical region to another by having each class send data on its region on a regular basis. The data can be compiled and sent back to each of the other classes participating in the project.

More network-experienced teachers or teachers with some local technical support could also use another teacher or teachers to set up their own learning project with other classrooms. One example of such use is a Spanish teacher in Ohio who linked with a Spanish teacher near Los Angeles to set up pen pals from their respective classes. Students communicate in Spanish. This project gives students not only additional practice using the Spanish language in a practical way, but also a better perspective on their counterparts who live in a totally different area of the country. Another example is a teacher who linked with an individual in Saudi Arabia during the Persian Gulf War—the entire elementary school was soon involved in daily communications.

An elementary school followed the progress of a dog sled trip across the Arctic. The classes received E-mail messages from the team members describing their progress and giving accounts of their activities. Daily announcements kept the entire school posted on the team's progress. Classes studied about the Arctic region—its geography, animal life, and weather. A dog sled team even visited the school. This was a project that spurred a great deal of interest and all that was involved was E-mail.

To communicate with someone on the Internet all you need to do is send a message, called electronic mail, to their Internet address. An example of an address is: wl_cay@mavca.ohio.gov. In this example, the user is identified by "wl_cay." The @, usually read "at," indicates that what follows is the electronic location of the user. "mavca" is the name of the computer where the user account is located and "ohio" is the agency where that department is located. "gov" indicates that this connection is through a government agency. Many addresses you may see will have "edu" as the last part, indicating that it is an educational organization that provides the service. Some addresses end in "com" indicating a commercial organization. Electronic mail or E-mail can be sent on the Internet by using the mail program and send commands with the address. Mail from another person can be accessed by using the read command.

MAILING LISTS AND DISCUSSION GROUPS

Information about various projects may be available to the individual teacher through E-mail based **mailing lists**, news groups, or **discussion groups**. One really good source of information is Classroom Connect's mailing list. To subscribe send a message to

crc-request@classroom.net

in the body of the message type

subscribe

After sending this message, you will be added to the list of subscribers. You will begin getting mail once or twice a day. This is a moderated mailing list geared to the K-12 classroom. They write about things that work and things that don't. This is a great source of information about projects, answers to questions, and just general resource information.

There are also USENET groups that are accessible through an Internet connection's News function or through an automatic news browser function that is available in some programs, such as Eudora. There are thousands of USENET groups on a wide range of topics. There are several dozen education USENET groups available. To read information posted in a USENET group, you must subscribe. Lists of groups may be found in journals or from sources on the Internet.

COMMERCIAL SERVICES

Several commercial services were listed earlier in the text. America Online, CompuServe, Microsoft Network, and Prodigy are the most widely used services. In additional there are smaller local or regional service providers that have some features found in the larger services. Generally each service offers the following options: a News feature with U.S. & World News, Business, Sports and Entertainment; Business and Professional areas featuring reference areas, forums, and chats; Homework Helping Tools including research tools; Computer Help with problems you may be having with your computer or software; and Sports and Games for entertainment.

Most of these options are a part of your normal monthly billing costs. In addition, other services are often available, such as tracking an investment portfolio, that require an additional charge.

Many services offer a no-charge trial period during which you may explore the service to see whether it has features that appeal to you. Using this free trial can help determine whether one of the services is right for you. See the resources at the end of the chapter for additional information.

INTERNET RESOURCES AND TOOLS

The Internet is a network of networks that seems to be growing all the time. If your school does not currently have an account, check with your local university or with a regional computer center organized by your state department of education to see whether you can obtain free access. A tremendous variety of resources is available through the Internet, and entire books have been written about the Internet. *Zen and the Art of the Internet, Educators World Wide Web Tour Guide*, and *Educators Internet Companion* are only a small sampling. Most universities and many state and regional teachers' networks are available through Internet.

You can also access resources through Internet by using either the telnet or the connect command with an account address. These addresses have both a numeric format as well as the name (or domain) described previously. Usually it is best to use the domain format in case the service may have been moved to a different location. Consult the Resources at the end of the chapter for information and addresses.

THE WORLD WIDE WEB

Of all the many features that telecommunications offers, none are quite as alluring to the educator as the World Wide Web. The **World Wide Web** (also referred to as WWW or just The Web) allows information to be intertwined in multiple directions. Text and links to other information can be presented on the same screen. It offers ease of navigation and also a multimedia format. A Web page may have text, graphics, audio, and even video. Essentially a Web site can easily look like a multimedia CD-ROM.

The user may begin with a Home Page, but may then branch to the information connections offered on the Home Page in any order based on his or her interests or preferences. There are various **Web Browsers** available that allow you to search for specific information. Currently Netscape is one of the most popular browsers. Using it you may type in keywords that allow you to search for information about a topic. Sometimes it takes some thought to find the right combination of keywords to focus in on a topic without eliminating any references to the topic at all.

You may explore on the Internet by using addresses, called URLs (Universal Resource Locator). Using Web Browser software, you can access sites with URLs that begin with an http:// prefix. A URL address should be entered with no spaces between characters—as an unbroken string. A sample URL address is

http://www.fedworld.gov

The following sites have information that may be of interest to educators. Sites change frequently on the Internet. If you do not find information using these URL addresses, try searching with a search engine using keywords such as "education," "K-12," or subject-specific references such as "mathematics" and "problem solving" or "science" and "cell division."

Fed World—a federal government system of government-related databases of information http://www.fedworld.gov

Global Network Navigator—contains education, business, and travel information that may be of interest to teachers and students http://gnn.com

ERIC— information service for ERIC (Educational Resources Information Center) http://www.ericir.syr.edu/

EdWeb—a variety of K-12 education resources and information on the impact of the Information Highway on education http://k12.cnidr.org:90

NASA SpaceLink—information on NASA activities including shuttles and lesson plans http://hypatia.gsfc.nasa.gov/NASA_homepage.html

Global SchoolNet Foundation—assists K-12 teachers and students in designing collaborative projects that encourage use of the Internet http://www.gsn.org/web

The Smithsonian—provides a virtual tour of the Smithsonian museums http://www.si.edu

With the current interest in "interactive" learning, the Web offers many possibilities for education. Through the use of goal-based scenarios, a teacher may allow students to explore a subject from their own point of reference. The Web is just one more tool available to the teacher to "engage" students as active learners.

Other technologies such as **Chats** (real-time discussion groups) and **CUSEEMe** (a teleconferencing program that allows users to see and hear each other through use of a video camera) offer additional possibilities for students and teachers to access scientists, researchers, other teachers, and other students. Many of these technologies are relatively inexpensive to set up once you have Internet access. In the future, more technologies will be available that will allow teachers to further expand the learning experience beyond the traditional four walls of the classroom.

Conclusion

In this chapter, additional features of ClarisWorks and the use of the ClarisWorks communications application have been introduced. More information on these features and additional details about each ClarisWorks application are available in the ClarisWorks Help window and the manuals. Also, a journal subscription can be obtained to the ClarisWorks Journal, which has articles on various uses and features of ClarisWorks (see the Resources section at the end of this chapter for information).

These features may offer some help with the initial frustrations of creating certain types of documents. Telecommunications, however, can be aggravating because of the constant changes in networks and the lack of standardization, not to mention problems with phone connections and off-line computers. You will discover, however, that with minimal practice and experience, you will become more efficient and effective with all the applications and will wonder how you ever taught without these resources.

KEY TERMS

Assistants	discussion groups	Save Lines Off Top
baud rate	electronic mail	session
bulletin board	Hide Scrollback	Settings
Capture to File...	local area network	Show Scrollback
Chat	(LAN)	Stationery
Close Connection	mailing lists	telecommunications
communications docu-	modem	template
ment	network	Web Browser
CUSEEMe	Open Connection	World Wide Web

REFERENCES

Editor, *The Educator's Internet Resource Handbook*. Lancaster, PA.: Wentworth Worldwide Media, Inc., 1995.

LaQuey, Tracy. *The Internet Companion: A Beginner's Guide to Global Networking.* Reading, MA: Addison-Wesley, 1993.

Panepinto, Joe, et al. "Online Service Report Card." *Family PC*, February 1996, pp. 43-56.

Venditto, Gus. "Online Services: How Does Their Net Access Stack Up." *Internet World*, March 1996, pp. 55-65.

RESOURCES

America Online, Vienna, VA 22182. Phone: (800) 827-6364. Dial (800) 977-1436 for AOL software and free trial hours.

ClarisWorks Journal, ClarisWorks Users Group, Box 702020, Plymouth, MI 48170. Phone: (313) 454-1969.

Classroom Connect, Wentworth Worldwide Media, Lancaster, PA 17605-0488. Phone: (800) 638-1639 or E-mail: connect@classroom.net or Web site: http://www.classroom.net

CompuServe, Columbus, OH 43220. Phone: (800) 848-8990. Dial (800) 487-0588 for free software and 10 free hours.

Cruisin' the Information Highway: Internet in K-12 Classroom, Annette Lamb, Vision to Action, 10732 E. Sunset Dr., Evansville, IN 47712.

Educators Internet Companion, Wentworth Worldwide Media, Lancaster, PA 17605-0488. Phone: (800) 638-1639.

Educators World Wide Web Tour Guide, Gregory Giagnocavo, et al. Wentworth Worldwide Media, Lancaster, PA 17605-0488. Phone: (800) 638-1639.

Family PC, P.O. Box 400454, Des Moines, IA 50340-0454. Phone: (800) 413-9749.

Global SchoolNet Foundation, P.O. Box 243, Bonita, CA 91908-0243 Phone: (619) 475-4852 or E-mail:info@gsn.org

Internet World, P.O. Box 7461, Red Oak, IA 51591-2461. E-mail subs@iw.com or for information: info@mecklermedia.

Microsoft Network, Redmond, WA. Phone: (800) 426-9400. (This is shipped with Windows 95.)

National Geographic Society, Educational Services, Washington, D.C. 20036. Phone: (800) 368-2728.

Plugging In, NCREL, North Central Regional Educational Laboratory, 1900 Spring Road, Suite 300, Oak Brook, IL 60521-1480. Phone:(708) 571-4700.

Prodigy Services Company, White Plains, NY 10601. Phone: (800) 776-3449. Dial (800) PRODIGY ext. 1173 or E-mail: freetrial@prodigy.com for free software and 10 free hours.

Surfin' the Internet: Practical Ideas from A to Z, Annette Lamb, Vision to Action, 10732 E. Sunset Dr., Evansville, IN 47712.

Telecommunications in Education, a special interest group for International Society for Technology in Education (ISTE), 1787 Agate St., Eugene, OR 79403-1923. Phone: (503) 346-4414.

The JASON Project, Putnam/Norther Westchester BOCES Elementary Science Program, 200 BOCES Drive, Yorktown Heights, NY 10598. Phone: (914) 248-2349 or fax to: (914) 245-4540.

Zen and the Art of the Internet (4th ed.), Brenda Kehow, Prentice Hall. Phone: (800) 382-3419.

7 Introduction to HyperStudio

Introduction

Teachers today are looking for more effective methods to present material to students, to keep information about students, and to involve students in meaningful learning experiences using technology. **HyperStudio** and **HyperCard** are pieces of software that have the flexibility to address all these needs. HyperStudio was created by the Roger Wagner Company in 1988 first for the Apple IIGS and now for the Macintosh and for Windows-based machines. HyperCard was created in 1987 by Bill Atkinson as a tool for gathering, organizing, presenting, searching, and linking information. As versatile teaching tools, both can be used for such varied purposes as tutorials, drill and practice exercises, keeping grades and other information about students, and creating multimedia presentations.

Both are flexible enough to be used across the curriculum. For instance, they can be used in science to teach about the parts of the human body: The student might have a diagram of a skeleton on the screen and then click on a bone to see an explanation of that bone and its purpose, to see the muscles involved in the movement of that part, or to see how the circulation system nourishes that part. HyperStudio can be used in social studies to present issues concerning Desert Storm that could include pictures captured with a scanner, maps with explanations about various locations in Saudi Arabia, or, through an attached CD-ROM player, actual speeches made during that time. They can be used in math to explain the various formulas for area and perimeter by shading diagrams and giving an explanation of what is being done. They can utilize sound capabilities to teach foreign languages. Students can hear the words pronounced by their own teacher and then make a selection of the action or item that the teacher is saying. Students can use either program to make their own multimedia presentations with information they have researched. When the Macintosh is connected to an LCD unit, a device used to display the Macintosh screen through an overhead projector and onto a screen, the teacher can use either application in a classroom situation to stimulate class interaction and lively discussions.

Because both are very powerful tools, it is important to introduce you to both. This chapter will introduce you to HyperStudio. In HyperStudio and HyperCard, much of the terminology is the same — stack, card, button. However, there are also differences. HyperStudio is more menu-driven, choices are made by selecting from a list, whereas in HyperCard commands must be written out. This concept makes HyperStudio an excellent tool to use with elementary students; they can easily design impressive stacks. However, this places limitations on the capabilities of HyperStudio. In HyperCard you can program sophisticated commands for record keeping and calculations similar to any programming language. HyperStudio links very easily to laser disk players to create multimedia presentations or directly to a web page on the Internet; this is done with a menu selection. Each program has its advantages, and presenting both to you will allow you to decide which program is appropriate for your use. The following terms are used in both programs.

HyperStudio Elements

STACK

HyperStudio or HyperCard can be envisioned as a series of index cards, each card containing various types of information. In both, this series of index cards is called a **stack.** For example, a stack could be called Space Program and contain information about the U.S. space missions. A good way to understand a stack is to visualize it as a Rolodex; you can move through the entire stack of cards and eventually return to the beginning card, with the capability to continue through the cards again. However, one of the strong features of these applications is that they do not restrict you to sequential movement through the cards, but also allow movement directly to any card in the stack. This permits students to progress through the stack in a variety of ways, depending on their needs and interests. For instance, one student viewing a card related to an Apollo flight might go directly to details about the rocket used on that flight. Another student viewing the Apollo flight card might follow other interests and go directly to astronaut information.

CARD

A **card** is the fundamental unit of a stack. The term card is usually associated with what is seen on the screen at any point in time. The screen displays text or graphics or both. For example, in a stack about famous people, a card might have written information about one person. When you see the screen change, it is usually because another card is being displayed. For instance, clicking on the screen could cause another card showing the person's picture to be displayed.

TEXT OBJECT

Each card may contain text objects, buttons, and graphics. A text field, or **text object,** is an area that is established for entering text. Usually it contains most of the information typed on a card. This item can be any rectangular shape or size not larger than the size of the card. Text font, size, and style can be chosen for the text field.

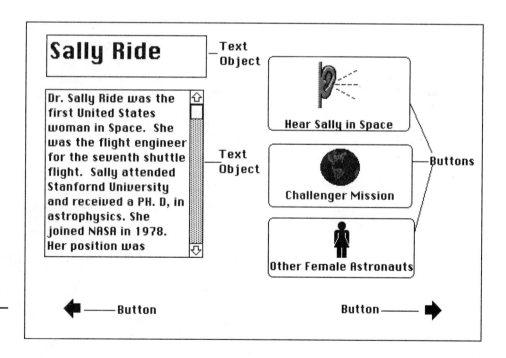

FIGURE 7-1

Sample of a card with buttons and text objects labeled.

BUTTON

Cards also contain buttons. A **button** is a specific area on the card that triggers an action when clicked. For instance, buttons can be used to move from card to card in a stack, allowing you to go directly to a card that has information you specifically want to see. In a stack about famous people, clicking on a button could allow you to get to the information about Daniel Boone. Another button may allow you to hear a part of a speech by Martin Luther King, Jr. Buttons often have icons, pictures that represent what they do. For example, a right arrow usually means to move to the next card; clicking the arrow will display the next card. Clicking a button icon of a musical note might cause a song to play. Buttons and text objects are labeled on the card shown in Figure 7-1.

Introduction to HyperStudio

The best way to learn about HyperStudio is to actually use it. In this chapter you will be introduced to some fundamentals of HyperStudio in a tutorial format. You will learn how to browse through a stack, how to edit text objects in a stack, how to create new cards, how to use the graphics tools, and how to create a new stack. This chapter is written based on HyperStudio version 3.0.6 using CD-Rom. See Appendix for non-CD-Rom versions. To use the stacks provided on the floppy disk accompanying this text, you need to have HyperStudio installed on your hard drive.

OPENING HYPERSTUDIO

1. To start HyperStudio, locate HyperStudio on your hard drive and double-click on it.

2. Once the program is loaded, the screen you see, also shown in Figure 7-2, is part of a stack called the Home Stack. The **Home Stack** is like a starting point, a table of contents. It contains buttons and text objects with information for you. This Home Stack was created by the Roger Wagner Company to introduce you to HyperStudio. Notice the text box on the right side of the card. It is a scrollable box because it contains a scroll bar and more text than fits in the box. Read the entire contents of this welcome box by clicking on the down arrow in the scroll bar.

3. Click on the picture above the words Show Me How to move to another card that will explain different parts of HyperStudio (see Figure 7-2).

FIGURE 7-2

Click on Show Me How.

4. On the Show Me How card, click on the picture above the words HyperStudio Step-By-Step.

5. On the Step-By-Step card, click on the picture above the word Introduction, as shown in Figure 7-3.

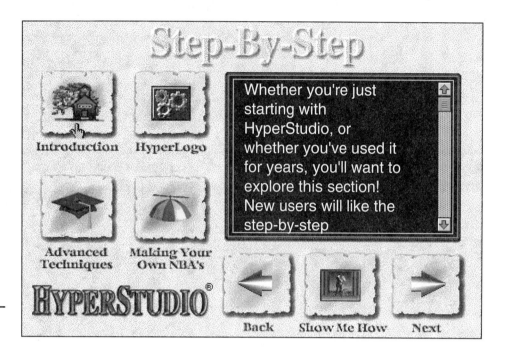

FIGURE 7-3

Click on the picture above the word Introduction.

6. Read all the information in the text box on the left side of the card before you begin. Continue to read and follow instructions in this section. This section demonstrates the concept of cards and buttons to you. You can see that information is placed on each card and buttons permit you to move from one card to another.

7. When you have finished the Introduction, you will begin the next tutorial section called How to Create a Project. This section will demonstrate many HyperStudio concepts to you including buttons, button activity, transitions, sound, and clip art. Follow directions carefully. Remember this is an introduction; you will see how things are done, but you will not actually be doing it yourself.

8. When you reach the last card containing the picture of the Solar System, do not choose Let Me Try!; instead click on the picture of the house in the lower left corner next to the words Step-By-Step.

9. You should be back on the Step-By-Step card.

10. Click on the Show Me How button located between the two arrows in the lower right corner of the card.

11. You should be on the Show Me How card.

12. Click on the Home button located between the two arrows in the lower right corner of the card.

13. You should now be back on the original Home card. If you are not there, select Home from the Move menu.

This is a good introduction into HyperStudio. You should now have a basic understanding of the concepts of stack, card, button, text object, and graphics. You are now ready to explore further. If you would like, take time to explore some of the sample projects included with your version of HyperStudio. If you have the CD version, make sure the CD-ROM is in the drive when viewing the sample projects.

CLASSROOM ◄──────► CONNECTION

To introduce the concept of a stack, demonstrate by using index cards. Use post-it notes on the cards for text objects and round stickers for buttons. Students will understand better if they can relate it to a real object.

Using Stacks

OPENING A STACK FROM HYPERSTUDIO

Once HyperStudio is opened, you can open any stack immediately. You will be working first with the stack named Machines on the Data Disk.

1. Place the Data Disk in the floppy disk drive.
2. Select Open Stack from the File menu.
3. Click on Desktop in the Open Stack dialog box.
4. Click on Data Disk and then click Open.
5. Click on Machines and then click Open.
6. You should now see the first card of Machines on the screen, as shown in Figure 7-4.

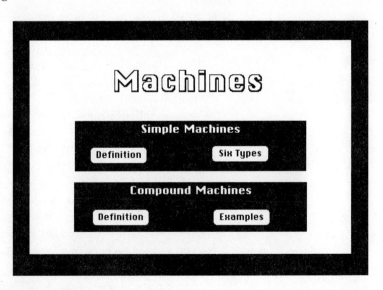

FIGURE 7-4

The first card in the Machines stack.

BROWSING A STACK

Browsing a stack refers to simply looking through the stack, moving from card to card; this is also referred to as **navigating.** Finding your way through a complex stack can sometimes be quite an adventure. You can browse this sample stack quite easily by using buttons that allow you to go from card to card, by using arrow keys, or by using the Move menu.

Using Buttons to Browse

Notice that as you move the mouse around on the card, the pointer is in the shape of a hand with a pointing finger. This is the icon for the **Browse tool**. With it you can activate buttons by clicking on them. As mentioned earlier, buttons are areas of the screen that can be clicked to cause actions to occur, such as movement to different cards. The first card of the Machine stack has four choices for finding information on machines. Each choice is a button. By clicking on one of the white ovals, you will "jump" to a certain card of the stack that has the information you want.

1. Click on the Definition button for Simple Machines. This puts you on the card that contains that definition.

2. Click on the Return to Main Menu button at the bottom of the card. This button takes you back to the first card of the stack. You are now on the title card once again.

3. Click on the button labeled Six Types. You should see a card with six simple machines listed on it, as shown in Figure 7-5. Each of these names is another button. Each button will move you to a specific card that contains information about that machine.

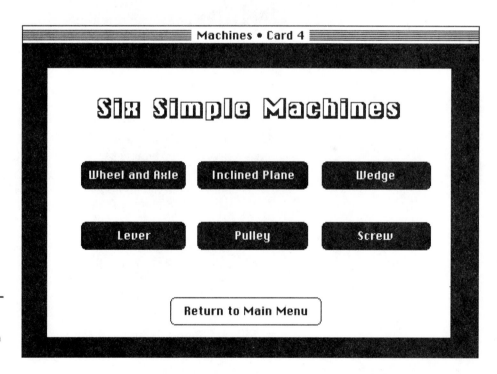

FIGURE 7-5

The Six Simple Machines menu card. Each labeled rectangle is a button to take you to cards with more information.

4. Click on Lever to see the definition and diagram of the lever, as shown in Figure 7-6. The right arrow icon is a button that will move you to the next card to see more information about levers.

5. Click on the right arrow icon to move to the next card. This card shows examples of a lever. Notice there are two buttons at the bottom of this card. In this case the left arrow is for moving back one card. As you can see, HyperStudio stacks allow flexibility; you can move to a variety of locations

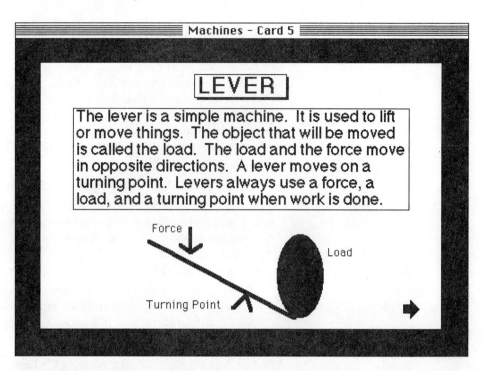

FIGURE 7-6

The Lever definition card has two fields with text and one button.

in a stack. Students can select the areas in which they need more practice and can bypass those they don't need.

6. Click on the left arrow. This takes you back to the first card that contains the definition for a lever. This movement allows the student to go back to read the definition a second time if necessary.

7. Click on the right arrow icon and then click on Return to Simple Machines to move back to the Simple Machines menu. Moving back to this screen allows the student to choose another machine, or even to choose the lever again, if needed. Without having to view the entire stack, students can go back to the same information time and time again, until they understand the material.

8. Click Inclined Plane to see the information about the inclined plane. Once again you will see a definition and a diagram about a simple machine.

9. Click on the right arrow. Samples of an inclined plane are now on the screen. Notice the two buttons at the bottom of the screen: the left arrow and the Return to Simple Machines menu. When the format on the cards is uniform, it is easier to browse the stack.

10. Click on Return to Simple Machines.

11. Take some time now to explore the rest of the Machines stack by clicking on the various buttons.

12. Return to the Six Simple Machines menu.

Using Keys to Browse

There are other ways to navigate through a stack that can be quite useful if you are creating or editing a stack. One of these is to use the ⌘ key and the > key. These keys move you through a stack sequentially—you see each card as it occurs in the stack.

CLASSROOM ◄────────► **CONNECTION**

Use HyperStudio to create a stack about a field trip. Assign one card to each student and create a class stack. If you have a QuickTake camera, take it on the field trip to record the trip and add these pictures to the stack. Record the students' voices talking about what they learned on the field trip. Use this stack during open houses and parent-teacher conferences.

1. Press the ⌘ key and the > key. This takes you to the next sequential card in the stack.

2. Press the ⌘ key and the > key repeatedly. Notice that eventually you return to the card you started on. This is one reason stacks are compared to Rolodex files—when you reach the last card in the stack, you can go right on to the first one and around again, and again, and again.

3. Press the ⌘ key and the < key. This takes you to the previous card in the stack. Pressing this key repeatedly would also take you through the entire stack and back again to the beginning.

Using the Move Menu

Another way to move through a stack is by using the **Move menu**. The Move menu offers you a variety of options, as shown in Figure 7-7. Next Card and Previous Card serve the same functions as the arrow keys, taking you to the next and the previous cards, respectively. But you can also move to other locations.

1. From the Move menu choose First Card. This should take you to the main menu of the Machines stack, the first card on the stack.

2. Choose Last Card from the Move menu. This takes you to the last card in the stack, the one listing types of compound machines.

3. Choose Jump to Card... from the Move menu. This allows you to type in a card number, similar to a page number, to move to a particular card. Type in **6** and click on OK. You should be on the Samples of a Lever card. This method will give you great flexibility in moving around a stack.

FIGURE 7-7

The Move menu can be used to navigate a stack.

PREFERENCES

HyperStudio allows you to set certain parameters that will always apply to any stack you create. These parameters will assist you in creating and editing your stacks.

1. From the Edit menu select **Preferences.** A dialog box will appear, as is shown in Figure 7-8.

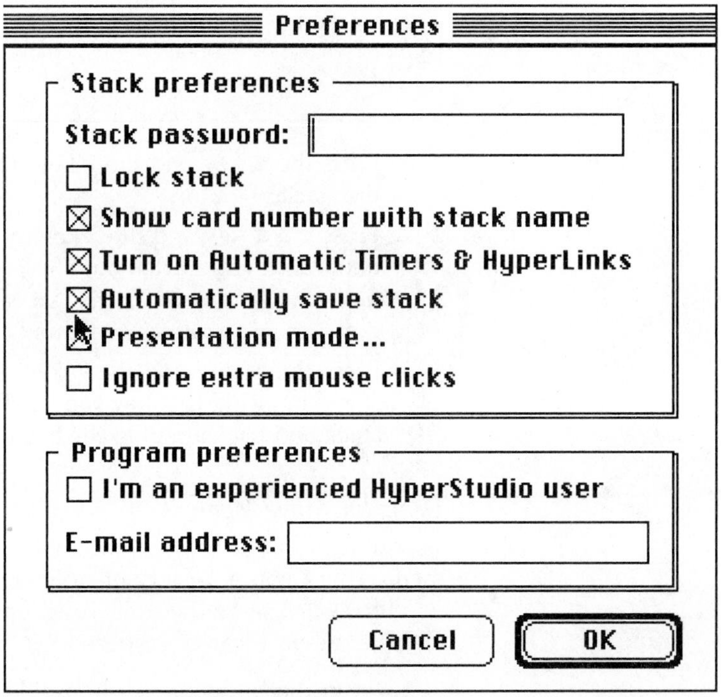

FIGURE 7-8

The Preferences dialog box with four preferences selected.

2. The following features are important to you:

   Lock stack - When you have finished the stack and you want no changes to occur to the stack, click this box.

   Show card number with stack name - This is a good feature to have on when you are creating a stack; it will help you stay organized.

   Automatically save stack - This feature saves the stack for you, so you do not need to worry about saving.

   I'm an experienced HyperStudio user - When you have used HyperStudio for a while and are comfortable with it, you can select this option and more features will be available to you.

   E-mail address - If you are using HyperStudio to connect to the Internet, you can fill in your E-mail address.

3. Click OK when you are finished.

SAVING A STACK

If you have clicked on the automatic save feature in the Preferences dialog box, you need not worry about saving the stack. If you did not select this feature, to save a stack select **Save Stack** from the File menu.

To save the stack with a different name or to save the stack to a different location, select Save Stack As from the File menu. When the dialog box appears, you can type in a new name for the stack and click Save. This is similar to what you did in Chapter 2 when saving word processing files with a new name. To save the stack to a new location, click on Desktop and select the folder or floppy disk you wish to save the stack to.

QUITTING HYPERSTUDIO

You will now be using another stack on your Data Disk. At some point, now or later, you may choose to take a break and quit using HyperStudio. Even if you are not going to take a break now, exit the HyperStudio program so that you will know how to do it later. Then you will be able to break at any time in the remainder of the chapter.

1. From the File menu choose Quit HyperStudio.

2. If the dialog box asks you about saving changes, click on Save No Changes. You should now be out of both the stack and the program.

Opening a Stack from the Desktop

When you first started HyperStudio, you launched the application itself. HyperStudio can also be launched by opening a HyperStudio stack. You will now launch HyperStudio by opening a stack called All About Me.

1. Place the Data Disk in the floppy disk drive.

2. If the disk doesn't open automatically, double-click on it to open it. Notice that many of the icons in the Data Disk window look like a stack of papers with a musical note, a film clip, and a CD-ROM above it. Locate the stack labeled All About Me and double-click on it to open the stack. This will also launch the HyperStudio program.

3. You will see the first card of the stack, as shown in Figure 7-9. This card contains one text object, the title, and one button, Next Card. Everything else is part of the background of the card.

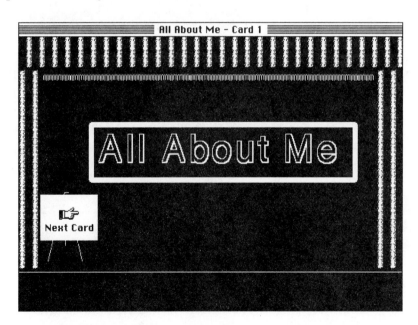

FIGURE 7-9

The first card of the stack, All About Me.

Editing a Text Object

As mentioned earlier in this chapter, a text object is an area for typing text. By using a text object, the typing can be edited in a manner similar to editing done in any Macintosh word processor. In the following exercise, you will be editing text objects.

1. Click on the pointed hand to move to the next card.
2. Move the mouse around on the card.
3. The rectangle containing the instructions marks the boundaries of the text object. Notice that, as you move the pointer within this rectangle, the hand pointer turns into an I-beam. This indicates that you can edit the text.

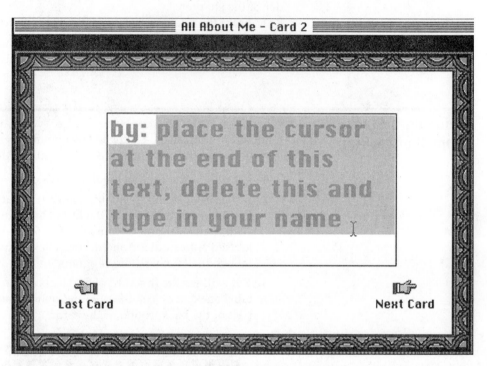

FIGURE 7-10

Drag the I-beam across the text and delete the instructions.

4. Position the I-beam at the end of the instructions for typing your name.
5. Drag the I-beam up and to the left to the beginning of the instructions, as shown in Figure 7-10.
6. Press the Delete key, or from the Edit menu choose Cut Text.
7. Type your name. You have just edited your first stack!
8. Move to each of the next four cards and fill in the information asked for on each card.

Adding Cards to a Stack

Cards can be added to a stack in a variety of ways. One method is to simply copy the card and then paste the new card. The advantage is that everything on the original card, including text objects, text, and buttons will be copied. The disadvantage could be that you will need to delete text and type in your own information. A second method is to use the command **New Card**. With this method, a totally blank card is created — no background graphics, no text objects, no buttons. If you are going to create a card very different from the rest of the stack, this is the method to use. There are also three **Ready Made Cards** functions that you can use. The first one is called **Blank Card** and is the same as New Card, totally blank. The second function is called **Same Background**; this will give you a card with all the graphics as the card you are presently on, but contains no text objects, text, or buttons. When you are trying to keep consistency in a stack, this is a useful function to use; it allows you to have the same background but change the text objects and buttons on a card. The third function is called **Group Card**. Grouping cards allows you to add background to all the cards of the group at the same time. What you draw on one card will appear on all the cards of the group. This can be very useful and time saving. In the following exercises, you will explore all of these possible methods of adding cards to a stack. Sometimes if you are creating a simple stack, a good practice is to create one card with all the necessary items, place it at the end of the stack, and copy and paste it.

COPYING AND PASTING CARDS

1. Move to card 7 of this stack.
2. Choose Copy Card from the Edit menu.
3. Choose Paste Card from the Edit menu.
4. Notice the card name now includes the number 8. Both buttons and the text field are also on this card.
5. Paste two more cards, and the stack will now have a total of 10 cards.
6. Move back to card 7.
7. Type in information about your family.
8. Move to card 8 and type in information about your neighborhood.
9. Move to card 9 and type in information about your favorite season of the year.
10. Move to card 10 and type in The End!

NEW CARD

1. Select New Card from the Edit menu; notice that card 11 is blank. New Card gives you a totally blank card with no background. If the background items are important, then Copy Card and Paste Card would be the method you would want to use.

DELETE CARD

If you accidentally add too many cards to the stack, you can remove them from the stack.
1. To delete card 11, choose Delete Card from the Edit menu.
2. When asked if you really want to delete this card, click Yes. You no longer have card 11.

READY MADE CARDS

To see the differences in the Ready Made Cards functions, move to card 10 of the stack.
1. Select Ready Made Cards from the Edit menu and hold down the mouse button. Notice that a submenu appears to the right of Ready Made Cards.
2. Slide to the submenu and select Blank Card. Notice card 11 is totally blank. This is similar to New Card.
3. Use Delete Card to erase card 11.
4. You should now be back on card 10. Once again select Ready Made Cards from the Edit menu and hold down the mouse button. This time select Same Background from the submenu. Card 11 should have the border on it, but not the text object and the buttons. Remember, this can be useful for consistency of a stack.

5. Again, use Delete Card to erase card 11.

6. You should now be back on card 10. Again select Ready Made Cards from the Edit menu and hold down the mouse button. This time select Group Card from the submenu. Card 11 should have the border on it, but not the text object and the buttons.

7. This looks the same as Same Background. To see the difference, select About this Card... from the Objects menu. Notice the X in the box in front of Group Card. Remember, this allows you to add paint features to all the cards of the group by painting on one card. If you wish this card to not be part of the group, click in the box in front of Group Card to deselect it. Notice the X disappears. Click OK to return to the card.

8. Delete card 11.

CLASSROOM ←——→ CONNECTION

Use HyperStudio as a story starter. Create the stack and one or two cards of the stack. By using Same Background the student can create similar cards and write the rest of the story. Use buttons and have students record sound effects on each card. Students could also record themselves reading the text they wrote on each card.

Practice Adding Cards and Editing Cards

1. Add two more cards to the stack and write on one card about your pets and on the other about places you have traveled to. Be sure you use Paste Card while on card 9.

2. Change the information on the card about your family to only your grandparents.

3. Change the last card to include a Thank you to the professor and then type **The End.**

Tools Menu

The **Tools menu** on the HyperStudio menu bar is important. Whenever you are in HyperStudio, you are using one of the HyperStudio tools. Figure 7-11 shows the icons used for these tools. Although you may not have realized it, you have been using the Browse tool. The Browse tool, represented by a pointing hand, is what has allowed you to move through the stacks and to edit fields. If you wanted to change a text object (in ways other than editing text), you would need to select the **Text object tool**, represented by the rectangular icon with dotted lines and a T. The Tools menu also has a **Button tool** for changing buttons, a **Sound tool** for changing sound effects, an **Edit tool** for editing, resizing, moving, or deleting objects around a card, and a **Graphic object tool** for manipulating graphics objects. The Tools menu also contains drawing tools that can be used to create and edit pictures in a stack. Graphics and sound add a dimension to a stack that can make an impact on a presentation, can increase the interest level of a learner, and can help the learner by associating a picture with a word or phrase.

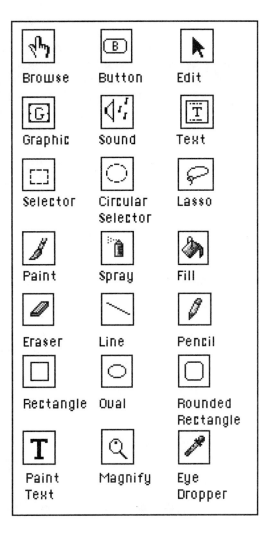

FIGURE 7-11

The HyperStudio tools.

TEARING OFF THE TOOLS MENU

There are times in editing stacks when you need to use the Tools menu frequently. To make it easier to access, you can "tear" the Tools menu off the menu bar so that it stays visible on the screen. This saves many motions of continually selecting the Tools menu. To place the Tools menu, also called the **tool palette**, on the Desktop, follow these steps.

1. While in the All About Me stack, position the pointer on the Tools menu.
2. While holding the mouse button down, drag through the menu and continue to slide down and to the right. A dotted rectangle should follow the pointer as you move it to the bottom right corner of the screen.
3. Position the pointer on the title bar of the tool palette.
4. Drag the title bar to another location on the screen. This is the same technique used to move windows around the Desktop. In this way you can position the tool palette wherever it is convenient.
5. If you wish to remove the tool palette from the Desktop, click the close box on the top left of its title bar.

Adding a Graphic Object

As you have seen in the HyperStudio Introduction, there is a large library of pictures that can be added directly to a stack. It is important to understand the difference between **clip art** and a **graphic object**. If you choose Clip Art from the File menu, that graphic becomes part of the background and will appear on all the cards. The only way to remove it is to erase the item. This can be devastating if you add clip art after much of your stack is created! The better method is to add a graphic object to a card. The graphic object will sit on top of the background and can be moved around the screen without altering the background. It can also become animated. This is chosen under the Object menu. In the following exercise, you will add a graphic item to two cards in the stack.

1. Move to card 3, I live at ....
2. Choose Add a Graphic Object... from the Objects menu.
3. A dialog box may appear showing possible sources of the graphic. If this dialog box does appear, make certain that Disk File is selected and then click OK.
4. Scroll through the list until you find Icon Library - Clip Art.
5. Click on this title and then click on Open.
6. Look for the house (row 2, item 7). The cursor is now a plus sign, which will allow you to draw a selection box around an item. Drag a dotted line rectangle around the house (see Figure 7-12).

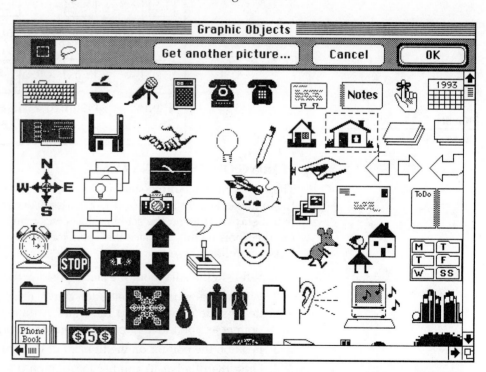

FIGURE 7-12

A Selection box dragged around the house.

7. Click OK. If a dialog box appears explaining what the difference is between a graphic object and clip art, read it and click OK.
8. You are now back on the card in the stack All About Me. A dotted rectangle appears inside the text box. The graphic object is "behind" the text object.
9. Place the pointer in the middle of the dotted rectangle and drag the picture to the bottom of the screen, as shown in Figure 7-13.

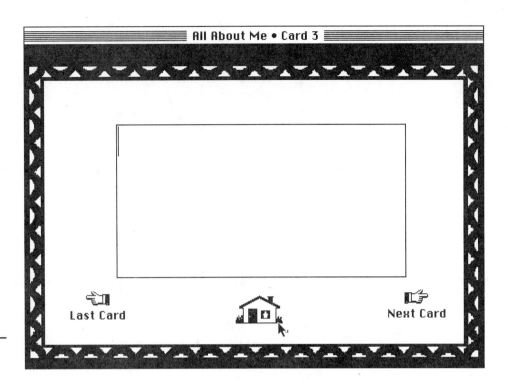

FIGURE 7-13

Drag the house to the bottom of the card.

10. Click outside the graphic to deselect it. The Graphic Appearance dialog box appears with information about the graphic. Click OK and the house is now part of the card.

11. Because this is a graphic object, you may move it at any time. Make sure the Graphic tool is selected (rectangle with a G) and click on the house. Once again the house is surrounded by a dotted line rectangle.

12. Drag the house to a new location.

13. Click outside the rectangle to deselect it. Be sure to place the house exactly where you want it before proceeding to the next step.

14. To place a school house on card 4, I work at..., you will repeat Steps 2 through 10. However, the school house is located in the file labeled Education 2, not Icon Library - Clip Art.

CLASSROOM ←——→ CONNECTION

Have the students create a family tree stack as their first stack. Baby pictures can be scanned in, a QuickTake camera can be used to take pictures of the student and his/her family, and tape recordings of relatives can be saved as sound buttons.

Editing a Text Object   The Text object tool allows you to see and edit information about a text object. You will be able to change the font, color, size, and style of the text. You will change the text on the second card of this stack.

1. Make sure the Browse tool is selected and then move to card 2.

2. On the tool palette click on the Text object tool (row 2, item 3).

3. Double-click within the text object that contains your name to select it. Notice that a moving border appears around the field to show that it is selected.

4. The **Text Appearance** dialog box should be displayed, as shown in Figure 7-14. The Text Appearance dialog box includes the title of the text object, color of the background and of the text, and options that put limits on the field. One of the important options is Read only. With this option checked, you (or your students) cannot accidentally erase or change text in that field. Don't select Read only in a text object until you have typed in the text.

5. Click on the Style... button and the **Text Style** dialog box appears; here you can select font type, style, size, alignment, and color.

6. Watch the words in the box on the top right of the dialog box as you do the following:

    a. Click the box beside Shadow.

    b. Click the box beside Italic.

    c. Click a font size of 36.

    d. Scroll down through the fonts in the top left scroll box until you see New York. Click New York.

    e. Click OK.

    f. You should be back in the Text Appearance dialog box.

7. Click on Read only.

8. Click on green for the text color.

9. Click OK to return to the card. You should see that the text has changed.

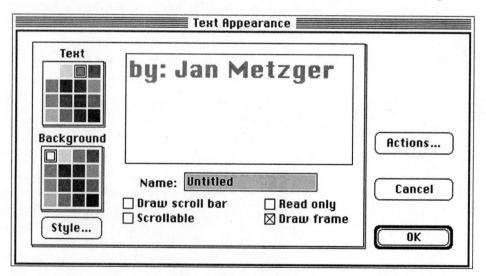

FIGURE 7-14

The Text Appearance dialog box.

Editing a Button

The sound on the button of the first card is applause. As you recall from the introduction, sounds can be added to buttons. Sounds can add greatly to a stack. You will be adding a sound to the second card of your stack.

1. Select the Button tool on the tool palette (row 1, item 2).
2. Notice the buttons on the card all have rectangles around them.
3. Double-click on the right-hand button.
4. From the **Button Appearance** dialog box, click on Actions....
5. From the **Actions** dialog box, look at the list called Things to Do. Click in the box in front of Play A Sound.
6. From the Sound dialog box, click on Disk Library.
7. A list of all sounds available is displayed, scroll down to Funky.Bells and select it.
8. Click Open.
9. To hear the sound, click Play on the Tape deck controls.
10. Now click on OK to accept the sound. This returns you to the Actions dialog box.
11. Click on Done to finish the button action.
12. If a dialog box appears to remind you to switch to the Browse tool, click on Change to Browse tool. Otherwise, click on the Browse tool when you are back on the card.
13. To check the new sound, click on the button.

C L A S S R O O M ←——→ C O N N E C T I O N

Use buttons to record oral directions for students who need extra assistance with work. Because the directions are on a button, it can be repeated an infinite number of times without losing patience!

Practice Adding Sounds and Graphics

1. Add sounds to the other buttons on cards 2 and 3.
2. Use the same sound process, but instead of selecting a sound, record your voice reading the text on one of the cards.
3. Add a new card after the travel card and add a map of the United States (graphic item USA) to it. (Hint: Select Import Background... or Select Clip Art options from the File menu to do this.)
4. Add a graphic object to two more cards in the stack.

Painting Tools

The remainder of the tools on the palette are **painting tools**, tools to actually draw objects. They are painting tools rather than drawing tools because they create bit mapped graphics — graphics comprised of dots, or pixels, that can be edited individually. As you look at these tool icons, notice that many are similar to the tools used in other paint applications. This is one of the features of Macintosh software: Commands carry over from one application to another so that fewer new sets of commands have to be learned with each new program. However, there are some differences between the painting tools in HyperStudio and those you may have used in other programs. You will now explore the different tools available in HyperStudio.

The Fill Tool

1. Move to card 2. This card would look better with more color. Click on the **Fill tool**; it looks like a spilled paint bucket (row 4, item 3).
2. From the Color menu, select a dark orange (row 1, item 3).
3. Move the bucket into the large area surrounding the text object and click. The area should now be orange.

If you made a mistake and what you see is not what you want, do not click anything! Choose Undo Painting from the Edit menu and the last action you did will be removed. Remember this— it will be very important to you!

The Rectangle, the Line, and the Spray Tools

Move to card 8, about your neighborhood. This card would look nice with a row of houses and trees at the bottom. By using different paint tools, we can draw a figure similar to the one in Figure 7-15.

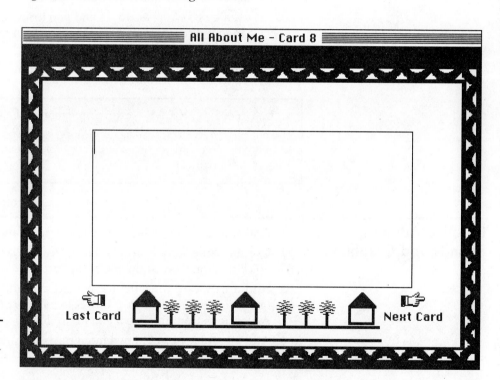

FIGURE 7-15

Trees and houses created with the Rectangle tool, the Line tool, the Fill tool , and the Spray tool.

1. You will need the line to be thick. To do this, double-click on the **Line tool** (row 5, item 2). A dialog box with line thickness choices appears. Click on the second one from the left for a medium thickness. Click OK.
2. Click on the **Rectangle tool** (row 6, item 1).
3. From the Colors menu, select black.
4. At the bottom of the card, draw a rectangle similar to the one in Figure 7-15.
5. To create the roof, you will draw two lines and then use the Fill tool. Click on the line tool (row 5, item 2).
6. Select gray from the Colors menu.

7. Draw a line from the upper left corner of the rectangle you just created, up and to the right until you are approximately half way.

8. Now draw another line from the end of the line you just drew to the upper right corner of the rectangle.

9. Select the Fill tool (row 4, item 3). Click inside the roof, and the roof should now be a solid gray color.

Remember, if you make a mistake, choose Undo Painting from the Edit menu immediately.

Copying and Pasting Graphics

To create more houses, all you need do is copy and paste the one you have. There is no need to draw another house.

1. Click on the **Selector tool**, the dotted rectangle (row 3, item 1). This tool allows you to select an item and then move it, resize it, or manipulate it. It is the same tool you used when selecting a graphic item earlier in the chapter.

2. Draw a rectangle around the house, as in Figure 7-16.

3. From the Edit menu, select Copy.

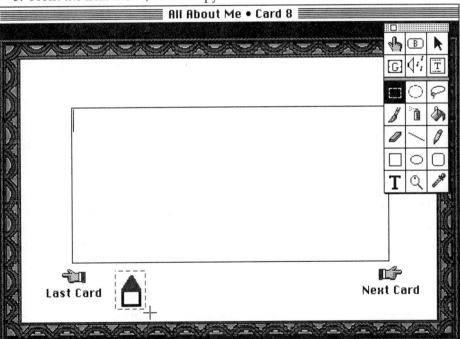

FIGURE 7-16

Use the Selector tool and draw a box around the house.

4. From the Edit menu, select Paste.

5. The new house is on top of the original house. Click on the house and drag it to the right, similar to Figure 7-15.

6. From the Edit menu, select Paste again and drag the third house further to the right.

Now it is time to draw a tree.

Now it is time to draw a tree.

1. Click on the Line tool (row 5, item 2).
2. Select brown from the Color menu.
3. Draw a straight line similar to the tree trunk in Figure 7-15.
4. Click on the **Spray tool** (row 4, item 2).
5. Select green from the Color menu.
6. Move the spray icon directly above the tree trunk and click once. Move the mouse slightly and click again. This should give a look of leaves on a tree.
7. To make the rest of the trees, once again you will copy and paste.
8. Click on the Selector tool (row 3, item 1). Draw a rectangle around the tree.
9. From the Edit menu, select Copy.
10. From the Edit menu, select Paste.
11. Drag the new tree to the right of the original tree.
12. From the Edit menu, select Paste again.
13. Drag this new tree farther to the right, so you now have a row of three trees.

To create the second row of trees, you will copy the three trees as a group and paste one time.

1. Click on the Selector tool (row 3, item 1). Draw a rectangle around all three trees.
2. From the Edit menu, select Copy.
3. From the Edit menu, select Paste.
4. Drag the new tree group to the right of the second house.
5. All you need is a street in front of the houses. Select the Line tool.
6. Select black from the Color menu.
7. Draw two lines similar to those is Figure 7-15. Hold down the Shift key as you draw the line to get a straight line.

Additional Graphics Features

You have used a variety of the painting tools: rectangle, line, spray, select, and fill. You can make many different pictures with just a few tools. There are some other graphics tools that haven't been presented in this chapter. When you feel comfortable with what you have learned so far, you may want to try these. Feel free to explore. If you are afraid you will destroy something important in a stack, create a copy of the stack and use it to play with the graphics. You won't be able to hurt anything, so experiment a little.

Here are a few tips to start you on your explorations:

1. The Pencil, the Paint, the Oval, and the Rounded Rectangle tools were not used. Try them.
2. Choosing **Magnify** from the Options menu (clicking the Magnify tool) "zooms in" to enlarge the part of a card where a painting tool was last clicked. This is valuable when it is necessary to work on small details of graphics. In Magnify you can see and edit the little squares called pixels that make up the graphic. Clicking the Pencil tool on a pixel erases it and clicking on a white area adds a pixel. Great detail work can be accomplished in

this mode. In the bottom, left corner of the screen a small box shows what the normal-sized picture looks like as changes are made to the pixels. To move to a different location of the card, first hold down the Option key to change the arrow to a hand; then hold down the mouse button and drag the mouse around. Notice the picture slides around. Envision your hand on a piece of paper sliding the paper around a desktop. If you continue to double-click on the Pencil tool, the picture will magnify up to 800 percent and cycle over again starting with 100 percent. To leave Magnify, you may double-click the small box with the normal-sized picture or select Magnify from the Options menu, and then select 100 percent from the submenu.

3. The Selector tool, the Circular Selector tool, and the Lasso tool all can be used to select objects on the screen, move them, resize them, and copy them. Experiment with all three. The Circular Selector tool is great for creating oval portraits.

4. A shortcut to copying and pasting a graphic is available. Select the graphic with the Select tool, Circular Select tool, or Lasso tool. Then hold down the Option key and drag the graphic. A copy of that graphic moves with the mouse. This saves the motions of using the Edit menu to create a copy and then paste a copy of the graphic. Holding down the Shift key as you drag moves the copy only in horizontal or vertical directions.

Practice with Graphics

1. On the travel card, mark each state you have visited with a circle.

2. On the favorite season card, draw a scene representing the season using snowflakes for winter, sun and water for summer, flowers for spring, and yellow and orange leaves for fall.

3. Draw a design on the first card of the stack.

Creating a New Stack

The power of HyperStudio is in being able to create your own stack, or project. You will now create a five-card stack about famous explorers. The stack will have a title card and four cards with the name of an explorer and information about the explorer on each card.

The stacks you have worked with so far were set for 16 colors. However, other settings are available. With more colors, you will have more options.

SETTING UP THE STACK

1. To begin your new stack, select **New Stack** from the File menu. You have a blank card. If card numbers do not show with the stack name, Untitled, select Preferences from the Edit menu and click on Show card number with stack name. Click OK.

2. From the Objects menu, select About this Stack. The **About Stack** dialog box, as shown in Figure 7-17, allows you to change the number of colors and the size of the card.

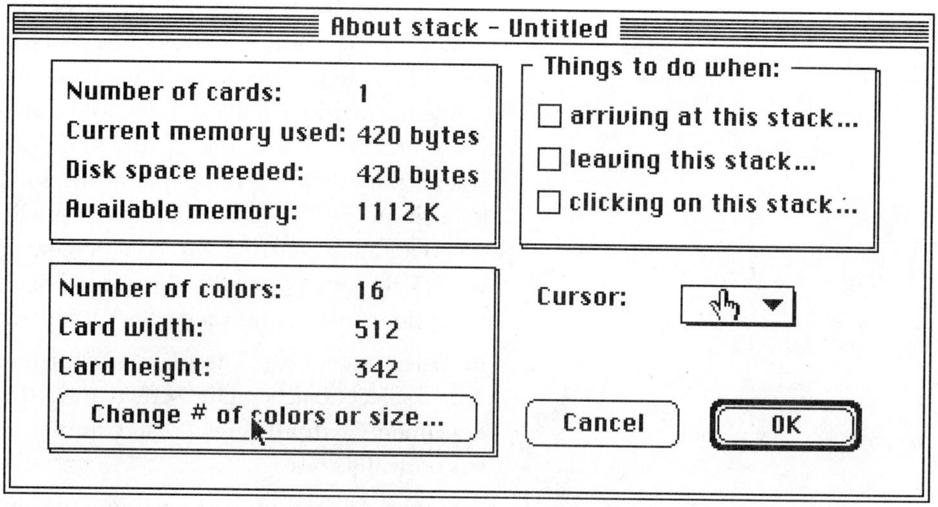

```
┌═══════════════ About stack – Untitled ═══════════════┐
│  ┌───────────────────────────────┐  ┌─ Things to do when: ─┐  │
│  │ Number of cards:      1       │  │ ☐ arriving at this stack... │ │
│  │ Current memory used: 420 bytes│  │ ☐ leaving this stack...     │ │
│  │ Disk space needed:   420 bytes│  │ ☐ clicking on this stack... │ │
│  │ Available memory:    1112 K   │  │                             │ │
│  └───────────────────────────────┘  └─────────────────────┘  │
│  ┌───────────────────────────────┐                           │
│  │ Number of colors:    16       │   Cursor:  [ 🖑 ▼ ]        │
│  │ Card width:          512      │                           │
│  │ Card height:         342      │                           │
│  │ [ Change # of colors or size... ] │  [ Cancel ]  [ OK ]   │
│  └───────────────────────────────┘                           │
└══════════════════════════════════════════════════════════════┘
```

FIGURE 7-17

Click on Change # of colors or size....

4. The colors are preset to 16; click on 256 to have a wider variety of colors.

5. Notice the pull-down menu of card size choices. The standard size is the present one, Standard HyperStudio Size, which is 512 pixels by 342 pixels. This is a good size for designing the stack. The Current Screen Size depends on the size of your monitor. This mode would be good to set after the stack is designed and is ready to be used. Select standard Hyper Studio card, and then click OK.

6. Another option on the About Stack dialog box is the cursor shape. Currently it is set as a hand pointing up; as you can see you have a generous number of options for this. If you change this, be certain that your students will have no problems recognizing the Browse tool. Click OK when you are finished.

7. When you are back on the card, pull down the Color menu. Notice the larger number of colors and patterns. This menu is similar to the Tools menu: You can tear it off and place it on the screen to make it more convenient to use. If you would be comfortable with it on the screen, drag through the Colors menu and drag it to a location on the screen convenient for you. If you place it on the screen, you will notice three new items at the bottom. These show you what color the Active tool, the Eraser tool, and the Text tool are. To change these colors, click on any tool in the tool palette and then click on the color you want.

8. Select Save Stack from the File menu and name the stack *Famous Explorers*. Click Save.

CREATING THE TITLE CARD

Because this stack is about explorers, a world map will be placed on the first card. There is a world map in the clip art folder. However, because it will be the background for this card, you will use Import Background instead of Clip Art or Graphic Object.

1. From the File menu, select Import Background.

2. If a dialog box appears, select Disk file and click OK.

3. From the HS Art folder, scroll down and select World Map. Click Open.

4. You should now have a world map on the first card of your stack.

PAINT TEXT TOOL

The title Famous Explorers needs to be added to this card. Since it is only two words, you do not need to create a text object to accomplish this. Rather, you will use the **Paint Text tool** and type on top of the map. Keep in mind that if you make a mistake, you can use the Delete key as long as you are still in the original Text tool mode. Once you leave that Paint Text tool mode, you will need to erase the letters like any other paint object. If you erase the letters, you will also erase the map, because the eraser erases the entire background at that location. If this occurs, simply reload the world map and try the text again.

1. Click on the Paint Text tool on the tool palette (row 7, item 1).
2. From the Options menu, select Text Style.
3. Select a size of 48 and the color black for the letters. Click OK.
4. To type directly on the map, you need the cursor. Move the mouse to a location on the map where you want to begin typing. Refer to Figure 7-18 for an appropriate location for the title. Click the mouse.
5. You should now have a cursor. Type **Famous** and press Return.

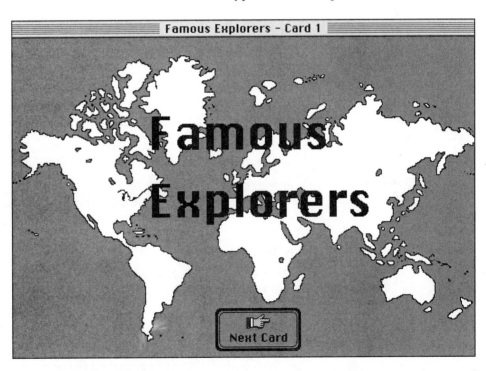

FIGURE 7-18

The title card for the Famous Explorers stack created with Import Background and the Paint Text Tool

6. Type **Explorers,** and you are finished. Remember this is not a text object, and you cannot go back and edit. If you make a spelling mistake, you need to correct it before clicking somewhere else and deselecting that paint text item. If it is too late, you will need to import the background again and try again.

ADDING A BUTTON

To navigate to the next card, a button is needed.

1. Choose Add a Button... from the Objects menu.
2. On the Button Appearance dialog box, type in the button name Next Card.

3. Click on the box Icons... to get the choices of icons.

4. A screen of possible icons appears. Click on the picture of the right hand and then click OK.

5. You are now back on the Button Appearance dialog box. Click OK. A dialog box may appear containing information about moving and sizing the button, simply click OK.

6. The button is now on the card. Move it to a good location on the card (see Figure 7-18).

7. Click outside the button.

8. A new screen appears with choices of Places to go and Things to do.

9. Click in the box in front of Next Card and click OK.

10. A transition screen appears. **Transitions** are the effects shown when moving from one card to another. Several transitions were used in the All about me stack, including Barn Open and Fade to Black. On this button, select Barn Open and click for Medium speed. Click OK.

11. You are back at the Places to go screen. Click Done. Your first card is now finished.

Creating the Cards for the Stack

NEW CARDS

The rest of the cards will be identical, containing two buttons and two text objects. One text object will contain the explorer's name and the other will contain information about the explorer. You will now be creating a card and then copying it three times to have enough cards for the stack.

1. From the Edit menu, select New Card. This card is all white. A blue background would be appropriate. Select the Fill tool from the tool palette.

2. From the Color menu, select the blue closest to the blue on the first card.

3. Click anywhere on the card, and the card should now be blue.

NEW TEXT OBJECTS

There will be two text objects on the card, one for the explorer's name and one for information about him.

1. From the Objects menu, select Add a Text Object.... A dialog box may appear containing information about moving and sizing the text object, simply click OK.

2. A dotted rectangle appears on the card. Use the mouse to move the text box higher on the card. Resize the card by placing the arrow on the bottom line of the text box until the arrow turns into a line with two arrows. Hold down the mouse and drag that bottom line up until the size of the text box is similar to the one in Figure 7-19.

3. Click outside the new text box and the Text Appearance dialog box appears. Click Scrollable and Draw scroll bar so that those choices are off, not selected. If you were typing a large amount of information in this text box, then the scrollable text box would be better. However, the information you enter will be rather short in this exercise.

4. Click on Style…. When that dialog box appears, set the font size at 48 and the font color at black. Select Center from the Align submenu. Click OK.

5. Click OK on the Text Appearance dialog box. This text box will contain the explorer's name.

6. The second text object will contain information about the explorer. To create the text object, repeat Steps 1 through 6 but use a font size of 14 and align left. Refer to Figure 7-19 for size and placement.

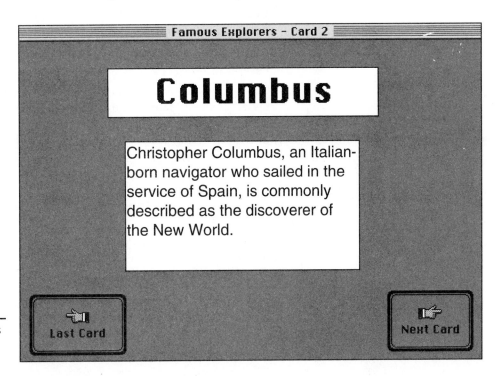

FIGURE 7-19

The second card of the Famous Explorers stack containing two text objects and two buttons.

ADDING BUTTONS

1. This card needs two buttons: one for going to the next card and one for going to the previous card. To create the button to go to the next card, repeat Steps 1 through 11 in the section "Adding a Button." Instead of placing it at the bottom middle of the card, move it to the bottom right corner, similar to Figure 7-19.

2. To create the button to move to the previous card, repeat the steps you just completed to create the button to go to the next card, with three exceptions: on the Button Appearance dialog box, type in the name Last Card, click on Icons… and select the left hand, and when you are on the Places to go dialog box, click in front of Previous card. Everything else is the same. Be sure to place the button in the bottom left corner.

ADDING THE INFORMATON TO THE CARDS

1. Your card should now be ready. To create three more identical cards, select Copy Card from the Edit menu.

2. Then select Paste Card three times. You should now be on card 5 of the stack. The stack is ready; all that is needed is for the current information to be entered.

3. Move to card 2 of the stack and type **Columbus** in the first text box. In the second text box, type the following: **Christopher Columbus, an Italian-born navigator who sailed in the service of Spain, is commonly described as the discoverer of the New World.**

4. Move to card 3 and type in the information for Magellan.

   Magellan - Ferdinand Magellan was the leader of the first expedition to circumnavigate the world.

5. Continue to cards 4 and 5 and type in the information for Cartier and Champlain.

   Cartier - French navigator Jacques Cartier is recognized as the European discoverer of the St. Lawrence River.

   Champlain - Samuel de Champlain is known as the founder of Quebec, the father of New France, and the discoverer of the Ottawa River and Lakes Champlain, Ontario, and Huron.

Your stack is now complete. Test it out. You added a background, text objects, buttons, and text. You also copied and pasted cards. These are the fundamental elements in creating a stack.

CLASSROOM ←——→ CONNECTION

Have students create stacks to introduce their parents to your classroom. The students can design the stack any way they wish. Present the stacks at parent-teacher conferences. If a student has a computer at home, you may legally give him/her a copy of the HyperStudio Player and a copy of the stack to run on a computer at home.

Storyboard

Many times when you are working with a stack, you may decide the order of the cards needs to be changed. Perhaps card 3 is better after card 7 and card 9 should be card 2. HyperStudio makes these changes very easy for you to do with a function called **storyboard**. When using the storyboard, you can move the cards to any location in the stack. You can completely change the order of all the cards if you wish to. Let's move the Champlain card before the Columbus card.

1. From the Extras menu, select StoryBoard. You will see a miniature version of all the cards in the stack.

2. To change the order, you simply move the card to the location you prefer. Place the arrow on card 5 - Champlain. Notice the red box that appears around the card. Drag the card up between card 1 and card 2. Look at the text in the upper left-hand corner of the storyboard. It will tell you where the card will be placed. When it states "Insert between cards 1 and 2" release the mouse. The card has been moved, as shown in Figure 7-20.

3. Click on OK and browse the stack to make sure the cards changed positions.

4. Remember to save the changes if you did not set the Preferences for automatic saving.

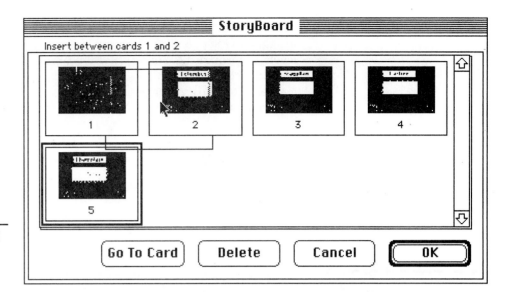

FIGURE 7-20

Drag the card between cards 1 and 2 until the message "Insert between cards 1 and 2" appears.

CLASSROOM ←——→ CONNECTION

Create a stack of a mixed-up story to have the students practice putting events in sequence. Have the students use the storyBoard to put the story in correct order and then print it out. This stack can be very simple, with a picture or one sentence on each card. Have the students create their own story and use the storyBoard to mix up the story and then have another student put it in the correct order.

Practice Changing Card Locations and Adding Cards

1. Move card 4 in front of card 2.
2. Add two more explorers to the stack.
3. Add a blank card between each explorer and use Import Background to place the world map on each of the new cards. Draw lines to show where each explorer is from and where he traveled.

Conclusion

You have accomplished quite a lot in this chapter. You have learned some of the basic vocabulary for using HyperStudio, navigated through stacks, and learned how to create new cards and add, edit, and delete text. You have also used most of the painting tools available in HyperStudio to create and edit graphics and discovered how even simple graphics can enhance the information in a stack. You have also learned how to create a new stack and design cards by adding text objects and buttons.

If you are a beginner, you may feel clumsy when using the painting tools or confused by the variety of options available in HyperStudio. You may also feel that you are working slowly. However, as with any new tool, the more you use HyperStudio the easier it will become. With practice you will be able to navigate through your stacks quickly and create very sophisticated drawings for your cards.

From what you have done in this chapter you may already have gained some insight into the potential of this program for your classroom. It can be used at all levels, K through 12. Young children can use tutorials created in HyperStudio. For older children it can be a discovery tool or a presentation tool. For you, as a teacher, it can be a management tool. In the next chapters, you will learn about the features of HyperCard, its similarities to HyperStudio, and its potentials.

KEY TERMS

Actions…	Home Stack	Save Stack
About Stack	HyperCard	Selector tool
Blank Card	HyperStudio	Sound tool
Browse tool	Line tool	Spray tool
browsing	Magnify	stack
button	Move menu	StoryBoard
Button Appearance	navigating	Text Appearance
Button tool	New Card	text object
card	New Stack	Text object tool
clip art	Paint Text tool	Text Style
Editing tool	painting tools	Tools menu
Fill tool	Preferences	tool palette
graphic object	Ready Made Card	transitions
Graphic object tool	Rectangle tool	
Group Card	Same Background	

EXERCISES

1. Open the stack called Classroom Rules on the Data Disk. Using Copy Card and Paste Card, add six cards to this stack and write your own classroom rules. Illustrate each card. Add sound to the buttons.

2. Open the stack called Parent Welcome on the Data Disk. Use the function Ready Made Cards and add four group cards that will contain information about the coming year and add two cards that will contain the same background but not be part of the group. Add text objects and graphics objects.

3. Find journal articles about specific HyperStudio stacks that have been used in classrooms. Use the Articles stack on the Data Disk to store resource information about the articles. Add a new card for each article.

4. Create a stack and call it Books. The first card should be a title card. Add five more cards that will contain information about books. Include three text objects: title, author, and summary. Make the summary text object scrollable. Add two buttons to navigate forward and backward through the stack. Make the background of the cards pleasant.

5. Create a stack and call it My Adventure. The first card should be a title card. Add six cards that tell a story. Use buttons to create sound effects appropriate for each card. Include graphics on each card.

6. Create a stack of ten cards, call it My Words. Write one word in very large letters on each card. Create a button and record the pronunciation of the word and a sentence using that word. Have all the words in the stack relate to the same topic or the same letter sound.

8

HyperCard— Introduction to Stacks, Fields, and Buttons

OUTLINE

Introduction

HyperCard is a program similar to HyperStudio. It has **cards**, **stacks**, **buttons**, graphics, and text objects called **fields.** If you did not work through Chapter 7, read the first three pages of Chapter 7 for the explanations of these fundamental concepts. They are the same for both HyperCard and HyperStudio. Many other features of HyperCard are either the same or very similar to HyperStudio. If you did work through Chapter 7, you will find it easy to move into HyperCard. The fundamentals are the same. One of the main differences is that button action in HyperCard can become very sophisticated when using the language called HyperTalk. The best way to learn about HyperCard is to actually use it. In this chapter you will be introduced to some fundamentals of HyperCard in a tutorial format. You will learn how to browse through a stack, how to edit fields in a stack, how to use the graphics tools, how to create buttons and fields, how to copy buttons and fields, and how to print a stack. The HyperCard chapters of this text are written based on HyperCard version 2.3. To use the stacks provided on the floppy disk accompanying this text, you need to have HyperCard installed on your hard drive.

Using Stacks

OPENING A STACK FROM THE DESKTOP

Opening a HyperCard stack will also launch, or begin, the HyperCard program. You will be working first with the stack named Machines.hc on the Data Disk.

1. Place the Data Disk in the floppy disk drive.
2. If the disk doesn't open automatically, double-click on it to open it. Notice that many of the icons in the Data Disk window look like stacks of paper or cards.
3. Double-click on the icon named Machines.hc to open the Machines HyperCard stack. This should also launch the HyperCard program.
4. You will see the first card of the stack, as shown in Figure 8-1.

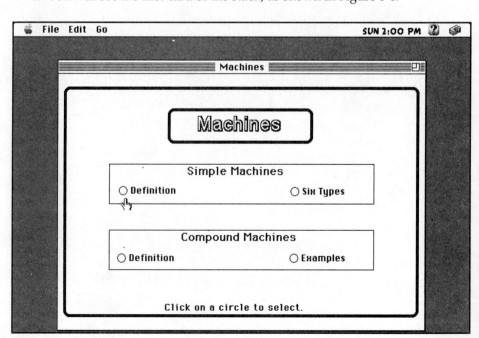

FIGURE 8-1

The first card in the Machines stack.

BROWSING A STACK

In HyperCard **browsing** a stack refers to simply looking through the stack, moving from card to card. This is the same as HyperStudio. Browsing is also referred to as **navigating**, and finding your way through a complex stack can sometimes be quite an adventure. You can browse this sample stack quite easily by using buttons that allow you to go from card to card, by using arrow keys, or by using the Go menu.

Using Buttons to Browse

Notice that as you move the mouse around on the card, the pointer is in the shape of a hand with a pointing finger. This is the icon for the **Browse tool**. With it you can activate buttons by clicking on them. As mentioned earlier, buttons are areas of the screen that can be clicked to cause actions to occur, such as movement to different cards. The first card of the Machines.hc stack has four choices for finding information on machines. Each choice is a button. By clicking on one of the circles, you will "jump" to a certain card of the stack that has the information you want.

1. Click on the Definition button for Simple Machines. This puts you on the card that contains that definition.

2. Click on the Return to Main Menu button at the bottom of the card. This button takes you back to the first card of the stack. You are now on the title card once again.

3. Click on the button labeled Six Types. You should see a card with six simple machines listed on it, as shown in Figure 8-2. Each of these names is another button. Each button will move you to a specific card that contains information about that machine.

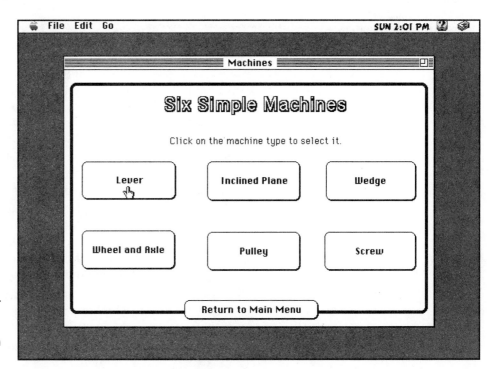

FIGURE 8-2

The Six Simple Machines menu card. Each labeled rectangle is a button to take you to cards with more information.

4. Click on Lever to see the definition and diagram of the lever, as shown in Figure 8-3. This card contains two fields and two buttons. The first field contains the title. Notice that the font is rather large. The second field contains the definition. Because each field can have its own font, size, and style of type, the font size of the second field can be smaller. The right arrow icon is a button that will move you to the next card to see more information about levers. The rounded rectangle at the bottom of the card containing the words Return to Simple Machines is a button to take you back to the Six Simple Machines menu.

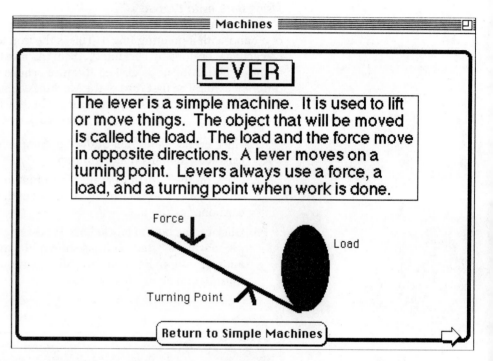

FIGURE 8-3

The Lever definition card has two fields and two buttons.

5. Click on the right arrow icon to move to the next card. This card shows examples of a lever. Notice that there are two buttons at the bottom of this card. In this case the left arrow is for moving back one card. As you can see, HyperCard stacks allow flexibility; you can move to a variety of locations in a stack. Students can select the areas in which they need more practice and can bypass those they don't need.

6. Click on the left arrow. This takes you back to the first card that contains the definition for a lever. This movement allows the student to go back to read the definition a second time if necessary.

7. This time click Return to Simple Machines to move back to the Six Simple Machines menu. Moving back to this screen allows the student to choose another machine, or even to choose the lever again, if needed. Without having to view the entire stack, students can go back to the same information time and time again, until they understand the material.

8. Click Inclined Plane to see the information about the inclined plane. Once again, you will see a definition and a diagram about this simple machine.

9. Click on the right arrow. Samples of an inclined plane are now on the screen. Notice the two buttons at the bottom of the screen: the left arrow

and the Return to the Simple Machines button. When the format on the cards is uniform, it is easier to browse the stack.

10. Click on Return to Simple Machines.

11. Take some time now to explore the rest of the Machines stack by clicking on the various buttons.

12. Return to the Six Simple Machines menu.

Using Arrow Keys to Browse

There are other ways to navigate through a stack that can be quite useful if you are creating or editing a stack. One of these is to use the arrow keys located on the bottom row of your keyboard or in a cluster on the right side of the alphabetic keys. These keys move you through a stack sequentially—you see each card as it occurs in the stack.

1. Press the right arrow key. This takes you to the next sequential card in the stack.

2. Press the right arrow key repeatedly. Notice that eventually you return to the card you started on. This is one reason stacks are compared to Rolodex files—when you reach the last card in the stack you can go right on to the first one and around again, and again, and again, if you want to.

3. Press the left arrow key. This takes you to the previous card in the stack. Pressing this key repeatedly would also take you through the entire stack and back again to the beginning.

However, when you click in a field and the Browse tool has changed to an insertion point, the arrow keys will not work. You must click outside the field to make the arrow keys effective.

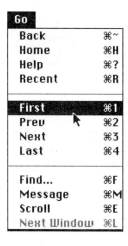

FIGURE 8-4

The Go menu offers a variety of options for moving through the stack.

Using the Go Menu

Another way to move through a stack is by using the **Go menu**. The Go menu offers a variety of options, as shown in Figure 8-4. Next and Prev serve the same functions as the arrow keys, taking you to the next and the previous cards, respectively. But you can also move to other locations.

1. From the Go menu choose First. This should take you to the main menu of the Machines.hc stack, the first card on the stack.

2. Choose Back from the Go menu. Notice this command takes you back to the card you were just on, not necessarily back one card in the stack. HyperCard remembers the order of the cards that you have just moved through. Be careful not to confuse Back with moving backward through a stack, even though the results could be the same if that is the order of cards you just browsed through.

3. To demonstrate how HyperCard remembers the order of the cards, choose **Recent** from the Go menu; a very different screen appears, as shown in Figure 8-5. The Recent window displays an array of all the cards you have seen. If you return to a card, it is not added to the array again. The card you were last on is framed. By clicking on one of these cards you will go directly to that card in the stack. This feature becomes important when you are creating your own stacks and you need to move around quickly instead of moving through the entire stack sequentially and wasting time. The Recent window can also include cards from other stacks that you have recently been in, so you can move easily between stacks as well as between cards.

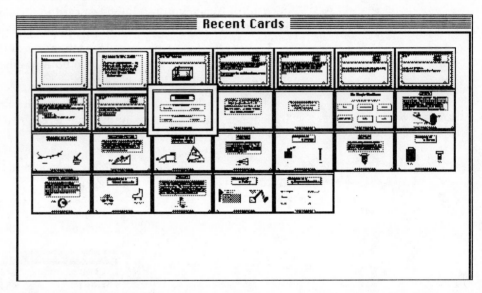

FIGURE 8-5

Selecting Recent from the Go menu displays a screen showing all cards recently viewed. The framed card is the one just viewed.

4. Click on any card to get out of the Recent window. You should go directly to that card.

5. From the Go menu choose Last. The last card in the stack, the one listing types of compound machines, should now be on the screen. Similarly, choosing First moves to the first card in the stack. Be careful not to confuse Back with Last!

QUITTING HYPERCARD

You will now be using another stack on your Data Disk. At some point, now or later, you may choose to take a break and quit using HyperCard. Even if you are not taking a break now, exit the HyperCard program so that you will know how to do it later. Then you will be able to break at any time in the remainder of the chapter.

From the File menu, choose Quit HyperCard. This takes you out of both the HyperCard stack and the HyperCard program.

SAVING STACKS

Before you continue on you should be aware that HyperCard is very different from other Macintosh tool applications in the way it saves files. In a word processing program, for example, if you don't tell the computer to save your edits, they will not be saved, and the document on the disk will remain as it was before you started those edits. When you edit a HyperCard stack, however, the changes are automatically saved. For instance, if you add a graphic to a card, type text in a field, or change the way a button works, those changes will be saved by the time you leave the card. Therefore, if you are concerned that you may make errors in your edits and may want to return to the way the stack was before it was edited, you should save a backup copy of the stack before you make the changes. If the changes are good, you can always delete the backup stack (and then, of course, it is always good to keep a copy of your good stack).

Because the Data Disk is locked and you cannot change any files on it, you will want to copy the remaining stacks you will be working on from the Data Disk to another disk. To copy the stacks to either the hard drive or another disk, review Chapter 1, "Copying and Removing Files on the Desktop."

CLASSROOM ←——→ **CONNECTION**

Use HyperCard to create a presentation of famous African Americans. Each student in the class is assigned a different person to research. The information is then placed on cards, one per person. This stack can then be used for a Black History event during the month of February.

Launching the HyperCard Program

HyperCard can be launched by opening the HyperCard program icon, as well as by opening a stack.

1. Find the HyperCard program icon on your hard drive.
2. Double-click on the program icon, or click once on the icon and choose Open from the File menu, to launch the program. When you start HyperCard, you see the first card of a stack called the Home stack.

THE HOME STACK AND THE HOME CARD

The **Home stack** is a very important stack—the HyperCard program cannot run without it. This stack has special properties that will be helpful to you in the future. The first card of the Home stack is called the **Home card**. It usually displays icons of other HyperCard stacks that can be clicked to open these stacks. The Home stack and the Home card will vary with the different versions of HyperCard. You can also customize the Home card to include icons for your own stacks. In Figure 8-6, two different versions of a Home card are shown. Your Home card may look completely different from these, but every Home card should display the word Home.

You can go to the Home card by launching HyperCard, as you just did, by opening the Home stack, or by choosing Home from the Go menu of any stack.

1. Browse your Home stack by using the arrow keys.
2. Return to the Home card when you finish browsing.

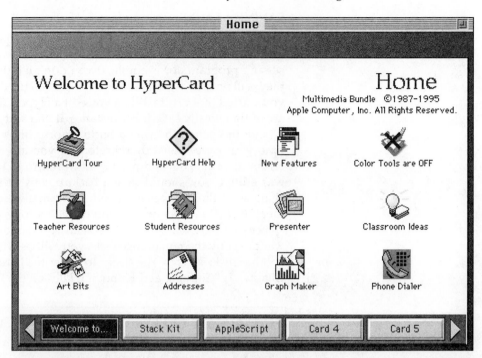

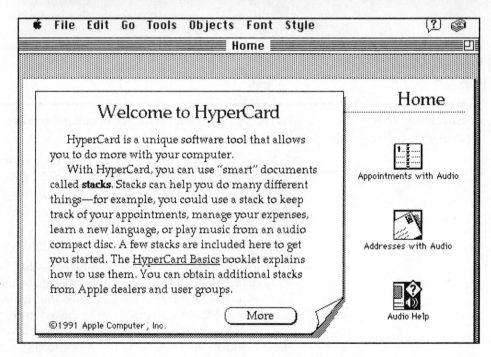

FIGURE 8-6

Two samples of Home cards. The Home card varies with the version of HyperCard you are using.

THE USER LEVEL

Use the left arrow key to move to the last card of the Home stack or select Last from the Go menu. This card, the **Preferences card**, indicates what **user level** you are presently on.

There are five different levels of HyperCard use: Browsing, Typing, Painting, Authoring, and Scripting. Level 1, Browsing, is the lowest user level. At this level you can move through the stack looking at cards, but you cannot make changes to the stack. The highest level, Scripting, allows you full freedom to make stack changes. **Scripting** refers to writing commands that instruct HyperCard to perform specified programming types of activities, such as displaying a particular card, playing sound, or manipulating data.

The menu bar at the top of the screen gives you a hint as to what your user level is; the higher levels have more menu options. Notice the differences between the menu bars shown in Figure 8-7, where the user level is set for Scripting, and that shown in Figure 8-8, where it is set for Browsing. When you are creating and editing a stack, you will want the user level to be set at one of the highest levels. However, to avoid accidental changes to a stack you will probably want stacks you have created and edited to your satisfaction to be set at lower user levels.

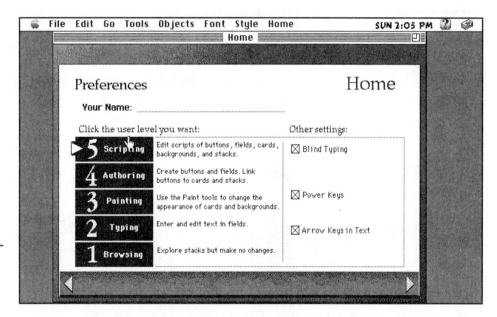

FIGURE 8-7

The Preferences card of the Home stack showing the five user level definitions. This stack is set for Scripting.

In the remaining exercises in this chapter, you will primarily be typing text into fields (Level 2) and painting (Level 3), but you will also be adding new cards to the stack and viewing information related to the higher user levels. So you'll need to set the user level to the highest level, Level 5.

You can set the user level with the last card in your Home stack, if you have a user level card in your Home stack and if it has the fifth level on it, but this will not necessarily control the user level of a particular stack. Stacks often have instructions within them for setting their own levels. You will set the user level after you have opened the Art Museum stack.

Opening a Stack from HyperCard

You can open a stack at any time in HyperCard by using the File menu. Opening a stack automatically closes the stack you are in and opens another.

1. Choose Open Stack... from the File menu to see the Open dialog box.

2. If the Data Disk files are not displayed:

a. Be sure the disk is in the floppy drive.

b. If it is still not displayed, click on Desktop, click on Data Disk, and click on Open.

3. Scroll until you see the name Art Museum in the list of Data Disk files.

4. Double-click Art Museum, or click Art Museum and click Open to open the Art Museum stack.

Setting the User Level

Now that you have a stack opened you will set the user level to Scripting. These instructions allow you to set the user level from any location in a stack, and they will work with most stacks—though not all stacks, because stacks can be protected from changes in a variety of ways.

1. From the Go menu choose Message. The **message box** should appear at the bottom of the screen. The message box is an area for giving scripting (programming) commands directly to the HyperCard.

2. Type **set userLevel to 5**, as shown in Figure 8-8. The word userLevel must be one word with no space between user and level, but capitalization of any or all the letters is optional. HyperCard users often capitalize in this way to make commands easier to read.

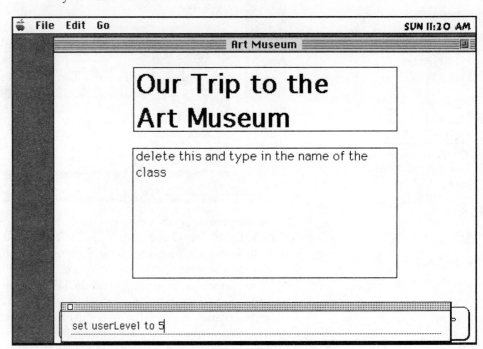

FIGURE 8-8

The command to change the user level has been typed in the message box.

Note: You may type and edit text in the message box as you do in a word processor, except that arrow keys will not move the insertion point—they are for navigation and will take you to another card.

3. Press Return.

4. Your menu bar should now be similar to the one displayed in Figure 8-7, except that the Home menu will not appear, but a Color menu may appear. The color menu will be explored in the next chapter.

5. To hide the message box, click in the close box at the top left of the message box. The user level is now set to 5. Refer to this set of instructions when the user level of the stack you are on does not allow you to make the changes you want.

Information Dialog Boxes

As you work on stacks, there will be many times when you will want information, or need to change specifications, concerning the stack you have open and the objects in it. Choices on the Objects menu display **information dialog boxe**s in which you can see and change this information.

STACK INFORMATION

Information such as how many cards are in the stack and where the stack is located (what disk and folders it is in) can be found in the Stack Info dialog box.

1. From the Objects menu choose **Stack Info...**, as shown in Figure 8-9, to see information about this stack.

FIGURE 8-9

Select Stack Info... from the Objects menu.

2. The Stack Info dialog box indicates, as shown in Figure 8-10, that this Art Museum stack has three cards and one background and is located on the Data Disk.

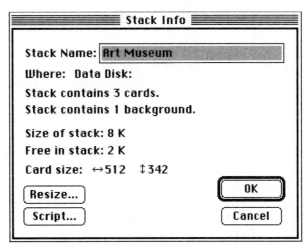

FIGURE 8-10

The Stack Info dialog box indicates there are three cards and one background in this stack.

3. Click on OK or Cancel to return to the stack. Cancel would ignore changes to the stack information, if you had made any, and OK would save the current stack information.

BACKGROUND INFORMATION

You may have noticed in the stack information that the stack has one background. **Background** refers to any fields, buttons, or graphics that were created in the background—in effect, behind the cards. Background can be thought of as lying underneath every card. Objects on the background level are displayed on every card. For instance, in this stack the right and left arrow buttons and the text fields are needed on every card, so they were created in the background. To see just the background, or to work with the background, follow these steps:

1. From the Edit menu choose Background.

2. Notice that the text that was previously on the screen is no longer there and that the menu bar has hatching marks on it, as shown in Figure 8-11, to tell you that you are looking only at the background, not at any particular card.

3. Point to the Edit menu and hold the mouse button down.

4. Notice that on the Edit menu Background has a check mark beside it, as seen in Figure 8-11.

5. From the Edit menu choose Background again to go back to the card.

FIGURE 8-11

The Background command has a check mark in front of it and the menu bar is surrounded with hatching marks when the background is being displayed.

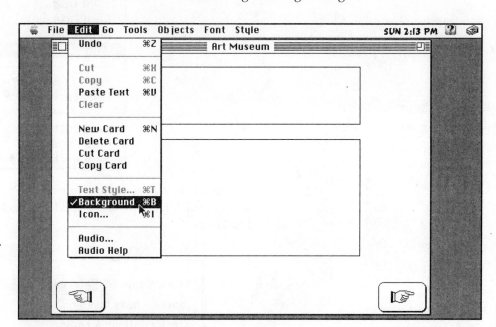

Information such as how many fields and buttons are on the background can be found on the Background Info dialog box. Take a look at the Background Info dialog box for the Art Museum stack:

1. From the Objects menu choose **Bkgnd Info...** to see information about this card's background.

2. The Background Info dialog box indicates that this background has two fields and two buttons, as shown in Figure 8-12.

3. Click on OK to return to the stack.

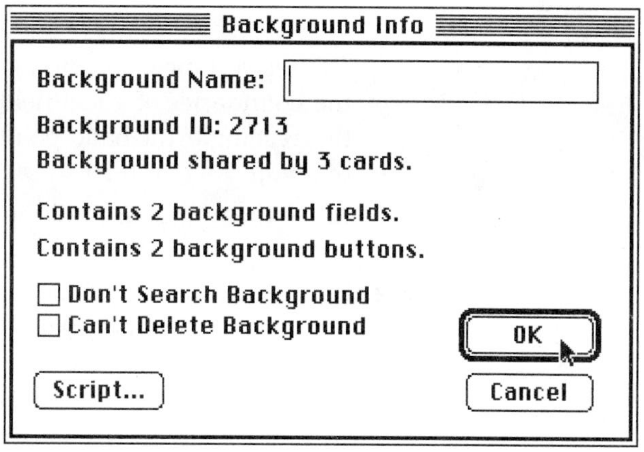

```
╔═══════════════ Background Info ═══════════════╗
║                                                 ║
║  Background Name: [                         ]   ║
║                                                 ║
║  Background ID: 2713                            ║
║  Background shared by 3 cards.                  ║
║                                                 ║
║  Contains 2 background fields.                  ║
║  Contains 2 background buttons.                 ║
║                                                 ║
║  ☐ Don't Search Background                      ║
║  ☐ Can't Delete Background      ┌─────────┐     ║
║                                 │   OK    │     ║
║  ┌─────────┐                    └─────────┘     ║
║  │ Script...│          ┌─────────┐              ║
║  └─────────┘          │ Cancel  │              ║
║                        └─────────┘              ║
╚═════════════════════════════════════════════════╝
```

FIGURE 8-12

The Background Info dialog box indicates three cards, two background fields, and two background buttons.

CARD INFORMATION

Information regarding the card you are on is also sometimes necessary when you are creating or editing a stack. The Card Info dialog box shows, among other things, the card name, if it has been named; the card number, determined by its sequential location in the stack; and the card ID, created internally by the computer. Card names and numbers are useful when you link cards using buttons.

1. To see information about this card, from the Objects menu choose **Card Info...**.

2. As shown in Figure 8-13, the Card Info dialog box indicates that this card is the first of three cards, that it is not named, and that there are no fields or buttons on the card.

3. Click on OK to return to the card.

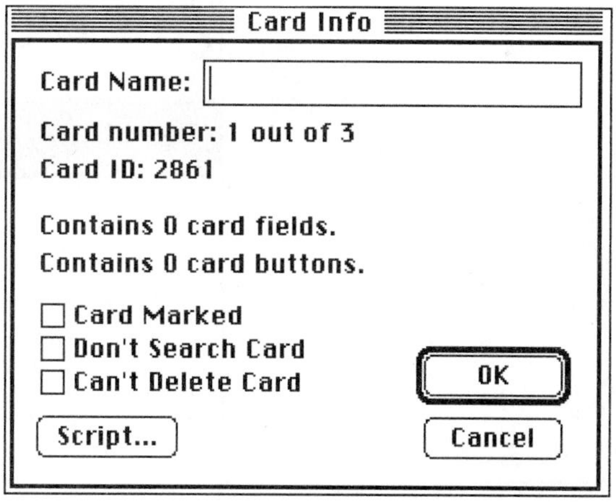

```
╔═══════════════════ Card Info ═══════════════════╗
║                                                   ║
║  Card Name: [                              ]      ║
║                                                   ║
║  Card number: 1 out of 3                          ║
║  Card ID: 2861                                     ║
║                                                   ║
║  Contains 0 card fields.                           ║
║  Contains 0 card buttons.                          ║
║                                                   ║
║  ☐ Card Marked                                    ║
║  ☐ Don't Search Card          ┌─────────┐         ║
║  ☐ Can't Delete Card          │   OK    │         ║
║  ┌─────────┐                  └─────────┘         ║
║  │ Script...│         ┌─────────┐                 ║
║  └─────────┘         │ Cancel  │                 ║
║                       └─────────┘                 ║
╚═══════════════════════════════════════════════════╝
```

FIGURE 8-13

The Card Info dialog box indicates that this is the first card of a three-card stack.

Information dialog boxes can be very useful as you are editing stacks, especially as stack size increases. Remember to refer to these information dialog boxes when you are unclear about card numbers, backgrounds, fields, and buttons.

Editing a Field

A field is an area for typing text. By using a field, the typing can be edited in a manner similar to editing done in any Macintosh word processor. In the following exercises you will be editing text fields.

1. Move the mouse around on the first card and watch the pointer.

2. The top rectangle containing the words Our Trip to the Art Museum marks the boundaries of a text field. Notice that, as you move the pointer within this rectangle, the hand pointer turns into an I-beam pointer. This indicates that you can edit the text.

3. Move the mouse around the lower box and the hand turns into an I-beam again.

4. Editing text fields is done in a manner similar to editing in any Macintosh word processing program—text can be inserted, cut, copied, pasted, and deleted. (Note: The arrow keys cannot be used to move the insertion point, however, because in HyperCard they are used to navigate through the stack.) One way that you can replace the instructions with the class name follows.

   a. Position the I-beam at the beginning of the instruction for typing the class name and click the mouse button.

   b. Hold down the mouse button and drag the I-beam down and to the right to the end of the instruction, as shown in Figure 8-14.

   c. Press the Delete key, or from the Edit menu choose Cut Text.

   d. Type **Grade 5** and press Return. Type **Mr. Andrews** and press Return. Type **Fall Elementary School** and press Return.

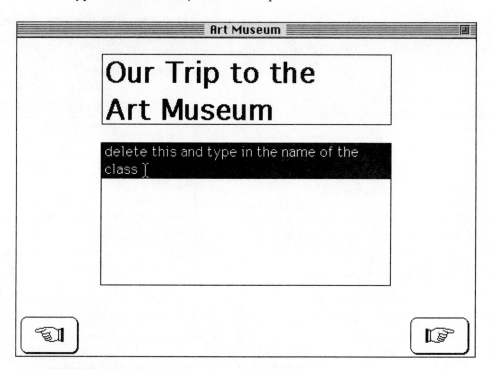

FIGURE 8-14

Highlight the text and press the Delete key to remove the instructions.

5. Click the right arrow button to go to the next card.

6. The second card of the stack describes the Egyptian room and the sentences were written by Justin. You will continue this format for the rest of the cards. Click the right arrow button to go to the next card.

7. The third card has a blank field where you are going to type in information about the class trip to the art museum. The information for this stack will be written as if a different student wrote each card.

a. Click in the upper left hand corner of the lower text field to get an I-beam.

b. Type the following information on this card:

We visited the Swiss room.   This is a real room. It contains a ceramic furnace that is painted with great detail. The furniture in the room is all wood, even the walls are all wood. It is amazing to believe that a family could live together in such a small room! Allison

Your card should look like Figure 8-15.

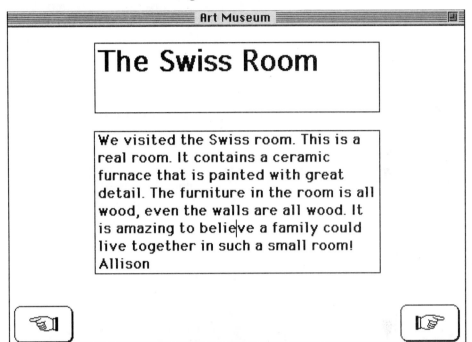

FIGURE 8-15

Text has been typed in the two fields on the third card of the Art Museum stack.

Adding Cards to a Stack

This stack has no more cards, but more are needed. Cards can be inserted any-place in a stack, except before the first card. The following steps place a new, blank card in the stack immediately behind, or after, the current card.

1. Make sure you are on the third (and last) card in the stack.

2. From the Edit menu choose **New Card**.

3. You should see the new card on the screen. It should contain only the back-ground objects, with no text in the text field.

4. Check to be sure it is the fourth card: from the Objects menu choose Card Info… and look to see that the card number is 4.

5. Click on OK to return to the new card.

6. Type the following information in the top field on the new card (remember to click in the upper left corner of the field to get an I-beam first):

The Glass Room

7. Type the following information in the second field on the new card (remember to click in the upper left corner of the field to get an I-beam first):

The art museum has a large glass exhibit. There are glass containers from 3000 B. C. A glass punch bowl used at a World's Fair is also displayed. It is huge! There are many glass mugs with drawings that tell stories on them. Julius

8. From the Edit menu choose New Card again. This will create another card, which should be card 5. Type in the following:

Top field: **The Cloisters**
Second field:

One of the most inspiring rooms in the art museum is the Cloisters. It is a darkened courtyard with arches made of different styles with a fountain in the middle. It really feels like you are in a real courtyard in the Middle Ages! Rosa

9. Repeat Step 8 to make one more card and place the following information on it.

Top Field: **The Modern Art Room**
Second Field:

There were many different kinds of paintings in this room. Some were just colors and not pictures. Some were sculptures. I liked the bright colors in some of these paintings. Mary

10. Browse through your stack with the arrow keys. If you created too many cards, you may want to delete them. With the extra card displayed on the screen, choose Delete Card from the Edit menu.

CLASSROOM ←————→ CONNECTION

Create a stack containing your classroom rules. Use an overhead projector and an LCD unit with the computer to have the students develop the rules as a class. Type in the rules as the class agrees on them. Refer to this stack during the year to reinforce the rules or have this stack available for open house or parent-teacher conferences.

Practice with Adding Cards and Editing Fields

1. Add at least two new cards anywhere in the stack, using your own knowledge about an art museum.

2. Edit the text in the card fields. If you find typing errors, phrasing that could be better, points that could be clearer, or grammar that needs correcting, fix what you find.

3. Add new cards to the stack Favorites on the Data Disk. Type in some of your favorite nursery rhymes—or change the theme and type in your favorite poetry, your favorite quotes, your favorite sayings, or just your favorite facts or ideas.

The Tools Menu

The **Tools menu** on the HyperCard menu bar is important. Whenever you are in HyperCard, you are using one of the HyperCard tools (Figure 8-16 shows the icons used for these tools). Although you may not have realized it, you have been using the Browse tool. The Browse tool, represented by a pointing hand, is what has allowed you to move through the stacks and to edit fields. If you wanted to create a field or change a field (in ways other than editing text), you would need to select the **Field tool**, represented by the rectangular icon with dotted lines representing text. The Tools menu also has a **Button tool** for creating and changing buttons and painting tools that can be used to create and edit graphics in a stack. Graphics add a dimension to a stack that can make an impact on a presentation, can increase the interest level of a learner, and can help the learner by associating a picture with a word or phrase. You will be using the Field tool, the Button tool, and the painting tools in this chapter.

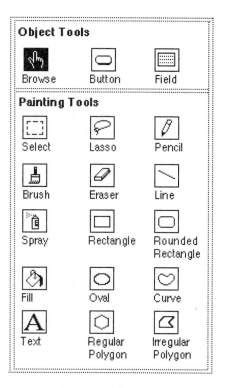

FIGURE 8-16

The HyperCard Tools menu with all tools labeled.

Sometimes when editing stacks you will need to use the Tools menu frequently. To make the tools easier to access, you can "tear" the Tools menu off the menu bar so that it stays visible on the screen. This saves many motions of continually selecting the Tools menu. To place the Tools menu, also called the **tool palette**, on the Desktop, follow these steps.

1. In the Art Museum stack, position the pointer on the Tools menu.
2. While holding the mouse button down, drag through the menu and continue to slide down and to the right. A flashing rectangle should follow the pointer as you move it to the bottom right corner of the screen. Release the mouse button. The tool palette will stay on the screen in the new location.
3. Position the pointer on the title bar of the tool palette.
4. Drag the title bar to another location on the screen. This is the same technique used to move windows around the Desktop. In this way you can position the tool palette wherever it is convenient.
5. To remove the tool palette from the Desktop, click the close box on the top left of its title bar.

The Field Tool and Field Information

The Field tool allows you to see and edit information about a field. You will take a look at the information available for one of the fields you used in the Art Museum stack.

1. Go to the third card, the Swiss Room, of the Art Museum stack. (Use the arrow keys or the Recent option of the Go menu.)

2. Tear off the Tools menu, so that it is easy to access.

3. On the tool palette click on the Field tool (row 1, item 3). When the Field tool is selected, lines appear in every field on a card—two fields in this case—to show you where the fields are.

4. Click within the field that contains the student comments to select it. Notice that a moving border appears around the field to show that it is selected.

5. From the Objects menu choose **Field Info...**, as shown in Figure 8-17. This option is only available when you have chosen the Field tool and selected a field. The Field Info dialog box should be displayed, as in Figure 8-18.

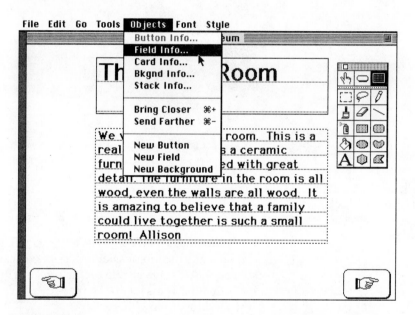

FIGURE 8-17

Select Field Info... from the Objects menu only after you have selected a field.

The Field Info dialog box includes the name of the field, the field number, and field ID, and a preview box to see how your text will appear on the card. A Style pop-up menu is located on the right side of the card.

Other options on the right allow you to put limits on the field; one of the important ones is **Lock Text**. With this option, you (or your students) cannot accidentally erase or change text in that field. Don't select Lock Text in a field until you have typed in the text for that field.

6. Click on the small box containing Text Style... and you will see the Text Properties dialog box with choices of font style, type, and size, as shown in Figure 8-19. The number and kind of fonts depends on your computer.

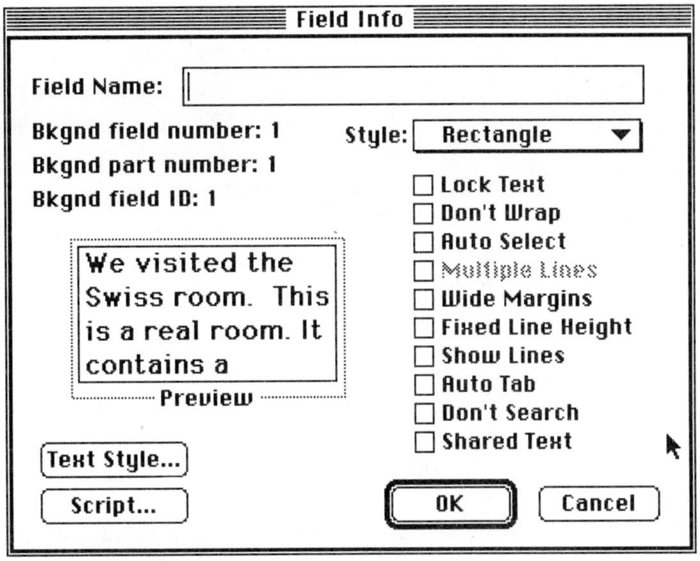

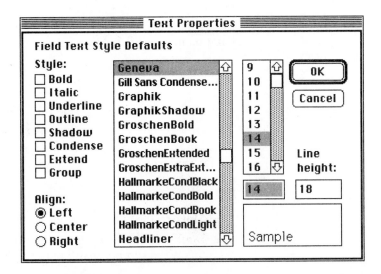

FIGURE 8-18

The Field Info dialog box showing preview text and a rectangle style.

7. Watch the word Sample in the box on the bottom right of the dialog box as you do the following:

   a. Click the box beside Bold.

   b. Click the box beside Italic.

   c. Click a font size—such as 10 or 18—that is not currently highlighted.

   d. Click a font—such as Helvetica or New York—that is not currently highlighted.

   e. Choose a font, size, and style that you would like to have for this field in your stack. Remember that this field is a background field, so changing these characteristics of the field will affect text on all the cards in your stack.

   f. Click OK when you are happy with what you have chosen. You should be back on the card with the Field still selected.

FIGURE 8-19

The Text Properties dialog box. The word Sample shows how the choices will affect the text.

You used the Field Info dialog box to change the text styles. You can also change the style of the text box.

8. If the field is not selected, click on the field. Again choose Field Info… from the Objects menu to see the Field Info dialog box.

9. Currently, the style of the field is a rectangle. Move the mouse to the word Rectangle and hold down the mouse. A pop-up menu of styles will appear. Drag the mouse down and select Shadow. If you find later that you like the field better with the rectangle, you can change it again.

10. Click OK to return to the card.

11. Click the Browse tool (the pointing hand on the tool palette). Remember: This is necessary if you want to edit fields or to use buttons to browse through your stack. Browse your stack to see how the field changes affected it.

PRACTICE WITH FIELD INFORMATION

1. Try other font and style changes for the fields: Select the Field tool and the field again and go back to the Field Info dialog box to change your field. Then browse the stack again. Repeat these procedures until you are satisfied with the stack and feel comfortable with using the options.

2. Review: Add another card to your stack that states how helpful the Art Museum guide was to the class.

Enhancing a Stack with Graphics

The top three tools on the tool palette are considered to be object tools, because they deal with objects such as buttons and fields. The remaining tools are painting tools for graphics. They are considered to be painting tools rather than drawing tools because they create bitmapped graphics—graphics comprised of dots, or pixels, that can be edited individually. As you look at these tool icons, notice that many are similar to the tools used in other paint applications. This is one of the features of Macintosh software: Commands carry over from one application to another so that fewer new sets of commands have to be learned with each new program. However, there are some differences between the painting tools in HyperCard and those you may have used in other programs. You will now explore the different painting tools available in HyperCard.

THE RECTANGLE TOOL, THE PATTERN MENU, AND THE BRUSH TOOL

The Art Museum stack can be greatly enhanced with pictures. You will notice that many of the painting tools are the same as the tools in HyperStudio. You will briefly explore some of the painting tools. The Cloister card would look good with a picture of arches on it. You will create the arches by using the Rectangle and the Brush tools.

1. Move to the Cloister card.

2. Double-click on the **Rectangle tool**. Notice the rectangle became shaded, this is the symbol that the rectangle you draw will be a solid color.

3. From the **Pattern menu**, select black (row 2, item 2).

4. At the bottom of the card draw a rectangle similar in size and location to the one in Figure 8-20.

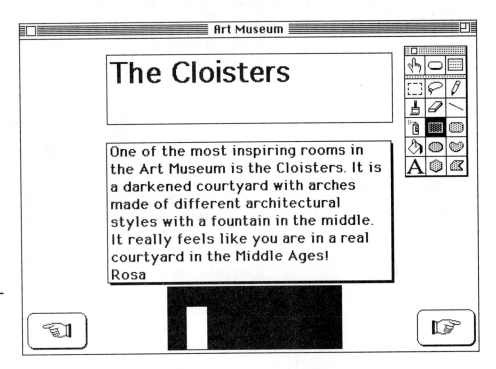

FIGURE 8-20

Create a rectangle at the bottom of the card. Draw a white rectangle on top of the black rectangle.

To draw the arches, you will draw a white rectangle inside the black rectangle and then top the white rectangle off with a circle.

1. From the Pattern menu, select white (row 1, item 1).

2. Draw a white rectangle inside the black one similar to Figure 8-20.

3. To create the curve at the top of the arch, double-click on the **Brush tool** (row 3, item 1). This dialog box contains choices for the brush shape. Because you need a curve, click on the largest circle. You are now back on the card.

4. Move the circle to the top of the white rectangle and click when half of the circle is in the white rectangle and half is above the white rectangle. Refer to Figure 8-21 for help. This should create the arch. If your circle is smaller than the white rectangle, hold down the mouse button and slide gently to fill in the gaps. If you make a mistake, select Undo from the Edit menu before pressing any other keys.

FIGURE 8-21

Click the mouse when half of the circle is in the white rectangle and half is above the white rectangle. Move the circle to the right and click again to create the arch.

COPYING AND PASTING GRAPHICS WITH THE SELECT TOOL

Your cloister needs a few more arches. You will create the rest by copying the one you have created. By using the **Select tool** and the Option key, you can create the rest of the arches.

1. From the tools palette, click on the Select tool (row 2, item 1).

2. Surround the arch you created with the flashing rectangle similar to Figure 8-22.

FIGURE 8-22

Surround the arch with the select box.

3. Hold down the Option key, place the arrow inside the flashing rectangle, and drag the flashing rectangle to the right. Notice the original arch is in place and a second arch is in the flashing rectangle.

4. Move the arch until it is positioned next to the original. Refer to Figure 8-23 for placement.

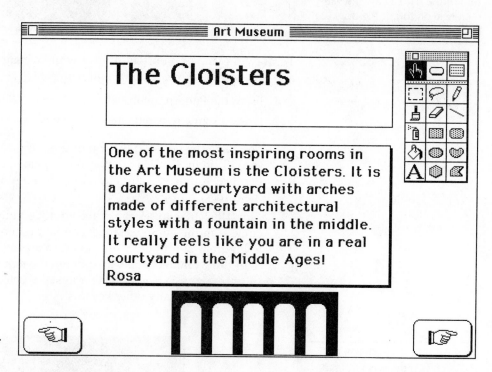

FIGURE 8-23

The completed arches.

5. Continue to hold down the Option key but let go of the mouse button. Your arch is in place. Do not click anywhere else.

6. Continue to hold down the Option key, click on the flashing rectangle containing the arch, hold down the mouse button, and drag to the right of the

second arch to create the third arch. If you let go of the Option key or you do not have the flashing rectangle, simply repeat Steps 1 through 5.

7. You now have the three arches in the cloister. By using the Option key, you eliminated the need to use the Edit menu option of copy and paste. The Option key method is quicker. Make as many arches as you need.

THE SPRAY TOOL, THE LINE TOOL, AND THE OVAL TOOL

The Modern Art card can use a painting representative of modern art. To accomplish this, you will draw a rectangle at the bottom of the card and then use your own artistic talent to create a modern art painting by using the **Spray tool**, the **Line tool**, the Brush tool, and the **Oval tool**.

1. Move to the Modern Art card.
2. Select the Rectangle tool. If the tool is shaded in, double-click on it to change it to outline.
3. Draw a rectangle at the bottom of the card.
4. Use the following tools and create your own design: Spray, Line, Brush, and Oval. Use the Pattern menu to select different patterns for each tool. Remember to double-click on the Brush tool to select a smaller brush size. Have fun and be creative!

PRACTICE WITH GRAPHICS

1. Create a mummy on the Egyptian card.
2. Create a building on the title card.
3. Create a punch bowl on the Glass Room card.

C L A S S R O O M ←——————→ C O N N E C T I O N

Have the students use the painting tools to draw a picture to go with their written story. Or have the students draw a diagram of a cell and label the parts or create different kinds of bacteria diagrams. The students could draw pictures to demonstrate the orbits of the earth and the moon.

ADDITIONAL GRAPHICS FEATURES

Some other graphics options are available that haven't been presented in this chapter. When you feel comfortable with what you have learned so far, you may want to try these. Feel free to explore. If you are afraid you will destroy something important in a stack, create a copy of the stack and use it to play with the graphics. You won't be able to hurt anything, so experiment a little.

A few tips to start you on your explorations:

1. Try some of the tools that were not used. Many will be simple to use. Use the **Pencil tool** on both white and black areas to see what it does. With the **Irregular Polygon tool**, click at the ends of each side of the polygon you draw, and for the last side either return to the beginning point or double-click.

2. On the HyperCard menu bar, the Paint, Options, and Patterns menus appear whenever any painting tool is selected. Pull down the Paint and Options menus and try the choices on them. (Keep in mind that a selection is frequently required for a menu choice to work.)

3. Many of the menu choices have keys on the keyboard that you can use as an alternative to using the menus. For instance, by holding down the Command key (the key with the and ⌘ symbols on it, on the bottom row of the keyboard) as you type M, the message box will be displayed, just as if you selected Message from the Go menu. On most pull-down menus, you will see these alternative keys displayed to the right of the menu options. Using these keys is frequently more efficient than using the pull-down menus.

4. Most of the painting tools perform somewhat differently if you hold down the Shift key while using the tool. Figure 8-24 tells what each tool does and also lists the effects double-clicking has on each tool.

5. Choosing **Fat Bits** from the Options menu (or double-clicking the Pencil tool) "zooms in" to enlarge the part of a card where a painting tool was last clicked. This is valuable when it is necessary to work on small details of graphics. In Fat Bits you can see and edit the little squares called pixels that make up the graphic. Clicking the Pencil tool on a pixel erases it and clicking on a white area adds a pixel. Great detail work can be accomplished in this mode.

   In the bottom left corner of the screen a small box shows what the normal-sized picture looks like as changes are made to the fat bits. To move to a different location of the card, first hold down the Option key to change the arrow to a hand; then hold down the mouse button and drag the mouse around. Notice the picture slides around. Envision your hand on a piece of paper, sliding the paper around a Desktop. To leave Fat Bits you may double-click the Pencil tool, choose Fat Bits again from the Options menu, or click inside the small picture in the bottom left hand corner.

6. Holding down both the Option and Shift keys as you drag a selected graphic moves the copy only in horizontal or vertical directions. Holding down both the Option and ⌘ keys as you drag a selected graphic copies the graphic repeatedly and leaves the copies on the card as you drag. (Try this—it's fun!)

FIGURE 8-24

Added features of the painting tools.

Tool	Double-clicking on Tool	Holding down Shift key while using mouse
Select	Selects entire graphic layer	Drags vertically or horizontally only
Lasso	Selects all graphics	Drags vertically or horizontally only
Pencil	Changes to and from Fat Bits	Moves vertically or horizontally only
Brush	Choice of brush width	Moves vertically or horizontally only
Eraser	Erases all graphics	Moves vertically or horizontally only
Line	Choice of line width	Angles in increments of 15 degrees
Spray	None	Moves vertically or horizontally only
Rectangle	Pattern-filled rectangle	Draws Perfect Squares
Rounded Rectangle	Pattern-filled rectangle	Draws Perfect Squares
Fill	Choice of pattern	None
Oval	Pattern-filled oval	Draws Circles
Curve	Pattern-filled curve	None
Text	Choice of font, size, & style	None
Regular Polygon	Choice of polygon type	Rotates in increments of 15 degrees
Irregular Polygon	Pattern-filled polygon	Angles in increments of 15 degrees

7. The Select tool and **Lasso tool** can also be used to enlarge and shrink selected graphics, if the ⌘ key is held down while you drag. Hold both the ⌘ and Shift keys as you drag one side of a graphic to enlarge or shrink in only horizontal or vertical directions. Hold both keys and drag a corner to enlarge or shrink proportionally, so that your graphic won't be distorted in height or width. (There is always some chance of distortion of bitmapped graphics when their size is changed, because the program has to decide which pixels to add or delete.)

This chapter is not divided into lessons, because everyone varies in pace, endurance, and interest. If you need or want to take a break, you can do it at the end of almost any section. If you must quit HyperCard, simply open the same stack when you return, be sure the user level is set to 5, and go to the card you were last on.

The basic steps for opening stacks are outlined here for a quick reminder. Any time you need to open a stack, you can refer back to these steps. For more detailed instructions, see the beginning of this chapter. The next stack you will be using is the Welcome stack.

1. If you are starting a new session:
    a. With the computer on, put the Data Disk in the floppy drive.
    b. Open the Data Disk by double-clicking on it.
    c. Double-click on the stack labeled Welcome.
    Or, if you are already in HyperCard:
    a. Select Open Stack… from the File menu.
    b. Open the Data Disk, if it's not already open.
    c. Double-click on the stack labeled Welcome from the list of stacks.
2. You should see the title card of the Welcome stack.
3. If you do not have all the menus showing, set the user level to Scripting by doing the following:
    a. From the Go menu choose Message.
    b. Type **set userLevel to 5.**
    c. Press Return.
    d. Close the message box or choose Message again from the Tools menu.

Working with Buttons

Buttons provide control to the users of the stack who may know nothing about HyperCard. By simply clicking buttons, users can have a wealth of options, such as moving through a stack, displaying different information, hearing sound, and even viewing animation. As a HyperCard author, you make these options available to the users of your stacks by creating and editing buttons. This section shows you how to create and edit buttons and define what the buttons will do.

CREATING A NEW BUTTON

In this exercise, a shell stack for a school welcome is available, but elements are missing: buttons to navigate through the stack and fields containing information about the school are needed.

The first card of the stack is a title card. Notice there is no button that allows you to move to the next card. You must create one.

1. Tear off the Tools menu (drag it down and to the side as you did earlier). This will give you easy access to the Button and the Field tools.

2. Click on either the Browse tool or the Button tool. From the Objects menu, choose New Button. A new button will appear in the center of the card, as shown in Figure 8-25. Notice that a flashing dotted line appears around the button. This means that the button is selected and can be worked with.

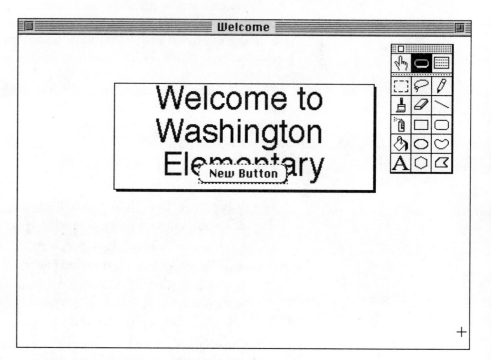

FIGURE 8-25

The New Button option on the Objects menu places a new button in the middle of the card.

3. Drag the new button down to the bottom of the card.

CHOOSING A BUTTON ICON

1. The next thing you want to do is set up the button and choose an icon to represent this button. The button should still be selected. However, if the button is not still selected, select it by clicking on it once.

2. From the Objects menu, choose **Button Info...**. You should see the Button Info dialog box. This is only available when the Button tool has been chosen and a button has been selected.

3. Type **Click Here to Continue** in the Button Name box. By doing this we will give instructions to the user.

4. Hold down the mouse on the Style pop-up menu (a pop-up menu can be recognized by the solid triangle facing down) and drag up to select Transparent. This will hide any box around the button.

5. Click on Icon.... You should see a dialog box with a choice of icons, as shown in Figure 8-26.

6. Look for a picture of the house similar to that shown in Figure 8-26. If it is not visible, scroll through the array until you locate one.

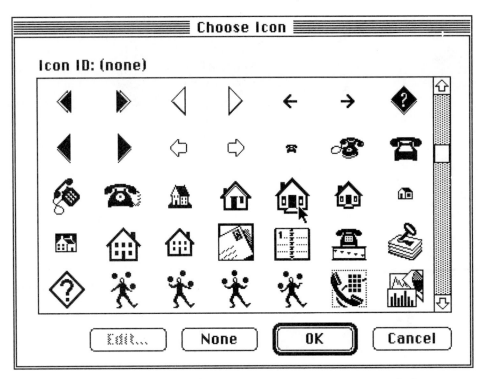

FIGURE 8-26

The Choose Icon dialog box shows an array of various icons. Click on the house icon.

7. Click on the house icon. This selects the icon to display over the button.
8. Click OK. You should return to the card and see the selected button with part of the house displayed on it.

MOVING AND RESIZING A BUTTON

You need to reshape the button to the shape of the house icon and the instructions.

1. With the Button tool still selected, position the pointer on a corner of the flashing box around the selected button. (Position the tip of the pointer just inside the corner for best results.)
2. Drag the corner of the button until the entire button name and house are visible.
3. If the shape of the button did not change, you missed the corner. Just try again.
4. Continue to reshape the button until the entire button name and house are visible.

SETTING TASKS FOR A BUTTON

Now it is time to script the button. Scripting is the method of telling the stack what to do; it is a form of programming. Simple scripting can be chosen from a menu of items. More sophisticated scripting must be written in the Script window. This will be addressed in the next chapter.

1. If the button is not still selected, select it by clicking on it.
2. From the Objects menu, choose Button Info… to get the Button Info dialog box.

3. Click on Tasks…. There are eight sets of **tasks** available in HyperCard: Go to Destination, Visual Effect, Launch Applications, Movie, Sound, Speak Text, CD Audio, and Laser Disc. Each task has its own menu of choices. You will be working with only the Go to Destination and Visual Effect tasks now. The rest will be explored in the next chapter.

4. You are presently on the Go to Destination menu. A list of places to go are displayed under Choose a destination on the right. Because this button will move to the next card, click in the circle in front of Next Card. By clicking on this choice, actual script is written in the script window. This is a short-cut for scripting.

ADDING A VISUAL EFFECT TO A BUTTON SCRIPT

The next step is to add a **visual effect** to the script. A visual effect is the visual impression you get as the screen changes to a new card. For instance, the visual effect you will use here is scrolling—when you go to a new card, it will appear as though the new card is scrolling onto the screen.

1. Notice the second icon on the left side is Visual Effect.

2. Click on the Visual Effect icon. A long list of visual effects appears on the right side of the screen.

3. Use the scroll bar and locate scroll left.

4. Click on scroll left, as shown in Figure 8-27.

5. Click on Assign Tasks.

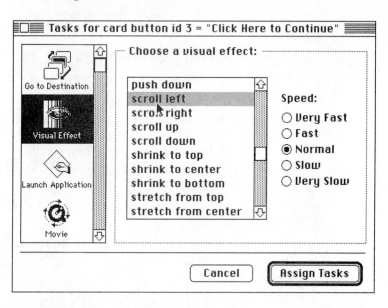

FIGURE 8-27

The Visual Effect task choices with the effect scroll left and the speed of Normal selected.

This automatically places the script for the visual effect into the button script. To see what that script looks like, you can return to the Button Info dialog box.

1. With the button still selected, from the Objects menu choose Button Info….

2. Click on Script…. Notice the commands "visual effect scroll left" and "go to next card" are now part of the script of this button. You could also type

these commands in directly without choosing Tasks… from the Button Info dialog box.

3. Close the script by clicking in the close box. You are now back on the title card.

TESTING A NEW BUTTON

1. Click on the Browse tool. Buttons can only be activated from the Browse mode.

2. Click on the button to see the effect in action. The next card should appear to scroll onto the screen.

3. If it does not work, make sure you selected the Browse tool before clicking the button. If you are still having difficulty, repeat the steps above to determine where the mistake was made.

The Message Box

Because you clicked on the new button, you are now on the second card with no apparent way to get back. However, you have three different ways to return to the first card. Two are familiar to you: you can choose Back from the Go menu or use the left arrow key on the keyboard. A third method is to use the message box, as you did when you set the user level. Through this box you give HyperTalk commands directly to HyperCard. HyperTalk is the programming language you saw in the script of the button you made. It will be discussed in more detail in the next chapter.

1. Choose Message from the Go menu. The message box appears at the bottom of the screen, as shown in Figure 8-28.

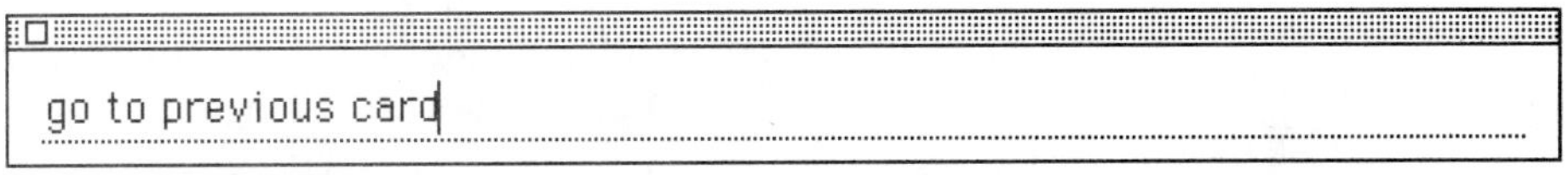

FIGURE 8-28

The message box with a HyperTalk command typed in it.

```
go to previous card
```

2. Type **go to previous card.** (Remember that the arrow keys are used to take you to a new card—if you make an error, do not use them to edit.)

3. Press Return. You should now be on the first card of the stack.

4. Choose Message from the Go menu—or click on the close box—to make the message box disappear.

The message box is useful when you are creating stacks or browsing stacks. You should recall that the message box was used to set the user level in the first lesson. The keyboard shortcut for activating the message box is ⌘ M (hold down the ⌘ key and type M); this will show or hide the message box, depending on whether it was previously hidden or shown.

Copying a Button

The second card needs a button to connect it to the third card. The button used on the first card would work very well. This section shows you how to copy a button from one card to another.

1. Make sure you are on the first card.

2. Click on the Button tool.

3. Click on the button to select it.

4. From the Edit menu choose Copy Button.

5. Move to the second card. (Using the right arrow key on the keyboard avoids the extra step of changing back to the Browse tool.)

6. From the Edit menu, choose Paste Button. The button should appear in the same location that it appears on the first card. You have now copied your first button!

Working with Buttons and Fields

COPYING A FIELD

A field like the field on the first card is needed on the second card. You may have noticed that the field on the first card is unlike those you worked with in the Art Museum stack—it does not appear on all cards in the stack. The reason for this is that it is a card field, rather than a background field—it was not created on the background and can only be seen on one card. Likewise the buttons you have created are card buttons. In this exercise you will copy the field from the first card to the second card.

1. Return to the first card.

2. Select the Field tool.

3. Click on the title field to select it.

4. Choose Copy Field from the Edit menu.

5. Move to the next card.

6. Choose Paste Field from the Edit menu. Notice that the text did not copy, only the field itself.

7. Type the following information into the new field, as you did in the prior field: **A School of Excellence**. (Remember, this must be done with the Browse tool.)

So far, you have created and copied buttons and fields. While creating the button, you chose the icon to use for the button and then resized it. You chose the visual effect for the movement from one card to the next and also chose the destination for the button. You copied a field and pasted it onto another card. These are very important concepts necessary for working with HyperCard. They will be used continuously in this chapter and in the next. You will now create buttons and fields for the rest of the stack. The instructions will be more concise than the previous instructions. You may need to refer to the lessons you just completed when going through the following steps to place buttons and fields on the rest of the stack.

CREATNG MORE BUTTONS

The rest of the cards in this stack will contain information about Washington Elementary School. These three cards have the same format, and they all need buttons and fields added to them. Two buttons are needed on these cards: one to designate going to the next card and one to designate going to the previous card.

1. If you are not presently on the third card, Academic Clubs, use the arrow keys on the keyboard to move through the stack until you are there. Remember the arrow keys will not work if the cursor is in a field.

2. A new button needs to be created to represent moving forward through the stack. A typical icon for this button would be an arrow facing to the right.

Because the arrow will indicate the action of the button, the button name does not need to show.

    a. Create the button. Hint: New Button is on the Objects menu.

    b. Hide the button name. Hint: Show name… is on the Button Info dialog box.

    c. Choose a button shaped like an arrow pointing right. Hint: Icon… is on the Button Info dialog box.

    d. Resize the button appropriately and place it in the bottom right corner.

  3. Add the button task to go to the next card. Hint: Task… is also on the Button Info dialog box and the selection is next card.

  4. Choose the zoom open effect for this button. Hint: Back again to the Button Info dialog box, Tasks…, and Visual Effect.

  5. Now the button is complete. Test it. Remember, you need the Browse tool to make it work.

  6. Because this button is needed on the next two cards, copy this button and paste it on the rest of the cards. Hint: You need that Button tool again.

    a. Copy the button. Hint: Use the Edit menu.

    b. Move to the next card.

    c. Paste the button.

    d. Repeat Steps b and c one more time until all the cards contain the right arrow button.

EDITING A BUTTON

These cards in the stack also need a left arrow button. Rather than creating a new button from scratch, you can copy the right arrow button and modify it.

  1. Use the left arrow key on the keyboard to move back to the Academic Clubs card.

  2. Choose Paste Button again. (The copied right arrow button should still be on the clipboard.) Although two buttons are not visible, they are there; one has been pasted on top of the other.

  3. Drag the top right arrow button to the bottom left corner of the screen.

  4. Change the icon to a left arrow icon with the following:

    a. While the button is still selected, from the Objects menu choose Button Info….

    b. Click on Icon… to see the choice of button icons.

    c. Click on the left arrow icon that corresponds to the right arrow you chose.

    d. Click OK. The button icon now faces in the opposite direction from the original button.

  5. Now the script needs to reflect that change.

    a. With the button still selected, from the Objects menu choose Button Info….

    b. Choose Tasks….

    c. Click on Previous Card.

    d. Click on Assign Tasks.

6. The new button is now ready to be copied to the other cards. Remember the process: Select the button, choose Copy Button from the Edit menu, move to the other cards, and choose Paste Button from the Edit menu while on each successive card.

7. When all the buttons are in place, select the Browse tool and test all the buttons you created.

ADDING A SCROLLING FIELD

Information concerning the school needs to appear on the cards. A new field must be added to each of the cards starting with the Academic Clubs card. Because this field will hold more information than can be visible at one time, a scrolling field is needed.

1. Move to the Academic Clubs card.

2. Select the Field tool from the Tools menu.

3. Choose New Field from the Objects menu.

4. With the new field still selected, from the Objects menu choose Field Info… to see the Field Info dialog box.

5. Select the pop-up menu for Style. Drag the mouse down and select Scrolling. This type of field is useful when there is more information than can fit on the card.

6. Click on Text Style… to see the Text Properties dialog box.

7. Click on Helvetica. (Choose another font if you don't have this one available.)

8. Click on 14.

9. Click OK to return to the card. Notice the scroll bar on the right side of the field, as shown in Figure 8-29.

10. Drag the new field below the title field and enlarge it until it is about the size and position shown in Figure 8-29.

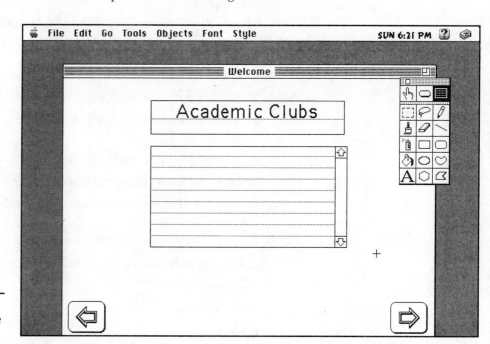

FIGURE 8-29

The Academic Club card with two buttons and two fields. The lower field is a scrollable field.

11. This same field can be used on the next three cards. By now you are familiar with the process of copying a field. (Make sure that the field is selected, copy the field, move to the next card, and paste the field. Repeat the last two steps twice to copy the field onto the last two cards.)

ENTERING AND LOCKING TEXT

Information now can be entered in the fields.

1. Click on the Browse tool and browse until you are on the Academic Clubs card.

2. Click in the new field to get the I-beam.

3. Type in the following information:

   The Washington Elementary School is proud of its Academic Clubs. The sixth grade has a Quiz Bowl club and competes with other schools. The fifth grade has a Geography Club and uses Carmen Sandiego for its practice. All grades have teams that compete in the Odyssey of the Mind contests. Last year our third grade team took first place! We also have an Academic Boosters Club formed by parents and supportive community members.

4. Scroll back through the field and edit your typing.

5. Move to the next card and type in the following:

   The Washington Elementary School believes that music is a very important part of every student's life. This is why all students learn how to play a musical instrument by third grade. Lessons are given during the school day. The students attend three symphonies a year, and many times the musicians will come to school and talk to the students. The fifth and sixth grade band performs for community organizations.

6. On the next card, type:

   The Washington Elementary School believes that sports play a very important role in every student's life. Emphasis is on learning a sport that they can do for their entire life. The Physical Education classes include golf, tennis, aerobic dancing, running, volleyball, basketball, and soccer. The Annual Sports Day draws athletes from the local university to demonstrate skills to the students.

7. This stack is one in which you would not want the information shown in these fields to be changed accidentally. These fields need to be protected from accidental changes. To do this, you need to lock the text. Start with the Academic Clubs card.

   a. Click on the Field tool.

   b. Click on the scrolling field to select it.

   c. From the Objects menu, choose Field Info… to see the Field Info dialog box.

   d. Click on Lock Text. This places an X in the box, indicating that the text is locked. Click on OK.

    e. Repeat these steps for the rest of the cards in this stack.

    f. If you decide later to edit text in any of these fields, repeat this process. Clicking on Lock Text when the text is already locked will unlock the text.

Notice that now when you move the Browse tool over this field, no I-beam appears. No one can change the information in this field. This is a good way to safeguard your information.

The Welcome stack is now complete. With this stack you explored the process of creating and copying buttons and fields to different cards. These processes are very useful and timesaving when you are making your own stacks. And—who knows—maybe you will want to edit this stack for use at your own school!

CLASSROOM ←——→ CONNECTION

Create a Book Report stack that all students can use during the year. Include fields for title, author, summary, and student name. You could also include a field for rating the book and for type of book. As students read a book, they can fill in the information on a card of the stack. This is a good way to record the number of books read during Right to Read month. When students are looking for a book to read and cannot decide on a book, have them browse the stack to find an interesting book.

Printing in HyperCard

Many times you will want to actually print out the stack. Several options are possible to print the stack, ranging from two cards per sheet of paper up to many on one page.

PRINTING A STACK

1. To print a copy of the Welcome stack, make sure that you still have it open.

FIGURE 8-30

Print Stack... is selected on the File menu.

2. Prepare your printer for printing. The necessary steps for this vary from system to system. You may need to turn on your printer, select the specific printer using Chooser on the Apple menu, or perform other steps. Check with your instructor if you are not sure what needs to be done.

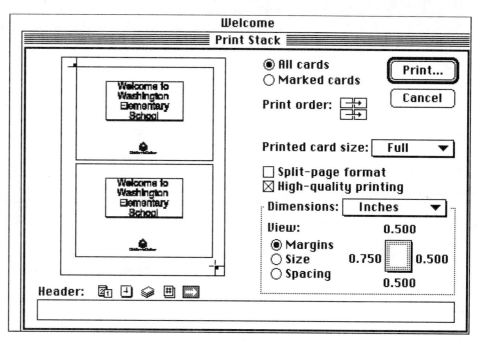

FIGURE 8-31

The Print Stack dialog box with two cards per page selected.

3. Choose Print Stack... from the File menu, as shown in Figure 8-30. (You may get an alert box with a warning about changing margins or other warnings, depending on your setup. If so, click whatever is needed to continue.) The Print Stack dialog box should be displayed, as shown in Figure 8-31.

Cards per Page

The diagram on the left of the Print Stack dialog box is a sample page showing how the cards will print. Figure 8-31 shows Full in the Printed card size box. This means that one card covers the full width of the paper, resulting in two cards on a page. The sample page on the dialog box demonstrates how the cards would be arranged. Two cards per page would show the cards in good detail, but if the stack is rather large, it could take a lot of paper. If you don't need that much detail, you might prefer more cards on a page.

1. Position the arrow on the box beside Printed card size.

2. Hold down the mouse button to see all the options for card size.

3. Choose Quarter and release the mouse button; notice that thirty-two cards now appear on one sheet of paper. One card covers one-quarter of the width of the paper. This certainly can save on paper and on printing time, but the detail may not be very clear.

4. Choose Half for Printed card size.

Margins

The number of cards per page can be adjusted by moving the margins on the paper. The margins are identified by the crosshairs located in the upper left and lower right corners of the sample page. Drag them around and watch the number of cards on the paper change. Drag them back until eight cards reappear.

Order

The order in which cards are printed on the page can be of two types: The cards can go down the page in column sequence or across the page in row sequence. This option is chosen by clicking on the icon next to Print order. Notice that in Figure 8-31 the Print order icon has arrows going across. Clicking on this icon changes the arrows to point down. By clicking again, the arrows return to indicate row sequence.

Headings

You can include information in the top margin of the print page. Figure 8-32

FIGURE 8-32

Choices of header icons for the printed stack.

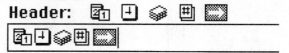

shows a closer view of the icons representing header options that are found in the bottom left corner of the dialog box. The first symbol represents the date, the second represents the time, the third is for the stack name, the fourth is for the page number, and the arrow is a tab button.

1. Press the Delete key to delete anything that might already be entered in the selected box under Header. Notice that the top margin (header) on the sample page is empty.
2. Click on the stack icon (the third one). Notice that the icon appears in the box. Also look at the top of the sample page and you will see, in very small (probably illegible) print, the name of the stack.
3. Click on the arrow icon to insert a tab in the header.
4. Click on the date icon (the first one). The date appears in the middle of the header because the tab was used.
5. Click on the arrow icon again.
6. Click on the page number icon. The second tab moves the page number to the right side of the heading. You may need to readjust the margins to show eight cards again.

This stack is now ready for printing, so click on Print... to see the printer dialog box for your printer. (These will vary depending on your printer.) Click Print or OK, depending on your dialog box, if all choices are appropriate. The stack should print.

PRINTING A CARD

CLASSROOM ◄————► **CONNECTION**

Print out stacks that the students have created, two cards per page. Laminate these pages and cut the cards to create books for the students to display or take home. Have the students create a stack with only one sentence or picture on each card. Print these stacks and cut the cards apart to have the students practice sequencing skills. A fun project would be to have intermediate classes create these stacks and help primary students put the stories in the correct order.

Conclusion

If you want a large printed copy of a single card, then choose Print Card from the File menu. There are no selections after this choice, the printing process starts immediately.

You have accomplished quite a lot in this chapter. You have learned some of the basic vocabulary for using HyperCard, have navigated through stacks, and have learned how to create new cards and add, edit, and delete text. You also learned how to create graphics and so discovered how even simple graphics can enhance the information in a stack. You also learned how to create, edit, and copy buttons and fields. By creating buttons you were introduced to HyperTalk scripting. More of this will be addressed in the next chapter.

If you are a beginner, you may feel clumsy when using the painting tools or confused by the variety of options, and you may feel that you are working slowly. But, as with any new tool, the more you use it the easier it will become to use. With practice you will be able to navigate through your stacks quickly and to create very sophisticated drawings for your cards.

As you saw in Chapter 7, there is great potential for both HyperCard and HyperStudio in your classroom. They can be utilized at all levels, K through 12. For young children they can be used for tutorials. For older children they can be discovery tools or presentation tools. For you, as a teacher, they can be management tools. In the next chapter you will learn more HyperCard features that relate to the classroom.

KEY TERMS

Background	Go menu	Pencil tool
Bkgnd Info…	Home card	Preferences Card
Browse tool	Home stack	Recent
browsing	HyperCard	Rectangle tool
Brush tool	information dialog box	scripting
button	Irregular Polygon tool	Select tool
Button Info…	Lasso tool	Spray tool
Button tool	Line tool	stack
card	Lock Text	Stack Info…
Card Info…	message box	tasks
Fat Bits	navigating	tool palette
field	New Card	Tools menu
Field Info…	Oval tool	user level
Field tool	Pattern menu	visual effect

EXERCISES

1. Open the stack called Classroom Rules.hc on the Data Disk. Use the function New Card and add as many cards to this stack as you need to write your own classroom rules. Illustrate the cards.

2. In the Aquarium stack on the Data Disk, add fish to the title card's aquarium. Add four cards to the stack that give information on various tropical fish. Draw a fish on each of those cards.

3. Find journal articles about specific HyperCard stacks that have been used in classrooms. Use the Articles.hc stack on the Data Disk to store resource information about the articles. Add a new card for each article.

4. Open the Counting stack on the Data Disk. Add graphics to each card to graphically represent the number on each card. Add more cards to the stack so the numbers from 1 to 10 are included. Keep in mind this is a stack for preschool.

5. Print a stack with eight cards on a page, with print order top to bottom. Include a header with the date, stack name, and page number.

6. Print a stack with full-size cards. In the header place the stack name on the left side and the page number on the right.

9

HyperCard–Backgrounds, New Stack, and Added Features

Introduction

In Chapter 8 you learned how to edit a stack, including creating cards, fields, and buttons. In this chapter you will explore the meaning of the background and learn how to create a new stack. You will also learn about several HyperCard features that are beneficial to teachers. More complex button scripting will be addressed, and an explanation of the button tasks not used in Chapter 8 will be demonstrated.

Background was mentioned briefly in the last chapter. A graphic, field, or button on a background is displayed on each card of a stack. Graphics on a background cannot be erased or changed when you are working on a card—you must choose Background from the Edit menu to work with background graphics.

When you create a background, you are creating the lowest layer of the stack. **Layer** is a term used to describe at what level an object, such as a button or field, is created within a stack. A new layer is created every time you add a graphic, field, or button to a card. Envision layers of transparent material, such as transparencies for an overhead projector, on top of each other. All graphics that you create are automatically placed on the bottom layer. The levels of other objects depend on the order in which you create them. If you create a new button, then it is in the second layer. If you create a field after that, then that field is in the third layer. Another button would be in the fourth layer. Each item is in a different layer, as if each were a different transparency.

Exploring Background and Layers

To better understand the concepts of background and layers, experiment with the stack Layers on the Data Disk.

1. Open the Layers stack.
2. Tear the Tools menu off and place it at the bottom left of your screen, if it is not already there.
3. Choose Background from the Edit menu. Hash marks appear on the menu bar to indicate that you are working on the background, and only the background objects and graphics are displayed.
4. Select the Field tool from the Tools menu.
5. Drag the field to cover the graphic circle. The graphic is the lowest layer—the field, in a higher layer, hides the graphic. Notice that the field is also in a higher layer than the button that it was hiding.
6. Select the Browse tool.
7. Click on the button. If your Macintosh has its volume on, you should hear a "boing" sound.
8. Now select the Button tool and try to move the button on top of the field and on top of the graphic. Notice that it will only move under the field and over the graphic, as shown in Figure 9-1. It is in a lower layer than the field and in a higher layer than the graphic. Leave the button partially hidden by the field for the next step.
9. Select the Browse tool again and try to click on the part of the button covered by the field. Nothing happens. Now click on the part of the button not covered by the field. You should hear the "boing." The button cannot be clicked through the field, but it can be clicked in an area where it is not covered.
10. Now select the Field tool.

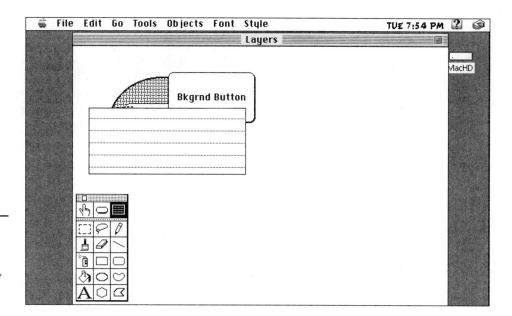

FIGURE 9-1

The button is on a higher level that the graphic and a lower layer than the field. When the button moves over the graphic, it hides the graphic but not the field.

11. Double-click on the field to see the Field Info dialog box.

12. Select Transparent from the Style pop-up menu and then click OK.

13. Select the Browse tool and try again to click on the part of the button covered by the field. You cannot click on any part of the button that is under the field, even when the field is transparent and you can see the button.

USING BRING CLOSER AND SEND FARTHER

As you have seen, if you create transparent objects (buttons and fields), the object positioned directly on the layer below the other object can be seen through the object on the higher layer. However, an opaque (solid) object will hide any lower layer objects that are directly under it.

Also, the pointer (tool, I-beam, etc., that is controlled by the mouse) is always on the highest layer. If a button is directly under a field, the mouse will always click on the field, not on the button. The same is true if a button is on top of a field, or a button is on top of a button. This is true even if the field, or button, is transparent.

Sometimes you will need to change these layers to get to a button or a field. This can be done by using two commands from the Objects menu. This exercise will have you move a button closer and then farther.

1. Select the Button tool.

2. Click on the button to select it.

3. Choose **Bring Closer** from the Objects menu. Now the button covers the field and the graphic. The button will work if you click (with the Browse tool) on the area that was previously hidden by the field. Because the button is now on a higher level, you cannot click on the field through the button. You cannot type text in the field.

4. Repeat Steps 1 and 2, and this time choose **Send Farther** from the Objects menu. The button is now back on a lower layer.

BACKGROUND LAYERS AND CARD LAYERS

You have been working on the background. Any graphics or objects on the background are at the lowest levels of the stack's layers. The absolute bottom layer of a stack is the graphics on the background. The rest of the objects on the background make up the next higher layers. If you then add items to an individual card, you are adding layers on top of the background layers. All the graphics and objects on a card are at higher layers than those in the background.

1. Select Background from the Edit menu to return to the card level.

2. As you look at this card you see a card button and a background button. Select the Button tool, click on the card button and drag it over the background button. The card button will be on top of the background button, because all card buttons are on a higher layer than background buttons.

3. Repeat this activity for the two fields. You will discover that card fields are always on a layer higher than background fields.

4. Drag the card field to the card graphic. The field will be placed on top of the graphic. Remember the card graphic is on the lowest layer of the card. Drag the card field back.

5. Now drag the background field to the card graphic. This time the field is under the card graphic. Remember, background objects are all on lower layers than any card object. Even using Bring Closer cannot bring a background object above a card object.

6. Select the Button tool and drag the card button on top of the card graphic. Use the Send Farther from the Objects menu to move the button to a layer below the graphic. You will not be able to do this no matter how many times you select Send Farther. The graphics layer is always the lowest layer of the card. Only buttons and fields can change layers.

Layers are not noticeable to HyperCard users but can be very important for a HyperCard author. When you first use HyperCard, layers will not be as important as when you create more complex stacks. As your stacks become larger it becomes more important to understand layers. Keep in mind the following ideas:

1. The background layers are always lower than the card layers.

2. The background graphics layer is the lowest layer of all.

3. The card graphics layer is always the lowest card layer.

4. Higher layers can hide lower layers, unless the higher layers are transparent.

5. Card level graphics will hide background buttons and fields but will not prevent the pointer from working.

6. Objects, even transparent objects, will prevent the pointer from working on lower level objects that they cover.

7. Bring objects forward or send them back to higher or lower levels by using Bring Closer and Send Farther.

8. A background layer cannot be brought forward to become a card layer nor can a card layer be sent back to become a background layer.

Working with the background is valuable for creating consistent effects that show up on every card. This consistency can make it easier for a student to navigate through a stack. The more you work in HyperCard, the more these layers and their uses will become apparent to you. Remember to check layers if problems arise, and also remember that you can move layers farther or closer by using the Objects menu.

Using Keyboard Shortcuts

Because some of the procedures in this chapter are a repetition of previous work, you may feel comfortable enough with them to start using some of the keyboard shortcuts. You have already used one shortcut: double-clicking to view Button and Field Info dialog boxes. You may also want to start using keyboard equivalents of menu commands. The symbol ⌘ represents the Command key, the key on the bottom row of your keyboard that has the same symbol on it. Try the following:

1. Hold down the ⌘ key as you type the letter M. The message box should appear, just as it would have if you had chosen Message from the Go menu.
2. Hold down the ⌘ key and press the space bar. This should make the menu bar disappear.
3. To have the menu bar reappear, simply hold down the ⌘ key and press the space bar. These two keys allow you to toggle back and forth between hiding and showing the menu bar.

Keyboard Shortcuts	
Keys	Command
⌘ B	Background
⌘ C	Copy
⌘ F	Find
⌘ H	Home
⌘ M	Message Box
⌘ N	New Card
⌘ O	Open Stack
⌘ P	Print Card
⌘ Q	Quit HyperCard
⌘ R	Recent
⌘ V	Paste
⌘ W	Close Stack
⌘ X	Cut
⌘ Z	Undo
⌘ 1	First Card
⌘ 2	Previous Card
⌘ 3	Next Card
⌘ 4	Last Card
⌘ +	Bring Closer
⌘ –	Send Farther
⌘ ?	Help
⌘ ~	Back
⌘ space bar	Menu Bar
Note: ⌘ Shift-space bar is required on some keyboards for Menu Bar.	

FIGURE 9-2

Keystroke equivalents for HyperCard menu commands.

Keyboard shortcuts are available for many, though not all, menu commands. If you look at the menus, you can see that all the Go commands have keyboard shortcuts, some of the Edit commands have them, and none of the Font or Style menus in HyperCard have them. Shortcuts are also available for some HyperTalk commands, as you saw with the HyperCard command "show menuBar." As you become comfortable with HyperCard, you will find using the shortcuts is quicker. If you prefer to use the menus, please continue to do so. A summary of keystrokes for HyperCard commands you have worked with is listed in Figure 9-2.

Exploring Hidden Fields

So far you have used button tasks to move from card to card. You will now be using HyperTalk commands. There are many other HyperTalk commands that are quite useful, yet simple to use. You will explore a few of these in the next exercises—one will erase text in a field; others will cause a field or button to appear or disappear on the card as needed; and still another is a variation of the **go to** command that will display a particular card (other than the next or previous card, which you have already used).

For an example of how disappearing text and fields can be used, take a look at the Vocabulary stack on your Data Disk.

1. Open the stack Vocabulary that is on your Data Disk. (If you are still in HyperCard, you can just choose Open Stack… from the File menu to get an Open dialog box. If not, you can open the stack by double-clicking on it.)

2. Read the directions on the first card.

3. Go to the next card. (Remember, the Browse tool is needed for buttons to work.)

   a. Type in your answer to the definition. (Remember to click in the field first to get an insertion point.)

   b. Click anywhere on the definition. You see another field displayed on the card with the correct answer, as shown in Figure 9-3.

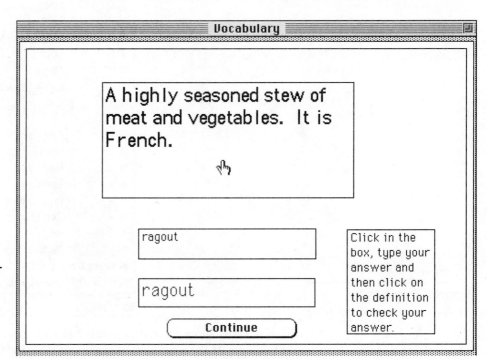

FIGURE 9-3

A card in the Vocabulary stack with a field for the definition of the word, a field for a student to type in the word, and a field for the correct answer to be displayed.

c. Click on Continue to move to the next card. Notice that the word you typed and the field with the correct answer disappear as you move to the next card. Try a few more of the cards to see how the stack works.

To make the text and field disappear, three new commands were used: **hide field**, **show field**, and **put empty into** field. Stacks created with these commands could be useful for drill for students in any subject area. To see how these work look at the fields and buttons:

1. Go to any card in the Vocabulary stack showing a definition.

2. Click on the definition so that the correct answer is showing on the card.

3. Select the Field tool. (The user level in this stack should already be set to 5.) You should see three fields with dotted lines in them.

4. Double-click on the field with the correct answer—or click once and choose Field Info… from the Objects menu—to see the Field Info dialog box.

   Double-clicking on a field when the Field tool is selected is an alternative to selecting the field and then choosing Field Info… from the Objects menu. Likewise, double-clicking on a button is an alternative to selecting the button and then choosing Button Info… from the Objects menu. Because this takes fewer steps and is generally considered to be easier than using the menu, this procedure will be used in the remainder of the chapter. You may continue to use the menu to view the Button Info and Field Info dialog boxes if you prefer.

5. Notice that this field has been named VocabularyWord. The field above this one, where the student enters an answer, has been named Response.

6. Click OK to return to the card.

7. Select the Button tool. There are two buttons on the card—one directly over the definition field and the other at the bottom for continuing to the next card.

8. Double-click on the button over the definition—or click once and choose Button Info… from the Objects menu—to see the Button Info dialog box.

9. Click on Script… to see the button script. The commands in this script cause the field named VocabularyWord to show on the screen when the button is clicked.

10. Click on the close box to return to the card.

11. Double-click on the Continue button—or click once and choose Button Info… from the Objects menu—to see the Button Info dialog box.

12. Click on Script… to see the button script, as shown in Figure 9-4. When this button is clicked, these commands cause the text in the field named Response to be erased, the field named VocabularyWord to be hidden, and the next card to be displayed on the screen. In this way the student can again enter a response and check the answer.

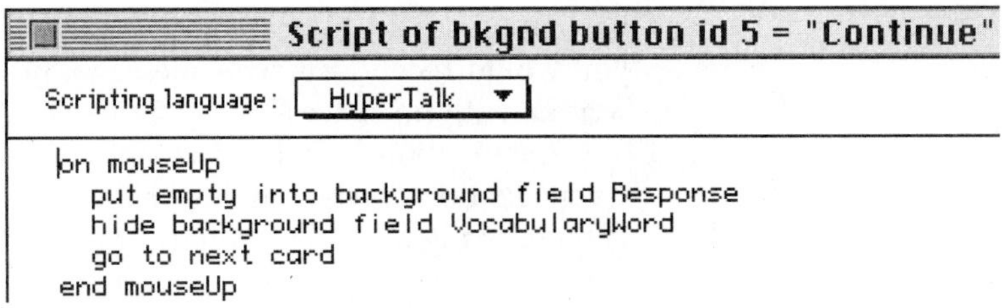

FIGURE 9-4

Script of a button that erases text in a field named Response, hides the field named VocabularyWord, and goes to the next card when the button is clicked.

```
Script of bkgnd button id 5 = "Continue"

Scripting language :  [ HyperTalk  ▼ ]

on mouseUp
    put empty into background field Response
    hide background field VocabularyWord
    go to next card
end mouseUp
```

Practice Editing Stacks with Hidden Fields

1. Modify the Vocabulary stack by deleting the words and definitions presently in the stack and typing in vocabulary words and definitions from a subject you teach. Remember to move the transparent button off the field before you attempt to type in new text.

2. Modify the Vocabulary stack by deleting the words and definitions presently in the stack and creating questions and answers relating to your teaching field.

Hiding, Showing, and Emptying Fields

You will be setting up similar buttons and fields in another stack, the Area stack. The purpose of the stack is to provide drill with formulas for the area of various plane figures. When the stack is complete, students will able to enter formulas for the area of a displayed figure, then click on the figure to see the correct answer, as in the Vocabulary stack. To show the correct answer field, you must name the field and script a button to show it. With another button you must hide the correct answer field and empty the student's response field, so that the fields will be ready to use again.

The stack you will be using is the Area stack on your Data Disk:

1. Open the stack called Area. The first card is a menu card, similar to the Simple Machines menu card.

2. Set the user level to 5, if it is not already set to 5, with the following steps:

   a. From the Go menu choose Message.

   b. Type **set userLevel to 5**.

   c. Press Return.

   d. Close the message box or choose Message again from the Go menu.

3. Go to the second card with the rectangle drawn on it.

NAMING FIELDS

When a script refers to a field, such as to hide or show the field, it must indicate to HyperCard what field is being referenced. Field numbers and field ID numbers can be used for this purpose, but field names are more frequently used—a script that says hide card field id 23 is not as easy to understand as a script that says hide card field Formula, especially if there are also many other references to different fields.

When you choose names for fields, buttons, or cards almost any name can be used, but names that make sense to you are best. If you choose names that are more than one word, references to that name must be put in quotes. For instance, if the VocabularyWord field were named Vocabulary Word with a space, hide background field "Vocabulary Word" would be the script. Without the quotes you would receive an error message. In most cases a two-word name should be written with no spaces between the words as was done with VocabularyWord.

Capitalization of names is optional—you may capitalize any or all letters. Capitalization is used only to make it easier for you to read your script, because HyperCard ignores the capitals. It treats all letters as lowercase.

To name the field that will contain the correct formula:

1. With the rectangle card displayed, select the Field tool. There are three fields on this card — a field at the top for instructions, another below for the student to type in a response, and a field below the student response for the correct answer to be displayed, as shown in Figure 9-5. The correct answer field is the one you want to show when the transparent button on top of the rectangle is clicked. You need to name the student response field and the correct answer field so that you can hide and show them.

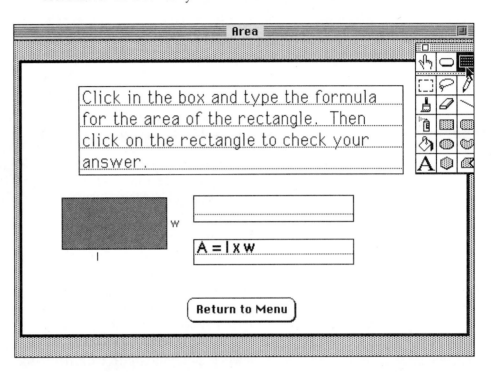

FIGURE 9-5

Three fields are on the rectangle card of the Area stack.

2. Double-click on the correct answer field to see the Field Info dialog box (or choose Field Info... from the Objects menu).
3. Name this field Formula.
4. Notice that the field information indicates this is a card field rather than a background field. It can be seen only on this card. All the buttons and graphics on this card were created at the card level.
5. Click OK to return to the card.
6. Double-click on the student response field to see the Field Info dialog box (or choose Field Info... from the Objects menu).
7. Name this field StudentResponse.
8. Click OK to return to the card.

USING SHOW FIELD SCRIPT

Now the transparent button on top of the rectangle needs script so that the student can click on it to have the correct answer field show.

1. Select the Button tool.

2. Double-click on the button over the rectangle to see the Button Info dialog box. Notice that this button is transparent so the rectangle can be seen, and it has no icon—an icon would cover the rectangle.

3. Click on Script… to see the button script.

4. An empty line is needed to type in the new command. One way to get an empty line is to click after on mouseUp and then press Return. On that new empty line type: **show card field Formula**.

5. Close the Script window and save changes. You cannot test the button yet— the field is already displayed. You wouldn't be able to see if it worked.

USING HIDE FIELD SCRIPT AND PUT EMPTY SCRIPT

Now that the show field button is ready, you need to make sure the field gets hidden whenever anyone leaves the card, so that it will be hidden the next time the card is viewed by either another student or the same student again. One way to do this is to put the script to hide the card in the only button that is available for leaving the card, the Return to Menu button. To clear the formula entered by the student so that it won't show when the card is viewed again is also done by adding script to the same button. You will add these two lines of script to the Return to Menu button.

1. With the Button tool still selected, double-click on the Return to Menu button to see the Button Info dialog box.

2. Click on Script… to see the button script.

3. Click at the beginning of the visual effect command and press Return. This is another way to get an empty line for typing in script. Now click on the empty line and add the following line of script: **hide card field Formula**. Press Return.

4. The second line of script needs to be inserted on the next line. Type the following: **put empty into card field StudentResponse.**

5. Click on the close box, save the script, and return to the card.

6. Select the Browse tool. Now you can test your buttons.

7. Try clicking on the Return to Menu button. It should take you to the first card. Return to the Rectangle card to see if the Formula field was hidden. If not, check the button script and the field name for typing errors. (Beware: Spaces accidentally typed in or after the field name will be considered part of the name. Everything may look right if extra spaces are there, but it won't work. Try highlighting the whole name box and retyping the name if you think this is a problem.)

8. Try clicking on the rectangle button on the Rectangle card to see the Formula field displayed. (Remember, the Browse tool needs to be selected for buttons to work.) If it doesn't display, check the button script and the field name to see if you typed correctly.

9. Type an answer in the Student Response field. Remember that you need to click in the field to edit it.

10. Click on the Return to Menu button and then return to the Rectangle card. Did it erase your answer? If not, find your error. Then test everything again. If your script doesn't work, don't panic. Errors are almost always very simple, but they are not always easy to find. Make sure you are using

the Browse tool when you test the buttons, check your field and button names (remember to watch for extra spaces, both in and after names), and check your scripts carefully for typing errors (extra spaces could be after names here, too). With just a little patience you will find your problem.

Up to this point most of the stacks you have used have been sequential stacks—you used the cards in their physical order. One of the great advantages of HyperCard is that the cards do not have to be viewed sequentially—you can have any card of the stack go to any other card. In the Area stack the title card has been set up as a menu card to allow students to go directly to particular cards. However, the buttons for this card have not been completed. For these buttons you will need script that tells HyperCard to go to the correct card; you won't be able to say simply go to next card. One way to do this is to name each card and to use button script to go to each card by name.

NAMING CARDS

To name each card, follow these steps:

1. Use the right arrow key to move to the Circle card.
2. From the Objects menu choose Card Info… to view the Card Info dialog box. (Notice that this can be done with any of the three Object tools at the top of the menu selected.)
3. Type **Circle** in the name box and click OK to return to the card.
4. Repeat for the remaining cards with figures on them. Name them according to their shapes: Triangle and Square.

USING GO TO CARD SCRIPT

The title card of the Area stack has a button and script that will take you to the appropriate card on the rectangle. You will need to copy this button and modify the script for the three remaining figures.

1. Go to the title card. As shown in Figure 9-6, this card has all the figures drawn on it.
2. Tear off the Tools menu and place it in a convenient location on the screen.

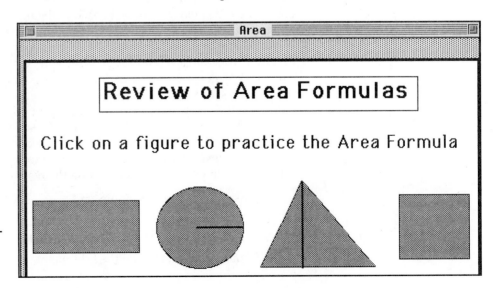

FIGURE 9-6

The title card of the Area stack with the four figures. This is also called a menu card.

3. Select the Button tool.

4. Click on the button surrounding the Rectangle.

5. Select Copy Button from the Edit menu.

6. Select Paste Button from the Edit menu.

7. Remember the pasted button will be on top of the copied button. Drag the new button to the circle and resize it to fit around the circle.

8. If the script is not changed, this button will go to the Rectangle card. Because it needs to go to the Circle card, the script must be modified.

9. Double-click on the new button to see the Button Info dialog box.

10. Click on Script... to see the button script.

11. Change the word Rect to Circle.

12. Close the Script window and save the script.

13. Repeat Steps 6 through 12 to create two more buttons, one for the triangle and one for the square.

14. Test the buttons. If any don't work, check to be sure you selected the Browse tool, that you typed the script correctly, and that the card name in the script matches the name on the card. (Once again, remember to check for extra spaces in or after the name, as well as for other typing errors.)

The go to command has many variations. For instance, you can also tell HyperCard to go to card 5 to get to the fifth card in the stack or go to card id 1234 to get to the card with that ID number. You may use any of these variations that you find useful.

FINISHING THE AREA STACK

The Circle, Triangle, and Square cards in the Area stack need to have buttons and fields added. They each need: (1) a field for the student response, (2) a field with the correct formula, (3) a field for the directions, (4) a button on top of the figure to show the correct formula, and (5) a button to empty text in the Student Response field, hide the correct formula field, and return to the menu card. Use the copy and paste functions to place these items on each of the cards. For example, go to the Rectangle card, click on the Field tool, click on the field for directions. Copy the field and move to each of the next three cards and paste the field.

Notice that on the remaining cards you may leave the field names the same as on the Rectangle card. Because they are on separate cards, the names are unique for any particular card, and HyperCard will be able to tell what field to show or empty. Type in the correct area formula on each card. The formula for area of a circle is $A = \pi \times r \times r$. (To get the π symbol, you can hold down the Option key and then press the P key in some fonts. If you can't do this, just type the name Pi.) The area of a triangle is $1/2 \times b \times h$. The area of a square is $s \times s$.

You may have noticed that copying a field does not copy text within the field. To copy the text, you must use the Browse tool. You will copy the instructions from the Rectangle card and paste it on the rest of the cards.

1. Move back to the Rectangle card.

2. Select the Browse tool.

3. Highlight the text that gives directions for what to do on the card.

4. Choose Copy Text from the Edit menu.

5. Move to the next card.

6. Click in the field when you see the pointer turn into an I-beam.

7. Choose Paste Text from the Edit menu.

8. A small amount of editing must be done to this text. Replace the word rectangle with the word circle in two locations.

9. Move to the next card and paste the text again.

10. Replace the word rectangle with triangle.

11. Move to the last card and paste the text again. Replace the word rectangle with square.

12. Test your stack.

Practice with Hide, Show, and Empty Fields

1. Modify the Area stack by using chemical formulas instead of area formulas.

2. Add cards to the stack that will explain each of the formulas.

3. Add cards with practice problems for each formula; include the ability to see the answers to these practice problems.

CLASSROOM ←——→ CONNECTION

Use HyperCard to create a stack that has pictures on each card. When the student clicks on the picture, show a hidden field with the word for that picture. In a primary class use the same idea and have the field show only the first letter of the word.

About HyperTalk

As you know, the script you have been using is written in the programming language used with HyperCard, called **HyperTalk.** A very English-like language, HyperTalk is user friendly. For example, spaces placed in a command do not always return an error and using capital letters instead of lowercase is not a concern.

A series of HyperTalk commands is called a **script** and the process of writing the HyperTalk commands is called scripting. Scripting allows you to control what is to be done in a stack. A script is typed in a window called the **script editor**, which you used when scripting buttons. The script editor makes it easy to edit commands and also checks for some types of errors.

When commands are typed in the script editor, they are not executed immediately. Specific actions that occur, such as releasing the mouse button, cause HyperCard to access and perform the commands. Notice that the script in Figure 9-7 begins with on mouseUp and ends with end mouseUp. The word **mouseUp** is an action that HyperCard knows is happening in the stack. Other samples of actions could be **openStack**, openCard, or openBackground. All scripts begin with **on (action)** and close with **end (action)**. In contrast, HyperTalk commands entered in the message box, as when you set the user level, are executed immediately.

HyperTalk script can become very complex. A sampling of things that can be done by scripting are looking up information elsewhere in a stack or in other stacks; calculating amounts, such as grades; putting information in fields; moving to another stack, application, or device; creating animation; and prompting the user to type in information. However, you can successfully use the language with

FIGURE 9-7

The script begins with on
mouseUp and ends with end
mouseUp.

```
on mouseUp
   visual effect dissolve
   go to next card
end mouseUp
```

knowledge of just a few commands, as you have already seen. By using the scripting commands previously introduced in this chapter, you can create a series of review lessons or informational stacks for almost any subject and create a great many other types of stacks.

You have used HyperTalk commands in button scripts. Scripts can also be written for entire stacks, for fields, for backgrounds, and for cards. In the next exercises you will be working with stack scripting.

WRITING STACK SCRIPT

You can improve the Area stack by hiding the menu bar when the stack is opened. This makes the cards fill more of the screen and also keeps students from accessing the menus.

1. Choose Stack Info… from the Objects menu.
2. Click on Script….
3. Type in the following:

    on openStack
      hide menuBar
    end openStack

    This script will do exactly what it says: hide the menu bar when you open this stack. Notice that when you type the second and third lines of the script, they indent automatically. However, if you save the stack or type Return at the end of the third line the script editor automatically corrects the alignment of the line.

4. Click in the close box to close the script editor.
5. When asked to save changes, click Yes.
6. To test this command you need to close, then reopen the stack.
7. It is a good idea to write this script when the stack is finished to avoid having to make the menu bar reappear each time you open the stack. Two ways to have the menu bar reappear are:

    a. Hold down the ⌘ key (with the Apple on it) and continue to hold it as you press the space bar. (On some keyboards, the Shift key must also be held with the ⌘ key as you press the space bar.)

    b. Hold down the ⌘ key and type M to show the message box and then type **show menuBar** and press Return.

Creating a New Stack

At this point it will be assumed that you are familiar with the menus and will not need the specific directions that have been given in the past. For example, rather than saying: "Choose New Field from the Objects menu," the directions will be: "Create a new field." If necessary refer back to a previous section or chapter on how to do a specific procedure. This stack will also be used to introduce you to various features that can add to the learning value of a stack. These new instructions will be in detailed format. This new stack will give high school students information about the guidance department. It will be a nonsequential stack containing information about colleges, courses, and personal help. This new stack will be small, but it will be a shell for you to continue enhancing.

1. To create a new stack you must be in the HyperCard program. If you are not currently in HyperCard, open the HyperCard program by double-clicking on the program icon.
2. From the File menu, choose **New Stack...** to see the New Stack dialog box.
3. Type **Guidance Dept** for the stack name.
4. Click New. You now have a new stack and are viewing a blank screen, except for the menu bar.
5. If the user level is not set to 5, set it by using the message box.

CREATING BACKGROUND GRAPHICS

A border will be created in the background so it will appear on all the cards of the stack.

1. Choose Background from the Edit menu (⌘-B). You should see the hatch markings on the menu bar indicating the background.
2. Pull down the Tools menu and position it on the screen for your use.
3. Select the **Rounded Rectangle tool** (row 4, item 3) and make a large rectangle, almost the size of the screen, for the border, as shown in Figure 9-8.

FIGURE 9-8

Create the background by using the Rounded Rectangle tool and the Fill tool.

4. Select the **Fill tool** (row 5, item 1).
5. From the Patterns menu select the pattern in row 9, item 2.
6. Click in the area between the edge of the card and the rounded rectangle to fill in the area outside the rectangle. If you make a mistake, select Undo from the Edit menu and try again.
7. Choose Background from the Edit menu (⌘-B) again to leave the background.

TITLE CARD

The first card will be a title card, as shown in Figure 9-9. It will have one field and one button.

FIGURE 9-9

The first card of the Guidance
Dept stack contains one field
and one button.

1. Using Figure 9-9, create a field with the following specifications: Rectangle style, bold text, Geneva font at 30 points, and centered. (Hint: Select the Field tool and double-click on the field to get the Field Info dialog box.) Type in the following text: **The Downtown High School's Guidance Department Assistance**. Remember, the Browse tool must be selected before text can be typed.

2. Create a new button on this card with the following specifications: Icon — face, Rounded Rectangle shape, Tasks: Next card, visual effect — dissolve slow. More will be added to the button later.

CREATING THE SECOND CARD

1. Add a new card to the stack for the menu card. Create a button with the following specifications: Rounded Rectangle. Shape the button to resemble the button in Figure 9-10. Copy and paste this button twice. Drag the buttons to locations similar to Figure 9-10. Add the correct icon and name to each button.

2. Create a field on the card similar to the one in Figure 9-10. The field specifications include Shadow and Geneva, 18 points and bold. Do not type any text in the field yet.

3. You will need three more cards for this stack. These cards will contain information about colleges, group counseling, and schedule changes. Add a new card and name the card **College**. (Hint: Go to Card Info... to name the card.)

4. This card will contain one field and one button. The field has a Rectangle style and a Geneva font of 14 point.
5. This card will contain one button—a rounded rectangle that has the name Return. More will be added to the button later. See Figure 9-11 for size and location.

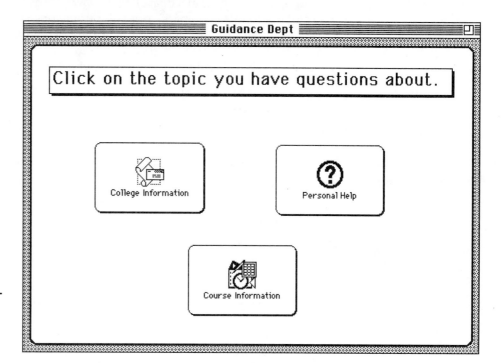

FIGURE 9-10

The second card of the Guidance Dept stack is a menu card, and it contains one field and three buttons.

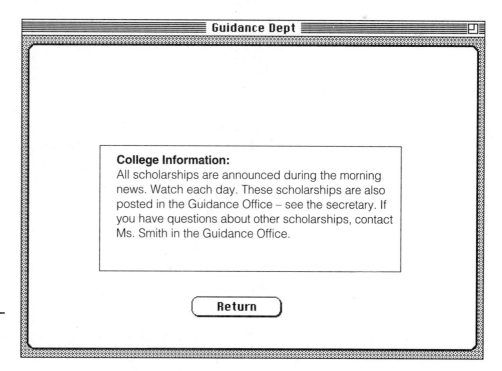

FIGURE 9-11

The third card of the Guidance Dept stack contains one field and one button.

Using Push Card and Pop Card Commands

By clicking on the button for college information, you will move to the College Information card. By clicking on the Return button, you will return to the menu card. For this you will use two new commands: **push card** and **pop card**. The push card command tells HyperCard to remember the "pushed" card; think of it as putting a bookmark on that card to remember to come back to that exact card. The pop card command signals HyperCard to "pop" that card back on the screen, to return to that bookmark. You will put the push command in the script of each of the buttons on the menu card and the pop command in the script of the Return button on each card. Each click on a menu button will "push" the menu card so that each click of the Return button will "pop" back to display the menu card.

1. Move to the second card of the stack by using the arrow keys.
2. Select the Button tool from the tool palette. The buttons on this card are card level buttons, not background. You add to the script of these buttons while on the card. Do the college button first.
3. Double-click on the College Information button and then click on Script....
4. On the line after on mouseUp, type **push card** and press Return.
5. On the next line, type **go to card College**.
6. Click on the close box and save changes to the script.
7. If you would like to add a visual effect to the button, double-click on the button and choose Task.... Click Visual Effect, and then select Zoom Open and Slow. Click Assign Tasks.
8. Now the button on the College card needs to be set to return to the menu card. Move to the College card.
9. While the Button tool is selected, double-click on the button and then click on Script....
10. On the line after on mouseUp, type **pop card** and press Return.
11. Click on the close box and save changes to the script. This button will now return to the menu card.
12. You need two more cards in this stack exactly like the College card. Copy this card and paste it twice. (Hint: use the Edit menu.) You now have three blank cards. If you are having difficulty determining which card you are on, check Card Info....
13. Name the new cards Help and Courses, respectively.
14. Repeat Steps 3 through 6 to change the script of the two buttons on the menu card to allow you to move to the correct cards.
15. Type in the following information on each of the three cards.

College Information:

All scholarships are announced during the morning news. Watch each day. These scholarships are also posted in the Guidance Office see the secretary. If you have questions about other scholarships, contact Ms. Smith in the Guidance Office.

Personal Help:

If you are having a problem with drugs, alcohol, or anything else that is keeping you from doing your best in school and you want help, give a

note to Mr. George to let him know. He will place you in one of the many group counseling sessions that are held here in the school every week.

Course Information:

If you are interested in adding or dropping a class, sign up to see your counselor before September 15. September 15 is the deadline for dropping without a late fee. The late fee charge is $10.

Now it is time to test all the buttons. Check to be sure that each button takes you to the expected card. If not, proofread your scripts, and check card names in the script and on the cards where they are required, remembering to watch for extra spaces and making sure that the name is the correct one for the card and that other cards do not have the same name.

This is a very simple use of push and pop card scripts. This example was given to show you the basics of how it works, but it is more frequently used to take you back to a prior card when there are a number of possible cards that you might have viewed previously. For instance, suppose this stack were a part of a larger stack about the entire high school, the teachers, and the administrators in the school. In addition to the Guidance menu card already in the stack, there might be other menus, including a College menu that would take you directly to the information card about college scholarships. When you write the stack, you would not know which menu card a student would be coming from to get to the College Scholarships card. By using push card commands on all menus, pop card would take the student back to the most recently pushed card, which would always be the menu card used by that particular student.

CLASSROOM ←——→ CONNECTION

Create a stack for a thematic unit. Each button can send the student to an activity in a different curricular area. For example, use the theme of community. One button can go to a card that willl have the student calculate population per square mile, another button can send the student to a card with instructions to write a story about the history of the community, and a third can address air pollution in the community.

Adding Sound to a Script

You can add sound to a stack. You will add music to the first card of this stack.

1. Move to the first card of the Guidance Dept stack.
2. Click on the Button tool.
3. Double-click on the button to get the Button Info dialog box.
4. Click on Script…. Currently there are two lines of commands in this script; you will be adding a third line.
5. Place the insertion point after the word slow in the second line and press Return. You now have a blank line to type in a new command.
6. Type **play harpsichord tempo 180 c#3e d# f**. Harpsichord is the name of a prerecorded sound available in the HyperCard Home stack. (Boing, Silence, and Dialing Tones are other available sounds, if your Home stack has not been altered.) This command should play three notes when the button is clicked. Refer to Figure 9-12 for a little more detail on the **play** command.

7. Close the window, choosing Yes when asked to save changes to the script.

8. Click on the button. You should hear it play. If nothing happens or not all the notes play, check your script for typing errors.

If you decide to try other tunes with HyperCard, you might find it easier to try each one out in the message box before you enter the command in the script. Choose Message from the Go menu. Press Return after you enter the command to test your tune. Then when you like your tune, highlight the command in the message box, copy it, go to the stack's or the specific button's Script Editor, and paste it.

9. Add music to the buttons on the menu card.

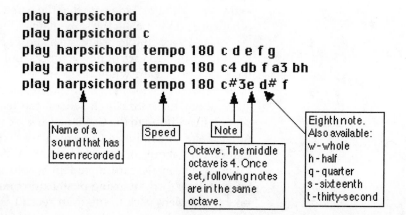

FIGURE 9-12

The play command plays a pre-recorded sound. The tempo and notes are optional.

Creating Audio Buttons

Most versions of HyperCard have audio capabilities. These versions allow you to record sounds and add them to a stack. This is a very useful tool for foreign language, preschool, primary, and special education classes. You can include verbal instructions and explanations in a stack. The instructions can be played as many times as the student needs to listen to them (something that a teacher may tire of after several times). To determine whether your version of HyperCard does have these capabilities, pull down the Edit menu and see if the last two items refer to audio, as shown in Figure 9-13. Some versions of HyperCard have certain audio stacks appear on the Home card. You can also check this.

FIGURE 9-13

The Edit menu with audio capabilities.

If your Macintosh has a microphone, you can record sound. When recorded with the HyperCard functions, sound is placed in a stack as a button. Once this button is placed on a card, the button can be edited like any other button, including scripting and adding icons.

You will add a sound button to the third card of this stack:

1. Move to the College card of the stack.
2. Choose **Audio...** from the Edit menu.
3. Notice the Audio window, called the **audio palette**, is similar to a cassette player in appearance. The normal functions — record, stop, pause, and play — are here. The speaker on the right demonstrates how loud the sound is as it is being recorded.
4. Place the microphone 9 to 12 inches away from you.
5. Click on the Rec. button and say something into the microphone for a test run. Notice the bar moving across the Seconds box to show how much time the recording takes. Keep in mind that sound uses a very large amount of memory. A 30-second sound will require 660 K of memory.
6. Click the Stop button, if the recording has not already stopped.
7. Click the Play button to hear the recorded sound.
8. Click the Edit button at the top of the dialog box. The audio palette is extended to show additional options, as shown in Figure 9-14.

   Along with the recording functions, the audio palette includes a graphic representation of the sound, a waveform, that you can edit. At the bottom of this palette there is a scale for volume. Sliding the bar on the scale to the right will increase the volume; sliding to the left will decrease the volume. You can adjust this bar and click Play again until the volume is appropriate for you.

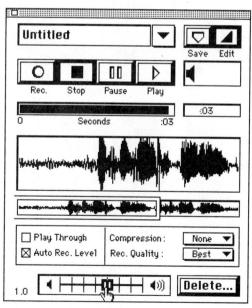

FIGURE 9-14

The audio palette with an extension for editing your recorded sounds. The editing options appear when Edit (top right corner) is clicked.

9. Click the Edit button again to close the edit functions of the audio palette.
10. Click the Rec. button to record over the old sound. This time, record a sentence as if you were the counselor in charge of college scholarships. Note:

If the edit portion of the audio palette is left on the screen when you record, the new sound is added to the end of the old sound. The old sound is not erased. Be cautious when you do this.

11. When you are satisfied with the recording, click Save to save the sound.
12. Name the sound Ms. Smith. This name will be the button name. Click OK.
13. The sound is now a button. You are back on the third card of the Guidance Dept stack, and a message appears at the bottom of the card to instruct you on how to move the button.
14. Close the audio palette and the message box.
15. Select the Button tool from the Tool menu.
16. Reposition and resize the button. If you wish, hide the name and choose an icon for it.

As you can see, adding sound to a stack is a simple process and can be a very useful tool. There are several other features included in the audio palette. Refer to Audio Help on the Edit menu for an in-depth explanation of those features.

Practice Adding Sound to Buttons

1. Add music to the buttons on the rest of the cards.
2. Add a recorded sound button on the first card welcoming students to Downtown High.
3. Add a recorded sound button on the rest of the cards.

CLASSROOM ◄─────► CONNECTION

Use HyperCard to create a stack with buttons that you previously recorded with the spelling words. The student will click on the button, hear the word and a sentence, and then spell the word. Students who need the word repeated can simply click on the same button to hear the word again. Use this same stack for students who are absent on the test day.

Animation

Another useful feature of HyperCard is animation, making pictures or drawn objects appear as though they are moving. Among many other possibilities, animation could be used to enhance a science presentation on cell mitosis, to help beginning readers understand action, or to help foreign-language students understand vocabulary, especially prepositions. You will explore a stack that demonstrates animation, and then you will create your own animation stack.

EXPLORING AN ANIMATION STACK

1. Open the stack Eclipse.
2. Click on the right arrow button to move to the second card.
3. Follow the directions to click and watch the moon move into position for a solar eclipse.
4. Notice that the moon steadily moves around the Earth. The illusion of animation is created by having several cards appear in rapid succession with

the moon redrawn in a new position on each card. This is the same concept as drawing little figures in the corner of every page in a notebook and flipping through the pages. The figure changes on each page. This is how the moon was moved.

5. To look at how this actually came about, move to the first card of the stack.

6. Instead of using the buttons, use the right arrow key on the keyboard to move slowly through the stack. Now you can see that the diagram stays the same and only the moon is redrawn in a different location on each card, as shown in Figure 9-15.

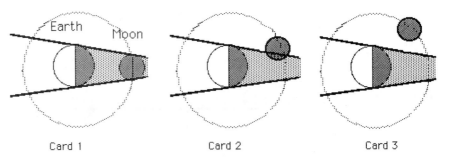

FIGURE 9-15

A series of drawings used to produce animation in the Eclipse stack.

7. Move to the second card of the stack.

8. Select the Button tool, double-click on the button in the upper right corner of the card, and click Script... to see how the animation was done. The script is shown in Figure 9-16.

FIGURE 9-16

The repeat command is used here to display nine successive cards.

```
 Script
on mouseUp
   repeat 9
      go to next card
   end repeat
end mouseUp
```

The HyperCard command used was **repeat**. Repeat 9 tells HyperCard to do the following command or commands nine times, in this case to go to next card nine times. There were nine cards used to move the moon around to the solar eclipse position. Notice the repeat command closes with end repeat. This tells the stack that there are no more commands to carry out nine times. The usual on mouseUp and end mouseUp is still necessary.

9. Close the script editor.

CREATING ANIMATION

The Eclipse stack was a simple demonstration of how animation could be used in a classroom situation. In the next set of exercises, you are going to create another simple stack with animation. Your own ideas for animation will undoubtedly be more involved than this one, once you have used the process.

The stack will be a series of cards that demonstrate what action occurs when the like poles of two magnets are close together and then again when their unlike poles are close together. The first two cards of the stack, an introduction and a card containing a graphic of two magnets, have been created for you. You will create four cards that will show the like poles moving away from each other and four that show the unlike poles moving together. You will then add script to the button on the second card. As mentioned earlier, HyperCard is very English-like and the repeat command will simply say repeat 4, tell what is to be repeated, and then close with end repeat.

1. Open the stack Magnetism.
2. Move to the second card of the stack.
3. Choose New Card four times. You now have four blank cards.
4. Type Like Poles in the title field on all the new cards (or copy and paste the text).
5. Move to the second card of the stack again.
6. Use the Select tool to select both magnets labeled N and S, as shown in Figure 9-17.

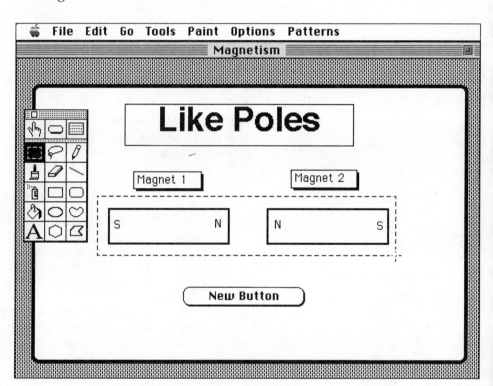

FIGURE 9-17

The graphic of the two magnets is selected for copying.

7. Choose Copy Picture from the Edit menu.
8. Move to the third card of the stack.
9. Paste the picture on each of the four new cards.

Moving the Magnets Separately

The magnets need to be moved a little farther apart on each successive card. This time the magnets will be selected separately and moved.

1. Move back to the third card in the stack.
2. Use the Select tool to select only the magnet on the left.
3. Hold down the Shift key as you drag the magnet about one-half inch to the left. The Shift key "locks" the motion so that the selection can only be moved

horizontally or vertically, depending on your initial movement. This ensures that the magnets always stay on the same horizontal level on all cards, so the movement looks more realistic.

4. Select the magnet on the right.

5. Hold down the Shift key as you drag the magnet about one-half inch to the right.

6. Repeat Steps 2 through 5 for the next three cards keeping in mind that the magnets need to be farther apart on each successive card.

7. On the last card, add a button that allows movement to the next card.

8. On the last card, also add a field to contain an explanation about like poles, as shown in Figure 9-18.

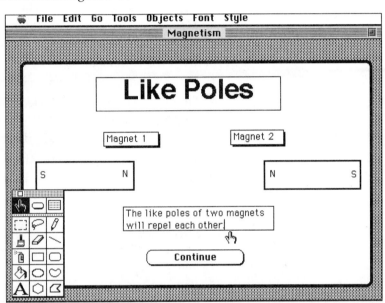

FIGURE 9-18

The last card of the series about like poles contains an explanation and a button to go to the next card.

Writing the Repeat Script

Script must be added to the button on the second card involving the repeat command to cause the animation.

1. Move to the second card of the stack again.

2. Select the Button tool and double-click on the New Button.

3. Change the button name to Click Here to See.

4. Type the following script between on mouseUp and end mouseUp:

```
repeat 4
        go to next card
        wait 25 ticks
end repeat
```

5. Close the script editor and save the changes.

The **wait** command causes the computer to wait before moving on to the next command. Here, the command is a way of having a card remain briefly on the screen—the larger the number of ticks, the longer the card remains on the screen. The time for a tick varies with different computers. Sometimes this is very useful in a stack, particularly if you have a powerful and quick Macintosh and the animation occurs too quickly.

Completing the Stack

The second half of this stack will demonstrate what happens when unlike poles come in close contact: they attract each other. This half will need to have the magnets start farther apart and come together. To accomplish this, do the following:

1. Select **Copy Card** from the Edit menu to copy the second card. Select **Paste Card** from the Edit menu to paste the copy of the second card after the last card presently in the stack. Notice that Copy Card creates a complete duplicate of the card including all the text in all the fields, both background level and card level. Remember New Card copies background objects only.

2. Change Like to Unlike in the title.

3. Erase the magnets. Because the animation will show the magnets coming together, the magnets must start farther apart.

4. Move to the last card of the Like animation sequence. Here the magnets are the farthest apart. Select the two magnets with the Select tool.

5. Copy the two magnets.

6. Move to the new card and paste the magnets on this card.

7. Because the poles are opposite, erase the N and S on one of the magnets and use the Paint Text tool to reverse the letters to S and N.

8. Once again, use the New Card command to create four more cards.

9. Type Unlike Poles in the title field on each.

10. Again, the graphic must be copied on each card. Select the two magnets on the first card of the Unlike series.

11. Copy the magnets and paste them on each of the next four cards.

12. Select each magnet separately on the second card of the Unlike series, hold down the Shift key, and drag the magnet about one-half inch closer to the other magnet.

13. Repeat Step 12 for each of the remaining cards, bringing the magnets closer on each card until the two magnets are touching on the last card.

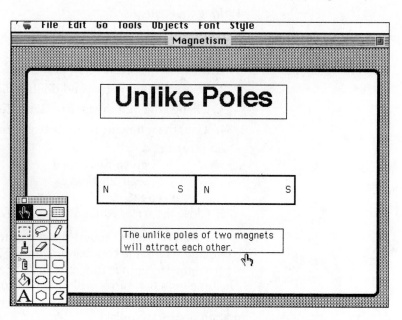

FIGURE 9-19

The last card of the Magnetism stack.

14. On the last card, add a field for the explanation, as shown in Figure 9-19.
15. Test your stack.

As you can see, animation can be a useful tool in the classroom. Animation can be used in almost any subject area—even math, for drawing a graph or watching parts of a pie (fractions) come together to create a whole. Also, students enjoy creating animation for projects—models of molecular movement or capillary action, historic scenes, or definitions of foreign-language words for up, down, in, and out are just a few of the possibilities.

The Answer Command

Another way to use HyperCard in the classroom is by allowing students to choose or type in answers to questions and receive immediate feedback. The next stack will demonstrate how this can be accomplished.

1. Open the stack Quiz Review.
2. Read the directions on the first card, then move on to the questions. Explore all the possibilities on each of the cards.
3. Now take a closer look at how this stack works. The user level of this stack is set at 3 so students cannot change anything. To change that level, open the message box and type: **set userLevel to 5**.
4. Notice there is no menu bar. Type **show menuBar** in the message box, or use ⌘-space bar to see the menu bar.

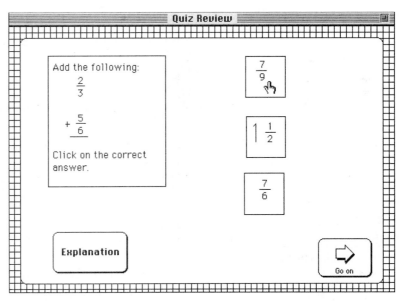

FIGURE 9-20

The first card of the Quiz Review stack. There are five buttons and one field on this card.

5. Move to the second card of the stack. As shown in Figure 9-20, on the first two questions the student could choose one of three possible answers. A student who needed more help could see an explanation on how to work that specific problem.
6. Look at the button script. (Select the Button tool, double-click on the first answer, and then click Script....) Notice a new command: answer "Oops! Try again," as shown in Figure 9-21.

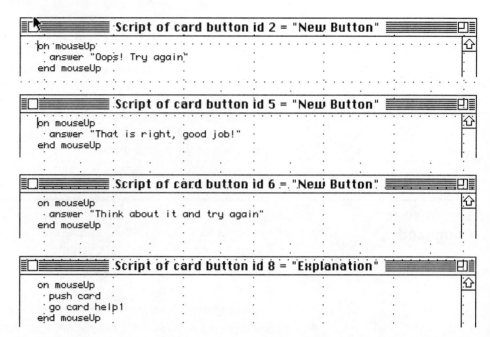

FIGURE 9-21

The script for the three answer buttons and the explanation button on the second card in the Quiz Review stack.

The **answer** command produces a dialog box with the specified comment in it, as shown in Figure 9-22. Whatever you place in the quotation marks in the script will appear in the dialog box. The student can click OK to close that box. This is a simple command that can be used for many purposes.

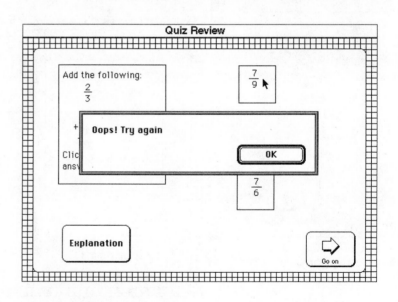

FIGURE 9-22

A dialog box produced by an answer command.

7. Close the script editor.

8. Look at the button script for the remaining two fraction buttons to see similar script. As you can see, the answer command gives you the ability to communicate different messages to students depending on their choices.

9. Look at the script for the explanation button, as shown in Figure 9-21. Notice push card is used here in a way similar to its use in the Guidance Dept stack.

The Ask and If/Then/Else Commands

On the third question card in the Quiz Review stack, the method of questioning is quite different from the first two question cards. Here the question appears in a dialog box. The student has no choices; a specific answer must be given. To accomplish this, the scripting becomes a little more involved.

1. Move to the fourth card of this stack. It should look similar to Figure 9-23.

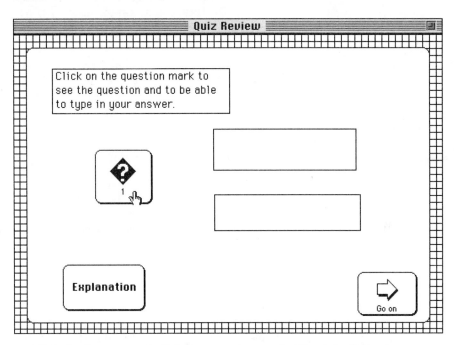

FIGURE 9-23

The second type of question card in the Quiz Review stack.

2. With the Browse tool click the question mark. The Ask dialog box appears, as in Figure 9-24, with a question in it.

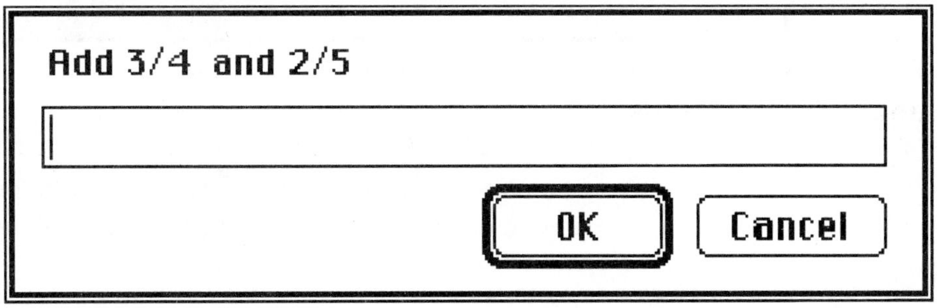

FIGURE 9-24

The Ask dialog box contains a question that was written in the button script.

3. Type in an answer and observe the response.

4. With the Button tool, look at the script for the question mark button. The script is shown in Figure 9-25.

The first command is **ask.** This causes a dialog box to appear with the specified question in it, as shown in Figure 9-24. As usual, the dialog box expects an answer.

The next command, **put**, is used to place text in a particular location. In this case the answer from the student (**it**) is placed in Card Field 1. Now the student can see the typed answer. Also, now that answer can be checked.

The **if/then/else** command is used to decide what to do if the answer is right and what to do if the answer is wrong. Here, if the answer is right, the put command places Correct answer in a second field. If the answer is wrong, the put command places No, try again, in the second field to give the student feedback. An end if command is used to end the if/then/else action.

FIGURE 9-25

The script of the question mark button.

```
▤□▤▤▤▤▤▤▤▤▤▤▤▤▤▤▤▤  Script of card button id
on mouseUp
   ask "Add 3/4  and 2/5"
   put it into card field 1
   if card field 1 = "1 3/20"  then
      put "Correct answer"into card field 2
   else
      put "No, try again." into card field 2
   end if
end mouseUp
```

5. Close the script editor.
6. Check the script on the right arrow button. Notice that the **put empty** commands are used to clear out the two fields that held answers and comments. This is similar to the put empty commands you used in the Area stack in Chapter 8.
7. Close this script editor.

This demonstrates two very powerful methods to create interactive stacks for students. Foreign-language vocabulary studies, decision-making exercises, and book review questions are possible uses for this technique. It can be a study or review tool for almost any subject area. For example, students studying the rules of volleyball could use a stack like this to prepare for a test. Students also enjoy using these methods to create their own stacks.

Practice with Answer and Ask Commands

1. Add another question card of each type to the Quiz Review stack to provide more practice questions.
2. Modify the Machines stack to show the motion of levers and pulleys.
3. Modify the Quiz Review stack to use it for grammar questions.
4. Create a stack to demonstrate electrons moving around the nucleus of an atom.

Color Tools

INCREASING MEMORY ALLOCATIONS FOR HYPERCARD

HyperCard 2.3 has color capabilities. Color can certainly enhance a stack. You can color buttons, fields, or graphics. However, using the Color Tools requires more memory for the HyperCard application. To change the amount of memory, do the following:

1. Quit HyperCard.
2. Locate the HyperCard application on the hard drive.
3. Click on it once to select it.

4. From the File menu, select Get Info.
5. Delete the number in the Preferred size box and type in 4500 as shown in Figure 9-26.
6. Close the window.
7. Open HyperCard.

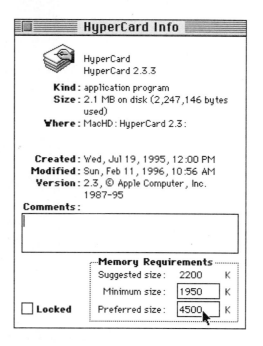

FIGURE 9-26

Delete the number in the Preferred size box and type in 4500 to be able to work with color.

TURNING THE COLOR TOOLS ON

HyperCard typically opens with the Color Tools turned off. You will need to turn them on.

1. From the Go menu select Home.
2. Notice the icon at the end of the first row of icons on the Home card. It probably says Color Tools are Off. To turn Color Tools on, click on the icon. It will take a few minutes for the change to be made.
3. A new menu item called Color will appear in the menu bar.
4. Open the Welcome stack.
5. From the Color menu, select Open Coloring Tools. The **Coloring tools** is a separate part of HyperCard. Notice the menus have changed. You will not be able to use the typical HyperCard menus when the Coloring tools are open.
6. To color a field, click on the Field button on the Coloring tools.
7. Click on the field Welcome to School.
8. Click on any color on the palette. The field should now be that color.
9. The same process can be used to color buttons. Color the button on this card.

EXPLORING THE COLORING TOOLS

These two features of the Coloring tools are the simplest to use. As you become more proficient at using HyperCard, you may want to explore the other tools. The Rectangle tool will create a rectangle of any color you choose. It can then be

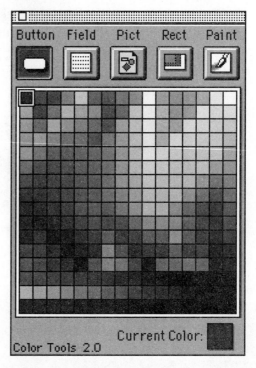

FIGURE 9-27

The Coloring tools palette. The Button coloring tool is selected.

resized and also moved anywhere on the card. The Picture tool allows you to import pictures from other programs. By double-clicking on the Paint tool, a painting tool palette is placed on the screen and you can draw any type of figure you need. However, the more color items placed on a card the more memory the stack needs. Be cautious in the amount of coloring you add to a stack.

Button Tasks

As you created buttons, you used two tasks: Go to destination and Visual effect. HyperCard 2.3 includes several more tasks that eliminate the need to write the actual script. These tasks can be useful to the classroom teacher. To explore each of these tasks, you will create a one-card stack and create buttons on it. The purpose of this exercise is to familiarize you with these tasks and their possibilities for the classroom.

LAUNCH APPLICATION

1. From the File menu, select New Stack and call it Task Exploring.
2. Place six buttons on the card.
3. With the button tool selected, double-click on one of the buttons.
4. Title this button Application.
5. Click on Tasks... in the Button Info dialog box.
6. Click on Launch Application in the Tasks dialog box. New choices are presented on the right side of the dialog box. This task will launch any application on the hard drive. You can set it to open ClarisWorks or any other program.
7. To designate the application you want to open, click on choose... under the Launch Application option on the right side of the Tasks dialog box. A dialog box containing folders on the hard drive appears. Scroll through and select

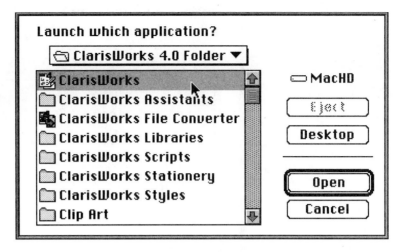

FIGURE 9-28

Click on the application
ClarisWorks, and then click
Open.

ClarisWorks, as shown in Figure 9-28. Notice you could even select a specific document in ClarisWorks if you choose to. Click Open.

8. Click on Assign Tasks. Try out the button. To return to HyperCard, quit ClarisWorks.

A stack could give instructions on math skills and then use a button to launch Math Blaster to practice those skills. When students quit Math Blaster, they are returned to the same card that launched Math Blaster. Students could then progress through the stack. Instructions could be given on writing an opinion paper, and then a button could open ClarisWorks and allow the student to write immediately. Information on how to create a graph could be given in a HyperCard stack, with a button sending the student to a specific spreadsheet in ClarisWorks to do the actual graphing.

MOVIE

You will use the second button to play a QuickTime movie.

1. With the Button tool selected, double-click on the second button.
2. Click on Tasks....
3. Click on Movie. A new list appears similar to the Launch Applications list. This task is used to place movies on a card. If you have a QuickTime movie on your hard drive (if you have HyperStudio installed on your hard drive, there are several movies in that folder), you can try out this task.
4. Click on Play Movie. Once again a dialog box listing items on the hard drive appears.
5. Locate a QuickTime Movie and click on it (see Figure 9-29).
6. Click Open.
7. Click on Assign Tasks and try out this button.

Videos of students on a field trip or working in the classroom can be placed in a HyperCard stack. The Welcome stack could show videos of sporting events or a welcome speech by students presently attending the school. Videos of chemical reactions could add to the explanation of chemistry concepts. Student interviews can be added to stacks about the community. Remember to keep the movies short because movies use quite a bit of memory.

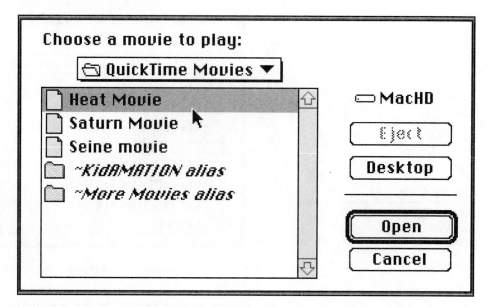

FIGURE 9-29

Click on the QuickTime Movie
you wish to add to the stack and
then click on Open.

You have now set the task for two buttons, so the instructions for the rest of this
section will assume you know how to select the button and get to the Task... dialog box. Refer to previous instructions if you need help on this.

SOUND

1. The third button will place sound on the card. When you are on the Tasks...
   dialog box, scroll down and select Sound.

2. You will see that you have three options: choose a sound to play, record a
   sound, or import a sound, as shown in Figure 9-30. Recording a sound is
   similar to the activity you did previously in the sound buttons section.
   Sounds saved on the hard drive can be imported to this stack.

3. Select the How are you? sound and click Assign Task. Try out the button.

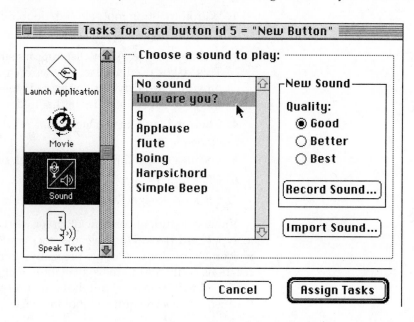

FIGURE 9-30

The sound dialog box with the
prerecorded sound: How are
you? You can also record sounds
from this dialog box.

Sound capabilities greatly enhance a stack. By using this task you can record your voice to reward a student who gets a right answer. Think back to the Quiz Review stack. If the student selects the correct answer, the dialog box could come up and the sound could play to them. This sound task is very important for primary students who cannot read. Your voice would tell them whether they selected the right or wrong answer. Oral instructions are very important to poor readers or those just learning to read.

SPEECH

The fourth button will demonstrate the speech capabilities of HyperCard. Speech capabilities refers to the fact that typed text can be read by the computer.

1. The fourth button will place speech on the card. When you are on the Tasks... dialog box, scroll down and select Speech.

2. The important choices are Speak Currently Selected Field and Speak String. Click in the circle in front of Speak String.

3. Type in a few words that the computer will speak, as shown in Figure 9-31.

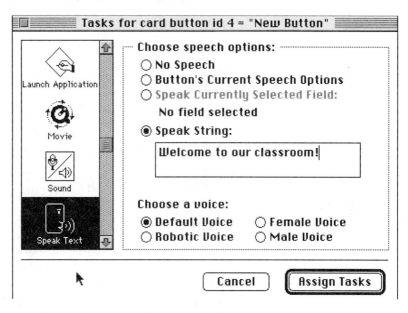

FIGURE 9-31

The speech options with Speak String selected. You can choose one of four voices to speak the string.

4. Click on Assign Tasks and try out the button. Notice the voice is mechanical. There are four choices of voices. Go back to the Tasks... dialog box and experiment with all of the voices.

5. If a field were placed on this card, the Speak Currently Selected Field would have the text in that field read to the student. Keep in mind that this voice too would be mechanical. If you wish to try this, add a field to the card and type in some text. While you are on the Tasks... dialog box, drag the Tasks... dialog box down to the bottom of the screen until you can see the field on the card. Click on the field to select it and then click in the radio button in front of Speak Currently Selected Field in the Tasks... dialog box.

Although the speech quality is not as good as a recording of an actual voice, this option has several classroom applications. To save time and memory, this option could be used to allow students to have information in the field on each card read to them. If you recorded your voice for every card in a 15-card stack, the size of the stack would be very large and may inhibit use of it. Using this task would keep the stack's memory small and still have the text read to the student. This option could also be used to have students type in a sentence and then have the sentence read back to them to determine whether it is a complete sentence and sounds correct. In addition, students could compare how they think a word is spelled with the way the word is pronounced by the computer once they type it in. This would provide an auditory prompt along with the visual representation. Since most people do not feel comfortable with their spelling skills, this could be helpful. Students with learning disabilities may benefit from this feature to overcome reading and writing difficulties.

CD AUDIO

Certain sections of an audio CD can be played in HyperCard. If your computer has a CD-ROM either attached or built in, you may use this task.

1. The fifth button will demonstrate CD capabilities. Place an audio CD in the CD tray.
2. When you are on the Tasks... dialog box, scroll down and select CD Audio.
3. The list of choices on the right side of the Tasks... dialog box, shown in Figure 9-32, refer to the CD. Click on the ? to determine the Disc ID. A series of numbers will now appear in the box.

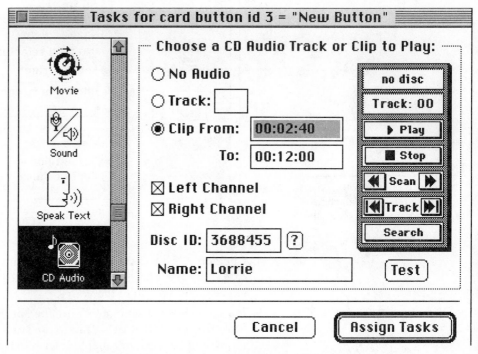

FIGURE 9-32

The CD Audio Track dialog box with a clip selected.

4. You can select a track to play or you can type in actual numbers for a clip to play. To determine these numbers, play the CD and watch the numbers in the box change. Typically a clip does not start at 0; try starting with 00:03:00. Type in some numbers to hear a small clip of the CD.
5. Assign the task and try out this button.

There are times when music enhances learning. This could be used to set the mood of a stack. It could be used to teach about music, or it could play a famous speech.

LASER DISC

In the past interfacing a laser disc player with HyperCard was difficult. Now, using the task for the laser disc has made this process simple. If your computer is not connected to a laser disc player, you will only be able to look at the choices.

1. The sixth button is for laser disc.
2. When you are on the Tasks... dialog box, scroll down and select Laser Disc.
3. A screen similar to the CD Audio screen appears. You can see the options allow you to display a still from a laser disc or a clip. The clip can be set by watching the video with the numbers displayed. Select the numbers you want and type them in the Clip From: and To: boxes.
4. If you attempt to play a laser disc and none is attached, a message will appear informing you that HyperCard is unable to determine what videodisc is attached. Click No Player to return to the Laser Disc Task screen. Click Cancel if you do not have a laser disc player attached.

Creating multimedia by attaching a laser disc player to the computer can greatly enhance learning through the use of video segments. A stack about tornadoes becomes dynamic when a click of a button shows an actual tornado crossing fields and towns. Laser discs are available in every subject area. Students can create dynamic presentations that include video clips to demonstrate science principles, such as mitosis. Lessons come alive when you can show students laser disc motion sequences with the click of a button.

Tips

Here is a basic list of tips on the material contained in these two HyperCard chapters.

- If there are too many fields on a card or on a background, select the Field tool, click on the field you don't want, and press the Delete key. That field will now be gone. For background fields, a message appears that asks if you want the background field to be removed from all the cards. Make sure that you really want it to be removed.

- If there are too many buttons on a card or on a background, select the Button tool, click on the button you don't want, and press the Delete key. That button will now be gone. Once again, make sure that you really want the background button removed.

- If a card has no buttons and you want to move to another card, use the right and left arrow keys to navigate through a stack.

- If the menu bar is not showing, hold down the ⌘ key (or, if that doesn't work, the ⌘ and the Shift keys) and press the space bar.

- To get to the message box, choose Message from the Go menu or use the keys ⌘-M.

- If you need to set the user level, use the message box to write the command **set userLevel to 5**, where 5 is the highest level of 1 through 5.

- If you want to remove a card from a stack, choose Delete Card from the Edit menu.

- If a field is hidden and you want to see it, use the message box and type **show card field "name"** or **show card field 2** or **show background**

field id 4379, varying the command based on whether your field is a card or background field and whether you want to use its name, number, or id.

- If a field or button or graphic is on top of or below other objects, use the Send Farther or Bring Closer commands on the Objects menu to move the object to another layer. You may need to repeat the command a number of times to get to the desired layer.

- If the option you want is not available on the menu bar, click on a different tool and see if it appears. For example, the Objects menu only appears when the Browse, the Button, or the Field tool is selected.

Conclusion

After concluding this chapter, you should now be able to create a new stack, use HyperTalk to hide and show fields, play and record sounds, go to various cards, and work with card and background layers. You learned script that allows you to return to previously viewed cards, to display a dialog box in response to questions, and to display a dialog box asking a question. And you learned how to use color in HyperCard and how to use the button tasks to enhance teaching and learning in your classroom.

Although these two chapters covered much material, this is just the beginning of the potential of HyperCard. There are many other possibilites for using HyperCard and HyperTalk that could not be presented here. For instance, you can search stacks for information and sort stacks. In addition, scanners can be used to copy pictures into HyperCard—students can see themselves in a stack, and detailed pictures can illustrate concepts and student stacks. And the list goes on. (To learn more about HyperCard, you may want to refer to the books listed at the end of this chapter.) As with any tool, HyperCard has strengths and weaknesses that make it more appropriate for some purposes than others, but you will find that the flexibility of HyperCard generally makes it a valuable educational tool. For classroom management and curriculum areas; for presentations, tutorials, and review; for student reports and projects; or for special events, HyperCard can be a useful tool in the classroom.

KEY TERMS

answer	hide menuBar	pop card
ask	HyperTalk	push card
audio palette	if/then/else	put
Audio...	it	put empty into
Bring Closer	layer	repeat
Coloring tools	mouseUp	Rounded Rectangle tool
Copy Card	New Stack...	script
end (action)	on (action)	script editor
Fill tool	openStack	Send Farther
go to	Paste Card	show field
hide field	play	wait

EXERCISES

1. Edit the stack Layers. Create a few cards that would explain one or more of the following to novice HyperCard users: (a) What layer means; (b) How to create buttons and add script to go to cards; (c) How to create or use fields; (d) How to hide and show fields; or (e) How to add sound to a button. Some graphics have been put on extra cards in the stack—they can be edited, copied, cut, moved, and pasted from card to card. Cut cards, buttons, fields, and graphics that you do not need, or edit them to suit your needs.

2. Open the stack Books. On the background create a **scrolling field** that can be used to write a summary and create buttons to go to the previous or next card. If necessary, change the title card so that the scrolling field is hidden on that card. Add any other fields or buttons that you think will improve the stack. Fill in the cards with appropriate books. Include appropriate graphics.

3. Create a stack Diagram. Draw a diagram of a plant, an animal, a map, or anything that is appropriate to your area of teaching. Create fields and buttons that will allow a student to click on a part of the diagram and see an enlarged diagram, a definition, or a label appropriate to that part. For example, on a diagram of a cell with buttons covering the different parts of the cell, when the student clicks on the nucleus, a small field shows that says nucleus or another card displays more details of the nucleus.

4. Create a stack explaining erosion; use sound and animation and any other features to demonstrate how erosion wears down mountains.

5. Create a stack that uses animation to demonstrate the relationships between fractional parts and a whole.

6. Create a stack to provide students with practice on phonics, such as reading words with short vowel sounds. Use the audio capabilities of HyperCard.

7. Add a card to an information stack you have already created. The card you add will be used to check what was learned from the stack. Use the ask or answer HyperTalk commands. Send students back for the appropriate review if they are unable to answer the question or questions on the card correctly.

8. Create a stack in a foreign language that lets the students hear the language; include question cards to quiz students on comprehension.

9. Develop a stack, with a minimum of 15 cards, of your own design. Have it approved by your instructor.

REFERENCES

1. Beekman, George. (1994). *HyperCard 2.3 in a Hurry.* Belmont, CA: Addison-Wesley (International Society for Technology in Education, 1-800-336-5191).

2. Bull, Glen and Harris, Judi. (1992). *HyperCard for Educators: An Introduction.* Eugene, OR: International Society for Technology in Education.

3. Culp, George H. and Watkins, G. Morgan. (1993). *The Educator's Guide to HyperCard and HyperTalk.* Boston, MA: Allyn & Bacon.

4. Goodman, Danny. (1990). *The Complete HyperCard 2.0 Handbook, 3rd Edition.* Toronto: Bantam Books.

5. Hofmeister, Joseph F. and Rudowski, Joyce B. (1992). *Learning with Hypercard.* Cincinnati, OH: Southwestern.

6. Lamb, Annette and Myers, Dennis. (1991). *HyperCard Creativity Tool for Writing, Organizing, and Multimedia.* Orange, CA: Career Publishing.

7. Ventura, Fred, and Marilyn Grover. (1991). *HyperCard Projects for Teachers.* Grover Beach, CA: Ventura Educational Systems.

8. Turner, Sandra and Land, Michael (1994). *HyperCard - A Tool for Learning.* Wadsworth. (International Society for Technology in Education, 1-800-336-5191).

9. Yoder, Sharon and Smith, Irene (1994). *HyperTalk for Educators - An Introduction, Second Edition.* Eugene, OR: International Society for Technology in Education.

10

In the Classroom

343

Introduction

As seen in the previous material, there is a great range of useful things a teacher can do with a Mac. This book only begins to touch on all the creative ways teachers and computers may come together. In this last chapter, a brief overview of other software available for the Mac is presented. Please note that the examples given here are not comprehensive; the amount of quality software available for the Mac is growing daily. Rather, the examples below are intended to provide you with an introduction to the many uses to which a Mac may be put by a teacher. As you grow in your experience with computers, you will discover unique ways to use technology for yourself and with your students. Often teachers find that the greatest strength they have in applying technology to their activities is their previous experience with students and teaching—their hard-won knowledge about teaching and students naturally drives their initial use of technology. Ultimately, as teachers' experience and technology interact, the technology may help them explore and discover new insights into what is possible in the classroom.

One theme of this book is that the best first place for a computer is on the teacher's desk. By using computers for their own specialized tasks, such as the applications covered in this book, teachers often become aware of the possibilities computers provide. Another important view of technology is as a tool for student use—as a way to learn content (facts and concepts), to practice processes such as problem solving and writing, and to learn and apply computer skills such as using a database or spreadsheet. As you read through the following material, consider which software you might use to prepare materials or organize information, which software students might use (such as for drill and practice), and which software you and your students might both use. As an example of the last case, consider spreadsheet software. A spreadsheet might be used by a teacher to keep grades, but a spreadsheet might also be used by students to record and analyze data in a social studies or science experiment. A HyperStudio stack could be used by the teacher to present a concept or a stack could be created by a student to report to the class.

Thinking About Software: Tutor, Tool, Tutee

Software is available for a wide variety of purposes. In education, one valuable way to think about software is in terms of the modes of educational computer use presented by Robert Taylor in his book, *The Computer in the School: Tutor, Tool, Tutee* (Teacher's College Press, 1980). Taylor proposes that computers may be used in education in one of three modes: tutor, tool, or tutee (student). In the **tutor mode**, material is presented to the student, the student is questioned about the material, the student's responses are evaluated by the computer, and then, based on that evaluation, the computer presents additional content. The tutor mode is the mode in which the computer has greatest control .over the interactions between the user and the computer. Tutorials are clear examples of tutor mode. Other examples of tutor mode applications include instructional games, simulations, and drill and practice programs. These examples are familiar to teachers, because they employ methods similar to noncomputer instructional methods.

In the **tool mode**, the computer provides a service that extends the computer user's capabilities in some way. Unlike the tutor mode, the computer does not act as a teacher. Rather, it lets computer users apply capabilities they already have in a way that may lead to increased efficiency or quality in the work produced.

Users have more control over interactions than in the tutor mode, but they must remain within the confines of the program's structure and responses. A word processing program is a good example. Word processors allow users to electronically create, edit, save, and print documents, but they do not teach how to write. Users bring their writing ability to the computer and apply that ability. The fact that it will be much easier to revise the document created may lead to a better finished product, but no writing instruction is offered by the word processor. Database programs, spreadsheets, and grade-keeping programs are some other types of programs that can be classified as tool mode software.

Tutee mode software allows the user to treat the computer as a student—to "teach" the computer. Teach is used here in the sense that a computer requires instructions (a program) to work. The acts of deciding what the computer will do and then writing the instructions to make the computer do it can be thought of as teaching the computer to do the task. In the tutee mode, the user controls the interactions with the computer and provides instructions for what the computer will do. Most examples of software in the tutee mode are programming languages. For example, a teacher may want a drill and practice program to present exercises on the addition of the numbers 1 through 9 and may write a program in a programming language to make the computer do that. In this case, the teacher has taught the computer to perform as a drill and practice program. HyperCard may be thought of as tutee mode software when the scripting language is used to create materials for use by others. Many educators support tutee mode uses of the computer in education as a way to teach problem-solving strategies, which the teacher can then actively help students apply outside of the computer programming environment. Applications in the tutee mode are also seen as a way to better understand how a computer works as well as a way to provide specific computer skills in programming.

Figure 10-1 depicts the modes of educational computer use with examples of software for each mode. This model of computer use is most valuable when the modes are thought of as being on a continuum from greatest computer control (tutor) through greatest student control (tutee). Programs may fit anywhere along the continuum, and in some cases a program may be used in more than one mode at different times. In Chapters 2 through 6 of this book, the uses of ClarisWorks were clearly presented as tool mode uses of the computer. Chapter 7 also presents HyperStudio as tool mode software. However, in Chapters 8 and 9, HyperCard and its scripting language is introduced as a means to program in HyperCard. When used in this way, HyperCard can be seen as an example of tutee mode software. Examples of tutor, tool, and tutee mode software for classroom use are found in this chapter.

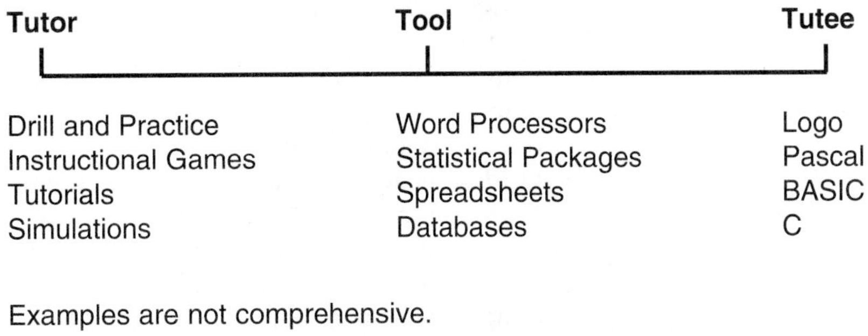

Tutor	Tool	Tutee
Drill and Practice	Word Processors	Logo
Instructional Games	Statistical Packages	Pascal
Tutorials	Spreadsheets	BASIC
Simulations	Databases	C

FIGURE 10-1

Examples of Taylor's three modes of software use.

Examples are not comprehensive.

Taylor's framework has held up very well over time as a way to begin thinking about computers in education. This is probably true because it places the focus on the use of the computer in education. As Taylor originally pointed out, the modes of educational computer use are designed to orient someone to a field that can initially be confusing, with its thousands of individual programs aimed at education. By considering the use of the computer in education, teachers who are already familiar with instructional methods and materials can readily relate to the possibilities computers offer.

These modes are intended to be a way to categorize the many programs available for educators, a way to begin to understand the possibilities technology provides to teachers and students. In fact, some programs may operate, at different times, in different modes. For example, a math tutorial program might provide a charting tool with which a student could create graphs to answer tutorial exercises. The charting portion of the program would be essentially tool mode software contained within tutor mode software. Another example is the variety of uses of HyperCard—when a teacher writes script to create a HyperCard tutorial on the Civil War, HyperCard is being used in the tutee mode by the teacher. However, when a student sits down to use the tutorial on the Civil War, the student will, at that point, be using HyperCard in the tutor mode. Keeping this in mind, consider the modes of educational computer use as you read and become familiar with the examples of programs for the Mac presented in this chapter.

As you think about computers and learning, keep in mind how you, as a teacher, will be using the computer with students. Such use will generally reflect your orientation to teaching and learning. If you believe in guided discovery as a beneficial instructional technique, you will likely be attracted to programs that fit into that approach. If a more structured, directed approach is your teaching style, you may find drill and practice and tutorial programs beneficial in your classroom. By thinking about the use of the computer in your classroom in relation to Taylor's modes, a framework is provided for reflecting on your practices as a teacher and their relationships to the use of technology. Many teachers also use technology as a way to explore alternate methods in the classroom, perhaps as a way to begin to implement discovery-oriented approaches or collaborative projects among students.

Evaluating Software

Just as with other materials used in the classroom, software should be reviewed by the teacher prior to purchase. No amount of reading about software is sufficient to qualify as software evaluation. Reviews of software, catalog descriptions, and recommendations from other professionals are good places to start, but you should always spend time with the software in a hands-on situation. Many of the things to be considered in reviewing software are also important in reviewing other types of educational material. The software must be accurate, should fit your teaching style, and must avoid stereotypes, as well as be engaging to the student and, in some cases, useful in a variety of grouping situations. Further, the documentation (written materials that come with the software) should ideally be written for teachers: It should contain educational goals and objectives, suggestions for extension and enrichment activities, and an outline of necessary prerequisite skills the student needs to be successful with the software.

Because the computer is a medium quite different from print media, a number of additional considerations need to be made when reviewing software. Is the software free of programming errors (bugs), in other words, will it operate smoothly? Are graphics and sound used appropriately? If a program contains too many "bells and whistles," too much use of graphics and sound to the detraction of its educational intent, look elsewhere. A good example of this is a program that presents an engaging graphics sequence when a wrong answer is entered. Students have been known to purposely enter incorrect answers over and over again just to see engaging graphics! Screens should be presented so that material is clear and accessible to the student. Also, the addition of a management system that can automatically store a file of student responses as well as allow a teacher to tailor the difficulty of material presented can be of great value. Further, provision by the software publisher of a backup copy, or the ability to make a legal backup copy, is important.

When considering software adoption, be careful to consider the type of software reviewed in the context of the software's possible educational use. A drill and practice program will be used for reinforcement of low-level cognitive skill, perhaps the bringing to mind of previously learned material. A word processing program, or a spreadsheet program, however, can be used to practice, develop, and provide evidence of the development of higher level skills, such as the ability to break down material into its underlying parts as a way to better understand the organization of the material. What is important is to be aware of the possibilities the software offers and then judge the software's value in the light of those possibilities. Taylor's framework, when coupled with an understanding of the types of cognitive development possible, can be a valuable tool in thinking about ways the computer might be used in the classroom.

Software Examples

The following software descriptions are intended to give an idea of the variety of educational uses to which a Macintosh may be applied. Generally, the software that teachers use will be proprietary—the rights to the software will be owned by an individual or a company and the software will be sold commercially. It is illegal to make copies of such software, except for the purpose of keeping an archival or backup copy of the software. Software piracy (illegal copying of software) is a crime and certainly has no place in the schools.

A second type of software is called public domain. These programs may be legally and freely copied. **Public domain software** varies in quality from the truly exceptional to the absolutely dismal. A third type of software is called **shareware**. This software may be freely copied, but if a user finds the software desirable and intends to make use of it, a small fee (generally between $5 and $25) is sent to the software author. With two exceptions, the programs cited below are all commercial software.

The following examples all come in versions that will run on the Mac.

TUTOR

Broderbund offers the Carmen Sandiego series of programs, including *Where in the World Is Carmen Sandiego?*, *Where in Europe Is Carmen Sandiego?*, *Where in the U.S.A. Is Carmen Sandiego?*, *Where in Time Is Carmen Sandiego?*, and *Where in America's Past Is Carmen Sandiego?* Students discover and analyze clues as they pursue a member of Carmen's gang who has committed a crime. Depending on the program, the gang member may flee through the U.S.A., Europe, the world, or history. Students can use various reference materials to decipher clues. A very popular program that can aid in both learning content (e.g., geography or history) and in practicing problem-solving skills, this series is useful for students in fourth grade and up. (This software even led to the creation of a television program!)

The Minnesota Educational Computing Corporation (MECC) provides a version of the time-honored favorite *The Oregon Trail* for the Macintosh. This simulation puts students in the position of making decisions that affect the survival of travelers journeying to Oregon in the mid-nineteenth century. Suitable for students in fifth grade and up, this program teaches students about conditions on such a trip and allows them to practice problem solving as they devise and implement strategies for survival. A newer implementation of this idea is also available from MECC. *Wagon Train 1848* will run on two or more Macs (to a maximum of 30) connected on an AppleTalk network. In this version, decisions made at one computer (wagon) can affect what happens at another computer (wagon). One intent in this package is to provide a set of materials to help implement cooperative learning strategies in the classroom.

Davidson offers *Math Blaster Plus* in a Mac version. This program has been popular for years in various versions. Students in first through sixth grades gain practice in a game setting in addition, subtraction, multiplication, division, fractions, decimals, and percents. *Math Blaster Mystery*, for fifth grade through adult, provides practice in whole numbers, percents, decimals, fractions, and pre-algebra skills through problem-solving activities including word problems.

MECC publishes *Number Munchers,* which offers students practice with multiples, prime numbers, factors, equalities, and inequalities. Students in third grade and up move Munchers through a grid by eating numerical expressions or numbers, while trying to avoid Troggles.

The *Geometer's Sketchpad*, published by Key Curriculum Press for eighth grade and up, offers students a set of tools with which to make and explore geometric constructions. Students can, for example, take measurements, perform calculations, animate a point on a line segment, and record sets of instructions. This is a powerful program that offers meaningful, motivating ways in which students can explore geometry.

Tom Snyder Productions publishes *Decisions, Decisions*, a software series that provides simulations designed for use by groups of students. Topics include *American History (Colonization, Immigration, Revolutionary War, and Urbanization)*, as well as *The Budget Process, Foreign Policy, Television, On the Campaign Trail*, and *The Environment*. The simulations, aimed at fifth through twelfth grade, give students the opportunity to participate in role-playing, debate, decision-making, and critical-thinking activities relevant to important curriculum topics.

Sunburst presents a number of interesting programs for the Mac, including *What Do You Do with a Broken Calculator?* for students in fourth grade and up. Students practice arithmetic skills and learn that there are multiple ways to solve problems as they attempt to find solutions to problems using a calculator that has some keys disabled. *The Factory*, for fourth grade and up, challenges students to use their problem-solving skills to construct a factory assembly line that will produce a particular product. In *Learn About: Plants,* for first through third grade, students plant a garden within the program and observe their simulated garden grow. They investigate, match, and label the parts of plants and learn about plant habitats and uses. In *Storybook Theater*, for first through fourth grades, students create animated stories by selecting a setting and adding characters, sound effects, props, and text. The stories may be printed out in a variety of formats including a big book, a storybook, a mini-book, and a coloring book.

Sim City is a simulation that places students in the position of city manager as they test their skills in managing a city or building a city from scratch. Available from Brøderbund, *Sim City*, appropriate for seventh grade and up, offers students an opportunity to learn relevant content and to practice problem-solving and strategy-building skills. *Sim Earth*, also from Brøderbund and aimed at sixth grade and up, gives students the opportunity to be in charge of an entire planet. Science content and problem solving are the areas in which students are engaged.

Wordtris, from Spectrum HoloByte for third grade and up, is a program that challenges students to form words, either horizontally or vertically, from falling letters. There are four difficulty levels and a built-in dictionary that checks the acceptability of words formed.

Math Connections: Algebra I, from Wings for Learning for students in eighth through eleventh grades, provides a series of tools with which students can explore the properties of and relationships among graphs, equations, expressions, variables, and numbers. This program is good for use both as a tool for students to use in explorations and as a presentation tool for teachers. *Math Connections: Algebra II* (ninth grade through college) is also available from Wings for Learning. Content covered includes multivariable expressions, conic sequences, matrices, and sequences.

The Playroom, by Broderbund, creates a positive environment where young children can explore a variety of activities. By clicking on an object in the room, a child may cause music to play or an action to occur. By clicking other objects, new environments appear that introduce the child to the alphabet, numbers, time, counting games, and creativity areas. *Sammy's Science House* by Edmark has similar activities for young children to explore and develop basic scientific skills.

A Fieldtrip to the Rainforest is a piece of software that serves several purposes: a child can visually explore the rainforest to see the diverse plant and animal life, but it also contains a sophisticated database of rainforest plant and animal life that allows students to search, sort, compare, and contrast the various life forms.

TOOL

Crossword Magic from Mindscape allows the user to create and print crossword puzzles. A program such as this can obviously be used by the teacher to create materials for student use relevant to any curriculum area. Another interesting use is to have students create puzzles and challenge other students. This program is appropriate for second grade and up.

WordSearch Deluxe, from Nordic for third grade and up, allows the creation of word search puzzles. Puzzles may be printed or can be solved at the computer. Graphics, as well as sound, can be added to the puzzles.

Certificate Maker, from Springboard, allows teachers (and students) to create certificates. Over 200 certificates cover a variety of categories. An additional disk is available, *Certificate Library*, that provides over 100 new certificates. *Certificate Maker* should be appropriate for students from the primary grades through adult.

Microlytics offers a computerized version of *The Random House Encyclopedia*. Appropriate for third grade and up, this software contains over 20,000 articles. Students can search the encyclopedia by category (such as history) or by date or simply enter a phrase.

Mac Timeliner, from Tom Snyder Productions, is a program that allows the creation of timelines to illustrate any series of events. Graphics may be incorporated into the timelines and data disks are available for a variety of topics, including *American History, World History, African American History, Women in History, The Great Ocean, Space,* and *Science and Technology. Mac Timeliner* should be suitable for students from the early elementary years up.

The Print Shop Deluxe, from Broderbund, lets teachers and students create signs, banners, greeting cards, and letterheads for stationery. This program is a great favorite of teachers. A variety of borders, type styles, and graphics comes with the program. Graphics can be edited and customized by using the included graphic editor option. *The Print Shop* is suitable for the early primary grades and up.

The Writing Center, by the Learning Company, is a desktop publishing program that allows the student to create newspapers, reports, and other documents that include text and clip art graphics. The student can easily design and modify work.

Kid Pix and *Kid Pix 2*, also from Broderbund and geared for first grade and up, is a paint program that allows the user to create artwork. Users have the option of using a variety of tools to draw (and color) pictures freehand, as well as the choice of a number of premade stamps to place pictures on the screen. Sound can be recorded on the computer and is associated with a particular picture. Text can also be included in the picture. Please note that there is a public domain version of *Kid Pix* available by the same author. The public domain version does not have as many functions (for instance, no color or sound) but retains most of the features that make *Kid Pix* such a valuable program.

PageMaker, from Adobe, is a desktop publishing program that lets the user create documents ranging from newsletters and manuals to entire books. For example, text may be created in a word processing program, and then that text and graphics from various sources can be imported into *PageMaker* where the layout of the material is accomplished. This is a powerful program that, when used with a laser printer, allows the creation of materials that are close to typeset quality. This program is appropriate for older students and adults, primarily for ninth grade and up.

Grammatik 6, published by WordPerfect Main Street, checks text the user creates in a word processing program for style, grammar, punctuation, usage, and spelling. Suitable for sixth grade and up, it offers what amounts to an automated copy editor, complete with explanations available of the rules on which it bases its suggestions.

When computers are left on for a long time with the same image on the screen, the image may burn into the screen resulting in a ghost image that will appear on the monitor even when the monitor is turned off. One way to avoid this is to use a **screensaver** program such as *After Dark* from Berkeley Systems. This program will automatically place a moving image on the screen. The image is chosen by the user from those available in the program, which include lightning bolts and flying toasters. The screensaver image starts after there has been no activity at the keyboard or mouse for a predetermined amount of time set by the user, for instance, a minute. Simply moving the mouse restores the screen the user was working on so that work can continue.

Jay Klein Productions provides a Mac version of the popular electronic gradebook *GradeBusters*. The Mac version, titled *Making the Grade,* allows teachers to enter, edit, and save grades and attendance records, as well as produce polished-looking reports.

A **computer virus** is computer programming code that may cause damage to files on your Mac or that may just cause a nuisance such as printing out unwanted messages on the screen at random times. Viruses can be spread through computer networks or by a disk containing the virus being inserted into a computer. The virus code contains instructions that allow it to make a copy of itself onto a computer without the user knowing it. Then, the next time a disk is inserted into the computer, the virus copies itself onto the new disk. When this disk is inserted into another computer, it can infect that computer. **Anti-virus programs** such as *SAM* from Symantec can protect a Mac from becoming infected as well as remove viruses from infected computers and disks. Because new viruses may appear at any time, updates to anti-virus programs become available as new viruses are discovered.

Viruses can be a serious problem in the world of computing. They can cost individuals and organizations both time and money. If you have ever lost an hour of work on the computer, you can imagine what it would be like to lose months or even years of work. It is hard to comprehend what would motivate a skilled programmer to want to set something loose that can potentially do so much damage, but unfortunately viruses do exist and it is safest to take steps to protect against them with a program such as *SAM*. There are also noncommercial anti-virus programs available such as *Disinfectant* by John Norstad of Northwestern University. *Disinfectant* is free and may be legally copied and distributed as long as author, copyright information, and disclaimer are included, and the software is not sold for profit or included with other software that is sold for profit. Your computer coordinator, an area Mac users group, or the computer services department of a local college or university will probably be able to tell you where to get a free copy of *Disinfectant*.

TUTEE

Any programming language available on the Mac can be classified as a tutee mode use of the computer. The following two pieces of software have had an important impact in educational computing across all grade levels and so are included here as tutee mode examples. For a thorough description of the ideas behind Logo, see Seymour Papert's books, *Mindstorms: Children, Computers, and Powerful Ideas* (Basic Books, 1980) and *The Children's Machine: Rethinking School in the Age of the Computer* (Basic Books, 1993).

Terrapin Logo, available from Terrapin, is an implementation of the Logo programming language developed at the Massachusetts Institute of Technology by Seymour Papert. Logo is a full-fledged programming language designed for use in education. Children as early as first grade can successfully learn and use Logo, but its useful range is certainly from first grade through adult. Logo is generally used for one or more of the following purposes: to provide practice in learning problem-solving skills; to offer practice in programming a computer and learning how computers work; and to give students opportunities to explore and learn mathematical concepts.

LogoWriter is a version of Logo available from Logo Computer Systems International. It incorporates, among other capabilities, a word processor that easily allows text to be associated with procedures students write. It has been said of *LogoWriter* that one aim in developing it was to offer learners a bridge from the verbal to the computational. *LogoWriter* is appropriate for first grade through adult levels. *MicroWorlds Math Links* helps students develop mathematical thinking, *MicroWorlds Languge Arts* encourages students to explore words, form, and images, and *MicroWorlds Project Builder* helps students build projects in any subject area.

   HyperStudio and *HyperCard* can also be part of the tutee group if designing and scripting are done.

Multimedia

The term **multimedia** refers to connecting together computers and other technology to provide material to individuals in more than one format. A **videodisc** (sometimes called a laserdisc) is a storage medium that uses a laser to store (encode) and play (decode) information such as audio, video, and text on a disc. A videodisc can store 54,000 images on each side of a 12-inch platter. The disc is simply inserted into a videodisc player for playback. Constant linear velocity (CLV) and constant angular velocity (CAV) are the two formats in which videodiscs are produced. CLV allows storage of up to 1 hour of full-motion video on one side of a disc; however, the user of the disc cannot access individual frames on the disc as is possible with CAV discs. One drawback of CAV discs, however, is that playing time on each side of the disc is reduced to 30 minutes.

   Instructionally, videodiscs are described in three levels, only one of which involves multimedia (Level III). Level I discs allow the use of this medium for presentation purposes: the teacher can present material from the disc, perhaps then engage in discussion with students, and then continue to present material from the disc. Level II discs add a computer program, encoded on the disc, which allows the student to switch from being a passive observer, as in Level I uses, to a more active participant. In Level II the student can interact with the videodisc by use of a hand-held controller. The program on the disc may interpret the students' responses and branch to specific information on the videodisc based on those responses.

   Level III use allows for even more interaction by the student and is the level where multimedia experiences are possible. In Level III, a computer may be connected to a videodisc player. The computer can run an interactive program that can present information both from the computer and from the videodisc. This information may be, from either the computer or the videodisc, in the form of audio, graphics, motion video, or perhaps text. For example, a student may work through a computer-based tutorial that requires a response to questions at different points but that also accesses the videodisc to show video clips of relevant events. If the student is studying Shakespearean plays, the videodisc may show scenes from relevant plays, or if the student is studying the Space Age, clips from different space flights may be available.

   Audio and video information may also be stored on a **CD-ROM (Compact Disc–Read Only Memory)** disc. Today most Macs have internal CD-ROM drives; older Macs may have an external CD-ROM connected to the computer. This medium allows much greater storage than disk. Because CD-ROM is a digital format, a computer can readily modify the way audio and video material stored on the disc is presented. For example, pictures stored on a CD-ROM disc can easily be resized and combined. CD-ROM discs, plus a computer, allow access to video and audio on the CD-ROM disc, as well as text, graphics, video, and audio from a computer, in an engaging educational format for learners. The student can access this information as needed, depending on the intent of the multimedia package utilized. One intent might be to present tutorial material to help instruct the student, followed by experiences in which the package is used as a tool for student research. An entire encyclopedia, complete with audio and video information, might be available to the student. The student might do needed research on the CD-ROM–based material and keep notes on the computer as the research progresses. (Note that CD-ROM–based materials can also be used solely for presentation purposes by teachers and students.)

Other items that are useful in creating presentations include scanners, cameras, and video cameras. **Scanners** are used to convert a picture into a digitized image to be used with the computer. There are a wide variety of scanners, ranging from hand-held to flatbed and black and white to color. With the right software, you can even scan old tests and save them as text files and then revise them in ClarisWorks. Scanners allow you to add students' drawings or significant pictures to any presentation.

The QuickTake camera by Apple Computer Company is a small camera that allows you to take up to 36 pictures, without film or disk, and then save the pictures on your Mac. These pictures can be placed in a document, such as a HyperStudio stack or a ClarisWorks file. Think how alive a field trip can become if this type of camera is taken along and then used to create a presentation back in the classroom. There are several other types of cameras that can also be used with the Mac.

By placing certain cards inside the Mac, movies from video cameras can be imported into a Mac. The AV Macs have this capability built in. Some cameras are so small they can be placed atop the computer. Student interviews can be made into QuickTime movies and placed in HyperStudio stacks or within reports done in ClarisWorks word processing. Visual teleconferencing through Internet can allow you to see and hear someone in another country.

Software is available to help you create multimedia presentations with the computer. You have already seen that this can be done in HyperStudio rather easily. Another example, *MediaText*, published by Sunburst, provides a means of creating multimedia documents with simplified links to sound clips, video clips, graphics, and QuickTime movies. Recommended for seventh grade and up, it allows both you and your students to produce interesting multimedia products. *My MediaText Workshop* is also available from Sunburst for kindergarten through sixth grades with the same features in an easier-to-use form.

More and more material becomes available on videodisc and CD-ROM all the time. The following are just a few examples of multimedia packages available for the Mac.

VIDEODISC

National Geographic publishes *GTV: A Geographic Perspective on American History*, for fifth grade and up. This package offers over 40 brief videodisc-based shows on important topics in American history. Teachers and students can access information and create their own presentations. National Geographic also offers *GTV: Planetary Manager*, for fifth grade and up. Students can investigate videos on major themes related to environmental issues including ozone depletion, deforestation, and air pollution, among others.

ABC News Interactive Laserdiscs offer videodisc-based segments of important topics and opportunities for students to interact with the video material in a variety of ways. Titles include *Martin Luther King, Jr; In the Holy Land; The '88 Vote;* and *Aids*.

Videodiscovery presents a number of packages, including the *Bio Sci II* (for eighth grade and up) videodisc. The *Bio Sci II HyperCard Stacks for Mac* videodisc, also from Videodiscovery, is available in conjunction with this disc. Students work with still photos, graphics, and video sequences that deal with all major biology topics.

The Discovery Channel Interactive presents *Investigating Science: Treasures from the Deep*, for students eighth grade and up. Students investigate how scientists locate and explore a 133-year-old shipwreck over a mile beneath the sea. Other titles include *Insects: Little Giants of the Earth,* in which students explore insect ecosystems and the basic characteristics of insects.

CD-ROM

Discis Knowledge Research offers the CD-ROM based series of *Discis Books* for kindergarten through sixth grades. Using well-written, established children's books, Discis has placed each book on a CD-ROM disc complete with speech, music, and other audio effects. The books are controlled by a computer program that offers the user a host of functions. For example, while reading the book silently the student may choose a word and have the computer pronounce it aloud, either as a whole word or syllable by syllable. The computer will also supply a definition of a word selected by the student. The student may also choose to have the entire book read aloud by the computer. In addition, teachers can customize the book for individual students by changing type size, style, and spacing. Some of the titles available, and the original authors, include *The Tale of Peter Rabbit*, by Beatrix Potter; *The Paper Bag Princess*, by Robert Munsch; *Heather Hits Her First Home Run*, by Ted Plantos; and *A Long Hard Day on the Ranch*, by Audrey Nelson.

Grolier offers its 21-volume *Academic Encyclopedia* on CD-ROM, *The New Grolier Multimedia Encyclopedia*. Over 30,000 articles including audio, illustrations, maps, and pictures are available. As a resource, this should be suitable for third grade and up. Other encyclopedias include *Encarta* and *Compton's.* Many of these also include video clips.

Living Books provides a CD-ROM based version of Mercer Mayer's *Just Grandma and Me* for prekindergarten through fifth grades. The animated book provides the student with sound effects, narration, music, and opportunities to interact with the software.

The Wayzata World Factbook, based on the *CIA World Factbook*, is available for fifth grade and up. It contains a variety of data on countries and offers color maps, as well as database files that may be imported into a number of database and spreadsheet programs.

How to Use the Computer in the Classroom

The number of computers accessible to a class varies. There could be one in the classroom or several in a classroom or a lab setting. There are different strategies on how to best utilize each situation. One computer in the classroom can be used in front of the classroom, in a learning center, or on the teacher's desk. The following suggestions involve using the computer with students.

ONE COMPUTER – LEARNING CENTER

Some classrooms have only one computer; however, it can be used in a variety of ways. One successful method is to create a learning center in your room using software that reinforces your curriculum. A tracking system can be created by using name cards or a checklist to ensure that all students have a turn and to keep track of the amount of time each student has on the computer. A writing center for students can be very successful. Story starters can be placed in a basket by the computer and the students can select one and begin writing. Students working with a partner at a learning center is a great way to utilize cooperative learning techniques. Teach two students how to use a piece of software and then let them teach other students.

ONE COMPUTER — PRESENTATION TOOL

Another way to utilize one computer in the classroom is to use it as a presentation tool. By connecting the computer to an **LCD panel** or connecting the computer to a television, all students can view the screen. The hardware needed to connect most Macintoshes to a television costs around $500. This is much cheaper than an LCD unit, which can cost up to $5,000. By creating a presentation machine, math demonstrations become clearer, notes previously written on a chalkboard become legible. Maps and statistical information about countries are current and readily available during class discussions. No longer do you need to turn your back to the class! Notes can be written before class so time is not lost writing during class. If you are using software that needs to be manipulated during class, assign a student with good typing skills to do it for you.

Class discussions can become exciting by using one computer in front of the classroom. Peer editing with the entire class can allow each student to receive numerous positive suggestions for improving a paper. There are many pieces of software that are written specifically for one computer and an entire class. Tom Snyder software is noted for this technique. Discussions are needed to make good decisions. All students' opinions become important, and they can see immediately the difference their opinion can make. Class brainstorming on classroom rules or a class newspaper can be effective in this mode of instruction. Discoveries in math with families of graphs can be directed using one computer. Use of probeware hardware that connects an object to the computer to record such things as changing speed or temperature can make science come alive. Watching the graphs on the screen change as the actual change occurs can increase student interest and stimulate immediate discussions about why and how these changes are happening. Writing a class story about a recent science unit, for example, the desert, together allows the teacher to direct the students and ensure that important ideas are incorporated in the story.

If you have more than one computer in your classroom, you could set up several learning centers around your room.

COMPUTER LAB

Some schools have full computer labs. Even in this "ideal" setting, it is important to develop a good lesson plan. By having students use only drill and practice software, they may never understand or take advantage of the real power of the computer. Students must learn that they are in charge of the computer, and this can be well demonstrated with tool software. Students need to have a definite purpose for being in a lab setting. Word processing is one good way to set this purpose. Because writing can be done in any subject area, the amount of possible topics is endless. Another good use of a lab setting is using discovery software such as Geometer's *Sketchpad*; each student, or pair of students, must see and discover the principles. Using Logo in the lab setting creates an atmosphere of collaboration among students. Keep in mind that it is hard work to structure lab experiences so students have a purpose for their experiences and explorations.

Some software is created to encourage cooperative learning in groups. For example, *Cross Country USA* is a simulation of a truck driver traveling across the United States, picking up specific commodities along the way. To utilize this program well, several students need to work together: a truck driver, a map reader, a commodities searcher, and a reporter. The activities created by this experience definitely encourage cooperative learning. HyperStudio and HyperCard can be used by groups to create presentations for class viewing. Several people working together can develop wonderful stacks.

Computers in any setting can be used for research by utilizing CD-ROM sources or Internet sources. In some cases, a lab setting is more useful because much research can be done simultaneously, and the teacher is available to assist.

As you can see, you can use the computer in your classroom or with your class in many different ways. As you become more comfortable with the computer and understand its potential, you will develop many teaching strategies using the computer.

Ethics and Equity

As we progress further and further into the Information Age, the ethical use of the machines and media that manage information becomes increasingly important. Teachers, as role models and members of society responsible for the learning of society's young, need to be especially careful in the ethical use of the materials available. On the simplest level, no teacher should engage in software piracy, the illegal copying of computer software. **Proprietary software** should not be illegally copied for use at home or at work. Software publishers often offer discounts for buying lab packs (perhaps consisting of 5 or 10 copies of the program) or may offer site licenses that provide for legal use of a program throughout a school or district. Such discounts are an attempt on the part of publishers to both sell more software and to meet the needs of the schools.

On another level, teachers should also take care to provide good role models regarding the use of information so readily available on computers in an Information Age. Just as grades are confidential, so is material gathered by administrators and teachers about students, even the material gathered about students and their families and stored in a database on a teacher's computer. These issues, and others dealing with citizens' rights to privacy as well as with who actually owns information about individuals, are important issues for teachers as professionals, but they are also important for society in general. As such, they can be the source of excellent, relevant material for learning at any grade level.

Another important issue is that of equity. As with science and math, computers and experiences with computers are in danger of being a white, males-only domain. If this is the case, we as a society lose a great resource: a pool of bright, eager people who may be kept from equal access to experiences that could lead to important life choices regarding careers that deal with technology. In addition, individuals, and not just society as a whole, will suffer as whole areas of possible personal and professional fulfillment remain unexplored by a large segment of society. Teachers must take care to ensure that students have equal access to computers and computing experiences. Further, materials used in relation to technology must be free of stereotypes (both racial and gender stereotypes). Such materials must also be chosen with care in terms of possible student interest. Software with male-oriented themes must not be the only software that makes its way into the classroom. As people with an opportunity to provide equitable experiences with technology to all segments of society, teachers are in a unique position to help shape the Information Age.

Important Sources of Information

There are many regional, state, and local organizations that deal with the general topic of computers and technology in education. Be sure to find out if there is an active organization of this type in your area—contact with other professionals knowledgeable about and interested in technology in education can be of great benefit. Also, find out if there is a Mac users group in your area. Such groups can be a good source of information specifically about the Mac. Also, you will almost certainly find other educators as members of such a group.

On the international level, the **International Society for Technology in Education (ISTE)** is a strong, active group that publishes journals, sponsors conferences, and offers relevant materials and training courses for educators. The group may be reached at the University of Oregon, 1787 Agate Street, Eugene, Oregon 97403. Membership in ISTE is a good way to keep up to date on what is happening in the technology and education field. Another important organization to become familiar with and perhaps join is the **Association for the Advancement of Computing in Education (AACE)**, which can be reached at P. O. Box 2966, Charlottesville, Virginia 22902. Both of these groups offer valuable services and information.

There are many journals aimed at technology and education as well as many magazines about specific computers and associated software. Following are just a few that will be of interest to educators.

ISTE publishes, among other journals, *Learning and Leading with Technology*, which is an excellent publication for teachers that includes instructional ideas, software reviews, and a host of other important material. ISTE also publishes an excellent research journal, *The Journal of Research on Computing in Education*.

AACE publishes a number of journals, including *The Journal of Computing in Childhood Education*, a well-done, useful publication with an emphasis on research on computers in the schools. AACE also publishes a journal on Hypermedia, titled *Journal of Educational Multimedia and HyperMedia*.

Scholastic publishes *Electronic Learning*, an excellent publication for teachers, and Peter Li, Inc., publishes *Technology and Learning* (which was previously titled *Classroom Computer Learning*). *Technology and Learning* is a practical, informative publication that teachers find very useful. It is filled with relevant information about software, technology applications in the schools, hardware, and current issues regarding technology and education.

A book entitled *The Macintosh Bible*, edited by Arthur Naiman and published by Peachpit Press, though not aimed specifically at educators, is an invaluable resource about the Mac in general. It provides many tips, tricks, and insights into working with the Mac and associated software and hardware. The magazine *MacUser*, geared for Mac users in general and published monthly by the Ziff-Davis Publishing Company, is another excellent publication with articles on Mac software, hardware, and applications.

Conclusion

This chapter has briefly introduced some examples of the software available to educators on the Mac. Often, many programs can be used productively by both students and teachers in a variety of ways. This chapter also showed you ways to incorporate the computer into your classroom. As you further explore the many possibilities the Mac provides for learning in your classroom, remember that the most important factor in bringing computers into the classroom is you, the teacher. Your experience, education, ideas, and energy are what will make learning come alive for students, whether learning takes place with or without a computer.

KEY TERMS

anti-virus program
Association for the
    Advancement of
    Computing in
    Education (AACE)
CD-ROM (Compact
    Disc–Read Only
    Memory)

computer virus
International Society for
    Technology in
    Education (ISTE)
LCD panel
multimedia
probeware
proprietary software

public domain software
scanner
screensaver
shareware
tool mode
tutee mode
tutor mode
videodisc

Appendix A
HyperStudio Version 3.0.5 (without CD-ROM)

This apendix is written based on HyperStudio version 3.0.5 for those of you who do not have a CD-ROM version of HyperStudio.

1. To start HyperStudio, locate HyperStudio on your hard drive and double click on it.

2. Once the program is loaded, the screen you see, also shown in Figure A-1, is part of a stack called the Home Stack. The **Home Stack** is like a starting point, a table of contents. It contains buttons and text objects with information for you. This Home Stack was created by the Roger Wagner Company to introduce you to HyperStudio. Notice the text box on the leftt side of the card labeled Welcome to HyperStudio! It is a scrollable box because it contains a scroll bar and more text than fits in the box. Read the entire contents of this welcome box by clicking on the down arrow in the scroll bar.

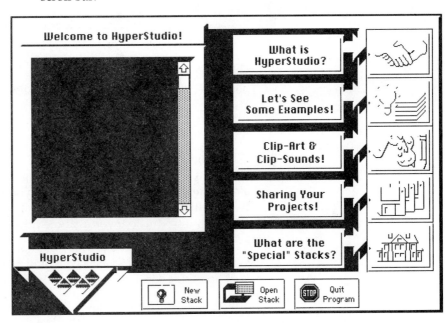

Figure A-1

The Welcome to HyperStudio! card for HyperStudio version 3.0.5.

3. Click on the rectangle with the words What is HyperStudio? to move to another card that will explain different parts of HyperStudio.

4. When you are on the What is HyperStudio card?, read the contents of the scrollable box on the left side of the card. When you have finished reading, click on HyperStudio Tour.

5. On this new card shown in Figure A-2, read all the information in the text box on the left side of the card before you begin.

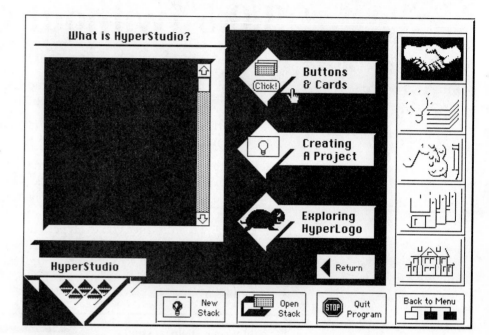

Figure A-2

Click on Buttons & Cards to begin the introduction to HyperStudio version3.0.5.

6. Click on Buttons and Cards. This section demonstrates the concept of cards and buttons to you. Read all information on the screen and click on the word Next in the bottom right corner when you want to move to the next card. You can see that information is placed on each card and buttons permit you to move from one card to another.

7. When you have finished Buttons and Cards, you will be returned to the card shown in Figure A-1. Click on Creating a Project. This section will demonstrate many HyperStudio concepts to you including buttons, button activity, transitions, sound, and clip art. Follow directions carefully. Remember this is an introduction; you will see how things are done, but you will not actually be doing it yourself.

8. When you reach the last card containing the picture of the Solar System, do not choose Let Me Try!; instead click on the Back to Menu button.

9. You should be back on the What is HyperStudio? card.

10. Click on the Back to Menu button again.

11. You should be on the Welcome to HyperStudio card! If you are not there, select Home from the Move menu.

This is a good introduction into HyperStudio. You should now have a basic understanding of the concepts of stack, card, button, text object, and graphics. You are now ready to explore further. If you would like, take time to explore some of the sample projects included with your version of HyperStudio. To see some samples, click on Let's See Some Examples!

When you have finished looking at the examples, you may return to Chapter 7 and continue working through the chapter. HyperStudio version 3.0.5 has a dialog box that version 3.0.6 does not. Whenever you are addingsounds from the disk library, graphic objects from a disk file, or clip art from a disk file, a dialog box will appear stating that you cannot save any changes. Simply click on OK and continue with the instructions.

Figure A-3

This dialog box will appear when adding a Graphic Object, cCip Art, or sounds from the Disk Library. Click on OK and continue with the instructions.

"Icon Library – Clip Art" is locked, so you will not be able to save any changes.

Cancel   OK

GLOSSARY

About Stack In HyperStudio, a dialog box selected from the Objects menu that is used to change the number of colors used in a stack or the size of the cards in the stack. Information concerning the number of cards in the stack and the size of the stack are displayed here. Actions occurring when the stack is opened or closed can be determined here.

absolute cell reference A spreadsheet cell reference that points to a specific cell address and does not change if the cell reference is copied to another cell. In ClarisWorks, a $ symbol is placed before the column and/or row parts of the cell address to designate that the column and/or row in the reference is absolute.

Accept button A checkmark icon near the top of a ClarisWorks Spreadsheet window that accepts data typed in the entry bar and places the data in the selected cell.

active window The window on the screen in which any actions, such as keystrokes or menu commands, take effect. When horizontal parallel lines are in the title bar, a window is active.

Address box The box at the top left of a ClarisWorks spreadsheet that tells which cell is selected. If a block of cells is selected it names the top left cell in the selection.

alert box A box on the screen that presents important information to the user, such as how to cancel the printing of a document.

align To line up. Objects can be aligned along edges or centers. Text can also be aligned at decimal points. See alignment.

Align Objects In ClarisWorks Draw, an option on the Arrange menu that displays a dialog box for aligning objects in various ways.

alignment The way in which lines of text are lined up with other text lines in a column or page. Or the way in which objects are lined up in columns or rows. In ClarisWorks Word Processor, the ruler has alignment options for text paragraphs and tabs have alignment options for text columns. In ClarisWorks Draw, the Align Objects... option on the Arrange menu allows objects to be lined up on their edges or centers.

answer A HyperTalk command that produces a dialog box with a specified comment in it. For example, answer "Try Again" produces a dialog box with the Try Again message.

anti-virus program A program designed to detect and remove viruses from computers—examples include *SAM* (a commercially available program) and *Disinfectant* (a program available at no cost).

Apple Guide A comprehensive built-in help system that includes Balloon help, tutorials, and the Macintosh guide. The menu to access this information is the question mark located on the right hand side of the menu bar.

application A program that allows you to do something with the computer, to use it in a particular way. An example is a word processing program. In ClarisWorks, there are six different applications, each of which has a particular use and its own set of menus.

Apply Ruler In ClarisWorks Word Processing, an option on the Format menu that applies previously copied ruler settings to the paragraph with the insertion point or to selected paragraphs.

Arc tool The Arc tool is a Drawing tool that enables you to draw arcs and wedges.

Arrange menu In ClarisWorks Draw, a pull-down menu that provides a variety of graphic options for arranging and moving objects in a document.

Arrow palette A part of the Pen palette controls, the arrow palette provides a way to have an arrow on one or both ends of a line.

Assistant A feature in ClarisWorks that guides you through a process by asking questions and then performs the work based on the answers to those questions.

ask A HyperTalk command that produces a dialog box with a specified question and provides a place for a response to be typed. For example, ask "What is your name?"

Association for the Advancement of Computing in Education (AACE) An organization that deals with issues related to technology in education. Among other activities, AACE publishes journals and sponsors conferences.

audio palette In HyperCard, a set of icons related to recording and editing sounds.

Audio... In HyperCard, an option on the Edit menu that opens the audio palette.

Autogrid In ClarisWorks Draw and Paint, an alignment feature that automatically aligns an object to a grid when moving or drawing it.

Average function In ClarisWorks, a function that calculates the average of a set of numbers.

background In HyperCard, the lowest set of layers in a stack. Buttons, fields, and graphics placed in a background will appear on every card with that background.

Balloon Help   A built-in help system that shows a description of an item on the screen when the mouse pointer is on that item.

baud rate   The speed at which data is received by and sent to a modem.

Bezigon tool   A part of the Draw tools palette, the Bezigon tool is useful for drawing straight lines and curves.

bit-mapped   A type of graphics that are created on the screen and in print by defining positions of dots, or pixels, that when combined create a design or image. Bit-mapped graphics are edited by working with the individual dots, rather than the whole graphic.

Bkgnd Info...   In HyperCard, an option on the Objects menu that displays a dialog box listing specific information about a background in a HyperCard stack.

Blank Card   In HyperStudio, an option on the Ready Made Card submenu that creates a card with nothing on it.

bookmark   In ClarisWorks Database, a portion of the File icon that can be moved to bring different records into view.

Bring Closer   In HyperCard, an Objects menu choice that will move an object up one layer.

Browse mode   In ClarisWorks Database, the Browse option on the Layout menu that displays a view in which field data can be seen, entered, and edited.

Browse tool   In HyperCard and HyperStudio, a tool (the hand pointer icon on the tool palette) that allows you to move through a stack, use buttons, and edit fields.

browsing   To look through a HyperCard or HyperStudio stack, moving from card to card, not necessarily sequentially. In HyperCard this can involve using buttons, arrow keys, or the Go menu. In HyperStudio this can involve using buttons, the > or < keys, or the Move menu. Also referred to as navigating a stack.

bulletin board   A computer network established to provide opportunities to share information, usually in a particular area of interest.

button   In HyperCard and HyperStudio, a specific location on a card that triggers an action when clicked. Examples of actions are movement to another card or playing a sound.

Button Action   In HyperStudio, a dialog box that allows the user to determine the action of the button.

Button Appearance   In HyperStudio, a dialog box that allows the user to name the button and select the type of button, color of text, color of button, and other options. It also contains a connection to the button actions dialog box and to the icon dialog box.

Button Info...   In HyperCard, an option on the Objects menu that displays a dialog box listing specific information about a selected button. Information includes button name, ID, number, and editing options.

Button tool   In HyperCard and HyperStudio, a tool that allows you to select and edit buttons.

byte   In general, one character's worth of data or information, where a character is a letter, numeral, space, or special character such as a period.

Calculate menu   A pull-down menu on the ClarisWorks Spreadsheet menu bar that includes options to move, fill, sort, insert, and delete cells as well as choosing to automatically or manually recalculate values within the spreadsheet.

calculation field   A database field containing data that is automatically calculated using information from other fields on the same record.

Cancel button   An X icon near the top of a ClarisWorks Spreadsheet window that causes edits made in the entry bar to be ignored.

Capture to File...   In ClarisWorks Communications, an option on the Session menu that places a copy of text displayed on the screen during a telecommunications session into a file that can be viewed later.

card   The fundamental unit of a HyperCard and a HyperStudio stack. A card may contain fields, buttons, and graphics.

Card Info...   In HyperCard, an option on the Objects menu that displays a dialog box listing specific information about the displayed card. Information includes name of the card, location in the stack, card ID, and editing options.

category   See **field**.

CD-ROM (Compact Disc-Read Only Memory)   A medium for storing audio and video (in digital format) on a disc.

cell   A rectangle created by the intersection of a column and a row in a grid.

cell address   The location of a spreadsheet cell, described by the names of the column and the row that the cell is in.

cell format   The way the contents of a spreadsheet cell are displayed. In ClarisWorks Spreadsheet, the Format menu allows changes to cell formats.

cell name   The cell address, which consists of a column name followed by a row name, such as A13.

cell reference   A cell name used in a formula to indicate that the data in the named cell is to be used in the calculation done by the formula.

center tab   A tab stop that aligns the center of text at the tab stop location.

chart   A graphic representation of data. In ClarisWorks Spreadsheet, the Options menu provides a Make Chart... choice.

Chat   In telecommunications, real-time discussion groups in which individuals type messages back and forth much as they would speak if they were in the same room.

Check Document Spelling... In ClarisWorks Word Processing, a part of the Writing Tools submenu on the Edit menu for checking spelling in a document. This option allows checking of the entire document while Check Selection Spelling... provides a means of checking a selected portion of the document.

click To press and release the button on the mouse.

clip art Sets of artwork on floppy disks or CD-ROM specifically designed to be "clipped out" and pasted into electronic documents. In HyperStudio, graphics that become part of the background of a card.

Close An option on the File menu that closes the active window, file, or disk.

close box A box located at the left side of a title bar. Clicking on the close box will close the window.

Close Connection In ClarisWorks Communications, a command on the Session menu that "hangs up" the phone to end connection for a telecommunications session.

Coloring tools In HyperCard, tools that allow the user to add color overlays to buttons and fields and create color backgrounds. The Coloring tools must be turned on from the Home Stack.

column In ClarisWorks Spreadsheet, a vertical set of cells, named with letters.

columnar layout In ClarisWorks Database, a layout that displays fields in columns.

Command key The key with the Apple (⌘) symbol and the command symbol on it on the bottom row of the keyboard. This key is held down while other keys are typed to perform specific commands.

Communications document In ClarisWorks, a document created to establish a telecommunications session with an online service or a remote computer.

computer virus Computer code that may cause damage to computer files. Computer viruses may infect a computer without a user's knowledge and subsequently damage files or just be a nuisance by, for example, printing out unwanted messages on the computer screen. See also, **anti-virus program**.

Copy In ClarisWorks and HyperCard, a command on the Edit menu that places a copy of a selected object, graphic, or text on the clipboard.

Copy Card In HyperCard, a command on the Edit menu for copying a card, including card level objects, background level objects, and background field contents. The copied card can be pasted into the stack using Paste Card on the Edit menu.

Copy Ruler In ClarisWorks Word Processing, an option on the Format menu that copies ruler settings of the paragraph containing the insertion point or the first selected paragraph.

The settings can then be pasted (using Paste Ruler) to other paragraphs.

crosshair When using certain Draw or Paint tools, the cursor becomes a crosshair (+), which provides a means of obtaining increased accuracy in creating the graphics object.

CUSEEMe A teleconferencing program that allows users to see and hear each other through use of a video camera.

Cut To delete a selected object, graphic, or text and place a copy of that selection on the clipboard at the same time. The Cut command is on the Edit menu.

data Information. In ClarisWorks Database, the information stored in fields that is made up of characters (letters, numbers, spaces, and so on).

data box In ClarisWorks Database, outlined boxes to the right of each field name where data is typed.

database A collection of data or a program used to store and organize data and perform functions on data, such as sort, find, match, and report.

decimal tab A tab stop that aligns decimal points in text at the tab stop location.

Define Fields... In ClarisWorks Database, an option on the Layout menu for creating and changing database fields.

Delete key A key on the Macintosh keyboard that causes selected items to be deleted. When editing text, if nothing has been selected it will cause the character to the left of the insertion point to be deleted.

Desktop A description of the Macintosh screen. The screen is presented as analogous to a physical desktop, with documents, folders, and office tools present.

desktop metaphor The comparison of a computer screen that uses icons to a desktop. See **Desktop**.

dialog box Provides the user with information and with one or more choices for action. For example, the dialog box displayed by choosing Save As... from the File menu in a word processing program offers information and choices related to saving a document.

discussion groups A group of people who communicate with each other through electronic mail about a specific topic.

disk A magnetic storage medium for computer data. Data can be written to (copied onto) a disk from a computer and read from (copied from) a disk to a computer.

Display... In ClarisWorks Spreadsheet a command on the Options menu that controls various display options for the document, such as display of the grid, of column and row names, and of formulas.

Distort In ClarisWorks Paint, an option on the Transform menu that distorts a graphic object when you drag a handle of the object.

document A set of data created by an application program such as a word processor. Also called a file.

Document... In ClarisWorks, an option on the Format menu that controls the sizes of margins, how a document is displayed, how footnotes are displayed and numbered, and what the first page number is.

double-click To click the mouse button twice in succession.

drag To hold the mouse button down as the mouse is moved. Dragging may be used to move an object, such as an icon, to a new location on the screen or to select text.

Draw environment The mode of ClarisWorks usage in which Draw tools are available.

Draw tools The tools that are available for use in the Draw environment. These include Line, Rectangle, Rounded Rectangle, Oval, Arc, Polygon, Freehand, Bezigon, and Regular Polygon tools.

Duplicate In ClarisWorks, an option on the Edit menu that puts a copy of whatever is selected into the active document. In ClarisWorks Draw and Paint, Duplicate is used to make an object identical to the current selected object. In ClarisWorks Database, Duplicate Record is available on the Edit menu. In the Macintosh Finder, the File menu has an option for duplicating files or folders.

Edit Master Page Edit Master Page, found on the Options menu, allows the user to create a background that will appear on all of the pages of a ClarisWorks Draw document.

Edit menu A pull-down menu that contains commands related to editing, such as copy, cut, and paste.

Editing tool In HyperStudio, a tool used to edit, move, resize, or delete text objects, graphic objects, and buttons.

electronic mail Electronic mail, or E-mail, is a means of sending messages to other individuals through the Internet. To send or receive electronic mail you must have an address and know the address of the person or group you wish to send the message to. An Internet address is comprised of the individual (or group) ID and the domain name of the computer that acts as the mailing agent.

end (action) In HyperCard, the HyperTalk command that terminates script associated with the specified action. The action includes such commands as mouseUp, mouseDown, openStack, closeStack, openCard.

entry Data that is typed into a database field or a spreadsheet cell.

entry bar The area at the top of a ClarisWorks spreadsheet in which cell data appears when typed and in which cell data is edited.

Eraser tool In ClarisWorks Paint and HyperCard, a drawing tool that can erase any paint graphic. In HyperCard double-clicking this tool will erase all graphics on a card.

Fat Bits In HyperCard, a choice on the Options menu that allows the user to magnify the screen to see and edit individual pixels of a graphic.

field In a database, a type of information—for instance, phone number, street address, or last name—for which data is entered on each record. Sometimes called a category. In HyperCard, a rectangular area on a card that is established for entering text. A field can be any regular rectangular shape.

Field Info... In HyperCard, an option on the Objects menu that displays a dialog box listing specific information about a selected field. Information includes title of the field, the field number, field style, and options for text.

field name The name given to a field in a database. For instance, Phone might be the name for the field that contains phone number data on each record.

Field tool In HyperCard, a tool (the rectangular shaped icon with dotted lines across it located on the top right of the tool palette) that allows you to select fields and use the Field Information dialog box.

File icon In ClarisWorks Database, the icon at the top left corner of the window that looks like a ringed notebook of index cards. It indicates the number of the record currently selected and can be used to move to other records.

File menu A pull-down menu that offers functions related to files or documents, such as opening, closing, saving, and printing files.

fill To put a graphic pattern or color into the area bounded by a graphic figure.

Fill color palette A part of the Fill tools, the Fill color palette provides a means of choosing a color to fill the interior of a selected graphic object or image.

Fill Down In ClarisWorks Spreadsheet, a command on the Calculate menu that fills each cell in a column (or columns) of selected cells with the contents of the topmost selected cell (or cells).

Fill gradient palette A part of the Fill tools, the Fill gradient palette provides a means of choosing a gradient to fill the interior of a selected graphic object or image.

Fill pattern palette A part of the Fill tools, the Fill pattern palette provides a means of choosing a pattern to fill the interior of a selected graphic object or image.

Fill Right In ClarisWorks Spreadsheet, a command on the Calculate menu that fills each cell in a row (or rows) of selected cells with the contents of the leftmost selected cell (or cells).

Fill tool In ClarisWorks, HyperStudio, and HyperCard, the paint-bucket-shaped icon used to fill figures with patterns is called the Fill tool. In ClarisWorks the icons in the tool palette that are used to control Fill color, pattern, and gradient are also considered to be Fill tools.

Find   In ClarisWorks Database, an option on the Layout menu that displays a find request view that contains all the fields of the current layout and is used to enter data that is to be searched for in the database.

Find/Change   In ClarisWorks, an option on the Edit menu that provides the ability to search a document for particular text and to automatically edit the found text.

Find mode   In ClarisWorks Database, a view of the database used to request a search of the database. It is displayed when the Find option on the Layout menu is chosen.

first-line indent marker   An upside-down, T-shaped marker on the text ruler that indicates where the first line of text in a paragraph begins on a page. See also **indent markers**.

Flip Horizontally   In ClarisWorks Paint, Flip Horizontally is found on the Transform menu, whereas in ClarisWorks Draw, it is found on the Transform submenu of the Arrange menu. Selecting Flip Horizontally will cause the selected graphic object to be flipped horizontally around an imaginary vertical line passing through the center of the object.

Flip Vertically   In ClarisWorks Paint, Flip Vertically is found on the Transform menu, whereas in ClarisWorks Draw, it is found on the Transform submenu of the Arrange menu. Selecting Flip Vertically will cause the selected graphic object to be flipped vertically around an imaginary horizontal line passing through the center of the object.

floppy disk   A disk that can be easily inserted and removed from a floppy disk drive. It is a circle of film-like material covered by a square made of either flexible or rigid plastic. A floppy disk drive, which reads from and writes to floppy disks, is often contained in the machine (internal) but may also be outside (external to) the machine.

folder   An icon that represents a location where documents, applications, and other folders may be kept. Analogous to a file folder inside which items may be kept.

font   A set of letters or characters with a particular design, such as Helvetica font.

Font menu   In ClarisWorks Word Processing, a pull-down menu on the menu bar that contains font options. In ClarisWorks Database, Draw, Paint, and Spreadsheet, an option on the Format menu that has a submenu of font choices.

footer   An area at the bottom of a page that contains information about the document, such as document title, chapter title, or page number. In ClarisWorks, footers are inserted from the Format menu.

format   The way numbers and text are displayed.

formula   A symbolic representation of how database or spreadsheet items are used in a calculation.

frame   In ClarisWorks, a rectangular graphics object that contains an application of one type within a document of another application. For instance, a spreadsheet frame can be in a graphics document. All the tools and menus of the frame's application can be used within the frame.

frame links   In ClarisWorks, connections between two or more frames of the same application. In linked word processing frames, text automatically flows or continues from one frame into the next. In linked spreadsheet frames, the frames display different portions of a spreadsheet.

Free Rotate   In ClarisWorks Paint, Free Rotate is found on the Transform menu, and in ClarisWorks Draw, it is found on the Arrange menu. Choosing Free Rotate will provide a means of rotating the selected graphics object by dragging one of its handles.

Freehand tool   In ClarisWorks Paint, the Freehand tool provides a means to draw irregular curves or lines as you would with a pencil.

function   In ClarisWorks Database and Spreadsheet, named operations that represent predefined formulas.

Go menu   In HyperCard, a pull-down menu that includes a variety of commands for movement in stacks.

Go to Cell...   In ClarisWorks Spreadsheet, a command on the Options menu that displays and selects a specified cell.

go to   In HyperCard, the HyperTalk command that allows movement. By adding "next card" to this command the button movement will be to the next sequential card of the stack. Likewise by adding "previous card," movement is to the previous card of the stack.

graphic   A pictorial representation; a picture.

graphic object   In HyperStudio, a picture or drawing that is treated as a single object. It can be moved, resized, or edited. It lays on top of the background and does not affect the background. It can be animated or hidden and shown.

Graphic object tool   In HyperStudio, a tool that allows the user to move, resize, delete, or edit graphic objects.

Graphical User Interface (GUI)   The way a user communicates with the Macintosh through selecting icons that represent desired functions. The icons on the screen are chosen for their familiarity to the user (i.e., a trash can, a file folder).

Graphics tool   In ClarisWorks, the arrow-pointer icon found in the upper-left corner of the tool palette, used to select, resize, and move objects.

grid   An area that has horizontal and vertical lines crossing each other at regular intervals. In ClarisWorks Paint and Draw, a grid can be automatically displayed as a guide for positioning graphics.

Group   Found on the Arrange menu in ClarisWorks Draw, the Group command allows selected objects to be grouped and treated as a single object.

Group Card   In HyperStudio, an option on the Ready Made Card submenu that creates a card containing the same graphic background as the card the user was on when selecting the this option and groups the new card with that original card. Graphic changes to one card will affect all cards in a group.

handle   A small square located on the outline of a selected object that can be dragged to change the size or shape of the object.

hard disk   A permanently mounted, rigid storage medium for magnetically storing and retrieving computer data and information. May be internal or external to the machine.

hardware   The physical components that make up a computer system, such as a monitor, keyboard, computer, and printer.

header   An area at the top of a page that contains information about the document, such as document title, chapter title, or page number. In ClarisWorks, headers are inserted from the Format menu.

Help   In ClarisWorks, an option on Guide (?) menu that provides information about how to use the program. In HyperCard, the option is on the Go menu (the HyperCard Help stack must be available to use it).

hide   In HyperCard, the HyperTalk command that will cause an object (a field, button, menu bar, etc.) to be hidden. The object must be specified, such as hide card field 3, hide menuBar, or hide background button "Student." See also **show**.

hide field   See **hide**.

Hide Graphics Grid   In ClarisWorks Draw, a choice on the Options menu that hides the grid.

hide menuBar   See **hide**.

Hide Scrollback   In ClarisWorks Communications, a command on the Settings menu that hides text that has been displayed with Show Scrollback.

Hide Selected   In ClarisWorks Database, a command on the Organize menu for hiding all selected records in the database.

Hide Unselected   In ClarisWorks Database, a command on the Organize menu for hiding all unselected records in the database.

highlight   To appear darkened. See **select**.

Home Card   The first card of the Home stack. It contains buttons to take the user to other stacks. The Home card can be customized for the user by adding buttons to link to specific stacks.

Home Stack   The stack that HyperCard and HyperStudio look for each time they start up. In HyperCard, it contains important information that HyperCard needs to run, including the Preferences card. In HyperStudio, it is a starting point

containing buttons and information. The Home Stack can be customized to include buttons the user wants.

horizontal scroll bar   A bar at the bottom of a window that allows the user to move the window contents horizontally. See also **scroll bar**.

HyperCard   A type of authoring software that can be used as a versatile teaching tool. It can be used to create tutorials, drill and practice exercises, classroom management applications, and multimedia presentations.

HyperStudio   A multimedia writing tool that can be used as a versatile teaching tool. It can be used to create tutorials, drill and practice exercises, classroom management applications, and multimedia presentations. It can easily be used by students and teachers.

HyperTalk   The programming language used with HyperCard.

I-beam   A pointer that resembles the letter I, which is moved by the mouse across the screen and appears when text can be edited. When an I-beam is displayed and the mouse is clicked, the insertion point is positioned where the I-beam is located.

icon   A graphic (pictorial) representation of an object.

if-then-else   HyperTalk commands that allow conditions to be required for other commands to be performed.

indent markers   Markers on the text ruler that indicate where lines of text begin on the left and end on the right of a page. These markers allow text in a paragraph to be indented from the margin. See also **first-line indent marker**, **left indent marker**, and **right indent marker**.

Info palette   Choosing Object Info from the Options menu will display the Info palette. Changing the measurements in the palette will resize or move the selected object.

Information dialog box   A dialog box in HyperCard that provides the user with information about a stack, a card, a field, a button, or a background. This information dialog box also allows the user the ability to change specifications of each.

inline graphic   In ClarisWorks, a graphic that is inserted or pasted into a document when the text tool is active. An inline graphic stays in the same position relative to the text—if the text moves, the graphic moves along with it. It can be selected, cut, and copied, but it cannot be resized or dragged to a new location.

Insert Cells...   In ClarisWorks Spreadsheet, a command on the Calculate menu that inserts one or more columns or rows into the spreadsheet.

Insert Footer   In ClarisWorks Word Processing, an option on the Format menu that inserts a footer at the bottom of every page of a document.

Insert Header   In ClarisWorks Word Processing, an option on the Format menu that inserts a header at the top of every page of a document.

Insert Page #   In ClarisWorks Word Processing, an option on the Edit menu that inserts a page number at the insertion point.

Insert Page Break   In ClarisWorks Word Processing, an option on the Format menu that inserts a page break at the insertion point.

Insert Part...   In ClarisWorks Database, an option on the Layout menu to create a header, footer, or summary part of a layout. This option can be used only in the Layout mode.

insertion point   The point where text will be entered when typed. Denoted on the screen by a flashing vertical line, it is positioned on the screen by clicking the I-beam.

Insert...   In ClarisWorks, a command on the File menu that places the contents of a file or document into the open document being displayed. You cannot insert a ClarisWorks document into another ClarisWorks document.

integrated software   A software package that includes a variety of applications and allows data to be easily transferred between applications. The applications are usually a word processor, spreadsheet, and database. Paint, draw, and communications applications may be included as well.

International Society for Technology in Education (ISTE)   An international organization that, among other activities, sponsors conferences, publishes journals and other materials, and offers training, all in relation to technology in the schools.

Irregular Polygon tool   In HyperCard, a tool with a six-sided, irregular polygon-shaped icon on the tool palette that creates irregular polygons with any number of sides.

it   A HyperTalk variable that temporarily contains the result of particular HyperTalk commands, such as the user response to the ask command.

laser disc   See **videodisc**.

Lasso tool   In ClarisWorks Paint or HyperCard, a drawing tool that is used to select a graphic precisely. Once selected with the Lasso tool, the graphic can be moved, copied, or cut.

layers   In HyperCard and in ClarisWorks Draw, the term used to describe at what level an object, such as a button, a graphic, or a field, exists in a stack or document.

layout   The way items are arranged on a page or a screen. In ClarisWorks Database, there can be a variety of layouts for each database.

Layout menu   In ClarisWorks Database, a pull-down menu that provides options related to the way data is displayed on the screen.

Layout mode   In ClarisWorks Database, a view of a database in which the arrangement of fields and field names can be changed and to which graphics and text can be added, if desired, for reports. This mode is displayed when the Layout option on the Layout menu has been selected.

LCD panel   An electronic device that attaches to a computer and is placed on an overhead to project the contents of the computer screen onto a wall screen.

left indent marker   A triangular marker on the text ruler that points right and indicates where lines of text, other than the first line of a paragraph, begin on the left of a page. See also **indent markers** and **first-line indent marker**.

left tab   A tab stop that aligns the left side of text at the tab stop location.

Library   In ClarisWorks, the Library command on the File menu opens a submenu of libraries and options. A library contains text or objects that can be used within a ClarisWorks document. New items can be added to existing ClarisWorks libraries or additional libraries can be created.

Line tool   In HyperCard, HyperStudio, and ClarisWorks, a tool (a straight line icon on the tool palette) that creates straight lines.

link indicator   The symbol that looks like three links of chain and is located at the bottom of one frame and the top of another to indicate that the frames are linked together. See also **frame links**.

List mode   In ClarisWorks Database, an option on the Layout menu that displays database records in list format, with records in rows and fields in columns.

local area network (LAN)   When computers within close physical proximity, as in a room or a school, are connected so that they may share peripheral devices or a file server.

lock text   In HyperCard, an option on the Field Info dialog box that "locks" the text, preventing any changes to the text within that particular field.

Lock Title Position   In ClarisWorks Spreadsheet, a command on the Options menu that locks rows or columns of cells, so that they remain in the window even if it is scrolled.

Macintosh Guide   A built-in guide that contains information about your computer and contains step-by-step instructions on a variety of tasks that can be performed on a Macintosh.

Macintosh Tutorial   Step-by-step training about the Macintosh system, the Macintosh desktop, and word processing features.

Magnify   In HyperStudio, a choice on the Options menu that allows the user to magnify the screen from 100% up to 800% to see and edit individual pixels of a graphic.

mail merge   Inserting database information into a form letter.

Mail Merge... In ClarisWorks, a command on the File menu that displays a Mail Merge window allowing you to place fields from an open database into a word processing or spreadsheet document or frame and to print the merged document.

mailing lists An electronic means of communicating with a group of individuals, generally with a common interest. Messages are generally sent to a moderator who then sends them on to others on the list.

Make Chart... In ClarisWorks Spreadsheet, a command on the Options menu that provides choices for making various charts using data in the spreadsheet.

margin The blank space on the edges of a page where nothing will be printed. In ClarisWorks, the margin sizes are set with the Document... option on the Format menu.

master page A master page is a background that repeats on all pages of a ClarisWorks Draw document. It can contain both text and graphics images.

Match Records... In ClarisWorks Database, an option on the Organize menu that allows records to be selected based on specified criteria. When this command is used, unselected records continue to be displayed along with selected records.

megabyte Approximately one million bytes, or characters.

menu bar The line across the top of the screen that begins with an apple (🍎) in the top left-hand corner. The entries on the line are choices for pull-down menus, such as File, Edit, View, and Special.

message box In HyperCard, a dialog box that allows the user to type HyperTalk commands that are executed immediately.

modem A hardware connection between a computer and a phone line that translates computer data into a format that can be transmitted over a phone line and transmitted data into computer data. Modem is an acronym for modulator-demodulator.

Modify Arc The Modify Arc command, found on the Options menu, provides a means of changing where an arc angle begins, the arc size, and whether it is a wedge.

Modify Chart... In ClarisWorks Spreadsheet, a command on the Options menu that provides choices for changing previously made charts.

mouse A peripheral device attached to the computer used to move a pointer icon, such as the arrow pointer and the I-beam, on the computer screen.

mouseUp In HyperCard, an action used with on and end commands that occurs when the mouse button is released after having been pressed down.

Move Backward In ClarisWorks Draw, an option on the Arrange menu that moves an object to a lower layer.

Move menu In HyperStudio, a pull-down menu that includes a variety of commands for movement in stacks.

Move to Front In ClarisWorks Draw, an option on the Arrange menu that moves an object to the top or front layer.

multimedia An application of computers and associated technology, such as videodisc and CD-ROM technology, to the presentation of materials which may include audio, video (still frame and motion), and text, often in an interactive format, to individuals.

navigating Looking through a HyperCard or HyperStudio stack, moving from card to card, not necessarily sequentially. In HyperCard this can involve using buttons, arrow keys, or the Go menu. In HyperStudio this can involve using buttons, the 🍎 key, and the > or < key, or the Move menu. Also referred to as browsing a stack.

network Computers that are connected to each other so that information can be passed between them.

New Card In HyperCard, a command on the Edit menu for adding a new card with the current background to the stack. In HyperStudio, a command on the Edit menu for adding a new blank card to the stack. In both programs, the new card is inserted immediately after the card being displayed.

New Layout... In ClarisWorks Database, an option on the Layout menu for creating a new layout for a database.

New Record In ClarisWorks Database, a command on the Edit menu for adding a new blank record to the database.

New Request In ClarisWorks Database, a command on the Edit menu that combines multiple Find requests to form more complicated searches in a database. This is often used when setting up either/or logical searches.

New Stack... In HyperCard and HyperStudio, a command on the File menu for creating a new stack.

New... In ClarisWorks, an option on the File menu that displays a New Document dialog box for selection of a document type and creation of a new document.

number format The way in which numbers are displayed. In ClarisWorks Database, the format for number fields is defined when the Layout mode is active by double-clicking the data box of a numeric field, or by using the Field Format... option of the Options menu when a numeric field data box is selected. In ClarisWorks Spreadsheet, number format is changed by using the Number... option on the Format menu.

Number... In ClarisWorks Spreadsheet, an option on the Format menu that allows you to change the way in which numbers are displayed.

object An icon, frame, button, or graphic on the screen that can be selected, moved around, resized, or otherwise manipulated as a whole unit.

Object Info In ClarisWorks Draw, selecting Object Info from the Options menu causes the Info palette to be displayed. Changing measurements in the palette will resize or move the selected object.

object-oriented A type of graphics program in which icons, frames, or graphic figures on the screen are selected, moved around, resized, or otherwise manipulated as a whole unit.

on (action) In HyperCard, the HyperTalk command that initiates script associated with the specified action. The action includes such commands as mouseUp, mouseDown, openStack, closeStack, openCard, openBackground.

open To make the contents of an application, document, or folder available for use. The Open… command is on the File menu.

Open Connection In ClarisWorks Communications, a command on the Session menu that dials the phone number to establish the connection for a telecommunications session. The phone number used is the one typed into the Connection Settings dialog box (from the Settings menu).

openStack In HyperCard, an action used with on and end commands that occurs when the stack is opened.

Options menu In ClarisWorks Draw and Paint, a pull-down menu that provides a variety of miscellaneous graphic options. In ClarisWorks Database, this menu is available in Layout mode. In ClarisWorks Spreadsheet, the Options menu contains commands for charting and changing the way the spreadsheet is displayed or printed.

Organize menu In ClarisWorks Database, a pull-down menu containing options for showing and hiding records, going to particular records, and sorting and matching records.

Oval tool In HyperCard and ClarisWorks, a drawing tool that creates a circle or oval.

page break The point at which text starts printing on a new page. In ClarisWorks, page breaks are automatically determined, but additional breaks can be inserted from the Format menu.

page guide In ClarisWorks, a line on the screen that indicates the inside edge of margins.

page indicator A box at the bottom of a ClarisWorks document that specifies the number of the page currently being displayed in the window. This is displayed when Page View is selected from the View menu.

Page View In ClarisWorks, a command on the View menu that displays a document on the screen with margins showing and pages separated, as it would appear when printed. Headers and footers, if any, and margins are displayed in Page view and Rulers can be shown, if desired. When Page view is selected, a checkmark shows on the menu and the

page indicator displays page numbers at the bottom of the window.

Paint environment The mode of ClarisWorks usage in which Paint tools are available.

Paint Text tool In HyperStudio, a tool used to place limited amount of text on a card. Once the mouse is clicked, the text cannot be edited.

Paint tools Tools that are available in ClarisWorks Paint. They include Selection Rectangle, Lasso, Magic Wand, Brush, Pencil, Paint Bucket, Spray Can, and Eraser tools. The Draw tools, Line, Rectangle, Rounded Rectangle, Oval, Arc, Polygon, Freehand, Bezigon, and Regular Polygon are also available in the Paint environment.

Painting tools In HyperStudio, tools on the tool palette used to draw objects. These objects are bit-mapped graphics.

Paste Paste is a command on the Edit menu that inserts a copy of what is on the clipboard into a document. In HyperCard, the menu will specify whether a stack, card, button, field, or picture is being pasted.

Paste Card In HyperCard, a command on the Edit menu for pasting a copied card. See **Copy Card**.

Paste Function… In ClarisWorks Spreadsheet, a command on the Edit menu that lists available functions and pastes them into the entry bar.

Patterns menu In HyperCard, a pull-down menu that includes a variety of graphic patterns that can be used with the graphic tools. These patterns are most commonly used with the Fill tool, any filled figure, and the brush tool.

Pen color palette A part of the Pen tools, the Pen color palette provides a means of choosing a color for the border of the selected graphic object or image.

Pen pattern palette A part of the Pen tools, the Pen pattern palette provides a means of choosing a pattern for the border of the selected graphic object or image.

Pen width palette A part of the Pen tools, the Pen width palette provides a means of choosing the width of the border of the selected graphic object or image.

Pen tools Icons at the bottom of the ClarisWorks tool palette representing tools that are used to control line width, pattern, and color and the placement of arrows on the ends of lines or borders of graphic objects.

Pencil tool In HyperCard and ClarisWorks Paint environment, a tool (a pencil icon on the tool palette) that draws a thin line. In HyperCard, double-clicking on this tool allows working in Fat Bits, a zoomed-in view.

peripheral device Any of a number of pieces of hardware that may be connected to a computer. Examples: disk drive, keyboard, printer, scanner, monitor, CD–ROM player.

play   In HyperCard, a HyperTalk command that will cause the computer to play a prerecorded sound. This command requires the name of the sound in quotes (as play "harpsi-chord"), and optionally the tempo, the note, the octave, and the type of note.

point   To move the pointer to a desired location on the computer screen through the use of the mouse.

pointer   The icon that moves on the computer screen when the mouse is moved. It is used to point to and select objects or portions of text to be worked with. The icon varies to represent the different functions being performed, such as an I-beam for text editing or an arrow for pointing to menu options.

Polygon Sides...   When the Regular Polygon tool is selected, choosing Polygon Sides from the Options menu allows you to enter the number of sides for the regular polygon.

Polygon tool   In ClarisWorks graphics, a tool with an irregular polygon-shaped icon on the tool palette that creates an irregular polygon. In HyperCard, a similar tool is called the Irregular Polygon tool.

pop card   In HyperCard, the HyperTalk command that returns to the card for which the push card command was most recently used.

Preferences   In HyperStudio, parameters that can be set to assist in creating and editing a stack. For example, one preference allows the user to include the card number with the stack name. Preferences are accessible by selecting Preferences from the Edit menu.

Preferences...   In ClarisWorks, an option on the Edit menu that allows you to change document defaults for a variety of miscellaneous options, such as Show Invisibles.

Preferences card   In HyperCard, a card in the Home Stack that lets the user set the user level and a few other options including blind typing, arrow keys in text, and power keys. This card is usually the last card of the Home Stack.

Print Merge...   In ClarisWorks, a command on the Mail Merge window that prints a merged document. It will print the document once for each database record.

Print...   In ClarisWorks, an option on the File menu that displays a Print dialog box for making printing choices and for printing documents.

probeware   External recording devices that attach to a computer to input data, such as temperature, recorded by the device. For example, a temperature probe can record the changing temperatures of a liquid over a time interval.

proprietary software   Software sold commercially. The rights to the software are owned by an individual or a company. Normally it can be copied legally only for backup purposes.

public domain software   Software that may be legally and freely copied.

pull-down menu   A set of command options that becomes visible when the pointer is located on the menu bar and the mouse button is held down. A selection is made from the menu by dragging the pointer down the menu and releasing the mouse button when the desired option is highlighted.

push card   In HyperCard, the HyperTalk command that specifies what card will be returned to when the pop card command is used.

put   In HyperCard, the HyperTalk command that will place a value in a memory location. Example: put it into message box.

put empty into   In HyperCard, a HyperCard command that deletes text from a card or background field, when the field is specified; as put empty into background field "Response,"put empty into card field 3, or put empty into card field id 56.

Quit   An option on the File menu that causes a program to stop running.

range   In ClarisWorks Spreadsheet, all cells within a selection. A range is named by specifying its top left cell and its bottom right cell, as A2..G15 or B3..B10.

read/write head   The mechanism in a disk drive that both writes data to, and reads data from, a disk.

Ready Made Card   In HyperStudio, an option on the Edit menu for creating predesigned cards.

Recent   In HyperCard, an option on the Go menu that displays a screen showing all cards recently viewed. From this screen the user can double-click on any card and move directly to that card.

record   A set of related data in a database, comprised of fields (categories). A database is a collection of records.

Rectangle tool   In HyperCard, HyperStudio, and ClarisWorks Draw and Paint, a tool (a rectangle on the tool palette) that creates a rectangle.

Regular Polygon tool   In HyperCard, a tool with a hexagon-shaped icon on the tool palette that creates a regular polygon. In ClarisWorks graphics, a similar tool is represented by a diamond-shaped icon.

relative cell reference   A spreadsheet cell reference that is based on its position in relation to another cell, rather than on the actual address of the cell.

repeat   In HyperCard, a HyperTalk command that indicates other commands are to be executed for a specified number of times.

Reshape   In ClarisWorks Draw, an option on the Edit menu. When it is selected (the checkmark shows), you can change the shape of objects by dragging their handles.

right indent marker   A triangular marker on a text ruler that points left and indicates where lines of text end on the right of a page. See also **indent markers**.

right tab   A tab stop that aligns the right side of text at the tab stop location.

Rounded Rectangle tool   In HyperCard and ClarisWorks, a tool (a rounded rectangle icon on the tool palette) that creates a rounded rectangle.

row   In ClarisWorks Spreadsheet, a horizontal set of cells named with numbers.

ruler   A bar near the top of a ClarisWorks window that shows a scale with the actual size of the page. A text ruler, displayed with ClarisWorks text documents and frames, also has icons for paragraph formatting options. In ClarisWorks, a ruler may be hidden or shown by using the View menu.

Rulers...   In ClarisWorks, a command on the Format menu that allows you to change the units displayed on the Ruler.

Same Background   In HyperStudio, an option on the Ready Made Card submenu that creates a card containing the same graphic background as the card the user was on when selecting the Same Background option. Text objects and buttons do not copy.

Save   An option on the File menu that saves a copy of a document on a disk.

Save As...   An option on the File menu that saves a copy of a document on a disk after providing an opportunity to change the document name and the disk drive.

Save Lines Off Top   In ClarisWorks Communications, a command on the Session menu that saves text that has scrolled off the top of the communications document. This text can be displayed with Show Scrollback.

Save Stack   In HyperStudio, an option on the File menu that saves a copy of a stack on a disk.

Scale by Percent...   In ClarisWorks Paint, an option on the Transform menu that displays a dialog box for changing the size of a selected object. This option is found on the Transform submenu on the Arrange menu in ClarisWorks Draw.

scanner   A computer peripheral that copies text or graphics from paper and translates it into a data format that a computer can use. Scanned pictures can be used for graphic illustrations in computer documents.

screensaver   A program that places a moving image on the screen when the computer is not in use. This prevents the burning into the screen of an image left on the computer for a prolonged time.

script   In HyperCard, a series of HyperTalk commands. A script is typed in the script editor. All scripts begin with on (action) and close with end (action).

script editor   In HyperCard, a window in which HyperTalk script can be typed and edited. The script editor does some automatic editing.

scripting   In HyperCard, writing a series of commands in the HyperTalk programming language.

scroll bar   A bar located at the right or bottom of a window with arrows on the ends used to change the portion of a document displayed in the window. When the scroll bar is gray, the document is larger than the window and can be scrolled by clicking the arrows or the gray areas, or by dragging the small square on the scroll bar. See **horizontal scroll bar** and **vertical scroll bar**.

scrolling field   In HyperCard, the field option that adds a scroll bar to the side of a field in order to allow the field to contain more information than is visible at one time.

select   To indicate that an object or text will be used or worked with by clicking or by dragging the mouse pointer over the object or text. Selected items are highlighted or darkened.

Select All   In ClarisWorks, an option on the Edit menu that selects all text or graphics in a document. Note: It does not select graphics in a text document.

Select tool   In HyperCard, a drawing tool that is used to select a graphic by surrounding it with a rectangular box. Once the graphic is selected with this tool, the graphic can be moved, copied, cut, enlarged, or reduced.

Selection Rectangle   In ClarisWorks Paint, the tool represented by a dotted rectangle that is used to select a graphic. Selection using this tool includes any white space around the graphic object.

Selector tool   In HyperStudio, a drawing tool that is used to select a graphic by surrounding it with a rectangular box. Once the graphic is selected with this tool, the graphic can be moved, copied, cut, enlarged, or reduced.

Send Farther   In HyperCard, an option on the Objects menu that will move an object down one layer.

Session   In ClarisWorks Communications, a pull-down menu that displays commands related to establishing and ending a session and to how data is handled during a session. A session is the time period when a connection is open and data can be passed between computers.

Set Field Order   In ClarisWorks Database, a dialog box that appears when a new layout is being created to set the order in which the fields will be displayed in the layout.

Settings menu   In ClarisWorks Communications, a pull-down menu that displays commands for setting connection, terminal, and file transfer specifications.

shareware   Software that may be freely copied, but for which a small fee (generally $5 to $25) must be sent to the software author, if the user intends to use it after trying it once or twice.

shift-click   To press the Shift key and continue to hold it down as you simultaneously click the mouse button. Shift-clicking on an object will select that object and keep previous selections, so that multiple objects can be selected. Shift-clicking text selects all text between the insertion point and the location of the shift-clicked I-beam.

show In HyperCard, the HyperTalk command that will cause an object (a field, button, menu bar, etc.) to be shown. The object must be specified, such as show card field 3, show menuBar, or show background button "Student." See also **hide**.

Show All Records In ClarisWorks Database, a command on the Organize menu for displaying all records in the database.

show field See **show**.

Show Graphics Grid In ClarisWorks Draw, a choice on the Options menu that displays the graphics grid.

Show Invisibles In ClarisWorks Word Processing, an option in the Preferences dialog box that displays invisible characters, such as returns, tabs, and spaces.

Show margins In ClarisWorks, an option in the Document dialog box (from the Format menu) that displays margins. Page View must be selected (from the View menu) if margins are to be displayed.

Show Multiple In ClarisWorks Database, when Show Multiple is selected on the Layout menu, multiple records will be displayed on the screen at the same time. Show Multiple can only be selected if Page View is not selected.

Show page guides In ClarisWorks, an option in the Document dialog box (from the Format menu) that displays page guides. Margins must be displayed for page guides to be visible.

Show Scrollback In ClarisWorks Communications, a command on the Settings menu that displays text that has scrolled off the top of the communications document. To use this command, Save Lines Off Top must be selected on the Session menu.

Show/Hide Tools control An icon at the bottom of a ClarisWorks window that alternates between displaying and hiding the tool palette when clicked. Show Tools and Hide Tools are also options on the View menu.

Shut Down A choice on the Special menu that performs operations to prepare for the power to be turned off, including positioning (or parking) the read/write head on the hard disk so it will not come into contact with the disk when power is turned off.

size box The box located at the lower right corner of a window. By dragging the size box the window can be made larger or smaller.

Size menu In ClarisWorks Word Processing, a pull-down menu on the menu bar that contains options for font sizes. In ClarisWorks Database, Draw, Paint, and Spreadsheet, an

option on the Format menu that has a submenu of font size choices.

slide show A presentation using ClarisWorks that can be run manually when speaking or can be self-running to create a demonstration. Any ClarisWorks document except a Communications document can be used in a slide show.

Smooth In ClarisWorks Draw, a choice on the Edit menu that rounds the corners on a selected graphic.

software A program, or set of instructions, that allows the computer to perform in various ways; for example, word processing software allows the computer to perform as a word processor.

Sort Records... In ClarisWorks Database, a selection on the Organize menu that provides options for arranging the records in numeric or alphabetic order, based on entries in the fields.

Sort... In ClarisWorks Spreadsheet, a selection on the Calculate menu that provides options for arranging selected cells in numeric or alphabetic order, based on entries in specified rows or columns.

Sound tool In HyperStudio, a tool used to edit, move, resize, or delete sound effects.

spacing The number of blank lines between lines of text in a word processing document. In ClarisWorks, this is controlled by clicking spacing icons near the center of the ruler.

Special menu On the menu bar of the Macintosh Finder, a pull-down menu that offers selections such as Empty Trash, Shut Down, and Restart.

spell checker Software that checks the spelling of text in word processing documents. In ClarisWorks, it is available through the Spelling option on the Edit menu.

Split Pane tool In ClarisWorks, a crossbar-shaped icon with arrows displayed when the mouse pointer passes over the black rectangle at the left of a horizontal scroll bar or above a vertical scroll bar. Available in all ClarisWorks applications, it can be dragged to split a document window into two horizontal or vertical sections, each with its own scroll bar.

Spray tool In HyperCard, HyperStudio, and ClarisWorks Paint environment, a tool (a spray-paint-can icon on the tool palette) that "spray paints" a selected pattern.

spreadsheet A document arranged in a grid with rows and columns, used primarily for calculations. Also, software for creating and using spreadsheet documents.

spreadsheet frame A frame containing a spreadsheet document. See **frame**.

Spreadsheet tool In ClarisWorks, the crossbar-shaped icon near the top of the tool palette that can be selected to perform spreadsheet operations and that is used for the mouse pointer when the Spreadsheet tool is selected.

stack   In HyperCard and HyperStudio, a series of cards that contain information on a specific topic and are stored on a disk as a single file.

Stack Info...   In HyperCard, an option on the Objects menu that displays a dialog box listing specific information about a HyperCard stack, including location and number of cards in the stack.

Stack Windows   In ClarisWorks, choosing Stack Windows from the View menu causes multiple open windows to be positioned over each other so that the active window fills most of the screen and a small portion of each of the other windows is always visible.

standard layout   In ClarisWorks Database, the layout that contains all the fields in the order in which they were created with field names displayed to the left of each field.

Stationery   A ClarisWorks document that has been saved as a template. The document itself cannot be saved with edits—any edits made in it have to be saved with a new document name—so that it can be used repeatedly in its original form.

status panel   In ClarisWorks Database, the File icon and record information displayed at the left of the window.

storage device   Computer hardware used to store and retrieve data and information, such as a floppy drive or a hard disk drive.

StoryBoard   In HyperStudio, an option on the Extras menu that allows the user to change the order of the cards in the stack.

Style menu   In ClarisWorks Word Processing, a pull-down menu on the menu bar that contains options for text styles, such as bold or italic. In ClarisWorks Database, Draw, Paint, and Spreadsheet, an option on the Format menu that has a submenu of style choices.

Sum function   In ClarisWorks, a function that adds (sums) a list of numbers.

Summary part   In ClarisWorks Database, a portion of a layout used for printing summary information. A summary part can be added to the layout by choosing Insert Part... from the Layout menu.

system software   The instructions that allow the computer to operate, to run programs, to store data and information, and so on.

tab   An invisible character inserted by pressing the Tab key that causes text to line up with a tab stop. Also used to refer to a tab stop that has been set using the ClarisWorks text ruler.

Tab key   The key on the keyboard that inserts an invisible character that causes the insertion point to skip to the next tab stop that has been set for that text line.

tab stop   A position on a text line, set by moving tab icons on the ClarisWorks text ruler, with which text can be aligned through use of the Tab key.

tasks   In HyperCard, actions for the buttons that do not involve scripting by the user. These tasks are selected from a list of possible tasks in the Task dialog box, which appears when Tasks... is selected from the Button Info dialog box.

telecommunications   Passing of information from computer to computer.

template   A document that contains graphics, formatting, and text that you typically use. When the document is opened, you may make changes for your specific application that do not change the original document.

Text Appearance   In HyperStudio, a dialog box that includes the title of the text object, the color of the background and text, and options that put limits on the text object. It also contains a connection to the Text Style dialog box.

text frame   A frame containing a word processing document. See **frame**.

text object   In HyperStudio, an area on a card used for entering text.

Text object tool   In HyperStudio, a tool used to edit, move, resize, or delete text objects.

text overflow indicator   The symbol that looks like an X and is located at the bottom, right corner of a text frame to indicate that the frame contains more text than can be displayed.

Text Style   In HyperStudio, a dialog box that allows the user to select font type, style type, size of font, alignment of type, and color of text and background.

Text tool   In ClarisWorks, a tool (an A icon on the tool palette) that produces an I-beam when clicked and is used to work with text.

Tile windows   In ClarisWorks, choosing Tile Windows from the View menu causes multiple open windows to be positioned next to each other so that each window is the same size and each is completely visible on the screen.

title bar   The top line of a window that contains the title of the document in the window.

Title Page   In ClarisWorks Word Processing, an option in the Section dialog box (from the Format menu) that keeps the header and footer from printing on the first page of the document.

tool   In ClarisWorks and HyperCard, an icon that represents a function that can be performed by moving the mouse pointer on the screen.

tool mode   A mode of educational computer use in which the computer provides the user with a service that extends the user's capabilities in some way, for example, a word processing program.

tool palette The set of icons representing tools used for drawing or painting and for changing application tools within a document. In ClarisWorks, the tool palette can be displayed at the left of a window or hidden by clicking the Show/Hide Tools icon at the bottom of the screen or by selecting Show Tools or Hide Tools from the View Menu. In HyperCard and HyperStudio, it is the pull-down Tools menu that can be "torn off" the menu bar by dragging the pointer beyond the menu.

Tools menu In HyperCard and HyperStudio, a pull-down menu that contains all the tools needed to work with buttons, fields, text, and graphics.

Transform menu In ClarisWorks Paint, a pull-down menu with options related to moving and changing a selected graphic. In ClarisWorks Draw, Transform is a submenu of the Arrange menu.

transitions In HyperStudio, the visual impression you get when the screen changes to a new card. Examples include dissolve, left to right, and zoom out.

transparent In ClarisWorks Draw and Paint, an icon on the Pen pattern palette that makes a line, object, or frame transparent. Also a choice for individual slides in a slide show presentation.

Trash An icon on the Desktop representing the disposal of objects. Documents, applications, and folders dragged to the Trash are erased from their disk. A disk icon denoting a disk in the floppy drive dragged to the Trash is ejected from the drive.

Turn Autogrid Off In ClarisWorks, the Autogrid feature is automatically turned on. For more flexibility in drawing or moving graphics objects, Autogrid may be turned off by choosing Turn Autogrid Off on the Options menu. See **Autogrid**.

tutee mode A mode of educational computer use in which the computer is used as a student, in which the computer is "taught" something by the user. Writing a program is an example of using the computer in the tutee mode.

tutor mode A mode of educational computer use in which the computer presents material to the student, asks for a response based on the material presented, evaluates the response, and based on that evaluation presents additional content.

Undo A command on the Edit menu that replaces the effect of the last action or edit with what was on the screen before that action.

user level In HyperCard, controls what a user is permitted to do with a stack. Levels range from 1, Browsing, to 5, Scripting. User level can be set by typing a command in the message box.

vertical scroll bar A bar at the right of a window that allows the user to move the window contents vertically. See also **scroll bar**.

videodisc A storage medium that uses a laser to store (encode) and play (decode) information such as audio and video on a disc.

View menu In ClarisWorks, the View menu provides options to create new views or ways to display a document in a window. A ClarisWorks document can be seen in multiple views at the same time with each view displaying a different portion or layout of the document.

visible records In ClarisWorks Database, the records that can be seen when the database is scrolled.

visual effect In HyperCard, the visual impression you get when the screen changes to a new card. Examples include scrolling, barn door open, and shrink. The visual effect is typed in a script directly or added to a script through the Button Info dialog box.

wait In HyperCard, a HyperTalk command that will produce a pause before the next command is executed.

Web Browser A program that allows a user to navigate through the World Wide Web.

window A rectangular view of data or information that appears on the computer screen. More than one window may be open at a time. Windows may be partially or completely superimposed over one another, moved around the screen, and resized.

World Wide Web The World Wide Web, often referred to as The Web or WWW, is a telecommunications feature that provides information linking in multiple directions. The multimedia format causes many Web pages to appear to be similar to CD-ROMs. Text and links to other Web pages may appear on the same screen.

word processing Use of a program that allows text to be typed, edited, saved, and printed.

wrap With reference to word processing, the automatic movement of text from the end of one line to the beginning of the next line.

Writing Tools A submenu of the Edit menu that contains Check Document Spelling..., Thesaurus..., and other useful writing tools.

zoom box The zoom box is located at the upper right corner of a window. Clicking within the zoom box will cause the window to become as large as possible on the screen. Clicking again will cause the window to return to its previous size.

zoom-in control To change to a closer, larger view. In ClarisWorks, this is accomplished with either the zoom percentage indicator or the zoom-in control at the bottom of the window. The zoom-in control is the larger of the two icons that look like mountains.

zoom-out control   To change to a more distant, smaller view. In ClarisWorks, this is accomplished with the zoom percentage indicator or the zoom-out control at the bottom of the window. The zoom-out control is the smaller of the two icons that look like mountains.

zoom percentage indicator   The box at the bottom left of a ClarisWorks application window that tells what percentage of actual print size is being displayed in the window and allows the percentage to be changed.

INDEX